Growth and Development
Planning in India

Growth and Development Planning in India

K. L. DATTA

OXFORD
UNIVERSITY PRESS

OXFORD
UNIVERSITY PRESS

Oxford University Press is a department of the University of Oxford.
It furthers the University's objective of excellence in research, scholarship,
and education by publishing worldwide. Oxford is a registered trademark of
Oxford University Press in the UK and in certain other countries.

Published in India by
Oxford University Press
22 Workspace, 2nd Floor, 1/22 Asaf Ali Road, New Delhi 110 002, India

© Oxford University Press 2021

The moral rights of the author have been asserted.

First Edition published in 2021

ISBN-13 (print edition): 978-0-19-012502-8
ISBN-10 (print edition): 0-19-012502-0

ISBN-13 (eBook): 978-0-19-099156-2
ISBN-10 (eBook): 0-19-099156-9

Typeset in ScalaPro 10/13
by Tranistics Data Technologies, Kolkata 700 091
Printed in India by Rakmo Press, New Delhi 110 020

Contents

Tables

Preface

Those who were born immediately after India's Independence have been both fortunate and unfortunate: unfortunate as they could not participate in the freedom movement, and fortunate as they could see the development of independent India unfolding before them. I was born in independent India in 1949 and hence my participation in the freedom movement was a mathematical impossibility. I had to learn about some of the early developmental efforts as part of history. So was the case with learning about the making of India as a republic, the first general elections to the Parliament and the state legislative assemblies, and the initiation of planned economic development. Some of these events entered into my memory from the animated discussions that were a routine affair in our household, where both like-minded people and people with conflicting ideas would be present. Among these, I vividly remember the discussions in the late 1950s that were centred on three issues: food crisis, price inflation, and corruption. There were mixed feelings about the application of planning to turn India into an industrially developed nation. It was a time when expectations were not very high and ideas about development remained strictly within the confines of food, clothing, and housing—the *roti–kapda–makaan* trilogy. It does not matter if the food consisted of coarse cereals, if cloth was coarse or hand-spun, or if the house was *kutcha* (not made of stones, tiles, and so on). But the ideas were rigid that these should be made available to all, and with the exception of none.

That is how my association with India's economic growth and development issues began. Though I missed the entire debate on whether planning should be used as a development strategy, and then the Mahalanobis model as a stepping stone for India's foray into the comity of developed nations, these were compensated many times in the course of my student days, when we were taught these subjects in great detail. In due course, I as a teacher passed on some of this knowledge to my students. The developments in the Indian economy began to unfold before my eyes from the late 1950s, as I witnessed food riots in Calcutta in 1959, became familiar with the border conflict with China in 1962, the war with Pakistan in 1965, and the unprecedented drought in the mid-1960s leading to a near-famine situation in large parts of the country. While this shock and horror was least expected, there was light at the end of the tunnel. In the late 1960s, India transformed from a food-deficit to a food-surplus nation, and in 1971 it earned a decisive military victory against Pakistan, heralding the birth of the new country Bangladesh in the Indian subcontinent. Though I do not find that military victory for anyone brings joy to me, that time was different, perhaps seeing the delight with which my parents embraced the news. They had reasons, emotions too, because Bangladesh was their place of birth, and they had spent their childhood days there.

In 1975, I entered the Indian Economic Service. It brought mixed feelings for me as it would mean leaving Calcutta, the city where I was born, educated, and began my professional career with sufficient contentment. It was a place where I learnt many things and made innumerable friends; and yet, there were hostilities too, in the field of history, literature, economics, and most of all, politics. During my student life, most of us were active politicians; there was no dearth of political parties or groups and their self-acclaimed leaders in Calcutta in those days. Then, there was the charm of teaching in a college in Calcutta. All these I had to forego for the sake of joining the government, whose office buildings I had detested for long—among them the Writers' Building, then the seat of the West Bengal administration, and also Lalbazar, the headquarters of the Calcutta Police. I wondered how people spent eight hours every day inside these buildings.

My first two years in the Indian Economic Service, in many ways, were a novel experience. Until then, my longest journey had been to the Visva-Bharati University, located in Santiniketan, West Bengal, for an interview that did not take place. I was paid the train fare and given free accommodation at their International Guest House. Frankly, that had been the motivation for the journey. My first two years working in the government, which was a probation period, involved structured training and travel across the length and breadth of the country. At the end of the probation, it was time to take a call about the place of my posting. I gave some thought to this issue, and requested for a placement with the Perspective Planning Division (PPD) of the then Planning Commission because I knew many of the mathematical models that they used. This work interested me. But, it was not an easy affair to get into the Planning Commission, and that too in the PPD. One of my seniors suggested that I should meet Division Head Y. K. Alagh. Alagh, a person with considerable knowledge in the area of mathematical modelling, told me straightaway that he would have to interview me to assess if I could fulfil the requirements of the posting. I had no reason not to agree.

The interview took place in Alagh's office at Yojana Bhawan and lasted for three hours. I cannot say that I was grilled, as the answers to the questions he asked were known to me, thanks to my teachers at Calcutta University. Nikhilesh Bhattacharya, my teacher in econometrics, and Asim Dasgupta, who taught me mathematical statistics, distribution functions, and growth models, helped me tide through Alagh's test; so much so that at the end of the session he threw his hands in the air saying I had wasted three hours of his time, and that I should have told him at the beginning that I was a student of Nikhilesh Bhattacharya. With this, my tryst with the Planning Commission began.

In the Planning Commission, I remained occupied with the work on multi-sectoral consistency models, which were being used at that time to formulate the Sixth Five Year Plan. For the most part of the next three decades I was engaged in this subject.

Over five spells I have spent seventeen years of my career in the civil services at the Planning Commission. And I have served this organization in different positions, including as adviser and head of the PPD, which I joined first in 1977. I consider such a long stay in the Commission a matter of luck and privilege. It gave me the opportunity to work on the application of mathematical models of growth and investment in the formulation of medium- and long-term plans, and understand the nuances of planning in determining the rate of economic growth and improving the levels of living and quality of life of people. This book, in some ways, is a culmination of my administrative and academic experience in the civil services in the past four decades on issues related to growth, equity, poverty, and deprivation. Writing this book has indeed been a task of tall order.

My friends and colleagues have been a source of inspiration in this endeavour. As always, I remain grateful to Y. K. Alagh, who inducted me into this complex and challenging area of research. In the Planning Commission, interactions with Arjun Sengupta and S. R. Hashim have been full of excitement and challenge. They reposed faith in me by entrusting me, among many other things, with the responsibility of leading a team of officers in the Planning Commission to prepare the 'Technical Note to the Eighth Five Year Plan'—a document which contains the mathematical models used to arrive at the macro-parameters for growth, its sectoral pattern, and allocation of resources for different sectoral activities of the Plan. My interactions with Montek Singh Ahluwalia and Saumitra Chaudhuri in the Planning Commission have been a rewarding experience. Others who have helped me in several ways include C. Rangarajan, Pronab Sen, Abhijit Sen, Arvind Virmani, Bibek Debroy, Kirit Parikh, B. N. Yugandhar, Mahesh Vyas, Sunil Khatri, Savita Sharma, K. Sundaram, Sabina Alkire, James Foster, Jugal Kishore Mohapatra, P. K. Padhy, Manjula Krishnan, Parthapratim Mitra, Himanshu, Rinku Murgai, and S. V. Ramana Murthy.

On the personal front, Amrita Datta and Sumeet Popli assisted me in a wide range of areas, which included hardware and software support. Embarking on such a project inevitably leads to a disruption of daily routine. My wife, Indu, tolerated my busy and irregular schedule that accompanied this research. For this, I am grateful to her. The errors and omissions, however, rest with me.

K. L. Datta

Introduction

India, after seven decades of independence, found itself in the position of the fifth-largest economy in the world, with nominal gross domestic product (GDP) of USD 2.94 trillion in 2019. It is also the fastest-growing trillion-dollar economy in the world. India's rank would have been third if GDP across the countries was compared in terms of purchasing power parity. But, in per capita terms, India falls way behind most of the member countries of the World Bank. However, this should not negate the expansion of the Indian economy that has taken place since Independence.

India adopted planning as an instrument of policy with rigid state control and regulation in economic activities after Independence. The degree of control may have varied within the first four decades of planning, 1951–90, but remained firmly in place. In 1991, when the policies of economic reforms and liberalization were initiated, state controls were either relaxed or dismantled, and planning became market-based. Finally, in 2014, planning was abolished, and along with it the Planning Commission, which was created in 1950 to formulate medium- and long-term plans for economic growth and development.

The institutionalization of planning in India became the subject matter of debate in India's post-Independence growth and development strategy ever since planners and policymakers began to realize that the growth rate of the Indian economy in the first three decades, 1951–80, was low (3.5 per cent per year). The experts believed that such low growth rate was below the country's potential. State control and regulation associated with planning was at its peak in this three-decade period, and this was considered to be the reason behind the growth rate being below the potential. In the 1980s, certain controls were relaxed, opening space for the private sector; and the growth rate picked up, for the first time, to a level of 5 per cent per year in a Five Year Plan period. Even after the initial few years of the economic reforms, the economic growth rate remained around the same level and there was not much change in the 1990s, which was the first decade of economic reforms. It was only in the twenty-first century that India's rate of economic growth attained a higher trajectory and reached the rate of 8 per cent per year. In view of the low rate of economic growth in the pre-reform period (1951–90) and the relatively high growth rate in the period of economic reforms (1991–2011), there has been a kind of convergence of opinion that planning and the associated state control on economic activities were responsible for the low growth rate in the pre-reform years.

It is in this context that a range of issues related to India's economic growth and development have been dealt with in this book. It focuses on the circumstances that led to the adoption of developmental planning after Independence. It begins by tracing the course of planning in India and analysing the manner in which planning was built into the strategy of growth and development. In the process, it discusses the rationality of application of planning in furtherance of economic growth, mentions some of the trials and tribulations encountered in the formulation of Five Year Plans, and the nitty-gritties of their implementation. It unveils the contours of the Plan by tracing the changing nature of planning over time from rigid state control on economic activities to reliance on the market and the private sector. Focusing on the growth debate, it presents a comprehensive analysis of the economic scenario that unfolded in India after Independence, documenting the shifts in growth and development strategy in the six decades of planning, 1951–2011, covering 11 Five Year Plans formulated and implemented during this period. In the end, an assessment of the Indian economy after the Eleventh Plan, that is, after 2010, has been made. The central theme of the book is to appraise the role of planning to maximize the rate of economic growth and improve the levels of living and quality of life of the people. There are four core areas, described in the following sections, that have been addressed in this book.

India's Planning Strategy

First, this book delves into the circumstances which led the political leaders to adopt a planning strategy and use it as a major instrument of policymaking in economic and social reconstruction after Independence. They looked for ways and means to maximize the country's overall rate of economic growth, and at the same time ensure that the benefits of growth percolated to all sections of the society. The issue before them basically was: how to maximize the rate of economic growth in a low-income capital-starved country so that the income of the people could be increased with minimum use of resources and within the shortest possible time? Economists and statisticians suggested that it could be possible through planning. The political leaders concurred.

The form of planning adopted in India in the 1950s entailed regulation of economic activities based on state control of the means of production and distribution. It was rooted in the concern that private ownership is concomitant with the prosperity of a few, notably the capitalists, and exploitation of the vast majority of the population— an idea that dates back to the days of the freedom struggle. It was favoured in independent India since the political leadership (among whom Jawaharlal Nehru figured prominently) was convinced that economic power should not be concentrated in the hands of capitalists, and especially in the private sector, because they operate exclusively for profit. This induced them to prefer the public sector.

There is no doubt that Jawaharlal Nehru was at the centre of the decision-making authority in the 1950s, when planning was initiated, and it was decided that the mixed economy approach within the framework of planning would be adopted. Planning may not have been the brainchild of Nehru but the mixed economy approach that was embedded into it certainly was. Taking recourse to history, the idea to use the instrument of planning to improve the economic fundamentals of a low-income, poor, and underdeveloped country such as India came from Netaji Subhas Chandra Bose. It dated back a decade before Independence, to be specific in February 1938, when Netaji Bose, the then president of the Indian National Congress, decided to constitute a National Planning Committee (NPC) under the chairmanship of Jawaharlal Nehru. At that time Nehru was in Europe, campaigning for Indian independence. Netaji Bose waited for about one year for Nehru to take up the job of chairman of the NPC, because he thought Nehru was the person most capable of understanding the nuances of planning in the context of India's economic development. This way, Nehru figured prominently in the endeavour of planning. The introduction of planning for India's growth and development in the 1950s was, without doubt, the handiwork of Nehru, but it may be a logical extension of the ideas originally conceived by Netaji Bose. This book makes an effort to first unearth why and then how planning came to be institutionalized in India in the 1950s, and, in this context, Nehru's role in devising the mixed economy approach within the framework of planning, instead of placing exclusive reliance on the public or private sector. Specifically, it makes an assessment of the role of Jawaharlal Nehru and identifies the events that may have shaped his decision to rely on planning.

Two events that may have shaped Nehru's decision to rely on planning and the antecedent role it gave to the state and the public sector can be identified. First, the pattern of growth and development in Europe and especially in England during the period of Industrial Revolution may have crystallized Nehru's ideas on capitalism and the private sector. Second, he was impressed by the economic development that unfolded from planning in the Soviet Union in the 1930s and 1940s as it filled certain critical gaps in the development of seventeenth- and eighteenth-century European society. However, it must be admitted that in the end, the idea of planning was not Nehru's alone, as it also came from contemporary political leaders.

Describing the circumstances under which planning was dovetailed with the mixed economy approach, this book dispels the notion that Nehru was influenced by the Soviet Union to adopt planning in India. The model of growth and development employed by the Soviet Union or the Soviet planning superstructure (Gosplan) was not implemented straightforwardly in India. The Soviet Union was dismayed with India adopting the mixed economy approach in the planning framework because they wanted India to adopt the 'public sector only' approach, which they were following. Yet, whether state control in areas of production and distribution associated with planning proved to be detrimental for India's economic growth is open to questioning.

This book analyses the features of the planning process in India, its form and content, and turns and twists in a bid to maximize the rate of economic growth and improve the standard of living of the people. It chronicles the change in the methodology of planning over time to contextualize it with regard to India's changing development strategy. It discusses the manner and method of formulation of the Five Year Plans, specifically underlining the roles of the central government and the state governments, and dwells on the high degree of centralization and administrative regulation in the first four decades of planning, 1951–90. Then, it discusses the planning process in the two-decade period of economic reforms, 1991–2011, which was grounded on a market-economy framework, traditionally known as the centrepiece of development strategy of the developed capitalist world.

This book does not support or make a case for continuance of planning in a rigid form that was a primary feature of the first four decades of planning, 1951–90, but argues that state intervention in the market may be a necessity so long as poverty and deprivation remain major economic concerns, and a section of the population is unable to afford market prices for essential goods and services. Such an idea, though it does not find favour with many, may only be effective in a democratic society when the state and the people have a socialist mindset.

The preparation of a Five Year Plan is a complex process. The analytical details of the planning process in this book give novel insights into the role of planning in India's economic growth and development. In the formulation of Five Year Plans, mathematical models were used to spell out development priorities and determine sectoral growth profiles. The features of the mathematical models are discussed to understand how intuitively the targets in different areas and sectors of the economy are fixed. The technicalities of the models are expressed in simple terms to expand the outreach of the study to a wider readership.

Planning and Economic Growth

The second core area of the book explores the rate and pattern of economic growth since the beginning of the planning era. A quantitative assessment of the growth performance of the Indian economy has been made and the reasons behind the shortfall in growth rate from the targets fixed in the Five Year Plans have been assessed. The issues that are specifically addressed here are whether planning has been able to raise the overall rate of economic growth to a certain level and in a manner that is necessary to improve the economic fundamentals, and has the increase in income enabled people to acquire the capacity to make a decisive impact on their levels of living and quality of life.

Pointing out the uneven nature of growth over time, it focuses first on the likely factors responsible for the low growth rate in the initial three decades, 1951–80, when planning was watertight in form and content, and its acceleration to a higher growth path afterwards, especially in the period of economic reforms, 1991–2011, when planning operated in a market-economy framework.

Citing the relatively lower rate of growth until the 1970s, it has often been argued that planning did not yield the desired rate of economic growth. This book takes a different route to deal with this issue and shows that despite the low growth rate, India gained certain solid ground in this period. It argues that the realized growth rate in the 1950s (First and Second Plans), which was 4 per cent per year on average, is by no means a mean achievement for a newly independent nation emerging from two centuries of colonial rule and decaying socio-economic condition. The consequent increase in per capita income was considerable by the standards prevailing then and particularly in view of the stagnancy in per capita income during the previous half a century, or even a century. Besides, the foundation of a strong industrial base initiated in the Second Plan was able to improve the fundamentals of the economy. These may be considered as major achievements of the planning era.

From the mid-1960s to the late 1970s, the government announced that in pursuance of the socialist policies, it was determined to capture the commanding heights of the economy. This suo moto meant that a larger proportion of the country's investment and income would accrue from the public sector. The reality is that even in the heyday of planning and state control, the share of the public sector rarely crossed half of the total investment. It shows that the socialist policies were there only in name.

The state control on economic activities was strengthened in the 1960s and 1970s, and the growth rate was low. Despite the low rate of economic growth, the Indian economy was placed on a sound footing. The book provides a perspective on planning and the food crisis in the context of the Green Revolution when India transitioned from a food-deficit to a food-surplus country. It is argued that throughout the 1960s and 1970s, the government pursued contrasting strategies in the areas of agriculture and industry; a potentially iniquitous policy was adopted in agriculture whereas promotion of equity was given a prime place in case of industrial development. It is believed that these policies contributed to the success of agriculture but retardation of the rate of industrial growth.

By the 1970s, the planners realized the limited effectiveness of a growth-centric strategy and, in the face of it, were not inclined to wait for the percolation of the fruits of economic growth for reduction in poverty. This led to a change in the development strategy, contemplating special measures to raise the income of the poor and the marginalized section of the population. By crafting a cohesive policy to tackle the menace of poverty through these measures, the issue of poverty was brought to the forefront of the development debate. These snow-balled into a major policy shift in the development strategy in the 1980s with special measures to increase the income of the poor and the marginalized, and it was dovetailed into the growth process. Such growth-cum-redistribution policies have become the order of the day. However, in the 1980s, it was a bold step in view of the stringent financial condition faced by the government.

Analysing the features of planning in this four-decade period, 1951–90, the book makes an effort to find out how far the reliance on planning is responsible for the low growth rate. It can be observed that more than the planning itself, it is the state control and regulation associated with planning that seemed to be responsible for retarding the growth rate. The policies in this four-decade period traversed from forceful attempts by the state to capture the commanding heights of the economy and nationalize private enterprises in industry and financial sectors in the 1960s and 1970s, to measures to widen the scope of the private sector and extend its area of operation in economic activities in the 1980s. It marked a visible shift in the growth and development strategy. Chronicling the circumstances which led to such a shift, it has been concluded that the 1980s marked the process of rolling back the frontiers of state intervention and reformulating the planning and development strategy. These changes in the 1980s have often been treated as the precursor of the economic reforms initiated in 1991.

Planning and Economic Reforms

Third, this book concentrates on the economic reforms and liberalization measures initiated in 1991, marking a paradigm shift in the approach to planning for growth maximization in which market mechanism replaced the different agents of the state as dominant decision-makers. State control and regulation on economic activities giving way to market mechanism, the hallmark of reform measures, proved to be a seismic change in economic policies with the opening up of the Indian economy to the world and heralding in of a new strategy of growth and development.

This book contextualizes the backdrop in which economic reform measures were introduced to understand how different areas and sectors of the economy were integrated with the reform process. Then, from the lens of economics and politics associated with the reform process, it outlines how India charted the course of economic reform. The process of institutionalizing the policies of economic reform shows that reforms did not move at a similar pace in all the areas and sectors of the economy. Together, their impact was not uniform, either at the level of sectors of the economy or for the income classes of the population. The transition from state control to an open market economy, which is central to the reform process, is effected by the government, in which the major actors are: (a) the Planning Commission, (b) the finance ministry, (c) the Reserve Bank of India (RBI), and (d) the state governments. Analysing the speed and intensity of the implementation of reform measures as well as the roadblocks these institutions faced, this book gives a graphic description of the dismantling of the planning apparatus and adoption of a market-based economic structure in its place.

It argues that in contrast to most developing countries, which pursued economic reform programmes at one go, the reform programmes in India were initially applied in selected areas. Based upon the result these were extended gradually to wider areas. There is a considerable gradualist element in implementing the reform measures.

In its critique of planning, this book points out that the acceleration of growth rate in the period of economic reform is driven by domestic investment, notably private sector investment, which, in turn, is the outcome of the increase in private sector savings. It shows how under economic reform, the space of production and trade relinquished by the state was filled by the private sector, and the major responsibility of growth was transferred from the state to the private sector. It identifies the factors that drove the growth rate to a higher level and, in the process, evaluates the impact of reform measures on the rate and pattern of economic growth and income distribution. Analysing the features of the growth process during the reform period, it pinpoints that the high growth rate in the first decade of the 2000s was inclusive, leading to considerable reduction in poverty.

After the economic reforms were initiated, the Indian economy by the first decade of the twenty-first century was sufficiently integrated with the global economy. Against this backdrop, the global economic and financial crisis that erupted in September 2008 was feared to have impacted the growth rate of the Indian economy in a major way. There are no studies which make an assessment of the impact of the global economic crisis on the different areas and sectors of the Indian economy. This book shows how the real and financial sectors were affected as a result of the global crisis. It makes a quantitative assessment of the impact of the global economic crisis on the rate of growth of the Indian economy. This book points out that the Indian economy was able to withstand the fallout of the global economic crisis quickly but soon after entered into a low growth phase. The factors responsible for retarding the growth rate of the economy after successfully withstanding the onslaught of the global crisis have been identified here. Tracing the cobwebs of economic policy and the decision-making process, this book shows that the slowdown of the growth rate of the Indian economy at this time was predominantly on account of the factors emanating from the domestic economy rather than the global economy.

There has been a denunciation of the economic policies in the pre-reform period, sometimes vehement. The denunciation, of late, has come by comparing the economic growth rate during the first four decades of planning, 1951–90, with the two decades of economic reforms, 1991–2011. This has been the dominant trend, ignoring the well-known dictum that it is not wise to judge the past by the standards of the present. This book focuses on the inappropriateness of judging the policies of the pre-reform era through the prism of contemporary market-led economic development. The suitability and appropriateness of planning in the Indian economy has to be judged based on the circumstances prevailing in the late 1940s and the early 1950s.

Planning and Poverty

The change in magnitude and structure of the growth rate is associated with the policy measures born out of the philosophy and ideological bent of the political party in power. How economic growth resulted in the increase in income of the cross section of the population, specifically those in the lower deciles, and altered the socio-economic scenario is the essence of the analysis presented in this book. It focuses on the strategic measures that resulted in increase in income and improvement in levels of living of the poor and the marginalized section of the population in periods of both low and high growth.

Describing the manner in which poverty was incorporated as a parameter in planning, this book delineates the use of poverty estimates in policymaking. It comments on the methodology of measurement of poverty, summarizing the debates surrounding it. It shows how (a) theoreticians and academicians, (b) administrators and civil servants, and (c) civil society and non-governmental organizations engage with the measurement-related issues on poverty and identification of poor households at the grassroots level. It goes on to show how poverty estimates have been used to formulate an effective plan for poverty alleviation and then to track the progress of development over time and space.

While analysing the features of poverty reduction, the book deals with the pertinent issues associated with planning in the Indian context—whether planning has been able to reduce poverty and improve the standards of living of the people, especially the marginal- ized groups. It analyses the levels and changes in officially measured poverty since the 1970s, and views poverty at the level of states and by socio-economic groups of the population. Further, it goes on to show the sensitivity of poverty to growth in income and equity in its class distribution.

Terming poverty reduction as an acid test of planning, the book demonstrates that the level of poverty reduced in the two-decade period of economic reforms, 1991–2011, and especially in the later part of the reform period, 2004–11, when the growth rate accelerated to a new high. A clinical examination of specific strategies to remove poverty, and the outcomes of these strategies, supported by a quan- titative assessment of growth and income redistributive anti-poverty programmes reveals that poverty reduction in this period took place almost exclusively due to increase in income and consumption as a result of economic growth rather than redistribution of income.

A feature of poverty reduction in the period of economic reform was that the interstate disparity in the level of poverty that existed ear- lier, when the growth rate was low to moderate, remained unchanged even when the growth rate became high. Poverty reduction was found to be associated with the change in the pattern of consumption, eventuated by rapid economic growth and growth-induced change in the socio-economic condition. Still, it is a situation where one in every five people is counted as poor, and pockets of poverty exist, affecting specific regions and classes of people who are unable to participate fully in the growth process. The analysis cautions that poverty remains a major economic and political concern.

Analysing the nature and pattern of growth at the regional level, it is concluded that the high growth rate in the period of economic reform has not been able to alter the pattern of development, if the state of poverty and the rate of its reduction is considered a guide. The pattern of consumption changed as a result of economic growth, but the structure of poverty remained unaltered. The per capita con- sumption in the poorer states increased, but this is a part of the global process as it increased in other states too, leaving their relative posi- tion completely unaffected. The gap between the poor and less poor states did not reduce. The level of poverty in the states reduced but their relative position did not change.

The latest officially measured estimate of the number of poor relates to the year 2011–12. It shows that 269.8 million people, or 21.9 per cent of the total population, are poor. Besides, a large number of people are subjected to transient poverty—a slight drop in their income or consumption is liable to raise the level of poverty. This can happen when the growth rate becomes low, as has been the case since 2017–18, and especially in 2019–20, when the growth rate dipped to less than 5 per cent. The analysis cautions that poverty remains a major economic and political concern in view of the large number of poor and also as they have been counted against a poverty line, which is viewed as a bare subsistence level of living, a level below which they are under severe stress and their survival is threatened.

Growth Scenario in the 2010s

The Eleventh Plan ended in 2011. The Twelfth Plan was formulated and set into motion before the Planning Commission was disbanded. In actuality, with the disbanding of the Planning Commission, the Twelfth Plan went into oblivion. This way, the economic growth in the 2010s became devoid of planning. The National Institution for Transforming India Aayog (NITI Aayog) prepared a vision document for the economy, but how this was integrated with the plans and programmes of the states is not sufficiently clear.

This book makes an asessment of the economic situation of the 2010s. Since there are no targets to be achieved, the state of the major macro-variables of the economy have been examined here. It finds that the growth scenario in the 2010s began with a promising note but ended in a bleak situation. The average growth rates in the two halves of the decade were close, but the yearly growth rates depict a U-shaped curve in the first half, 2010–11 to 2014–15, while sloping downward in the second half, 2015–16 to 2019–20. The two halves characterized contrasting features of the economy. In the first half, the price inflation was high and there was a kind of 'policy paralysis' affecting the decisions of the government on major economic issues whereas in the second half, the price inflation was low and there was plenty of 'policy activism', which impeded economic growth. It concludes that the retardation of growth rate in the second half was a part of the cyclical process that has been experienced at regular intervals since the initiation of economic reforms. This time, it may take more time to recover as the decline in the growth rate was eventuated by certain policies of the government in the second half, which had adverse impacts on the capabilities of specific sectors of the economy. Over and above this strategy to lift the growth rate to the trend level lacked consistency. Emphasizing on the fact that under similar circumstances, India had always used the monetary and the fiscal policies in tandem, this book points out that despite low price levels, the government waited for an unusually long time to set in motion the monetary policy, and there is still no sign of fiscal policy being put to action as the growth rate continues to dip to a level below 5 per cent. The government is also unable to take recourse to demand-side measures to restore the growth rate to the trend level, and that is likely to make the process of recovery more painful as well as lengthy for the people. It is necessary to prepare a concrete road map to lift the growth rate to the medium-term trend, taking the state governments on board, as they are the implementing agencies of the government policies to kick-start growth. The institutions that are associated with economic policymaking have either been abolished or weakened. In this respect, the government is certain to feel the absence of the Planning Commission, as its replacement, the NITI Aayog, has not been armed with sufficient power to deal with the situation. Some of the decisions of the government that are akin to throwing spanners in to economic growth have been identified here. Also identified are several opportunities that the government could not avail to raise the growth rate. Then, there was misplaced emphasis in areas that took the focus away from growth. Finally, the book brings out that lack of confidence among entrepreneurs and the business class that is impeding investment and growth.

The latest poverty estimates are available for the year 2011–12. These were estimated by the erstwhile Planning Commission using the National Sample Survey (NSS) consumer expenditure data. The next estimates of poverty were due in 2017–18. The National Statistics Office (NSO) has withheld the publication of the consumer expenditure data of 2017–18 citing technical issues related to data collection, preventing an assessment of the change in poverty situation in the 2010s. Several studies have brought out convincing evidence of decline in per capita consumption expenditure in real terms, in both rural and urban areas after 2015–16, and also stagnation and decline of real wages and salaries after 2011–12. The unemployment rate estimated by the NSO for the year 2017–18 was unusually high. These are reflections of the decline in growth rate and bring out symptoms of a deeper economic malaise.

1

Planning for Growth and Development

Planning and the Five Year Plans have been integral in the implementation of the growth and development strategy of India for a pretty long period of six decades, 1951–2011. In this period, India formulated and implemented 11 Five Year Plans.

The idea that planning can be used as an instrument of policy in the Indian context can be traced to the days of the freedom struggle in the pre-Independence era. In February 1938, Netaji Subhas Chandra Bose, as the president of the Indian National Congress, announced his intention to constitute the NPC under the chairmanship of Jawaharlal Nehru. Nehru was then in Europe to campaign for Indian independence. Bose waited for Nehru to return. Upon Nehru's return, the NPC was constituted in November 1938.[1] In the previous month (October 1938), Bose had organized a conference of the ministries of industries of the provinces in which the Congress Party was then in power. This conference adopted a resolution, which states: '[T]he problems such as of poverty and unemployment, of national defense and economic regeneration in general, cannot be solved without industrialization. As a step towards industrialization, a comprehensive scheme of National Planning should be formulated.'[2] In conformity with this, the NPC was asked to lay down the path for maximizing the rate of economic growth and, in this context, the 'industrial regeneration of the country'.

Bose and Nehru had very similar ideas about planning and its use-fulness to improve the economic fundamentals of a low-income, poor, and underdeveloped country such as India. The first meeting of the NPC was held on 17 December 1938 in Mumbai, where Bose delivered the inaugural address. Drawing upon the possibilities of industrial development, Bose emphasized the need for industrial regeneration, specifically of basic and key industries. While endorsing the use of planning for increasing production as well as improving the standard of living of the people, the committee emphasized that attainment of Independence is indispensable for taking necessary steps for carrying out the plans and programmes for growth and development.[3]

The NPC defined planning in a democratic system

> as the technical co-ordination, by disinterested experts, of consumption, production, investment, trade, and income distribution in accordance with the social objectives set by bodies, representative of the nation. Such planning is not only to be considered from the point of view of economics and the raising of the standard of living, but must include cultural and spiritual values and human side of life.[4]

This brings two prominent issues to the surface. First, the freedom fighters and national leaders decided that after Independence, India would be governed by democracy. Second, the deliberation on the use of planning for economic development began a decade before Independence.

In the process of transfer of power (from the British to indepen-dent India), an interim government was installed in September 1946, with the power of the prime minister effectively bestowed on Nehru.[5] Within a month, the Advisory Planning Board was created.[6] The All India Congress Committee (AICC) had set up an Economic Programme Committee (EPC) in November 1947 under Nehru's chair-manship.[7] A report of the EPC released in January 1948 mentioned that in order to establish a society based on social justice and equality, every man and woman should be provided with equal opportunity and freedom to work for the unfettered development of his or her per-sonality; and to extend democracy from the political to the social and economic spheres, it was essential to espouse planned central direction as well as decentralization of political and economic power so that an economic structure is evolved which can yield maximum production without the operation of private monopolies and concentration of wealth. The EPC maintained that such a structure could provide an alternative to the acquisitive economy of private capitalism and, at the same time, the regimentation concomitant with a totalitarian state. The idea to set up the Planning Commission and the perception that planning can be the best and the most efficient means to raise income of the people within a short span of time, and with minimum use of resources, is rooted in this contention of the EPC.

The government constituted the Planning Commission in March 1950 and tasked it with the responsibility to formulate medium- and long-term plans for economic growth and development.[8] The functions assigned to the Planning Commission included the following: (*a*) assessment of material, capital, and human resources, and investigating the possibilities of augmenting the resources; (*b*) formulation of Plan for effective and balanced utilization of the resources; (*c*) determination of priorities, defining the stages in which the Plan should be carried out and proposing allocation of resources for its implementation; (*d*) indicating the factors which tend to retard economic development, and laying down the conditions for successful execution of the Plan; (*e*) determining the nature of the machinery necessary to implement each stage of the Plan; (*f*) appraising the progress achieved in the execution of each stage of the Plan and recommending necessary adjustment of policy and measures. The functions of the Planning Commission also covered examination of issues specifically referred to it for advice by the central government or state governments.

Over and above, the Planning Commission was made a part of the decision-making process on how to distribute income among the different groups and deciles of the population. The entire process of income generation and its distribution among different sections of the population took place through planning. The intention was to ensure a process of income generation with equity in its class distribution at the core. It was considered indispensable to cope with the abject poverty and widespread hunger that afflicted India in 1950.

What exactly is expected from planning? The first and foremost is maximization of the rate of economic growth, and then, as far as possible, distribution of the fruits of growth equally among the cross section of the population. This is just the tip of the iceberg. The expectation is much more. The task of planning is to raise the standards of living of the people by increasing production by better distribution of what is produced, and eventually attaining a position where economic growth can be sustained. This spells out the purpose of planning, underlining the role it is expected to play in the production of goods and services so as to raise the income and standard of living of the people as well as the sustainability of the growth process. From this angle, planning is viewed as an intelligent and logical approach, in which certain objectives are set, and the method of attaining these objectives is specified. A pragmatic approach has been the hallmark of Indian Plans throughout, both in respect of formulation, as well as implementation.

Planning as an Instrument of Policy

The Five Year Plans facilitate to shape the course of development. The First Five Year Plan was launched in April 1951. Since then, the Planning Commission has formulated and overseen the implementation of 11 Five Year Plans between 1951 and 2011. The maxim of planning has been that the rate of economic growth be raised to a level and in a manner that it is able to improve the economic fundamentals, and increase the income of the people so as to acquire the capacity to make a decisive impact on the levels of living and quality of life.

The first and foremost target of planning is maximization of income, which is necessary to remove poverty among the masses of the population, and improve their standard of living and quality of life. India adopted democracy as the means through which political rights are expected to flow to individuals. Democracy was considered as the key to ensure political equality. The state engaged itself to build a wide range of institutions that are necessary for democratic governance. In tandem, economic equality was treated as an essential prerequisite to achieve political equality, and it (economic equality) became the cornerstone of the policy of growth and development. This is because democracy, despite fine institutions and ideals, may cease to be a living force if the people, in general, remain poor, and the social and economic indicators that define the standard of living and quality of life of the people remain at a low level. In order to ensure political as well as economic equality, it is necessary that there are no great differences in the interpersonal distribution of income in society and that opportunities are given to one and all.

It is believed that maximization of income and ensuring its equitable distribution among the people is contingent upon state control on economic activities, and especially on the means of production and distribution. The state, in such a situation, takes the responsibility of allocating resources (which, in the early stage of development, is scarce) between sectors and areas of activities in the economy so as to increase output, and devise a mechanism so that the output, as far as possible, is shared equally by the people. This entire process is conducted through planning.

The political leadership was convinced about the inevitability of planning for growth (income) maximization as it would be possible to utilize scarce resources efficiently and optimally to increase production and the system would be able to offer opportunities to all. In 1950, the Indian economy was underdeveloped with limited resources. Planning is considered more useful in such a situation for optimal utilization of resources. This induced the political leadership to pin their faith on planning for growth and development and to use it as a major instrument in economic and social reconstruction. The economic condition and social characteristics in Indian society, as in most countries, are inextricably linked. Hence, these are used as the basis for planning. It was envisaged that political, social, economic, legal, and related organizations would support the endeavours of planning and contribute to economic and social development. The perception is that planning would result in economic progress, which, in its due turn, would be able to satisfy the desire of the people across the social structure in which they live.

The formulation of a Five Year Plan has to encounter the changing conditions in domestic and international economies. It may often face uncertainties in areas such as domestic resources, foreign exchange, and import of machinery and equipment from abroad. The Plan, under the circumstances, is treated as a broad framework and is liable to alteration within the five years of the Plan. The changes are done through Plans for a shorter time frame of one year, which is termed as 'annual plan'. The annual plan is more detailed and precise in nature (as compared with the Five Year Plan) as it factors in the latest information and technology and facilitates their adaption in the economy. An annual plan entails a precise commitment for the later years within the framework of the Five Year Plan, and is a concentrated and detailed plan.

The Plan has an all-India approach. Behind the Plan lay the concept of India's unity, and a solid cooperative effort of its people. Before Independence, India consisted of two main entities: British India, which was the area under direct rule of the British government, and the Indian states, which were the 565 princely states of varying sizes in terms of area and population. The princely states were totally feudal in character. Besides pervasive poverty, social and economic inequality were equally at their peak in British India and the princely states. The exploitation by the British and the feudal nature of administration in the princely states perpetuated the process of economic inequality. Moreover, there was social inequality, which arose from age-old systems and traditions. It was a very different India back in the 1950s as compared to what it is in the twenty-first century. Stressing the interrelation of one part of India with another, the instrument of planning was used to tackle the disruptive tendencies associated with provincialism, communalism, and casteism. As a matter of fact, planning was used to bind the whole of India into one unit—a view often articulated by Prime Minister Jawaharlal Nehru in his fortnightly letters addressed to the chief ministers in the first half of the 1950s.

Planning in India is viewed as a process of assessment of a wide range of economic and social parameters and determination of targets, which are consistent with the available resources. In a multi-sectoral economy, the targets have to be made inter-sectorally consistent. In a sense, planning provides a guideline for the use of resources, which is usually scarce. Then, it is used as a means to sort out the prioritization issues, involved in making the choice between industry and agriculture, between consumption and investment, between investment in producer goods and consumer goods, and so on. The problems of choice are basically concerned with the inter-sectoral allocation of resources, and ensure that the resulting pattern of production fits into the consumption that is desired and demanded by the society. It is crucial to strike the right balance between material advancement viewed from the increase in income of the people, which is one of the prime objectives of the Plan, and the other prospective goals of the society. These processes, which are accomplished through planning, ideally should end up in the maximization of the rate of economic growth and at the same time facilitate the distribution of the benefits of growth fairly equally across different regions, and among the various groups and deciles of the population. The success of translating the theoretical frame of planning into fruition to a great extent depends on how pragmatic the planning process is at the ground level, balancing reality with ideas and coordinating aspirations with resources.

The form and content of planning in the 11 Five Year Plans implemented between 1951 and 2011 have not been the same. The planning process traversed from rigid state control on economic activities (in the first four decades of planning, 1951–90) to a liberalized economic management (from 1991 onwards, under the auspices of economic reform measures), in which the state eschewed from directly participating in production and trade, leaving these areas mostly to the private sector. The planning in the first four decades, 1951–90, is characterized by a high degree of centralization and administrative regulation, neatly fastened to state ownership and control of the means of production and distribution. It embodied rigid restriction on the activities of the private sector while the state-owned and -managed public enterprises were encouraged and empowered to scale the 'commanding heights of the economy'. The development policy (particularly in the early stages of planning) stressed on heavy industry, with agriculture generating surplus for industrial development. It is a model of economic development, which partly but not entirely resembles the growth model used by the Soviet Union in the 1930s and 1940s. Planning, in this case, becomes watertight and affects almost all the areas of economic activity and sections of the population, placing the state at the helm of the entire decision-making process. However, it is worthwhile to mention that the degree of state intervention varied in the first seven Five Year Plans formulated and implemented in 1951–90.

The state control on economic activities was moderated to some extent in the 1980s, when the private sector was allowed to gain access to certain areas of the economy, which were forbidden for them until then. The change in the role of the private sector was slow, and yet noticeable in the Sixth Plan (1980–85). This process was carried forward in the Seventh Plan (1985–90) while proposing a 'symbiotic and complementary relationship between public and private sectors'.[9]

The planning process witnessed a sea change from 1991 onwards with India embracing the policy of economic reform and liberalization. The economic reform measures placed reliance on market mechanism, traditionally known as the centrepiece of development strategy of the developed capitalist world. Planning during the two decades of economic reforms (1991–2011) was markedly different from the previous four decades 1951–90. The Eighth Plan (1992–97) was the last to be formulated under the aegis of state control on economic activities. But it was implemented against the backdrop of the liberal policies as part of the economic reform programmes. As a consequence, many of the plans and programmes in the Eighth Plan deviated from their blueprints. The connotation of planning became different from the Ninth Plan (1997–2002) and remained so until the Eleventh Plan (2007–12). Along with the withdrawal of the state from the areas of production and trade, the process of diluting the holdings of the public sector enterprises began in earnest from the Ninth Plan. Public sector enterprises were thus granted corporate freedom to operate in a competitive market. The earlier dominance of the public sector in India's economic superstructure began to fade from the Tenth Plan (2002–07). In the Eleventh Plan, the public sector enterprises were allowed to enter into the capital market to raise funds and forge partnerships with the private sector. In short, the state regimentation through planning gave way to a market economy.

In India's democratic set-up, the philosophy and ideological bent of the political party in power has largely been responsible in shaping the growth and development strategy. The prime ministers who presided in the six decades of 1951–2011 did not have the same world view on economic and social issues, and their ideas on the manner and method of maximizing the rate of economic growth often clashed. The common thread that runs between them is the unanimity about the role of planning to ensure economic growth and development, and reliance on the Planning Commission for the formulation of medium- and long-term plans. The growth and development strategy throughout 1951–2011 is guided by the basic principle of maximization of income and reduction in inequality in the class distribution of income. Improvement of living standards and quality of life of the people, especially of the poor and the marginalized, is treated as the principal milestone of progress. The ground reality is that the policies of the successive prime ministers in pursuance of growth and economic development are not very different. The difference, if any, is confined to the manner and method of implementing the policies and programmes in the Plan, which is formulated in furtherance of the strategy.

The process of planning was abandoned and the Planning Commission was abolished in August 2014, after 64 years of its existence. It was replaced by the NITI Aayog, which translated into English reads as 'Policy Commission'. NITI in this case is the abbreviated form of National Institution for Transforming India. It would be appropriate to mention that the functions and responsibilities of the NITI Aayog are much narrower in scope and content than the erstwhile Planning Commission. What is more is that in terms of power and authority, the NITI Aayog pales in comparison with the Planning Commission.

Four broad issues can be identified to judge the effectiveness of planning, inter alia, in the growth and development strategy pursued in the six decades between 1951 and 2011. These are: (a) level of income, employment, and output; (b) regional differential of major macroeconomic variables; (c) incidence of poverty and inequality; and (d) levels of living and quality of life of the people. The judgement at the first instance may come from the rate and magnitude of increase in income in conjunction with the class distribution of income over the Plan periods. Then, it is the issue of the extent of improvement in living standards of the people, which is mirrored in the level of and changes in poverty. It renders poverty reduction as an acid test of planning.

Planning Process: 1951–90

The Five Year Plans in the first four decades of planning were designed to set out the dimensions of economic growth and development. They postulated the macroeconomic features such as aggregate resources, savings, investment, GDP growth rate, and other broader economic and social requirements. The planning process focused on optimal deployment of investible resources, and at the same time (a) outlined the strategy of development and related policy issues; (b) worked out macro-parameters for economic growth and its sectoral pattern; (c) allocated resources between the central government and the state governments, and for different sectoral activities; (d) allocated budgetary support in detail; and (e) considered public sector projects and programmes which were implemented for making a positive impact upon the developmental process.

The Five Year Plans lay out a programme of investment and activities to steer the economy in the desired direction. The Planning Commission in this respect (a) estimates the size of national resources; (b) assesses balance of payments position; (c) takes stock of resources for development from external sources; (d) indicates the method by which resources can be augmented in a sustained manner; (e) estimates imports, exports, and inflow of foreign capital; and (f) assesses the incremental capital output ratio (ICOR), which is a summary expression of the existing technical conditions and structural configuration of the economy.

The target growth rate for the economy is determined from past behaviour and the need to meet the likely future demands for material production sectors (such as steel, cement, fertilizer, coal, petroleum, power, transportation, and so on) and social requirements (such as education, health care, sanitation, water supply, livelihood security, anti-poverty measures, and so on). The assessment of growth rate is made by matching resources and requirements, and consistent with the growth rate, the demand requirement for material production sectors is worked out. The demand for material production sectors is related to target growth rates and are worked out from the consistency-cum-investment model based on input–output. The social requirements at the sectoral level are assessed from a certain degree of judgement (a mix of demand and norms) as to the needs and affordability of resources. In other words, the social requirements are determined in a normative manner keeping in view the resource constraint. The growth rate that can be achieved is assessed by matching resources and requirements, and consistent with that rate of growth, the sectoral growth targets are worked out. Equivalently, it denotes that the overall growth rate is fixed matching the demand and supply of resources, and the sectoral targets of growth are made consistent with the aggregate growth rate.

The Plans have been functional within the confines of the entire economy, which consists of the public sector and the private sector in a mixed economy framework. Mathematical models have been used in several areas of Plan formulation in order to determine sectoral growth profiles, which are consistent with resource availability. These models are described in Chapter 2. The growth profiles are determined in a somewhat aggregative manner. Despite professing that the public sector would occupy the commanding heights of the economy, its share in aggregate investment throughout the first four decades of planning (1951–90) rarely surpassed 50 per cent. The planning is not oriented towards direct control on the private sector. The state control and regulation of the activities of the private sector is channelized through a set of instruments, such as industrial licensing, and monetary and fiscal policy. Such controls are usually indirect and used to induce the private sector to tread the path laid down in the medium- or long-term plans.

Preparation of a Five Year Plan

The formulation of a Five Year Plan began with the preparation of an approach paper, which contained the objectives, strategies, and macroeconomic dimensions. The approach paper discussed, among other things, the alternative feasible scenarios and policy implications. It was prepared by the Planning Commission after intense consultations with the Ministry of Finance, the RBI (or the central bank), and ministries of the central government (central ministries). The Planning Commission presented the approach paper to the National Development Council (NDC) for its consideration and eventual approval. On approval by the NDC, the approach paper was circulated among the state governments, the central ministries, and the institutions associated with Plan formulation, the leading among them being the RBI.

Based on the parameters postulated in the approach paper (as approved by the NDC), the central ministries and the state governments prepared their respective Five Year Plans in detail. The Plans prepared by the central ministries were called central Plans. Similarly, the Plans prepared by the state governments, and eventually implemented by them, were called state Plans. The objective of the central

Plan was to strengthen and support the states' Plans and to implement some of the important national priorities.[10] The Planning Commission played a coordinating role between the central and the state Plans in order to achieve the national objectives. The national Plan consists of central Plans and state Plans. The Planning Commission developed the national Plan by integrating these two Plans through a process of discussions and reviews at various levels, which included the bureaucratic and ministerial levels.

The basic modality of formulating the Plan involved setting up of a number of steering committees and working groups covering important areas and sectors of the economy. These committees/groups were composed of representatives of concerned ministries, selected state governments, academicians, private sector, non-governmental and civil society organizations, and so on. Based on the reports of these committees/groups, the state governments and the central ministries came up with their proposals of detailed plans and programmes and held discussions with the Planning Commission. The range of activities traversed by the steering committees and working groups for Plan formulation can be deduced from the fact that about 120 such committees/groups were constituted by the Planning Commission for the Eleventh Plan. The numbers in earlier Five Year Plans are not very different.

Through the discussions between the state governments and the central ministries, on the one hand, and the Planning Commission, on the other, a detailed Plan was evolved. Its main endeavour was to sort out the competing claims on resources, and, in the process, to ensure an element of consistency in resource allocation between the different sectors of the economy, and between the states as well. This was finally presented (by the state governments and the central ministries) to the Planning Commission. The Five Year Plan document was then prepared, clearly listing out the objectives and detailing the new Plan orientation, development perspective, macroeconomic dimension, the policy framework, financing of the Plan, and sectoral profiles. The Planning Commission presented the final Plan document to the NDC for its consideration and approval. A feature of the Plan was its unanimous approval by the NDC. In other words, the consent of all the chief ministers of the states was a necessary prerequisite for the finalization of the Plan.

Implementation of a Five Year Plan

Traditionally, the Planning Commission was responsible for the formulation of the Five Year Plans, and the implementation of the projects and programmes contained in the Plan rested with the central ministries and the state governments. The state governments used their own administrative apparatus to implement the projects and programmes contained in the Plan. In this regard, they could be assisted by the central ministries.

The projects and programmes contained in the Five Year Plan were implemented through the annual plan prepared by the Planning Commission. The requirement of investible resources for the Plan and its disaggregation between the central government and the state governments and among the ministries within the central government was decided in the annual plan. This way, the annual plan presented a detailed description of the allocation of resources between the central government and the state governments, and for different sectoral activities in the government, for one year. It was decided after a prolonged discussion with the central ministries (important among them being the finance ministry), the state governments, and the RBI, keeping in view the parameters postulated in the Five Year Plan.

As in the case of the Five Year Plan, the Planning Commission held discussions with the state governments to firm up the annual plan of the states. Similarly, the Planning Commission discussed with the finance ministry about the quantum of Plan expenditure to be incurred by the central government. The allocation of budgetary resources for the Plan is a component of the annual budget of the central government. Sanction of the government to finance the Plan expenditures was made through the annual budget of the central government (known as the central budget and falling in the domain of the finance ministry of the Government of India), which was passed by the Parliament every year. The allocation of resources and expenditure for a year was made by the government keeping the Five Year Plan in view. While presenting the budget to the Parliament, a review of the likely resource availability and investment was done and the size of the annual plan was determined in the light of such a review. The annual plan was not exactly one-fifth of the Five Year Plan, but it kept in line with it in general terms.

The amount of money allocated in the central budget in order to meet the growth and development objectives spelt out in the Plan was decided primarily keeping the resource availability in view. In this context, the amount of resources allocated for the Plan was decided jointly by the Planning Commission and the finance ministry of the Government of India. While there were indications from the mathematical models about the allocation of investible resources for the five years of the Plan, there was no such norm for annual phasing of the five-yearly investment from these models. The decision on the allocation in a year was rooted in the discussion between the Planning Commission, which would usually ask for more funds, and the finance ministry, which would make no mistake to squeeze it down to a reduced number. This was nothing unique in India. Such 'bargaining' takes place in almost all the countries where planning and finance departments are separate entities. Likewise, it is not different in countries where the responsibilities of the planning commission are subsumed in the finance ministry. In countries where these two organizations (planning commission and finance ministry) are contained within one department, there is somebody at the top—such as the president or prime minister, or the king or sultan, or the military dictator—who usually takes the call.

Civil servants who have the opportunity to experience the functioning of both the Planning Commission and the finance ministry are extremely rare. An envious exception is Montek Singh Ahluwalia, who participated in such 'bargaining' from both sides—first, from the finance ministry and then from the Planning Commission. Ahluwalia served as the finance secretary of the Government of India for six long years (1993–98)—long in view of the average time of an incumbent in the post, which until then had been less than two years. Then, he served as the deputy chairman of the Planning Commission for ten years in a row (2004–14)—the longest tenure for anyone in that capacity in the 64 years of its existence). In view of this, Ahluwalia's views on the roles of the finance ministry vis-à-vis the Planning Commission in the matter of allocation of resources for Plan projects are worthy of discussion here. When in the finance ministry, Ahluwalia was never shy of displaying a parsimonious attitude on the proposals of the Planning Commission for additional funds to finance Plan projects.

While in the Planning Commission, he reversed his role and began to negotiate with the finance ministry for enhanced allocation for Plan projects. On the issue of allocation of Plan funds, the duel between Ahluwalia, as the deputy chairman of the Planning Commission, and P. Chidambaram, the finance minister of the Government of India, is legendary. The whole process can be summed up as follows: demand from the Planning Commission for Plan funds always exceeded availability; the Planning Commission ended up pushing for a higher number and the finance ministry for a lower one. Ahluwalia says that in India, the prime minister typically makes the final call.

Planning Process under Economic Reforms: 1991–2011

The planning process until the 1980s embodied state control on economic activities. The state played a major role in production and trade and went all-out to support the public sector, and at the same time regulate the activities of the private sector. Trade policy tended to be inward-looking. The centrality of this policy was to pull off industrial development through import substitution, encouraged through a tight control over imports and high tariffs.

The growth rate in the first three decades of planning, 1951–80, never showed signs of coming out of the much ridiculed 'Hindu rate', a phrase coined by Raj Krishna, a member of the Planning Commission in the late 1970s, referring to the low growth rate of the Indian economy at this time, averaging 3.5 per cent per year, yielding growth in per capita income by as little as 1.1 per cent per year.[11] By the early 1980s, the limitations of the growth strategy pursued in the previous three decades, 1951–80, under the aegis of planning and state control were evident. It was recognized that the Indian economy lacked efficiency and competitiveness, and, as a result, was growing at a rate much below its potential. The low rate of economic growth was not sufficient to reduce poverty, and employment generation was inadequate. Besides, the economic growth was not regionally balanced. Whatever little growth had taken place in per capita terms, it was not distributed equally or even in a near equal manner, either between states or between regions, such as districts within a state or blocks within a district. The inequality in distribution of income remained high.

A wide-ranging economic reform was initiated in 1991. It culminated in deregulation of industry, liberalization of trade, elimination of protective tariff barriers, rationalization of the tax system, and privatization of state-owned financial institutions and public enterprises, among others. These are contingent upon relaxation of state control in economic activities, allowing the private sector to enter the space. In a broad alignment with these policies, whose authorship can be claimed by the International Monetary Fund (IMF) and the World Bank, the government adopted a series of sector-specific actions throughout the 1990s. In industrial policy, capacity licensing was largely dispensed with. The policy related to foreign direct investment (FDI) was liberalized and it was permitted through an automatic route to a range of areas and activities. The FDI limit was eliminated in virtually all areas in the manufacturing sector and in large areas of services. In trade, quantitative control on merchandise import was completely dismantled. The average rate of protective customs tariff was lowered to 10 per cent (from as high as 150 per cent in 1991–92, that is, at the time of commencement of the economic reform), and government control and regulation on use of foreign exchange was relaxed. The exchange rate (of the Indian rupee vis-à-vis major foreign currencies) came to be market determined. Free repatriation of profits and dividends was allowed. The process of ensuring a stable tax regime, rationalizing the structure of indirect taxes, and moderating the rates of direct taxation was initiated. In order to ensure fiscal discipline, legislations were framed to eliminate the revenue deficit and reduce the fiscal deficit. The monetary policy was characterized by deregulation of interest rate and making the money market sophisticated. There were attempts to strengthen the capital market so that it could be the source of investment funds for both the private and the public sector. With these, the Indian economy witnessed a gradual transformation in which a dominant and all-embracing public sector patronized by the state gave way to an enlarged private sector encompassing industry, trade, and services, which operated under market mechanism.

Economic reforms and liberalization allowed a greater play for the market, replacing the different agents of government as dominant decision-makers. The hallmark of economic reforms being market mechanism, the private sector as well as the public sector operates under market. The Five Year Plans were formulated and implemented in an environment where the private sector occupied a dominant position in the production of goods and services and there was pre-dominance of the market. In tandem, the public sector was exposed to market forces and made to function as an autonomous institution. This changed the manner and method of state intervention in the economy through planning, making the planning process under economic reforms vastly different from that in the pre-reform days.

Planning Methodology: Ninth (1997–98 to 2001–02) to Eleventh (2007–08 to 2011–12) Plan

The Eighth Plan (1992–97) was prepared in the pre-reform era, but implemented in the environs of the economic reforms. Under the economic reforms, three Five Year Plans, the ninth to the eleventh, covering the years 1997–2011, were formulated and implemented. These three Five Year Plans did not have a similar format and analyti-cal frame. The degree of state involvement (rather withdrawal) in the economy was not uniform throughout these three Five Year Plans as the process of implementation of the reform measures evolved over time. The economic reform measures were not implemented at one go; they were staggered over the years with varying intensity and, in consequence, the manner and method of internalizing the reform measures into the planning framework were not similar in these three Five Year Plans.

While implementing the policies of economic reforms, the state preferred to adopt a gradualist approach to replace the different agents of government in the decision-making process. It was necessary to grant autonomy to the public sector so as to enable it to operate under market forces, just as the private sector. The granting of autonomy to the public sector was a slow process. The dilution of holdings of the public sector enterprises began in the Ninth Plan, and it was not until the Eleventh Plan that they were permitted to forge partnerships with their counterparts in the private sector, and internationalize their operations with options for mergers and acquisitions. Because of the gradualist approach, it took one and a half decades to raise the share of private sector in total investment by 25 percentage points.

Before analysing the manner and method of formulation of the Five Year Plans in the era of economic reforms, it will be useful to take a look at some of the events that are considered to be important catalysts of the change that is found to have taken place in the planning process in the reform era. This will make keeping track of the process of change in the Plan formulation in the era of economic reforms rather easy.

The state was at the forefront of the decision-making process of economic activities in the pre-reform days whereas under the economic reforms, it withdrew from economic sectors and engaged itself in creating a suitable environment for growth and development. The state was not investing much in material production sectors, leaving that space to the private sector. Involving India's strong and vibrant private sector—its large, middle-sized, and small-scale enterprises—in the growth process dominated the agenda of economic reform.

The economy being market-driven, the state lost much of its authority to direct the flow of investment in the private sector compared to the manner and form it used to carry out this task in the pre-reform days. In the pre-reform era, the state used to derive enormous power from the trade policy by regulating exports and imports and especially the import tariffs, and from the price policy founded mainly on a system of administrative price mechanism, which ensured dual price of several products. In the era of economic reform, as trade liberalization took shape, and as the prices came to be determined in the market, the instruments associated with trade and prices could no longer be used by the state to control and regulate the activities of the private sector. In a similar way, the monetary and fiscal policies could not be used by the state in the way these were used in the pre-reform years to exercise control on large areas of economic activities through planning. The shift of investment from the public sector to the private sector, the loss of authority of the state to channelize the investment of the private sector in the direction the state desired, and the uncertainty that usually characterizes a market-based system compelled a change in the methodology of planning in the era of economic reforms.

The formulation of the Five Year Plans under economic reforms began with the assessment of (*a*) the size of national resources that could be made available for investment; (b) the balance of payments position; (c) imports and exports; and (d) the ICOR, which is a measure of efficiency of capital use. The values of these variables were assessed by the Planning Commission at the national level.

The aggregate investment requirement in order to meet the target growth rate in the Plan was worked out on the basis of past ICORs. Post 1991, the aggregate investment requirement was obtained from the sectoral investment profile. It was treated as an indicative forecast in light of the manner and method of arriving at the estimates of (a) domestic resource availability and (b) inflow of foreign capital—the two elements which govern the aggregate investment in the economy. The domestic resource availability was estimated separately, linking domestic savings by sector (for example, public sector, private sector, private corporate sector, and so on) and by its composition (for example, within the private sector, the savings made by households in financial instruments and physical assets). In this context, the estimate of domestic resources availability could be treated as more or less precise. But a similar degree of precision could not be achieved in the case of estimate of inflow of foreign capital as it depends more on factors that remain beyond the control of planners. As a result, the estimate of inflow of foreign capital had to be an indicative forecast. This was a natural outcome of the Indian economy opening up to international trade and capital flows.

The sectoral priorities in the Plan evolved as an outcome of the investment decisions. The sectoral investment was determined from the likely sectoral growth rate in the Plan and the sectoral ICORs. This way, the sectoral growth rates became more in the nature of extrapolated values from the previous Plans. In consequence, the sectoral growth rates in the Plan were not capable of adequately reflecting the structural changes in the economy that were generally believed to occur in the context of large inflow of foreign capital and increase in the share of private investment (to total investment) in the economy.

Aggregate investment is the sum total of the investment in the public and private sectors. Sectoral private investment was estimated first. The public investment at the level of sectors was obtained as a difference between the investment for the economy as a whole and that of the private sector. This, in a way, presumed that the public sector played the role of gap-filler in the sense that wherever the initiative for investment from the private sector was lacking, the public sector would reach out and fill the gap.

In the context of an open economy environment in which transborder capital flows are liberal, a large part of the Plan became indicative in nature. The sectoral growth profile prepared in the Plan was a part of this feature and, as a consequence, had to be an indicative forecast, with the market playing a lead role in determining its actual values. In view of this, the sectoral growth rates in the Plan were measured in broad categories, namely agriculture, industry, and services. In the Ninth and Tenth Plans, the sectoral growth rates were estimated as unique values, and in the form of a point estimate. In the Eleventh Plan, the growth rates of industry and services were given in a range instead of a point estimate. It was not possible to generate a point estimate for the growth rate of industry and services sectors with precision since market behaviour of most of the factors determining their growth could not be captured from the available information. The methodology of planning under economic reforms ordained that growth rate of only a few critical variables were determined quantitatively (using a mathematical model) while a large majority of them were allowed to be determined under the influence of market.

The estimates of sectoral growth rate and investment requirement in the Plan were derived from a fix-price model in which values of the variables are measured at the prices prevailing in a specific year (generally, the base year of the Plan). This meant that the estimates of resources and investment in the Plan were made at constant prices. Such estimation was based on the tacit assumption that the income–expenditure equilibrium at constant prices automatically ensures similar equilibrium at current prices. In the event of faster increase in the prices of capital goods than that of consumption goods, the realized real investment tends to be lower than the target of investment fixed in the Plan. Sectoral growth and aggregate investment requirement estimated from the fix-price model ignore the real effect of prices. Such an effect can be significant as the production decisions become more and more market-based. Its outcome is distortion in the efficacy of resource allocations.

With progressive deregulation of the economy, and a larger role of the private sector and market-based decision-making, planning methods based on input–output balances for each industrial sector as practised in the pre-reform days (that is, in the first four decades of planning, 1951–90) became less relevant. Planning under the economic reforms involved working out a consistent and desirable growth path, identification of emerging trends, and deriving policy measures to bring about a confluence between the two. The methodology was not based on a deterministic relationship between the Plan and the economic performance. The fact that in an open and global setting there are uncertainties in the planning system, which limits its ability to accurately predict future trends, is well-recognized. Under the circumstances, the effects of government policies and interventions in the economy were not entirely predictable. This is true more for economic variables, although it may be less for social sector variables, which usually has a direct bearing on levels of living of the people. The approach of the Planning Commission in the era of economic reforms was to set the broad targets for the economy and outline the policies needed to achieve them. This, in a way, pertains to broader government policies that affect outcomes in a market economy. This way, the planning focused on 'planning for policy' so that the signals that were sent to the economic system induced its various agents to behave in a manner consistent with the national objectives. Each of these policies being in the realm of one central ministry or the other, it was often not possible to offer an independent assessment by the ministry that was in charge of implementing the policy. The Planning Commission stepped in to provide a holistic view. Quintessentially, the details of the policies and the manner of their implementation were worked out from the interface between the concerned central ministries, the state governments, and the Planning Commission.

Projects and Programmes in the Plan

The end result of Plan formulation was a conglomeration of projects and programmes in a wide range of areas and sectors of the economy, judiciously chosen in keeping with the multidimensional objectives that the country set for itself, or in other words, the objectives set out in the Plan. The projects and programmes in the public sector were finalized after appraising from economic and social angles. In the pre-reform days, public sector projects were spread over large areas of the material production sector, such as coal, steel, power, cement, and so on. By the mid-1960s, the Planning Commission was equipped with the technical expertise to appraise these projects. Its talent pool was so vast that it could venture on deciding even the location of a project using what is known as integer programming models. Though most of these models were used to make decisions about the projects in the material production sector, there were others, such as animal husbandry (for example, Mother Dairy for milk production and more, its processing and distribution, and also social sector projects), which could benefit from similar appraisal techniques. With economic reforms, as investment in the material production sectors shifted to private sector, the role of the Planning Commission considerably waned in this regard.

In the pre-reform days, 1951–90, projects and programmes of the public sector found their way into a Five Year Plan through the central Plan and the state Plans. The central Plan was formulated, implemented, and financed by the central ministries. The state governments were basically in charge of the projects and programmes, which were contained in the state plan, and from this angle, they were responsible for their formulation and implementation. A large part of financing the projects and programmes in state Plans though comes from the central government in a variety of ways.

In addition to the state endeavours, the Five Year Plans had a private sector component, on which the central government or the state governments did not have direct control. The government in the pre-reform days could only induce the private sector to invest in certain areas and activities using price, and fiscal and monetary policy instruments. Of course, there was a major instrument at the disposal of the government to directly control the private sector investment in industry, and that is the industrial licensing mechanism.

Until the commencement of the economic reforms in 1991, the total investment earmarked in a Five Year Plan was shared almost equally by the public and the private sectors. The scenario changed under economic reforms, with the share of the public sector being lowered to about one-fourth of the total investment in the Tenth and the Eleventh Plans. In tandem, the focus of the public sector investment was changed from growth to poverty alleviation and social welfare programmes. The investment in growth-oriented areas, which were the forte of the public sector in the pre-reform days (1951–90), came to be dominated by the private sector in the era of economic reforms (1991–2011). In consequence, public sector projects and programmes lost much of their relevance in the maximization of the growth rate of the economy. It is a different matter that a large part of the investment in the private sector projects in the era of economic reforms was financed by the government, that is, the financial institutions in the public sector.

In the beginning of the planning (that is, in the 1950s) the location of the public sector projects was decided keeping in view the twin objectives: (*a*) maximization of the rate of economic growth; and (*b*) equitable spatial distribution of the fruits of economic growth so as to ensure balanced regional development. Putting it in an alternative way, the investment in public sector projects and programmes was guided by these two objectives. The investment flows (through the Five Year Plans) in actuality, took a different shape. As the resources were limited and the task of elevating the economy onto a higher growth path appeared imperative, the public sector investment surged in areas and regions which had the potential to grow more rapidly, or where growth potential could be developed quickly.

By the late 1960s, it was realized that the approach to investment in the previous one and a half decades was not compatible with the regional disparity in economic growth and development, which was evidently large and, according to many observers, on the upswing. It was prominent in the low living standards and degrading quality of life of a large section of the population. In order to counter this problem, balanced regional growth and development was made an indispensable component of the Five Year Plans. It is a fact that the investment decisions in the initial stage of planning could not pay much heed to regional equality ostensibly due to resource constraint. With economic growth, as additional resources became available, it was possible to channelize investment to the less developed areas and regions so that the regional disparity in growth and development is reduced. From the Fourth Plan (1969–74) onwards, transfer of investment funds from the central government to the state governments for the twin purposes of financing Plan projects in the underdeveloped regions and generating growth impulses within these regions became the major instrument of ensuring regional growth and equity under planning.

Flow of Funds from Centre to States

In the framework of planning, flow of investment funds from the central government to the state governments for the purpose of financing Plan expenditure was traditionally viewed as an instrument to guide and eventually shape the growth trajectory and development pattern of the states, particularly the relatively poorer states. Such a policy was pursued in the pre-reform years (1951–90), when the central government was at the forefront of the investment for growth maximization. The scenario changed when economic reforms were initiated in 1991, as the central government relinquished large areas of growth responsibility to the private sector.

Before the commencement of economic reforms in 1991, the transfer of funds from the central government to the state governments (to finance the Plan expenditure of the states) was based principally on the idea of benefiting the poorer and less developed states, more than others. The transfer mechanism, for several reasons, could not meet the development needs of all the states equally, much less the poorer states, for which it was largely intended. Economic growth was not regionally balanced and the growth rate failed to accelerate in some of the most backward regions. That many regions could not benefit adequately from the growth process was evident from the large regional disparity in growth of income and in the economic and social indicators that comprehensively defined the levels of living and quality of life of the people.

With the beginning of the economic reforms and the liberalization in 1991, the role of transfer of investible resources from the central government to the state governments for growth endeavour diminished as the state withdrew from production and trade, and confined its activities mostly to the social sector programmes and welfare services. The space of production and trade relinquished by the state was filled by the private sector, which shouldered the responsibilities for growth. In the era of economic reforms, state governments were empowered to decide about the area of investment, credit, and production. There was a decentralization of power from the central government to the state governments, and again from the state government to the grassroots-level administration, which comprises the three-tier panchayats (district–block–village) in rural areas and the local bodies in urban areas. Such empowering of the states and the local administration (within the state) allowed them greater manoeuvrability in managing their economic affairs, yielding plenty of space to chart their growth path. The growth and development of the states consequently became more associated with their own resource endowment and policy initiatives rather than the policies and finances of the central government. The lowering of central assistance to states that occurred in proportionate terms in the era of economic reforms should be viewed in this perspective.

Before the beginning of the Five Year Plans in 1951, there was a practice of extending central assistance to the state governments to implement earmarked development projects. Under planning, the flow of investment funds from the central government to the state governments generally took place through three routes: First were the block grants. These consisted of normal central assistance (NCA) and additional central assistance (ACA) for externally aided projects (EAPs) for special and other programmes. Second were the centrally sponsored schemes. These were joint efforts of the central government and the state governments in terms of financing. Third were the central sector schemes. These were formulated and implemented through the auspices of the central ministries.

In the first two decades of planning (1950s and 1960s), the investment funds (in the shape of central Plan assistance) used to be transferred from the central government to the state governments based on a schematic pattern. The interstate allocation of investment funds was decided on the basis of a set of parameters related to the state, which included its level of development, capacity to mobilize resources, size of population, level of income, ability to spend allotted investment fund (being a measure of performance in expenditure), and so on.

In the Fourth Plan (1969–74), the manner and method of allocating the central Plan assistance (or NCA) to the states was formalized through the 'Gadgil formula' (named after D.R. Gadgil, then Deputy Chairman, Planning Commission), the essence of which was to ensure equity in growth and development at the level of states. The formula was crafted with the purpose of canalizing more Plan assistance from the central government to the economically backward states so that they would be able to catch up with the developed states in economic growth and development within a reasonable time. The Gadgil formula was adopted for distribution of NCA to the states in the Fourth Plan, and continued until the Seventh Plan. A modified version of the Gadgil formula, known as Gadgil–Mukherjee formula, started being used for this purpose since the Eighth Plan. Since the 1990s, the allocation under ACA for EAPs was based on utilization of funds for projects. The allocation for special and other programmes is based on the needs of the states and sectoral priorities.

At the end of the Eleventh Plan, about 60 per cent of the Plan budget of the central government consisted of central assistance to state Plans and the remaining 40 per cent was allocated for central sector schemes. Of the total central assistance to state Plans, 25 per cent consisted of block grants and 75 per cent was earmarked for centrally sponsored schemes.[12] Under the economic reforms, the share of NCA in the flow of funds under central Plan was lowered and, in consequence, the Gadgil–Mukherjee formula lost much of its relevance in deciding the pattern of growth and development in the states.

Block Grant: Gadgil Formula

In the matter of allocation of funds under the Gadgil formula, the states were divided into two categories: 'general' and 'special'. The status of a state (general or special) was determined keeping in view the state of its economy and finances, and administrative parameters. The states that fulfilled the following conditions were identified as belonging to the special category: (*a*) low resource base and population density; (*b*) sizeable share of tribal population or hilly terrain; (*c*) backward economy and infrastructure; (*d*) international border; and (*e*) non-viable nature of finances. At the end of the Eleventh Plan, there were 28 states in the country; 11 of them were classified as special category states; the remaining 17 were termed as general category states. The 11 special category states were: Arunachal Pradesh, Assam, Himachal Pradesh, Jammu and Kashmir, Manipur, Mizoram, Meghalaya, Nagaland, Sikkim, Tripura, and Uttarakhand.

The special category states were allotted 30 per cent of the total central Plan assistance and 70 per cent was demarcated for the general category states.

There is a little bit of history associated with the classification of the special category states. The special category states did not figure in the Gadgil formula when it was put into operation for the first time in the Fourth Plan (1969–74). It was decided in 1969 that from the total central assistance earmarked for the states, the needs of Assam, Jammu and Kashmir, and Nagaland should be met first in consideration of the special problems they faced. In other words, these three states were granted liberal central assistance. The share of these three states in the total central Plan assistance during the three years preceding the Fourth Plan (that is, from 1966–67 to 1968–69) averaged around 10 per cent. In light of this, the Fourth Plan earmarked 11 per cent of the total central Plan assistance for these three states. In the Fifth Plan (1974–79), the share of these three states was raised to around 15 per cent. During the course of the Fifth Plan, another five states (Himachal Pradesh, Manipur, Meghalaya, Sikkim, and Tripura) were granted similar preferential treatment in the allocation of central assistance, taking the total number of such states to eight. In the Sixth Plan (1980–85), these eight states were defined as 'special category states' and 30 per cent of the central Plan assistance was set aside for them. The number of special category states was increased to 10 in 1990 with the inclusion of Arunachal Pradesh and Mizoram, and finally to 11 in 2010 with the inclusion of Uttarakhand.

The total central Plan assistance earmarked for the special category states was distributed among them mainly on the basis of their Plan size and their ability to spend the funds allotted in the past. The central Plan assistance across the general category states was distributed in the following way: (*a*) 60 per cent of total was distributed among the states on the basis of their population; and (*b*) the remaining 40 per cent was distributed using four factors—(*i*) per capita income, (*ii*) tax effort, (*iii*) ongoing irrigation and power projects, and (*iv*) special problems—among which the amount was divided equally.

In the course of implementing the Gadgil formula, some states pointed out that the criteria in respect of ongoing projects were weighted in favour of the relatively richer states. In response, the formula was modified in 1980 wherein the weightage for ongoing projects was merged with per capita income. The weight of per capita income as a result became 20 per cent. The fund earmarked for allocation with respect to per capita income was distributed among the states whose per capita income was less than the national average. This method of allocating funds to the states using per capita income as the criterion came to be known as the 'deviation method', as it is based on the deviation of per capita income of a state from the national average (of per capita income). Such a mechanism has the potential to assist the relatively poorer and less developed states more than others. This modified formula was used to allocate central Plan assistance among the states in the Sixth (1980–85) and the Seventh (1985–90) Plans, and in the annual plan of 1990–91.

In October 1990, the weights of the Gadgil formula were revised once again as follows: population 55 per cent, per capita income 25 per cent, fiscal management 5 per cent, and special development problems 15 per cent. Eighty per cent of the allocation under per capita income (which is equivalent to 20 per cent of the total central Plan assistance) was distributed among the states using the deviation method. The remaining 20 per cent of the allocation under per capita income (equivalent to 5 per cent of the total central Plan assistance) was distributed among the states using the distance method, which is based on the difference between the per capita income of the state and the highest per capita income among all the states. The Gadgil formula with these weights was used to distribute central Plan assistance for just one year (annual plan of 1991–92).

A committee was constituted in 1991 under the chairmanship of Pranab Mukherjee (then Deputy Chairman, Planning Commission) to evolve a suitable formula for distribution of central assistance to the states. Mukherjee stitched a formula, based entirely on the parameters used in the October 1990 version of the Gadgil formula (as mentioned earlier) with two changes. First, the weightage of population was raised from 55 per cent to 60 per cent. In tandem, the state-wise population estimates (used to calculate the interstate allocation of Plan funds) were frozen at the level of the 1971 census so that the states were not incentivized to increase population. The second change was associated with the treatment of special development problems of the states. Its weight was lowered to half, from 15 per cent to 7.5 per cent. The other 7.5 per cent of this fund was distributed among the states on the basis of their performance in tax effort, fiscal management, and progress in respect of four national objectives—namely, (a) population control, and maternal and child health; (b) universalization of primary education, and adult education; (c) timely completion of EAPs; and (d) land reforms. Notably, the manner in which per capita income was used in the Gadgil formula with 25 per cent weightage, and the combination of deviation (20 per cent) and distance (5 per cent) method, which were viewed as the main instruments to ensure equity in growth across the states, were kept unchanged by Mukherjee. This formula was endorsed by the NDC in December 1991 and came to be known as the Gadgil–Mukherjee formula. It was used to allocate central Plan assistance to the states from the Eighth Plan (1992–97) onwards.

In actuality, the Gadgil formula or its modified versions, including the Gadgil—Mukherjee formula, lacked quantitative reasoning. There was virtually no basis to earmark 30 per cent of the funds for the special category states. Many of the shares (such as tax effort and fiscal discipline) were not to scale and in that sense, the smaller and larger states (with respect to population or resource availability) were liable to be placed at the same footing. The link between Plan projects and central assistance was not transparent. Besides, the large number of parameters used to work out the Gadgil–Mukherjee formula made the entire exercise messy and cumbersome. The proof of the pudding is in the eating. The high regional inequality in income across the states testified to their inefficacy. The flow of funds through the Gadgil formula failed to assist the less developed states, that is, the special category states, in raising their rate of economic growth. It did not help the general category states to maximize their rate of economic growth either.

Centrally Sponsored Schemes

The projects and programmes contained in the central Plan were formulated and financed by the central ministries, and implemented by them in association with the state governments. These were known as central sector schemes and pertain to subjects covered by the Union List of the Constitution. The projects and programmes contained in the state Plans were formulated and implemented by the respective state governments. These were usually financed by the central government (some of these, either in full or in part were funded by the state governments themselves) through what were known as block grants, which were non-statutory transfers (from the central government to the state governments) flowing through the Gadgil (and later Gadgil–Mukherjee) formula.[13] Needless to say, the central Plan and the state Plans were prepared with the same objective in view, namely to meet the objectives of the Five Year Plan.

In addition, the Five Year Plans contained public sector projects and programmes that were implemented through centrally sponsored schemes. The centrally sponsored schemes cover areas and sectors of the economy which fall under the State List or the Concurrent List of the Constitution, and are formulated by the central government after appropriate interaction with the state governments. The expenditure in the centrally sponsored schemes is shared by the central government and the state governments in an amicably decided ratio. Usually, the central government shares a greater proportion of the project cost of the centrally sponsored schemes. The projects and programmes under the centrally sponsored schemes are implemented by the state governments using their own administrative apparatus.

The centrally sponsored schemes have a legacy. The projects and programmes covered by it were based on three main ideas: (*a*) national importance (such as family planning, resettlement of landless labourers, and so on); (*b*) specialized research (which usually benefits more than one state); and (*c*) pilot project for research and development. The origin of these projects can be traced back to the First Plan (1951–56), specifically in development schemes that were being executed then by the state governments outside the Plan. At the end of the First Plan, these schemes were transferred to the states and named centrally sponsored schemes. Over time, more schemes were incorporated within the centrally sponsored schemes. At the end of the Third Plan (1961–66), that is, after one and a half decades of planning, there were 92 centrally sponsored schemes, of which 35 were in agriculture (and cooperation) and 16 in general education.

The number of centrally sponsored schemes increased over time, but the irony is that most of these projects did not have a smooth run, perhaps ever. As early as the mid-1950s, the state governments began to point out the complications that they had to face to implement these projects. The problems originated mostly from procedural issues. The state governments found the staffing pattern, pay scale, design of building, equipment, and so on associated with the projects under the centrally sponsored schemes at variance with those prevalent in the case of the projects administered by themselves. Such mismatch in its natural course was enough to cause problems for the state governments.

On the centrally sponsored schemes, a more substantive issue relates to the difference between the central government and the state governments in their perception about the development priorities. The difference in this regard becomes discernible when the states' resources are scarce, and in consequence they have to alter the development priorities that they would have liked to pursue. The states often found it difficult to share the expenditure for the centrally sponsored schemes as they were perennially starved of funds. Besides, they argued that the centrally sponsored schemes have proliferated, resulting in thin spread of resources.

It becomes a sensitive issue when projects under the centrally sponsored schemes are instituted in areas which do not figure in the list of immediate priority of the state. The states would like to invest in projects which in their opinion are more important in the context of their development and can best serve the interest and well-being of their own people. As more of the Plan transfers (to the states) were routed through the centrally sponsored schemes, the amount of block grants under the Plan shrank, and that affected the room for manoeuvrability of the states in firming up their developmental plans.

The state governments desired a diminution in the area and coverage (and by implication, the number) of the centrally sponsored schemes because they felt that they had proliferated, resulting in a lowering of the block grant provided by the central government. For the states, block grants were essential to meet certain key objectives of the Plan. The states were also unhappy with the guidelines accompanying the centrally sponsored schemes and demanded flexibility in the implementation of these schemes. In direct contrast, at the insistence of the central ministries, the number of centrally sponsored schemes increased in almost every Five Year Plan, with the result that they spread over large areas and subjects as diverse as bovine breeding to modernization of police forces. In the era of economic reforms, the central government made a number of attempts to rationalize the centrally sponsored schemes, willy-nilly conceding that there is some truth about its proliferation. It is not certain how far the financial crunch faced by the central government around this time was responsible for this turnaround of ideas.

After several rounds of rationalization, the number of centrally sponsored schemes was curtailed to 66 in 2014. There is huge inequity in the allocation of funds across the types of schemes within the centrally sponsored schemes, as 17 of these 66 schemes, which are defined as 'flagship schemes' on account of their size and scale, subsume as much as 86 per cent of the total expenditure (central assistance) on the centrally sponsored schemes. These schemes are mostly in the Concurrent List of the Constitution, and cover wage employment, child development, rural road, social welfare, health care, primary education, mid-day meal, rural housing, and food security. That these are social sector schemes does not seem to be an appropriate riposte to the sensitiveness of the states.

A polar opinion with regard to the centrally sponsored schemes is that the projects and programmes which are in the realm of the states should be abolished altogether and the central fund on this count should be transferred to the state governments en bloc, without any conditionality so that they can decide about its sectoral or project-specific allocation. Most states prefer that the central funds for the centrally sponsored schemes be converted into grants to the states, leaving it to them to decide in which areas and sectors of the state economy they would like to park their money. In any case, opinions differ in this respect among major stakeholders, including the central government, peoples' representatives, and civil society organizations (which are mainly concerned about the social sector schemes). There is a concern that the state governments might resort to interdepartmental transfer of funds for short-term gains, ignoring the long-term needs for growth and development of the state.

The original idea behind the centrally sponsored schemes is to incentivize the states to spend more in areas and sectors of the economy which are critical for growth and development. Over time, the operation of the centrally sponsored schemes became cumbersome for many states, with 'one-size-fits-all' guidelines and their micro-managing by the central ministries. There have been attempts to reform the centrally sponsored schemes either by merging several of these schemes into one, by scrapping some, or by introducing some element of flexibility in the guidelines. These reforms failed to satisfy the states as their dependence on the central government for funds reduced in the era of economic reform, and they wanted independence in the formulation of projects and programmes to suit the developmental needs in their area. In such a situation, what was required was a deliberation on the futility of the centrally sponsored schemes in fostering growth and development in backward areas or in the specific areas of the states with preponderance of poor population.

Planning and Market

In the pre-reform years (1951–90), the state played an active role in the production and distribution of goods and services, and shouldered the major responsibilities for growth. In pursuance of the policies of economic reforms, the state withdrew from large areas of economic activities, allowing the entry of the private sector in that space. The main responsibility of growth in the process was shifted to the private sector. The abdication of the lead role by the state in economic activities in the era of economic reforms does not mean shirking its responsibility in areas that are important for growth and development of the economy and the welfare of the people. The state engages itself in areas where the private sector is not interested, and steps in for the supply of essential inputs and creation of infrastructure, where private initiative is either inadequate or not forthcoming at all. The role of the state and the private sector may be complementary in the reform era but the activities of both are governed by market forces.

In a low-income developing country such as India, where a sizeable portion of the population is afflicted with poverty and deprivation, the state cannot postpone the immediate needs for survival of the poor and the deprived. As per the latest official estimate (from the year 2011–12), one-fifth of the Indian population lives below the poverty line, which is defined as the bare minimum level of consumption expenditure—a level below which people are under severe stress. An estimated 40 to 60 per cent of the population is unable to access some of the basic services and facilities, such as health care, elementary education, drinking water, sanitation, housing, and so on. The state is required to plan and implement income generation programmes for the poor. The state also has to take care of the people who are just above the poverty line and often are painfully straitened in means so much so that they are unable to afford the market prices for many basic services. In a welfare society, the state cannot eschew the responsibility of providing for these services, and leave the destiny of the poor and deprived section of the population entirely at the door of the private sector or at the mercy of market forces.

A large number of people in India depend on agriculture for livelihood. The production decisions in agriculture are taken by millions of farmers in the countryside. But the entire agricultural operation is not left to the market forces. The state plays an active role in setting the input and the output prices in agriculture.

The policies associated with the economic reforms and liberalization gave the private sector the prime place in the area of investment and income generation. The growth and development under the economic reforms depended to a great extent on the efficiency and competitiveness of the private sector. The private sector needs well-functioning markets. It operates in a competitive market, which is open and free. In view of this, the Plan outlined instruments for the development of the market and to ensure its smooth functioning. The market in India is free but operates under the watchful eyes of the state. In order to foster efficiency, competitiveness, and economic growth, the state does not hesitate to intervene in the market, and in this way can act as a facilitator in its development. The state intervention in the market is considered as an instrument to make it work competitively and with accessibility to all its players—big and small. One of the important roles of planning in the era of economic reforms was to devise ways and means to make the least but the most effective state intervention in the market.

There is a traditional concern about social problems, which arises from the operation of market forces in its conventional form. This has made the government extremely careful in deregulating markets.

The trade-off between the efficiency gains out of the functioning of the market along with social problems ostensibly forced the government to slow down or even temporarily abstain from the process of reform in several areas. Its ripple effect was evident in the financial sector reforms, which were slow and tardy, when the truth is that reforms in the real sector of the economy need to be reinforced by reforms in the financial sector. There is no denying that the inadequacy of financial sector reforms, to some extent, retarded the rate of economic growth in India.

The development debate in the pre-reform days focused on whether equity should be preferred to growth in income, leading to a growth–equity trade-off. The answer is not straightforward because attainment of high growth rate and development of a modern industrial sector may often entail a compromise with egalitarian policies. The egalitarian policies preached and practised in India from the 1950s to the 1980s (prominent among these being the Monopolies and Restrictive Trade Practices Act, 1970) did not foster industrial growth as expected, and there was no perceptible improvement in equity in the class distribution of output or income. The issue, in the end, boils down to the level of income inequality that the economy can afford to tolerate in the course of development. The trade-off in this regard led to change in economic policies, and in tandem, the underlying model of economic growth and development. An important feature of this change is that the existing economic organizations were not disturbed in the wake of the economic reforms. In other words, the policy change was made within the confines of the economic organizations prevailing at that time. The manner and method of administering these organizations were changed to suit the demands of neoteric planning, which is to tend the functioning of the market for the best interest of the country. But the need to exploit the potential of the market was not disputed and, at the same time, never disturbed in a major way.

Balanced regional growth and development are regarded as indispensable elements of the planning and development strategy. The fact is that economic growth in India, either in the first four decades of state control and regulation of economic activities (that is, in the pre-reform years, 1951–1990) or in the two decades of economic reforms (1991–2011), was not regionally balanced. The interstate disparity in socio-economic variables that comprehensively define the leading indicators of growth and development has remained significant. There are certain regions which have not been able to benefit adequately from the growth process. The rate of economic growth failed to accelerate in some of the most backward regions. For a fairly long time, Bihar, Jharkhand, Madhya Pradesh, Chhattisgarh, and Odisha were classified as poor states. The level of poverty in these five states was much higher than in the rest. The level of per capita income in these five states was lower than in other states, and so was their rate of growth. The growth rate of per capita income in these five states was in the range of 1.5 to 1.7 per cent per year in the 1980s (1980–82 to 1990–92). This was less than half of the growth rate of per capita income that is realized at the national level. The growth rate of per capita income in these five states increased under the economic reforms, but in general remained lower than the national average. Planning is essential to achieve a certain degree of regional balance in the growth rate. The market on its own is incapable of performing this role. Since not all parts of India are equally well-endowed to take advantage of growth opportunities, and since historical inequalities have not been entirely eliminated, planned intervention by the state is required to generate the growth momentum, particularly in these areas. Likewise, state intervention is necessary to guide the market to achieve some of the societal objectives to which the market, being typically guided by short-term considerations, is not very sensitive.

The strong point of the market is efficiency. But the market always takes a short-term view, and that is considered its major weakness, especially in a developing market economy. Market prices are more influenced by available supplies and demand in a limited time horizon. As such, the price mechanism is inadequate to protect some of the areas such as environment and ecology, which have consequences for the long term. Some of these long-term costs can be built into current costs and prices, but that is possible mainly through state intervention and planning. In whichever area the society has to take a long-term view, state intervention and planning becomes necessary. Planning in this context means taking a long-term view, setting goals, and devising strategies to achieve these goals within the accepted paradigms.

The principal task of planning in a market-oriented economy is to identify the vulnerable areas that usually crop up from the range of uncertainties accompanying the market-based system, and to suggest measures to address them. This becomes necessary in view of the well-known fact that neither the state nor the private sector agrees with the notion that markets can convey all the necessary information that is required for making sound decisions with medium- or long-term implications. There are circumstances in which markets may not exist or, even if they do, may not work effectively and efficiently. Then, there are conditions under which unbridled operation of market forces may give rise to outcomes that may be deleterious when seen in a broader national and societal perspective. These can make state regulation and intervention in markets a justifiable necessity though this should not become an open-ended rationale for intervention. State intervention has to be strategic and should emanate from a vision of the role and responsibility of state policy and public action where markets are likely to be less perfect.

That the market, in the normal course, is not capable of taking care of a range of issues confronting the economy and the people was observed by Sukhamoy Chakravarty not many years before the economic reform measures were initiated in India.[14] Some of the issues Chakravarty mentioned in this context include: (*a*) raising the initial level of savings (which is usually low in developing countries) to finance investment in order to generate gainful employment and reduce poverty; (*b*) facilitating rapid spread of education, basic health services, and technical knowledge; (*c*) adopting, adapting, and initiating technological advances which can productively absorb the existing surplus labour; (*d*) removing institutional rigidities, including rural power structures, which limit society's creative responses to problems of low-end poverty;[15] and (*e*) ensuring environmentally sustainable development. These remain as important as ever and make the role of state intervention in the market (through planning or in some other form) a useful necessity for growth and development, especially if growth has to be sustainable and inclusive. India had to face these issues in a routine manner and devise suitable remedial measures in the course of its tryst with market mechanism in the era of economic reforms. The state, through planning, played an active role to frame and execute the remedial measures.

Notes

1. The members of the committee were K. T. Shah, Radha Kamal Mukherjee, M. Visvesvaraya, Ambalal Sarabhai, Purushottam Thakurdas, Walchand Hirachand, A. D. Shroff, Meghnad Saha, J. C. Kumarappa, A. K. Saha, Nazir Ahmed, J. C. Ghosh, V. S. Dubey, and N. M. Joshi.

2. K. T. Shah (Honorary General Secretary), *Being an Abstract of Proceedings and Other Particulars Relating to the National Planning Committee*, National Planning Committee, Bombay, p. 9, para 1.

3. The NPC could not function normally due to the frequent imprisonment of Jawaharlal Nehru. Nehru was in and out of jail until 1942, and during the Quit India movement he was imprisoned from August 1942 to June 1945, without a day's break. The work of the committee resumed in earnest in 1946 through its 29 subcommittees. It prepared papers on a range of issues before it was formally dissolved in 1949. Nehru seriously associated himself with this committee despite his political work, to which his time was devoted first and foremost.

4. Quoted by Jawaharlal Nehru in his fortnightly letter to the chief ministers on 28 September 1953 (Jawaharlal Nehru, *Letters to Chief Ministers*, Vol. 3, edited by G. Parthasarathi, Oxford University Press, 1987, p. 388).

5. In the Interim Cabinet, the British Viceroy was the prime minister and Jawaharlal Nehru was the deputy prime minister and minister of external affairs.

6. The Advisory Planning Board was constituted under the chairmanship of K. C. Neogy. It recommended the constitution of a non-political planning organization.

7. The members of this committee were Maulana Abul Kalam Azad, Jai Prakash Narain, N. G. Ranga, Gulzarilal Nanda, J. C. Kumarappa, Achyut Patwardhan, and Shankarrao Deo.

8. The Planning Commission was constituted with Jawaharlal Nehru as chairman, Gulzarilal Nanda as vice-chairman, and C. D. Deshmukh, G. L. Mehta, and R. K. Patil as members. The first meeting of the Planning Commission took place on 28 March 1950.

9. Policy Framework in the Seventh Plan, Chapter 7, Para 7.33, Seventh Five Year Plan, Vol. 2, Government of India, Planning Commission, New Delhi, November 1985.

10. Examples of central Plan are: (*a*) family planning, for which the state governments may have the intention but not the resources, due to which the central government comes up with a plan to implement family planning programme; and (*b*) power generation, for which, due to resource

constraint, the state governments may not be in a position to produce enough of it (the central government engages itself in power generation through its own projects).

11. The growth rate of the Indian economy is in no way connected with Hinduism. The low rate of growth of the GDP and its stability over a fairly long period of two to three decades may have motivated Raj Krishna to equate it with Hinduism, which as a religion and way of life is perceived to have remained stable for centuries.

12. Planning Commission, 'Report of the Working Group on State's Financial Resources for the Twelfth Five Year Plan', Government of India, May 2012, p. 34, Table 4.6.

13. These were part of the central assistance to state plans, which comprised centrally sponsored schemes, block grants, including NCA, and additional central assistance. Subsequently, such transfers were made under different nomenclature, such as one-time additional central assistance, special central assistance, special Plan assistance, and so on. In addition, there was statutory transfer of funds from the central government to the state governments, following the directive of the Finance Commission, which essentially met their non-Plan expenditure.

14. S. Chakravarty, 'Sustainable Development', paper presented at the EADI Conference, Oslo, Norway, July 1990, quoted in Servaas Storm and C.W.M. Naastepad, 'Sukhamoy Chakravarty: The Feasibility of Equitable Growth', *Development and Change*, Voi. 38, Issue 6, 2007, pp. 1173–85.

15. Low-end poverty is a situation of surviving with much less income or expenditure than the poverty line income or expenditure, bordering on destitution. The people at the low-end poverty group constitute the poorest of the poor and are unable to benefit from the income or employment generation activities of the state. They are located at the rock bottom of the income distribution. This term was first used by Professor Sukhamoy Chakravarty. India's Fifth Five Year Plan used this terminology to describe extreme poverty. The Ninth Plan also used this term in one instance to describe acute poverty.

2

Mathematical Models behind the Five Year Plans

The Planning Commission has extensively used mathematical models in the formulation of Five Year Plans. These models have been used in two major areas: (*a*) to spell out development priorities, that is, how to choose between agriculture and industry (and within industry, between heavy and light industry), between capital and consumer goods, and so on, and (*b*) to assess the various economic parameters and determine targets that are consistent with the available resources and, at the same time, inter-sectorally consistent. In other words, the mathematical models have been used to determine the sectoral growth profiles, which are consistent with the availability of resources.

It has been mentioned in Chapter 1 that planning until 1990 was watertight and the state was involved in almost all the spheres of economic activity. The first eight Five Year Plans (the First Plan to the Eighth Plan) were formulated in such environs of state control on economic activity. With the initiation of economic reforms in 1991, the state began to withdraw itself from directly participating in the areas of production and trade, and, in general, confined its activities to the creation of an environment that is conducive to the growth and development in a market economy framework. Under the economic reforms, Five Year Plans (the Ninth Plan to the Eleventh Plan) have been formulated and implemented in a market-based economy, assigning the private sector a prominent role in investment and income generation. In consequence, the treatment of mathematical models in the formulation of Five Year Plans in the era of economic reforms and liberalization (1991–2011) has been different from those in the first four decades of planning (1951–90).

This chapter gives an overview of the mathematical models that have been used in the formulation of Five Year Plans in the six decades, 1951–2011. The mathematical models used in the formulation of the Five Year Plans in the pre-reform days, 1951–90, belong to the family of growth and investment models. Three different models have been used in this period. These models can be classified into three groups. In the first group is the model that has been used in the First Plan (1951–56). Though the Planning Commission does not mention about the use of a specific mathematical model, theoreticians are of the view that the Harrod–Domar model, which is a model of economic growth, lies at the back of the quantitative calculations of the First Plan. In the second group comes the model used to formulate the Second Plan (1956–61), which is a growth model developed by Professor P. C. Mahalanobis at the Indian Statistical Institute (ISI), Calcutta (Kolkata). The third category covers the input–output based consistency model that was used from the Fifth (1974–79) to the Eighth Plan (1992–97).[1] Finally, the models used in the formulation of Five Year Plans in the era of economic reform have been discussed. The modelling exercises in the period of economic reform relies more on the macroeconomic model, even as the input–output-cum-investment planning model of the pre-reform era was used.

Model Used in the First Five Year Plan

There is no officially recorded model structure that was designed to formulate the First Five Year Plan, but it is generally agreed that the technical work behind the target setting in the Plan was inspired by the Harrod–Domar model.[2] The model is a highly simplified version of economic reality and has implications for policy. The growth path in the model is generated by capital accumulation and financed largely by domestic saving. The model is not given an explicit analytical form and is implicit in numerical figures which constituted the perspective Plan for developing the Indian economy.

The Harrod–Domar model was developed on the presumption that the product that is produced in an economy is homogenous. By implication, the model ignores the commodity composition of the total product. This, in turn, presumes absence of structural change in the economy during the planning horizon, even as the total product increases as a result of economic growth. The relative prices of commodities constituting the national product remain unchanged in the Plan under this model. The model assumes: (*a*) absence of foreign trade—it is based on the presumption that national product is either consumed or invested; (*b*) constant savings—it implies that the savings function is linear; (*c*) capital is the only factor of production; (*d*) capital goods have an infinite lifespan and, therefore, depreciation of capital stock is ruled out; and (*e*) technological relationships are fixed. In this case, the issue of inter-industry delivery (which is a feature of the Plan models that were used from the Fifth Plan onwards) does not arise. The time lag between investment and creation of productive capacity is not significant.

The linearity of the savings function in the model connotes equality between marginal and average propensity to save. The proportional rate of growth of income equals the product of the savings ratio, which is the savings as percentage of GDP and the inverse of capital–output ratio. The equilibrium rate of growth is determined from the savings ratio and the ICOR. The ICOR is treated as a measure of efficiency of capital use.

The Harrod–Domar model was modified, though marginally, for its use in the First Plan by distinguishing the average and the marginal propensity to save. The capital–output ratio was assumed to be the same on the margin as on the average. The model used in the First Plan was developed for a closed economy. It was used to determine the equilibrium rate of growth from the system, given the savings ratio and the ICOR. The model relies heavily on investment for capital accumulation on the presumption that production required capital and that capital can be accumulated only through investment. The faster the capital accumulation, the higher will be the rate of growth of the economy. The model is used to provide answers to questions such as: Given a certain ICOR, what is the required savings rate to realize a particular rate of growth? The model answers that the required savings rate is equal to the rate of growth multiplied by the ICOR.

However, application of the Harrod–Domar model for the purpose of planning for the economy is beset with problems for the underlying assumptions that there are no structural deficiencies in transforming savings into investment, and that too in the desired form (that is, in various sectors). In this, the model overlooks an important element of development planning. In addition, the model ignores the fundamental choice problem related to planning over time, which requires a weighing of present versus future gains, by assuming a constant marginal propensity to save for the economy. It lacks social objectives, considered to be an important element in planning for economic development of a low-income developing economy such as India.

The Harrod–Domar model principally indicates the problem of increasing per capita income in an underdeveloped economy. The model is highly aggregative in nature and that prevents its use as a tool in detailed quantitative policy-making. It conceals many structural aspects of the problem of a steady rate of growth. In view of the scarce availability of data in the early 1950s, and the simplicity of the model in answering broad policy issues in the Indian economy, the use of the Harrod–Domar model may have been considered appropriate.

Model Used in the Second Five Year Plan

The macroeconomic framework for the Second Five Year Plan was developed from a model of growth generated by capital accumulation based on domestic savings and foreign capital. In this model, the aggregate investment multiplied by the aggregate marginal capital–output ratio yields the increase in aggregate output. The formal relating of aggregate and sectoral investment allocation is carried out through a two-sector model, which later on was elaborated into a four-sector model developed by Professor P. C. Mahalanobis.[3] The four-sector model developed by Mahalanobis guided India's planning strategy in the Second Five Year Plan—a Plan for building up of a strong base for basic and heavy industry, which is the cornerstone of industrialization. To this extent, Mahalanobis's model emphasized the physical aspect of investment (in the Second Plan), marking a significant change from the mathematical model postulated in the First Plan.

Mahalanobis's Two-Sector Model

In the two-sector model, the economy is divided into consumption goods sector and capital goods (or investment goods) sector. Each sector is assumed to be vertically integrated. The sectors producing raw materials for consumption goods are aggregated with the sectors producing consumption goods. Similar is the case in the capital goods sector.

Investment is decomposed into two components as: (a) investment used in the capital goods sector, that is, investment used to augment productive capacity; and (b) investment used in the consumption goods sector.

The time path of income in the Mahalanobis model depends on a large number of structural coefficients (as compared to the Harrod–Domar model, which depends on aggregate savings rate and the capital coefficient, which is the output–capital ratio). The aggregate capital coefficient (incremental capital–output ratio, ICOR) in the Mahalanobis model is a weighted average of sectoral ICORs. The weights in this case are proportional to investment in the two sectors (capital goods and consumption goods sector).

The model is described by five elements—(a) the initial proportion of investment to income; (b) the output–capital ratio (that is, the inverse of ICOR) of the capital goods (or investment goods) sector; (c) output–capital ratio of the consumption goods sector; (d) the proportion of investment in the capital goods sector; and (e) the proportion of investment in the consumption goods sector. Among these five elements, the output–capital ratio of the capital goods and consumption goods sectors are technologically fixed. The proportion of investment in the consumption goods sector is determined as soon as the proportion of investment in the capital goods sector is known. If the constant ratio at which the initial investment is allocated (as proportion to income) is known, then the only policy instrument that the planners can play with is the proportion of current investment in capital goods (or investment goods) sector. With one instrument, only one target can be attained. The model treats the rate of growth of the economy as the target. Thus, income growth in the model depends on the initial proportion of investment to income and the proportion of investment allocated to the capital goods sector.

The relative rates of growth of consumption and output change over time. The asymptotic rate of growth of the system is given by the proportion of capital goods output devoted to further production of capital goods and the incremental output–capital ratio of the capital goods sector. A higher value of the investment devoted to the capital goods sector always has a favourable effect on the asymptotic growth rate of the system, irrespective of whether it is consumption or output. If a high value of the proportion of investment going to the capital goods sector is chosen, then in the beginning, the system grows at a somewhat slow rate, while it gains acceleration with passage of time. If the output–capital ratio of the consumption goods sector is greater than that of the capital goods sector, then a higher value of the proportion of investment devoted to the capital goods sector implies a lower immediate increment in consumption. Thus, there is implicit in the choice of the proportion of investment devoted to the capital goods sector a choice of alternative streams of consumption.

In the Mahalanobis model, one-third of the total investment is devoted to the capital goods sector. The model operates under a closed-economy assumption along with total non-shiftability of capital from the consumption goods to the capital goods sector. It implies that capital equipment once installed in any specific producing sector of the economy may not be shiftable.

Mahalanobis's Four-Sector Model

The four-sector model is an extended version of the two-sector model where the capital goods sector is kept unchanged but the consumption goods sector is split up into three sectors as (*a*) factory production of consumer goods; (*b*) production of consumer goods including agricultural products by small and household industries; and (*c*) service sectors such as health, education, and so on.

The time path for income in the four-sector model remains the same as in the two-sector model except that the output–capital ratio or the technological coefficient of the consumption goods sector (in the four-sector model) is a weighted average of the output–capital ratios of the three different consumer goods sectors, as mentioned earlier. In addition, a new variable, namely, employment, and a new set of parameters, namely, output–labour ratios, are introduced in the four-sector model. The output–labour ratios are assumed to be independent of productivity coefficients.

The four-sector model has two targets: (a) increment in income or, in other words, the postulated rate of growth of income; and (b) increment in employment. The instruments used in the model are: the proportion in which the investment is allocated among (a) the capital goods sector and (b) the three consumer goods sectors. The data given are: (a) aggregate investment; (b) output–capital ratios of the capital goods sector and the three consumption goods sectors; and (c) output–labour ratios for the capital goods sector and the consumption goods sectors.

The problem Mahalanobis set for the Second Plan was how to allocate the investment between the capital goods sector and the three consumption goods sectors when: (a) total investment to allocate is INR 56 billion; (b) total increment in income is INR 29 billion; and (c) total new employment to be generated is 11 million. From the consideration of long-term growth, Mahalanobis decided to allocate one-third of the total investment to the capital goods sector. It is assumed that for each sector, there is a constant incremental output–capital ratio and output–labour ratio. The resultant growth of national income becomes 25 per cent during the five years of the Second Plan.

As in the two-sector model, the growth rate in the four-sector model is determined by the share of investment in the capital goods and the consumption goods sector. A larger value of the share of investment in the capital goods sector (as compared to that in the consumption goods sector) results in a slower growth (of income) in the short run, but in the long run, the growth rate (of income) becomes higher, and, in tandem, the growth rate of consumption becomes higher. Conversely, a smaller proportion of investment in the capital goods sector at present does not slow down the growth rate in the short run, but it has implications for long-term growth. There is a choice between: (a) higher investment in capital goods sector at present leading to slower growth rate and slower consumption at present, laying down the basis for higher growth rate in future; and (*b*) lower investment in capital goods sector at present leading to higher growth rate and higher consumption at present. Clearly, the above-mentioned point (*a*) lays down the basis for higher growth rate in future at the cost of present consumption. It brings home the message that by investing more in the capital goods sector at present, the present growth rate slows down, but it promises higher growth rate in the future, when along with the high growth rate, the consumption growth rate will also be high. In plain terms, people have to sacrifice their present consumption to achieve a higher growth rate in future. Therefore, it boils down to a case of postponement of consumption from the present to the future. The relevance of the model in the context of the Second Plan lay in setting the paradigm of development in a low-income capital-scarce economy, which aptly described India at that time.

Assessment of the Mahalanobis Model

The Mahalanobis model was developed at the ISI, in the mid-1950s. The ISI at that time was famous for research in socio-economic fields. Truly, the fame of the ISI attracted people from far and wide, with visits of experts from national and international research institutions. Over and above, there was the demonstration of interest and encouragement by none other than Prime Minister Jawaharlal Nehru to develop a model of growth and development for the Indian economy for its application as the basis for the Second Five Year Plan, which the government decided beforehand would be a Plan for building up a strong industrial base. These factors together may be responsible for the wide range of discussion and debate on the theoretical and empirical aspects of the Mahalanobis model. The model structure and its solution procedure came under close scrutiny of contemporary planners and policy-makers.

The four-sector model was used for solving certain problems of policy. The model, as mentioned earlier, has two targets—the postulated rate of growth of income and increase in employment. The model's instruments are: the proportion in which investments are allocated (*a*) in the capital goods sector and (*b*) in the three consumption goods sectors.

On a theoretical plane, the model faced the critique that the sectoral values of income are not used as separate targets. All the four sectors in the model (the capital goods sector and the three consumer goods sectors) have independent output–capital and output–labour ratios. The model assumes a given total investment. The total investment is allocated between the four different sectors in such a way that the specified increase in income and employment (which are targets) are reached. The policy variables are the share of investment in each sector. The model is determined if and only if one of the investment shares is exogenously determined. Since there are two objectives (increase in income and employment) to be met, with the share of investment in the capital goods sector given a pre-assigned value (which Mahalanobis set as one-third of the total investment), the model is solved to allocate investment among the three remaining sectors.

The proportion of investment going to the capital goods sector is chosen from long-term considerations. The nature of these considerations has never been made clear by Mahalanobis, either in the two-sector or in the four-sector model. It is a pertinent issue as the system becomes indeterminate if this proportion is assumed to be a variable.

The manner in which sectoral investment allocation is made in the model suggests that investment is a single homogenous fund. Such an assumption is valid only when there is a single type of investment good. The assumption obviously is not rational with heterogeneous investment goods. With the presence of heterogeneous investment goods, the model would require the use of an investment matrix. In its absence, it is likely that investment allocation in the model may lack balance and optimality as well. However, lack of adequate data may have constrained the mathematical exercise in this respect.

Treatment of savings in the model is a debated issue. The Mahalanobis model shows no concern for savings constraint and assumes that savings comes from the industrial sector. In practice, the developing countries, however, do not display such a tendency, as the first stage of saving usually comes from the agricultural sector. The model does not mention taxation, an important potential source of capital.

The Mahalanobis model assumes a closed economy and total non-shiftability of capital stock from consumption goods sector to investment goods sector. Therefore, the model appears to provide the rationale for a shift in industrial investment towards building up of a capital goods base. The economic considerations underlying the choice behind the proportion of investment in the capital goods sector (to one-third of the total investment) were not spelled out by Mahalanobis. When the model-development work was going on at the ISI, J. B. S. Haldane showed through simulation exercises that over a period of 10 to 15 years, given certain reasonable data, the assumption of one-third of total investment devoted to the capital goods sector is the appropriate choice in maximizing inter-temporal growth.[4] Both the four-sector model and the findings of Haldane were published in the same issue of *Sankhya*, the house journal of the ISI.

Ryutaro Komiya found that Mahalanobis's solution is inefficient, in that it is situated in the interior of the feasibility locus between incremental output and incremental employment.[5] Thus, it is possible to generate greater employment and/or output by merely reallocating the given investment among the three sectors, although such a solution will not assign a positive fraction of investment to every sector. Shigeto Tsuru expressed the view that identification of investment with the output of a sector defined as basic investment goods is a mistake.[6] The output of such a sector, according to Tsuru, cannot be equivalent to investment, which is a complement to savings. Investment here in the latter sense can take various physical forms and not only that of production of new durable equipment. Thus, increase in inventories of all kinds of goods may constitute investment, though such increase does not constitute output of any sector.

Models Used in Fifth to Eighth Five Year Plan

The mathematical model used in the Fifth Plan (1974–79), and for that matter the models used in Indian planning from the Fifth to the Eighth Plan, was largely conditioned by what Professor Sukhamoy Chakravarty articulated in the form of integration of the models of the Harrod–Domar type and the Leontief input–output system in a demand–supply frame.

The mathematical model used in the Fifth Plan consists of: (*a*) a macro model of Harrod–Domar type; (*b*) a Leontief static terminal year input–output model; and (*c*) a consumption module. The model integrates macroeconomic parameters with consistency requirements at a disaggregated level of inter-sectoral relationship. The import requirements are endogenous in the model. Sectoral imports are estimated using an import-coefficient matrix. The model provides for redistribution of private consumption from the richer to the poorer section of the population. The redistribution is carried out in a fairly elaborate consumption module, in which the consumption demand of individuals is estimated.

The next three Five Year Plans—the Sixth Plan (1980–85), the Seventh Plan (1985–90), and the Eighth Plan (1992–97)—used the model developed by Professor Chakravarty for the Fifth Plan, with embellishments for investments at the sectoral level and derivation of consumption demand for the poor and the non-poor populations so as to derive a sectoral pattern of growth for ensuring a minimum level of consumption for the poor. In essence, the structure of the mathematical models covering the Sixth to the Eighth Plan remained faithfully weaved to the language and approach expounded by Professor Chakravarty for the Fifth Plan. For this reason, the mathematical models used in these four Five Year Plans, the Fifth to the Eighth, have been discussed together.[7]

While the basic structure of the model designed by Professor Chakravarty for the Fifth Plan remained unchanged, some change (addition) was incorporated in the Sixth Plan. The change in the Sixth Plan (vis-à-vis the Fifth Plan) was triggered by three factors. First, the planning methodology had to respond to the dynamics of the development strategy espoused by political authorities. Second, mathematical models had to incorporate new and emerging features of the economy. Third, the range of data availability from the country's statistical authorities expanded over time, permitting a closer examination of a wider range of issues. Under the impact of these three factors, two changes were made to the Fifth Plan model for the Sixth Plan. First, in order to assess separately the consumption demand of the poor and the non-poor groups of the population, the consumption module of the Fifth Plan was replaced by an elaborate consumption sub-model. Second, as additional data was made available by the Central Statistics Office (CSO), an investment model was developed with the help of a capital-coefficient matrix. It was useful to derive the estimate of sectoral investment to generate the desired level of output in a more precise manner.[8] In sum, the model used in the Fifth Plan was broadened in scope by introducing a consumption sub-model and adding an investment planning model developed with the help of a capital-coefficient matrix. These twin changes were incorporated in the model of the Sixth Plan and retained until the Eighth Plan.

The Sixth Plan model system (which was used until the Eighth Plan) was structured as a combination of a core model and a set of sub-models. The core model consists of the following: (*a*) macroeconomic model; (*b*) input–output model; and (*c*) investment model. The macroeconomic model and the input–output model were developed along the lines of the Fifth Plan model. The investment model is incorporated in the Sixth Plan to bring forth the interaction between a set of final demand elements and the input–output matrix, which represents inter-industry relationship and the state of technology. In the Sixth Plan, separate sub-models are developed for each of the elements of final demand—agriculture, financial resources, public and private consumption, industry, and trade. The (private) consumption sub-model in the Sixth Plan replaces the consumption module of the Fifth Plan.

As the mathematical models used in the Sixth Plan have been developed on the foundations of the Fifth Plan model, and this (Sixth Plan) model structure has been used in the Seventh and the Eighth Plans, the models used in the Sixth Plan have been discussed here, bypassing a separate discussion on the Fifth Plan model. Since the consumption module in the Fifth Plan model frame was replaced by a detailed consumption sub-model in the Sixth Plan, both have been discussed in order to underline the nature and pattern of change in the use of private consumption expenditure in the Plan.

Model System in the Sixth Plan: Core Model

The core model, as mentioned previously, consisted of the macroeconomic, input–output, and investment models.

1. Macroeconomic model: The medium- and long-term projections of GDP, which were consistent with the desired growth rate in the Plan and total investment, was estimated in the macroeconomic model. The projections were based on a set of structural relationships, most of which were in the form of income and expenditure identities developed within this model. The forecast estimates of the GDP and its growth rate, public and private consumption, savings, investment, and net inflow from the rest of the world were worked out by balancing income and expenditure for a series of alternative growth rates of income (that is, GDP) in the Plan. The set of estimates that was found consistent with the aggregate savings behaviour and domestic production possibilities was adopted. The model, in addition, provided separate projections for exports, imports, balance of payments, and for fiscal variables, that is, revenue, expenditure, savings, and borrowing of the government.

2. Input–output model: The core of the Plan model was a multisectoral input–output model. The input–output model used in the Plan was an open Leontief system with the explicit introduction of industry technology and fixed market shares. The model was used to derive mutually consistent sectoral output target and corresponding sectoral investment demand.

   The input–output model had an input-coefficient matrix, in which inputs used in an industry were expressed as quantities per unit of output of that industry. The input-coefficient matrix in the base year of the Plan was usually a calibrated version of the input–output transaction matrix of an earlier year since the basic input–output table was not available for the base year of the Plan. The basic input–output table represented the technology and product mix of that year, and at the prices prevailing in the year in which it was constructed. For this reason, this table (whatever was the latest available) was updated for the base year of the Plan after appropriate adjustment of input norms, commodity output and exports, imports, investment, and public and private consumption, each at the prices prevailing in the base year of the Plan. In this way, the input–output table took into account the economic flows of the base year of the Plan. The input-coefficient matrix for the terminal year of the

Plan was projected from the coefficient matrix of the base year, after incorporating the anticipated changes in the product and technology mix on the basis of information available for various sectors or industries in the economy. The supply and demand of the product of each input–output sector was balanced. The intermediate demand of each sector was obtained through interrelationships among different sectors using input–output coefficients representing the technology of the production process. The model assessed the requirement for consumption and investment demand (each separated into the public or the private sector), for export and import and intermediate goods in tune with the Plan objectives. These demand estimates (sectoral and aggregate) were worked out in the core model. The sectoral import was endogenously determined in the model through an import-coefficient matrix to give the total supply along with the estimated domestic production level to meet the total demand of products of each sector. Sectoral growth rates obtained through this model were thus mutually consistent.

The consistency of output levels was assessed through the input–output model and their supply feasibilities were checked mostly through the sub-models. The sub-models have been described later in this section.

3. Investment model: In the Sixth Plan, an investment model was added to the existing (Fifth Plan) input–output model in order to derive the investment required to generate the desired level of output at sectoral level. Investment requirement of a sector is known as investment by destination; the type of capital goods which form the investment is known as investment by source. The relationship between investment and output is assessed using the econometric method. Aggregate gross investment in a sector consists of new investment and replacement investment. New investment is geared to capacity creation. Sectoral investment is divided into (a) committed investment for ongoing projects; and (b) investment for projects initiated in the Plan. The investment to output relationship has a gestation lag as investment is spread over a number of years before a project or programme starts generating output. Investment by destination is converted into investment by source with the help of

the capital-coefficient matrix. Public and private investment is treated separately. Investment allocation in the public sector is treated as a target while investment in the private sector is an indicative forecast.

Model System in the Sixth Plan: Sub-models

The sub-models were formulated in order to accommodate some of the complex non-linear relations, covering various aspects of economic activities. These were used to unfold the intricacies of economic inter-dependence, and ultimately geared to the core model. Each sub-model was estimated separately, and its integration with other sub-models and the core model was achieved by an iterative process. The sub-models were developed for agriculture, financial resources, industry, and trade sectors.

1. Agricultural sub-model: The feasibility of the output level and its growth rate in respect of important agricultural commodities were checked in the agricultural sub-model. The impact of appli-cation of certain critical inputs such as land (type of land use), water, some of the input constraints (for example, fertilizer), and other infrastructure (in terms of quality and quantity) on agri-cultural production and productivity in the long- and medium-term could not be appropriately captured in the multi-sectoral input–output model. The sub-model filled this gap by checking the feasibility of agricultural output targets determined in rela-tion to type of land use, availability of irrigation, and fertilizer application levels.

   In the context of regional development, locational aspects of agricultural growth (in terms of crops and their input intensity) were not possible to be quantified under the input–output frame. In order to fill this gap, the parameters related to cropping intensity, area under irrigation and rain-fed crops, as well as area under high-yielding and traditional variety of seeds by major crops at the level of major states were measured in the agricultural sub-model. The sub-model determined crop output at the state level treating the area under different crops and between varieties of seed as exogenous. The supply at the state level was determined using land, water, seed, and fertilizer as explanatory variables. The demand for food grains was estimated from the consumption sub-model, using consumer demand function. The determinants of supply and the parameters affecting it were estimated separately for each major state. The feasibility of demand for food grains was tested with its supply estimated from this model.

The Plan objectives of growth and diversification of agriculture, self-sufficiency in food, and generation of surpluses for exports were assessed through the parameters estimated in the agricultural sub-model. Besides, several features of the agricultural plan such as development of rain-fed areas and agricultural planning in terms of homogenous agro-climatic regions were captured in this sub-model.

2. Financial resources sub-model: An assessment of resources availability in the Plan was made in the financial resources sub-model in great detail. This became important in the context of financing investment requirement (estimated in the input–output and investment model) to generate the desired growth rate in the Plan.

The level of domestic savings by sectors as well as in terms of its composition was worked out in the financial resources sub-model using an econometric estimation procedure. The gross domestic savings in the economy was composed of savings of the public sector and the private sector. The savings in the public sector comprised budgetary savings of the government and savings of the public sector enterprises. Within the private sector, savings were estimated separately for household, private corporate, and cooperative sectors. The household sector comprised individuals, non-government, and non-corporate private enterprises engaged in various economic activities as well as non-profit institutions such as charities and trusts. The gross savings of the households were made up of additions to financial assets net of financial liabilities, and additions to physical assets including depreciation. The financial assets of the household sector consisted of currency, deposits with the commercial banks and cooperative institutions and non-banking companies, investment in shares and debentures, mutual funds, pension funds, and so on. The savings of the households in the form of physical assets related to gross capital formation in terms of productive assets, such as machinery and equipment, and construction of residential and non-residential buildings. These estimates were consistent with the macro-aggregates of the Plan. The estimate of resources in this sub-model was procedurally recursive to the input–output cum investment model due to the simultaneity between savings and income.

3. Industry sub-model: The demand supply balance in case of important commodities (or industries) was checked through the industry sub-model. The approach of material balances lay at the heart of this sub-model. The production levels which enabled the final demands to be sustained, and at the same time meet the needs of input consumption, were defined as consistent. The consistent level of production (output) was derived from the core model, which had the input–output matrix at its base. The output level was determined for alternative sets of final demand inter alia alternative sets of growth possibilities. The feasibility of output target in industrial sectors obtained from the input–output model was assessed from material balances, which supplemented and cross-checked the results obtained from the input–output model.

The input–output model estimated sectoral output in the terminal year of the Plan. The output was based on inter-industry demand and final demand, and was estimated at the level of input–output sectors, which typically comprised an array of commodities and in most cases consisted of a group of non-homogenous products. The commodity-wise demand and supply within each input–output sector was obtained through material balance studies, in which the sectoral estimates of capacity and output, along with likely absorption of the commodity in major consuming sectors were worked out at a disaggregated level. The disaggregation was carried out at such a level that commodities became homogeneous in nature. The material balance studies were prepared for coal, electricity, petroleum products, heavy machinery, steel, petro-chemicals, sugar, cloth, cotton, jute, non-ferrous metals, and so on. The production target of the commodities within an input–output sector was fixed in such a manner that their aggregate growth rate was in conformity with that of the input–output sector comprising these commodities.

The material balance studies helped in estimating output for selected commodities and services (falling within the input–output sector) on the basis of independent demand–supply projection. The change in the process of production takes place at the level of commodity. Such change can be captured through commodity-specific studies of demand and supply. As a sector of the input–output table usually represents an aggregate of several commodities, it becomes difficult to account for technological changes at the level of input–output sectors. Hence, there was the need to use the material balances to supplement the input–output approach.

4. Trade sub-model: The final demand element of imports and exports along with balance of payments and current account deficit were projected in the trade sub-model.

   The import requirements for this sub-model were divided into two types: (a) imports required in the production process; and (b) imports which balanced the gap between demand and production for consumption purposes. Production-related imports were estimated through the import-coefficient matrix, which described imported input requirement for each industry. This was dealt with in the core (input–output) model, in which the import-coefficient matrix was made compatible with the input–output table and imports for each sector were estimated separately for intermediate use, consumption, and investment.

   The projected import in conjunction with the desirable level of current account deficit, which, in turn, had implications for foreign debt and debt servicing, determined the aggregate exports. The current account deficit, in effect, was the foreign component of investible resources in the economy.

   The aggregate export was decomposed at the level of commodities using feasibility studies based on past trends and future prospects, and taking into account policy changes and international trade environment. A detailed econometric analysis of commodity exports using appropriate demand and supply functions was conducted. Based on these, the export at the level of commodities and commodity groups was projected. These were fed into the input–output model for verifying their consistency with domestic demand and production profile. The projections were, however, adjusted in order to ensure consistency with the economy-wide projections obtained from the input–output model.

Net invisibles (that is, inflows net of outflows) included exports and imports of services, private transfers, and investment income. These were projected on the basis of recent trends.

Consumption Module in the Fifth Plan

The mathematical model of the Fifth Plan contained a 'consumption module', in which the private consumption demand for goods and services was estimated at the level of input–output sectors. This estimate of private consumption was used as the final demand in the input–output model.

The consumption module was built on three models: (*a*) migration model; (*b*) demography model; and (*c*) income differential model. The migration model captured the flow of population from rural to urban areas. The demography model captured the rate of growth of population in rural and urban areas in terms of age, sex, and activity. The income differential model tracked and tackled the urban–rural differential in per capita consumption.

The private consumption demand (for different goods and services) estimated in the consumption module took into account the growth pattern of the economy as postulated in the Plan, the rural–urban composition of the population, and the inequality in per capita consumption distribution. The consumption module, in effect, quantified the extent of the improvement in levels of living of the people as a result of increase in per capita consumption expenditure and reduction in inequality in consumption distribution.

In the consumption module, sectoral private consumption (that is, consumption by the input–output sectors) was estimated (separately for rural and urban areas) with the help of the base year consumption proportions (in 27 expenditure classes) obtained from the NSS consumer expenditure data and the total private consumption (that is, consumption for the country as a whole) as determined in the macroeconomic model. The process of estimating sectoral consumption began with the disaggregation of total private consumption (obtained from the macroeconomic model) into rural and urban areas using (*a*) projected population growth in rural and urban areas as assumed in the Plan; (*b*) base year (of the Plan) population in rural and urban areas; and (*c*) urban–rural differential in per capita consumption, which was expressed as a ratio of per capita consumption in urban areas to that in rural areas. The model was based on faster increase in per capita consumption in rural areas as compared to urban areas in order to fulfil the objective of narrowing the gap in the per capita consumption between rural and urban population.

The distribution of per capita consumption was assumed to follow a two-parameter log-normal distribution in rural and urban areas. The log-normal distribution was specified by its mean and standard deviation. The mean of this distribution was estimated from the total consumption obtained from the macro-model. The standard deviation, which was a measure of inequality in consumption distribution, was worked out from the class distribution of consumption obtained from NSS consumer expenditure data. These (mean and standard deviation) were estimated separately in rural and urban areas.

In the Fifth Plan, the increase in per capita consumption of the poor group (defined as the bottom 30 per cent of the population) was initially estimated on the basis of the target growth rate in the Plan and the prevailing inequality in the class distribution of consumption (that is, the inequality in the distribution of per capita consumption in the base year of the Plan). The resulting estimate of consumption of the poor group (that is, the bottom 30 per cent of the population) was so low that it is not considered adequate from nutritional angle.

The increase in consumption of the poor group was contingent upon increase in the GDP growth rate (that is, growth rate of income), for which it was necessary to increase investment. However, resource constraint came in the way of increasing investment. It was then decided to devise a growth structure that was egalitarian and was able to raise the income (and by implication, consumption) of the poor group, more than others. This was a kind of redistributive exercise, weaved into the process of growth, introduced in the mathematical model of the Fifth Plan in which the rate and pattern of growth was fixed after taking into account additional quantities of goods and services required to raise the consumption level of the bottom 30 per cent of the population to the minimum required level. The model results warranted 'more investment in food and energy production, and curbing the growth of luxury goods'.

The professed goal of poverty removal (by way of increasing the per capita consumption of the bottom 30 per cent of the population to a minimum level), therefore, demanded that the strategy must seek not only attainment of the rate of economic growth targeted in the Plan (which is considered higher in comparison to the prevailing trend growth rate), but also lower of the level of inequality in the distribution of per capita income (consumption). Therefore, increase in consumption of the bottom 30 per cent of the population in the Fifth Plan was made contingent upon a reduced level of inequality in the consumption distribution. Such an approach was considerably strengthened later in the Sixth Plan.

In retrospect, poverty was not used explicitly in the Fifth Plan, but consumption was endogenized by estimating separately the commodity-specific consumption demand of the bottom 30 per cent of the population, who without an iota of doubt could then be treated as poor. The consumption characteristics of the bottom 30 per cent of the population was factored in to decide the demand structure of the economy. Their consumption demand, assessed through the consumption module, was integrated with the Fifth Plan model, which, in turn, was an integration of the Leontief input–output system with the model of macroeconomic growth belonging to the family of the Harrod–Domar model. The mathematical quantification of the consumption demand of the poorer section of the population (bottom 30 per cent) and its integration with the overall rate of growth of the economy ensuring appropriate inter-sectoral consistency opened varied treatments of the concept of poverty in the planning exercises.

Consumption Sub-model in the Sixth Plan

An elaborate consumption sub-model was incorporated in the math-ematical model of the Sixth Plan so as to accommodate the changing development priorities, which demanded determination of the pat-tern of consumption separately for the poor and the non-poor groups of the population. The poor were separated from the total population using an exogenously determined poverty line.[9] The consumption sub-model developed in the Sixth Plan replaced the consumption module used in the Fifth Plan (discussed earlier). The main features of the consumption sub-model used in the Sixth Plan are described here first.

The sectoral consumption demand for four groups of population (poor and non-poor in rural and urban areas) was estimated in the consumption sub-model (in the Sixth Plan). The sectoral consumption demand was estimated by taking into account the growth pattern of the economy as postulated in the Plan, and the inequality in the distribution of per capita consumption. The aggregate (private) consumption estimated in the macro-model was bifurcated into rural and urban areas using the projected rate of growth of population derived from demographic parameters and the per capita consumption differential between rural and urban areas. The per capita consumption in rural and urban areas was assumed to follow a two-parameter log-normal distribution. The mean of the log-normal distribution was obtained from the aggregate consumption in the macro-model. The dispersion of the distribution (that is, the inequality parameter) was worked out from the Lorenz ratio of per capita consumption distribution derived from the NSS data on consumer expenditure. From this distribution, the per capita consumption within each area (rural and urban) was determined for the poor and the non-poor, using the exogenously determined poverty line (which is expressed in terms of per capita consumption). The private consumption of each of these four groups of population (poor and non-poor in rural and urban areas) were disaggregated into input–output sectors for their use as final demand in the input–output model. The disaggregation was done through a two-stage nested behaviouristic model, comprising a Linear Expenditure System (LES) for broad groups of commodities (11 sectors) and a set of best fitting Engel curves for different items of consumption (71 items) within each broad LES commodity group. The sectoral consumption of each of these four groups of population was added to obtain the sectoral consumption for the entire population, which was used as the final demand in the input–output model.

The LES parameters for rural and urban areas, and within each area for the poor and the non-poor groups of the population, were estimated from the time series of cross-section data of consumer expenditure obtained from the NSS (16th Round, 1960–61, to 28th Round, 1973–74). The consumer demand functions for the poor and the non-poor within rural and urban areas were estimated in the form of

Engel equations for disaggregated commodity levels applying single equation weighted least square method to the cross-section data on household consumption expenditure in 1973–74 (NSS 28th Round). Alternative forms of functions (linear, double log, log-inverse, log-log inverse, hyperbola, and proportions) were estimated in order to choose the best fitting Engel curve separately for each commodity, for the four population groups. The best fitting Engel curves among these were chosen on the basis of their coefficient of determination, adjusted for degrees of freedom and form of function.

The consumption sub-model depicted the consumption behaviour of the poor and the non-poor sections of the population in rural and urban areas. These were used to quantify the extent of improvement in levels of living as a result of increase in per capita consumption and reduction in inequality in its class distribution.

Measurement of Poverty

The task force estimated the poverty ratio (percentage of persons living below the poverty line) from the class distribution of persons obtained from the NSS consumer expenditure data and an exogenously determined poverty line. The NSS consumer expenditure data by expenditure classes were adjusted pro rata to the private consumption estimated by the CSO in National Accounts Statistics (NAS). This ensured correspondence between the total consumption estimated from the NSS and the NAS. The number of persons living below the poverty line was estimated from the poverty ratio by applying the estimated population of the year. The poverty line and the poverty ratio were estimated at the national level separately for rural and urban areas.

The task force estimated the poverty line in 1973–74 and updated it for price inflation measured from the wholesale price index (WPI) for use in later years. The choice of WPI was debated. It was argued that the WPI is unable to capture the price rise of goods and services constituting the consumption basket of the poor appropriately as it constituted a range of items (about one-third of its weight) not meant for private consumption at all, and that the wholesale prices are different from the price which the consumers face in the market.[10] In the mid-1980s, WPI was replaced by the private consumption deflator of the NAS. There were other problems too. The updating of rural and urban poverty lines by the same index ignored urban–rural price differential, which is large in India. The problem was compounded by the decision of the Planning Commission to use the national poverty line (though separate in rural and urban areas) uniformly for all the states, thereby ignoring the interstate price differential, which evidently is far greater than the urban–rural price differential.

The pro rata adjustment of NSS consumption to NAS level across expenditure groups of the population has been questioned as the discrepancy between the two consumptions could not possibly be similar for the lower and the upper deciles of the population. The task force decided to adjust the NSS consumption when the difference between the two consumptions (NSS and NAS) was small, less than 10 per cent. Such a small adjustment had a wider canvas. The Planning Commission was using poverty as a parameter in planning exercises. The Plan model in use then (in the Sixth Plan) integrated the Leontief input–output system with the models of macroeconomic growth belonging to the family of Harrod–Domar in a demand–supply frame. The solution of the model demanded balancing of macroeconomic variables (income, consumption, savings, and investment) and integration of macroeconomic parameters with consistency requirement at a disaggregated level of inter-sectoral relationship. Consumption in this model (besides investment and imports) was endogenous in the determination of the rate of growth of the economy and the basic parameters governing levels of living. This rendered the role of consumption critical in the Plan model by identifying it directly with the people's level of living.

At this stage, the task force faced a zero-sum game. The NAS consumption, which was available in the form of a scalar value with no disaggregation by class or region (except by broad commodity group) was not enough to estimate poverty whereas the NSS consumer expenditure data, which was available by expenditure class and region, was ideally suited for the purpose of estimating poverty. The poverty estimates could not be used in Plan models if they were divorced from NAS consumption. Being the only source of class distribution of consumption, the NSS consumption was used to estimate poverty. In tandem, the inclusion of poverty as a parameter in the Plan had to take cognizance of NAS consumption for ensuring consistency with macroeconomic balance. Faced with this dilemma, the task force adjusted the class distribution of NSS consumption proportionately to NAS consumption.

It recommended such an adjustment for poverty estimation at the national level, and not at the level of the states. The Planning Commission subsequently straightjacketed the task force's method to estimate state-wise poverty by (*a*) applying the national poverty line (in rural and urban areas) uniformly to all the states, and (*b*) adjusting the NSS consumption distribution of the states pro rata to the NAS consumption level across all expenditure classes of the population. The application of a single poverty line (the national poverty line) for all the states uniformly ignored the price differential of the goods and services constituting the consumption basket of the poor (which is the poverty line) across the states whereas the interstate price differential in the country was indeed large. The adjustment of NSS consumption at the national level, as was employed at the level of states, implied similar rate of adjustment for all the states (such as developed and less developed, high income and low income, rich and poor), and for all the classes of population (such as, lower and upper deciles). This was not considered a rational approach for the rate of adjustment cannot be similar for all the states and for all the income classes of the population even within the same state.

Poverty Block in the Sixth Plan

In the Sixth Plan (1980–85), income redistributive poverty alleviation programmes were launched in two major areas, namely asset generation and wage employment. These were meant to benefit poor families. In the mid-term appraisal to the Sixth Plan, a 'poverty block' was created within the consumption sub-model so that the impact of these income redistributive measures on the income of the poor and on poverty reduction could be assessed.

The assessment was carried out from the interrelationship among economic growth, Plan programmes, and poverty alleviation, and their integration with aggregated model structure. The variables related to income, consumption, and employment generation used in the aggregated model structure were divided into two separate blocks. The first block includes variables related to all activities of

the economy, barring those arising from income redistributive programmes. This block essentially captured the impact of growth on
poverty alleviation. The second block included the variables related
exclusively to the poverty alleviation programmes, and captured
their impact on poverty.

The distributional effect of all activities belonging to the first block
was estimated in the light of past observations regarding the pattern
of consumption distribution over time. In the second block, the distributional impact was assessed by identifying the beneficiaries of income
redistributive programmes and working out the net improvement in
their income and consumption (from the initial level) as a result of
these programmes. Their initial level of income or consumption was
assumed to be dependent on the activities covered in the first block.

The extent of poverty reduction as a result of general growth in
income was estimated in the first block. This was called the 'growth
effect' on poverty. The variables and parameters used to estimate the
percentage of people living below the poverty line and the number of
people crossing the poverty line were as follows: (a) poverty line; (b) gross
investment to net income ratio in the poverty alleviation programmes;
(c) gross level of investment; (d) total consumption of the households
or average propensity to consume; (e) total population; and (f) the
inequality parameter of the log-normal distribution function, which
is the consumption distribution parameter.

The extent of poverty reduction arising from income redistributive
programmes was estimated in the second block. For estimating income
generation and its effects on the people below the poverty line, the
additional parameters and variables estimated were: (a) number of
beneficiary families covered by poverty alleviation programmes;
(b) size of each beneficiary family; and (c) consumption distribution
parameter of beneficiary families.

It is worthwhile to mention that a watertight separation of the two
blocks is virtually an impossible task. These two blocks are interrelated
with the overall model frame through the inter-industry transaction
matrix. It is probable that some part of the income generation from
the programmes specifically earmarked for the poor might accrue
to the non-poor because of leakages. This can potentially make the
estimate of the income generation of the poor somewhat imprecise as
a result of income redistributive programmes.

The Model Solution: Summing Up

The solution procedure at different stages of the mathematical model consisting of the core model and the sub-models that were used to set the Plan targets has been chronicled in this section for the sake of clarity in exposition.

The requirements for consumption in the public and private sectors and investment in the public and private sectors, and the demand for export, import, and intermediate goods were assessed in tune with the various objectives set in the Plan. These estimates of requirement and demand, sectoral as well as aggregate, were worked out in the core model. The consistency of output levels was assessed through the input–output model and their supply feasibilities were checked through the sub-models. The sub-models played a crucial role in estimating the sectoral supply potentials. The sub-models were estimated separately and their integration with the other sub-models and the core model was achieved by iterative processes.

The domestic resource availability at the macro level, which is determined by domestic savings, was worked out in the macroeconomic model. Savings depend on the level of income and habits (that is, the observed behaviour) of different saving agents. Savings behaviour was assessed from the manner of response of saving agents to various savings instruments (that is, policies). The main saving agents were households, private corporate sector, public enterprises, and the government. The resources available from abroad were estimated. This is defined as foreign savings. The sum total of foreign savings and domestic savings yielded the amount of investible resources in the Plan.

Agents who generate savings do not necessarily make investments in equal amounts. A large part of savings of the households gets invested in the public sector or the private corporate sector. Savings change hands through financial institutions. An estimate of such flows among saving and investing agents was made by considering the investment capabilities and needs of various investing agents. These estimates served as a starting point of the model estimation and got revised in light of the final result of the model. The planning model was largely sequential. In actual working, the model became iterative because some of the variables were fed into the model system from outside, which means that they were not fully endogenized.

The ICOR, defined as the ratio of investment made in the Plan and additional output/income to be generated in the Plan, was estimated on the basis of past behaviour and future prospects. The rate of growth that could be targeted or was achievable was worked out from the investible resources and the ICOR. This point marked the beginning of the process of the model solution, usually, with a few alternative estimates of investible resources, ICOR, and targeted or achievable rates of growth.

Savings, investments, GDP and its growth rate, exports, imports, balance of payments, and fiscal variables (revenue, expenditure, savings, and borrowing of the government) were part of the macro-model. The final demand consisted of public and private consumption, exports and imports at the levels of disaggregation (or by as many industries and sectors) of the input-output table. These were worked out in keeping with the indicated levels of output in the macro-model.

The consistent production levels are those that enable final demands to be met, while at the same time fully meeting the needs of industrial consumption (input demands). This exercise was accomplished through the core model, which had the input–output matrix at its base and was undertaken for alternative sets of final demand, implying alternative sets of growth possibilities. The set of growth possibilities in which the detailed exercise was found to be consistent with the set of macro-parameters that were worked out in the beginning was finally considered feasible (or achievable).

A Five Year Plan was set within the perspective of long-term growth and constraints. The factors considered in the perspective Plan were demographic trends and basic resource endowments. The structure of population growth and the associated growth and size of labour force characterize demographic trends. Basic resource endowments are assessed in terms of land, water, energy, other essential minerals, and the environment. The perspective Plan checked that the requirement of output in the post-terminal year of the Plan (which was usually 10 years away from the terminal year of the Five Year Plan) was consistent with the long-term objectives of the economy and that it matched the growth potentials developed within the five years of the Plan. The Five Year Plans in India were always prepared with a 10-year perspective, which meant that the entire planning horizon was 15 years (five-year medium-term plan and ten-year perspective plan).

The Plan model was basically a production and investment model. The social objectives of the Plan (for example, the objectives set in the areas of education, literacy, health care, drinking water, sanitation, livelihood security, poverty alleviation, and so on) got integrated into the Plan model through additional consumption or through additional investment requirements in these sectors, both of which are components of the final demand in the model system. The instrumentalities of shifting people from below to above the poverty line are essentially social processes and necessitate social mobilization, institution-building, and adoption of a set of socio-economic policies. The policies and details of the programmes related to social objectives in a Plan were mostly worked out outside the model, and were not mathematically tractable.

Planning Models in the Era of Economic Reform

The planning models in India in the pre-reform era were used to determine sectoral investment in order to attain the desired sectoral rate of growth. The mathematical models used in different stages of Plan formulation to arrive at the values of the variables in the pre-reform years have been described in the previous sections. There was a change in the planning process or, in other words, in the methodology of Plan formulation in the era of economic reforms. This altered process of planning under economic reform resulted in the change in the manner and method of application of mathematical models in different stages of Plan formulation. In sum, the process of Plan formulation in the era of economic reform differed from that of the pre-reform days. Also, the role of mathematical models in planning in the era of economic reform became different.

The Eighth Plan (1992–97) was formulated under the framework of the consistency model of the pre-reform years, but not implemented in letter and spirit as it was overtaken by economic reform measures. Under these measures, the methodology of Plan formulation changed from the Ninth Plan (1997–2002) onwards, and so also the application of mathematical models. In the Ninth Plan, a macroeconomic model was added to the existing input–output-cum-investment planning model, which was a feature of the Plan model in the pre-reform days (and used in the Sixth to the Eighth Plan). This new macroeconomic model was designed to examine the implications of alternative growth target for the economy. It treated aggregate growth rate of GDP, unemployment rate, current account deficit, and government borrowing as the main target variables. Some of the variables that used to be controlled and regulated by the government in the pre-reform period were now determined in the market. The main purpose of this model was to capture the impact of these variables on the rate and pattern of economic growth.

Using the input–output model and the macroeconomic model, the sectoral growth rate of GDP was determined to be consistent with an exogenously determined (aggregate) GDP growth rate as target. Then, aggregate investment as well as its sectoral break-up was worked out. The investment requirement for attaining the target growth rate was computed on the basis of the likely sectoral growth rate in the Plan and the sectoral ICOR, which is a measure of the efficiency of capital use. The ICOR was estimated from past data. It should be noted that the sectoral growth rates used for deriving investment in the era of economic reform were not mutually consistent whereas in pre-reform days these were derived after ensuring appropriate inter-sectoral consistency, with the help of input–output based consistency-cum-investment model.

By relating investment to output in the private sector, its sectoral investment demand functions were estimated from an econometric model. Private investment at the sectoral level was estimated from these investment demand functions. Public investment bridged the gap between the required investment (for the economy as a whole) and the investment forthcoming from the private sector (as per the estimates yielding from the sectoral investment demand functions). Employment generation as a result of growth was computed from sectoral employment elasticities.

Current account deficit was obtained by calculating the difference between aggregate investment and savings. Exports of goods were estimated independently by relating it to the share of incremental manufacturing output that may have been available for export. Import was determined as a residual so as to maintain balance between projected current account deficit and exports. The ratio-nale was that the government in the reform era had better control over imports (through import policy, customs duties, and exchange

rates), than it had over exports. It is obvious that the planners preferred to set targets on the variables over which they could exercise
greater control.

In order to capture the impact of several variables which were
determined increasingly by the market forces, sub-models were
developed. The sub-models were not recursive to the macro-model
(a change from the practice in the pre-reform days) but its results
were factored in while deciding the aggregate growth rate. A sub-
model was developed for the measurement of poverty. It was used
to project the poverty ratios in rural and urban areas of the states.
Sub-models were also developed for external and fiscal sectors. The
external sector sub-model was developed to project imports and
exports during a Plan under alternative scenarios of growth in GDP
and tariff. Some of the parameters determining the fiscal balance in
the Plan, and mainly the parameters related to government finance,
were worked out in the fiscal sub-model. It was used to ensure consistency between the fiscal position of the government and the rate
of growth of GDP.

The mathematical model developed by the Planning Commission
and described earlier was used for formulating three Five Year Plans,
the Ninth to the Eleventh. Notably, in the finalization of the Eleventh
Plan, the results of the Planning Commission model were supplemented by specific results from four independent research institutes:
(*a*) National Council of Applied Economic Research (NCAER), New
Delhi; (*b*) Institute of Economic Growth (IEG), New Delhi; (*c*) Indira
Gandhi Institute of Development Research (IGIDR), Mumbai; and
(*d*) Indian Statistical Institute (ISI), Bangalore.[11]

The NCAER prepared a macro-econometric model. It is essentially
a structural model and provides medium-term assessment of macroeconomic variables of the Indian economy. The model is used to
assess specifically the impact of infrastructure development, agricultural growth, and FDI on the rate of growth of the economy. Using
this model, the implication of increase in international prices of
crude oil and petroleum products on growth and price inflation in the
Indian economy were examined in the context of the Eleventh Plan.

An econometric model that is Keynesian in outlook and at the same
time combines neo-classical and structuralist elements was prepared

by the IEG. They preferred to call it a structural macro-econometric model. Using simulations run by the model, the feasibility of an alternative growth target (of GDP in the context of the Eleventh Plan) was checked. The model is used to analyse the effects of domestic and global shocks on the growth rate, inflationary situation, and macro-balance of the Indian economy.

A computable general equilibrium (CGE) model was prepared by the IGIDR. It is a static model built around a social accounting matrix (SAM) with endogenous income distribution. The model specifically assesses the impact of changes in export, foreign savings, and international price of crude oil on the GDP growth rate and overall macroeconomic balance. It was used to assess the distributional impact of changes in some of these variables and of the policies which were considered to be the cornerstone of inclusive growth in the Eleventh Plan.

A vector auto regression (VAR) model developed by the ISI's Bangalore centre facilitated policy analysis. It is a macroeconomic simulation model concerned with the likely production performance, investment, price effects, and household savings and consumption patterns, with application in the Eleventh Plan.

The treatise on mathematical models and their application in the formulation of Five Year Plans in the Indian context may be wrapped up with a note of caution. The mathematical models were a crucial step in the process of Plan formulation. In the same breath, it must be stressed that the Five Year Plans were not formulated exclusively on the basis of the results obtained from these mathematical models. A large area of the Plan formulation was kept beyond the scope of mathematical modelling. The social objectives of the Plan, even in the heyday of state control, under state-regulated price, and fiscal and monetary policies were not mathematically tractable, and had to be kept outside the frame of the mathematical models. In the end, consensus determined a large area of Plan finalization. The different players in the Plan formulation, namely the central ministries, especially the finance ministry, the state governments, the Reserve Bank of India, and so on, built a consensus around the results that flowed through the mathematical models. This is more in evidence in the era of economic reform.

Notes

1. The economic growth in the 1950s led to diversification of the economy, and the planners felt the necessity to develop multi-sectoral and multi-period planning models in order to ensure an efficient resolution of the choice problems facing the economy. Such models were constructed by the Planning Commission for their possible use in the formulation of Five Year Plans. Pitambar Pant and I. M. D. Little prepared a model for the Planning Commission for use in the Third Plan. This is known as the Pant–Little exercise. The Planning Commission later prepared a consistency model for the Fourth Plan. The Third or the Fourth Plan did not explicitly mention use of any of these mathematical models and the linkage between the model results and the Plan, if there is one, is not explicit.

2. The discussion here is largely based on the description of the model given in Jagdish N. Bhagwati and Sukhamoy Chakravarty, *Contributions to Indian Economic Analysis: A Survey*, Lalvani Publishing House, Bombay, 1972, pp. 5–8.

3. The two-sector model was published in P. C. Mahalanobis, 'Some Observations on the Process of Growth of National Income', *Sankhya*, September 1953, pp. 307–12; and the four-sector model was published in 'The Approach to Operational Research to Planning in India', *Sankhya*, December 1955, pp. 3–130.

4. J. B. S. Haldane, 'The Maximisation of National Income', *Sankhya*, Vol. 16, December 1955, pp. 1–2.

5. R. Komiya, 'A Note on Professor Mahalanobis' Model of Indian Economic Planning', *Review of Economics and Statistics*, Vol. 41, February 1959, pp. 29–35.

6. Shigeto, Tsuru, 'Some Theoretical Doubts on Indian Plan Frame', *The Economic Weekly*, Annual Number, January 1957, pp. 77–9.

7. The mathematical models used in the Fifth to the Eighth Plans have been published by the Perspective Planning Division, Planning Commission, Government of India, New Delhi. These are as follows: *A Technical Note on the Approach to the Fifth Plan of India 1974–79*, April 1973; *A Technical Note on the Sixth Plan of India 1980–85*, July 1981; *A Technical Note on the Seventh Plan of India 1985–90*, June 1986; and *A Technical Note to the Eighth Plan of India 1992–97*, May 1995.

8. Absence of a capital-flow matrix had forced the investment estimate in earlier Plans to be one for the entire Five Year Plan, and that too at the aggregate level. The investment by sources under the circumstances used to be derived using aggregate investment and allocating them to

different sources, using parameters determined outside the model. In consequence, the impact of alternative investment allocations on sectoral growth profile could not be explored.

9. The poverty line is expressed in terms of per capita consumption expenditure. It was quantified by the Task Force on Projections of Minimum Needs and Effective Consumption Demand, constituted by the Planning Commission under the chairmanship of Y. K. Alagh. The poverty line was quantified in two stages. First, the average calorie requirement is estimated (separately in rural and urban areas) taking into consideration the age, sex, and activity distribution of the population and the associated calorie norm recommended by the Indian Council of Medical Research (ICMR). On this basis, the average calorie requirement is estimated as 2,400 kcal per capita per day in rural areas and 2,100 kcal in urban areas. Second, the poverty line is worked out as the consumption expenditure necessary to meet the calorie norm along with other non-food necessities (such as clothing, shelter, transport, education, health care, and so on.). Thus, the poverty line is defined as a level of per capita consumption, which meets the minimum calorie requirement along with specified non-food items of consumption. This makes the concept of poverty line partly normative and partly behavioural.

10. Two factors might have induced the task force to use WPI, ignoring sector-specific price indices such as consumer price index of agricultural labourers (CPIAL) in rural areas and consumer price index of industrial workers (CPIIW) in urban areas. First, the CPIAL and CPIIW had an older base (1960–61) in relation to the WPI (1970–71). Second, the time lag in release of CPIAL and CPIIW was a lot more than WPI. For these two reasons of having a more recent base and minimum time lag in availability, the task force chose WPI, despite the fact that it included some items not meant for private consumption.

11. The model descriptions can be found in Kirit S. Parikh (ed.), *Macro-Modelling for the Eleventh Five Year Plan of India*, Academic Foundation, New Delhi, 2009.

3

Growth, Investment, and Savings in Five Year Plans

Maximization of income has been at the centre of India's growth and development strategy. The issue of development is instinctively correlated with economic growth. In a low-income developing country such as India, it is only through rapid economic growth that the production base can be expanded to achieve and sustain a higher standard of living for the people. On attaining Independence, the political leadership adopted planning as the means to achieve a high rate of economic growth so that the income of the people could be increased to the maximum possible extent within the shortest possible time.

The GDP represents the total value of goods and services produced within the country. The increase in GDP is treated as a measure of economic growth. In India, the average growth rate of GDP (at factor cost) has been 5 per cent per year during the six decades of planning (1951–2011) since Independence. Whether this growth rate is high or low can be debated. An unwelcome feature of this long-term growth, however, is that it has been uneven over time. The GDP growth rate during the initial three decades of planning, 1951–80, was slower (3.5 per cent per year) as compared to that in the latter three decades, 1981–2011 (6.3 per cent per year). In per capita terms, the GDP growth rate in 1951–80 (1.3 per cent per year) was less than one-third of that in 1981–2011 (4.3 per cent per year). Again, the growth rate in the two decades of economic reform (1992–2011) was not uniform; the growth rate in the initial 11 years (5.9 per cent per year in 1992–2002) was about two-thirds of that in the latter 9 years (8.3 per cent per year in 2003–11).

Growth Performance in Five Year Plans

The growth target for the Indian economy was fixed by the Planning Commission in the five year plans. This was the only source of target growth rate for the economy. Throughout the first 10 Five Year Plans, that is, until 2007, the growth rate was fixed at the national level and was not available at the state level, despite the states being the main administrative unit. The target growth rate was fixed as an average of the five years of the Plan, and not separately for each of the five years. Therefore, annual phasing of the five-yearly growth target is not available. The Planning Commission disaggregated the national growth target (of the Plan) at the level of states in the Eleventh Plan (2007–12). But these national or state level targets were not disaggregated for each year of the Five Year Plan. The mathematical model that was at the base of the determination of the growth rate in the Five Year Plan was solved for terminal year configuration of input, output, and technology, and as a rule, the equilibrium values of the variables were not obtained in each of the five years of the Plan. As a result, the annual phasing of the growth rates could not be generated by the model. For operational purposes, the growth rate from the base year to the terminal year (of the Plan) was presumed to follow an exponential path. Alternatively, the growth rate in all the five years of the Plan was assumed to be the same.

The First Five Year Plan began in 1951–52. The Eleventh Plan concluded in 2011–12. These 11 five year plans spanned over 61 years. The six intervening years that were not covered by the five year plans are: 1966–67 to 1968–69, 1979–80, 1990–91, and 1991–92. The planning process was disrupted from 1966–67 to 1968–69 on account of uncertainty about availability of resources. A minority government at the centre was the principal reason behind the discontinuation of the process of planning in the other three years.

A quantitative assessment of growth performance of the Indian economy during the six decades of planning can be made by comparing the realized growth rate with the target set in the five year plans. The target and realized growth rate for the First to the Eleventh Plan have been given in Table 3.1. The growth rates relate to the average of the five years of the Plan.

The performance of a Five Year Plan at the first instance can be judged from the overall rate of growth of the economy. In the six decades of planning, there were two phases of failed growth rates, meaning the realized growth rate (in the Plan) fell short of the target. These two phases were (a) the Second Plan to the Fourth Plan, which were implemented in the two-decade period from the mid-1950s to the mid-1970s; and (b) the Ninth Plan to the Eleventh Plan, which spanned over one and a half decades, 1997 to 2011. Between these two phases of failed growth lies a two-decade period from the mid-1970s to the mid-1990s, when the target growth rate in the Plan was achieved. Four Five Year Plans, the Fifth to the Eighth, fall in these two decades.

The reasons behind the shortfall in growth rate in the five year plans were not similar. The shortfall in growth rate in the second to the Fourth Plan, spread over the years 1956 to 1974, was largely on account of poor agriculture. The GDP growth rate declined in at least one of the five years in each of these three five year plans. The shortfall in growth rate in the Second Plan was marginal. However, it was a different scenario in the Third Plan as the realized growth rate in the Plan was half of the target. The main reason behind the shortfall in growth rate in the Third Plan was the poor agricultural growth in four of the five years of the Plan period as a result of unfavourable weather. Besides, changes in inter-sectoral allocation of resources eventuating from the border conflict with China in October 1962 and the war with Pakistan in September 1965 were also responsible for this. The reasons behind the shortfall in the growth rate in the Third Plan have been detailed in Chapter 4 in context of the analysis of the first four decades of planning.

The growth performance in the Fourth Plan was not satisfactory; only about half of the growth target could be met. The Fourth Plan preceded three years of drought and crop failure (1966–67 to 1968–69), which left a devastating impact on agriculture and, in due course, on the entire economy. India was starved of foreign assistance largely on account of the discontinuation of financial aid from the

Table 3.1 Growth Rate in Five Year Plans (Per Cent per Annum)

Five Year Plan	Agriculture	Industry	Services				GDP (Total)
			Trade	Finance	Others	Total	
First Plan (1951–52 to 1955–56)	2.9	6.2	4.7	3.1	3.0	3.7	3.6 (2.1)
Second Plan (1956–57 to 1960–61)	3.5	6.5	6.1	2.8	4.3	4.6	4.3 (4.5)
Third Plan (1961–62 to 1965–66)	0.0	6.9	5.6	3.3	5.8	5.1	2.8 (5.6)
Fourth Plan (1969–70 to 1973–74)	2.7	3.2	3.8	4.0	4.3	4.0	3.4 (5.7)
Fifth Plan (1974–75 to 1978–79)	3.7	6.3	6.9	5.3	3.6	5.4	4.9 (4.4)
Sixth Plan (1980–81 to 1984–85)	6.0	5.0	5.4	7.4	5.1	5.8	5.5 (5.2)
Seventh Plan (1985–86 to 1989–90)	3.5	6.3	6.5	10.0	6.9	7.5	5.7 (5.0)
Eighth Plan (1992–93 to 1996–97)	4.6	7.6	8.8	7.0	5.6	7.3	6.6 (5.6)
Ninth Plan (1997–98 to 2001–02)	2.6	4.6	8.3	8.4	7.7	8.2	5.7 (6.5)
Tenth Plan (2002–03 to 2006–07)	2.7	9.7	10.5	9.4	5.2	8.8	7.6 (7.9)
Eleventh Plan (2007–08 to 2011–12)	4.0	8.1	9.1	11.0	8.0	9.4	8.0 (9.0)

Notes:

1. In the last column, the figures in brackets are the target growth rate of the Plan. The growth target in all 11 Five Year Plans is not measured in the same unit. The target growth rate is fixed in terms of national income from the First to the Third Plan, net domestic product (NDP) in the Fourth Plan, and GDP at factor cost from the Fifth to the Eleventh Plan.
2. The realized growth rate at the level of sectors and in the aggregate for the Plan periods is expressed in terms of GDP at factor cost, derived from 2004–05 as the base year.
3. Agriculture includes crop sector, animal husbandry, forestry, and fishing; GDP from mining and quarrying has been included in agriculture.
4. Industry covers manufacturing, construction, electricity, gas, and water supply.
5. In the services sector, trade covers hotels, transport, and communications; finance covers banking, insurance, real estate, and business service; other services cover community, social, and personal services, including public administration and defence.

Source: Author's computation based on data from 'Summary of Macro Economic Aggregates at Constant (2004–05) Prices, 1950–51 to 2013–14', Statement 12, 27 March 2015. CSO, Ministry of Statistics and Programme Implementation, Government of India. Available at mospi.gov.in.

United States of America (USA) and other European countries after the war with Pakistan in 1965. The balance of payments was in serious disequilibrium. The macroeconomic balance was distorted. The shortfall in the growth rate in the Fourth Plan has to be viewed against these circumstances.

The reasons behind the shortfall in growth rate from the Ninth to the Eleventh Plan are different than those in the Second to the Fourth Plan. The Ninth Plan witnessed two successive minority governments at the centre, each lasting less than one year, leaving their effects on the growth path. Then, there were two general elections within a period of one year. General growth and development projects could not be initiated when the process of election is underway. The shortfall in growth rate in the Tenth Plan was marginal and it was largely on account of a subdued agriculture. The target growth rate in agriculture in the Tenth Plan could not be met mostly due to unfavourable weather. In fact, in both the Ninth and the Tenth Plans, the realized growth rate in agriculture was less than the target, which itself was modest. In any case, the impact of agricultural growth on the overall rate of economic growth was less in the Ninth and Tenth Plans, for example, when compared with the Second to Fourth Plan, as the share of agriculture in aggregate GDP declined during the intervening four decades.

The growth rate in the Eleventh Plan was set at a high level—at 9 per cent per year. Such a high growth rate had not been targeted in any Five Year Plan before. However, the realized growth rate was 8 per cent per year, which was an all-time high, and had never been realized in any Plan before. The growth rate in the Eleventh Plan, though less than the target, was high and the high growth rate cut across major sectors, such as agriculture, industry, and services. Agriculture, which is often hit by adverse weather, in a rare exception yielded a growth rate of 4 per cent per year in the Eleventh Plan, equalling the Plan target.

The growth target was realized in four Five Year Plans, the Fifth to the Eighth, from the mid-1970s to the mid-1990s. Notably, these four Five Year Plans were formulated in a consistency Plan frame, with the public sector at the helm of investment and income generation. Traditionally, the growth targets in these Plans (with the backdrop of state control) were fixed at a modest level. This could have been one of the factors responsible for meeting the growth target. The realized growth rate in the Eighth Plan was a clear 1 percentage point more than the target, which is indeed large. The Eighth Plan was formulated in a consistency Plan frame in which the target was set at a modest level, but it was implemented under the aegis of the economic reforms and liberalization, when state control on economic activities was considerably relaxed and even eliminated in many cases. This could possibly have contributed to the large gap between the target and the realized growth rate in the Eighth Plan.

The realized or actual growth rates are available from the CSO for each of the five years of the Plan. The growth target in the Five Year Plan was fixed as an average of the five years of the Plan, and not separately for each of the five years. Under the condition of the actual growth rate being available for each year but the target growth rate being available as an average of five years, the growth performance in each year of the Five Year Plans has been assessed here by comparing the realized yearly growth rate with the five-yearly target. In other words, the target growth rate has been assumed to be the same in all the five years of the Plan. A Five Year Plan was implemented through annual plans. An annual plan was not exactly one-fifth of the Five Year Plan, but was close to it. In this context, such an approach—of equating the five-yearly growth target to annual target, and then comparing this target with the actual (realized) growth rate to assess the performance of yearly growth rate—to assess the annual performance may not be totally out of the way.

The realized annual growth rate of GDP from 1951–52 to 2011–12 has been given in Table 3A. The target growth rate in the First to the Eleventh Five Year Plan has been given in Table 3.1. An assessment of the growth performance for each year within the Five Year Plan has been made here by comparing the realized annual growth rate with the five-yearly growth target. The realized growth rate indicates that after the Fourth Plan, the GDP growth rate did not decline in any year of the Five Year Plans. Indeed, the Fifth to the Eleventh Plan, which means seven Five Year Plans in a row covering 35 years from 1974–75 to 2011–12, did not witness a single year when the rate of economic growth (GDP growth rate) declined. (This should not be confused with the decline in GDP growth rate by 5.2 per cent in 1979–80, which was not a part of any Five Year Plan.) The annual GDP growth rate during this 35-year range went up from a low of 1.2 per cent (in 1974–75 and 1976–77) to a high of 10.2 per cent (in 1988–89). Again, since the beginning of the Sixth Plan in 1980–81, the GDP growth rate was not less than 4 per cent in any year except 1982–83, 1987–88, and 2002–03. It shows that the GDP growth rate was at least 4 per cent in 27 of the 30 years covering the Sixth to the Eleventh Plan. Similarly, the GDP growth rate has been at least 5 per cent in 17 of the 20 years spanning from the Eighth to the Eleventh Plan. The two decades covering the Eighth to the Eleventh Plan, 1992–2011, coincide with the economic reform. In these two decades, the three years when the GDP growth rate could not attain the 5 per cent mark are 1997–98, 2000–01, and 2002–03. The low rate of growth in agriculture was singularly responsible for the overall rate of economic growth to fall below 5 per cent in these three years.

Sectoral Growth in Plans

The growth rates in the First to the Eleventh Plan at the level of major sectors, namely agriculture, industry, and services have been given in Table 3.1.

The performance of agriculture until the Fourth Plan was sub-par, the growth rate being 2.5 per cent per year, which was close to the rate of growth of population. It is relevant to mention in this context that agricultural production remained static in per capita terms until the Fourth Plan. It was not until 1980 that agriculture could attain the average growth rate of 4 per cent per year in a Five Year Plan. In fact, agricultural growth in only three Five Year Plans—the Sixth, Eighth, and Eleventh—exceeded 4 per cent per year. Of the four Five Year Plans in the two decades of economic reform, 1992–2011, agricultural growth rate was less than 3 per cent per year in two Five Year Plans (the Ninth and the Tenth) and exceeded 4 per cent per year in the other two plans (the Eighth and the Eleventh).

The agricultural GDP declined in at least two of the five years in each of the four Five Year Plans, the Second to the Fifth. Similarly, in eight Five Year Plans, there was at least one year in each Plan when the agricultural GDP declined. In contrast, the agricultural GDP did not decline in any of the three Five Year Plans—the Sixth, Eighth, and Eleventh, the latter two being in the era of economic reform.

The agricultural growth rate turned out to be the highest in the Sixth Plan (5.9 per cent per year). However, this high growth rate could be misleading as it was aided by an unusually high growth of 12.8 per cent occurring in the first year of the Sixth Plan, 1980–81. The high growth rate in 1980–81 was largely on account of the low base, with agricultural growth declining by 11.9 per cent in the previous year, 1979–80. Placing the agricultural growth in 1980–81 on the trend line, the average growth in the Sixth Plan would be in the range of 4 to 4.5 per cent per year. The low rate of growth in 1979–80 did not depress the average growth in any of the Five Year Plans, as it was not covered under any Five Year Plan.

The rate of industrial growth in the initial years of planning (from the First to the Third Plan) averaged 6.5 per cent per year. A series of factors adversely affected the industrial growth rate in the Fourth Plan. This was higher than the average rate of industrial growth of 5.8 per cent per year in the first seven Five Year Plans which were implemented before the initiation of economic reform. The rate of industrial growth was modest, averaging 6 per cent per year in the next few Five Year Plans, the Fifth to the Ninth, 1974–2002. Afterwards, industrial growth attained a higher trajectory and averaged 8.9 per cent per year in the Tenth and the Eleventh Plans, which span over a decade, 2002–12.

The growth of the services sector was modest until the Fourth Plan, averaging 4.4 per cent per year (from the First to the Fourth Plan). The long-term growth rate of the services sector was 5.2 per cent per year in the first seven Five Year Plans, which were implemented in the pre-reform era. The services sector expanded in the era of economic reforms and its growth rate became 9.4 per cent per year in the Eleventh Plan, though the kink in the growth rate of services sector surfaced earlier in the Seventh Plan when it touched 7.5 per cent per year. The growth of the services sector averaged 8.4 per cent per year in the four Five Year Plans implemented in the two decades of economic reform, 1992–2011. Notably, the growth rate of the services sector in the Five Year Plans accelerated in these two decades.

The growth rate of the services sector ranged from 8 to 12 per cent in 12 of the 61 years of planning, 1951–2011, and these 12 years fall in the era of economic reform. On the other hand, the growth rate of the services sector was less than 4 per cent in 11 years, and this was before the 1980s. Within the services sector, trade, including hotels, transport, and communications, increased relatively faster until the Fourth Plan. The rate of growth of financial services increased gradually from the Fifth Plan onwards, and reached a peak in the Eleventh Plan, when its growth rate became 11 per cent per year. Other services, which include public administration, increased relatively faster in the Seventh, Ninth, and Eleventh Plans, mainly as the salaries of government employees increased following the recommendations of pay commissions of the central and state governments, which were implemented periodically.

The pattern of sectoral growth rate had a consequential impact on the structure of the economy. This is discernible from the sectoral share of GDP in the Five Year Plans, as given in Table 3.2. The structure of the economy altered as a result of consistent decline in the share of agriculture in GDP and increase in the share of the services

Table 3.2 Structure of the Economy (Sectoral Share in GDP)

Plan	Agriculture	Industry	Services
First Plan (1951–56)	54.7	15.2	30.0
Second Plan (1956–61)	51.8	17.4	30.8
Third Plan (1961–66)	46.8	20.5	32.7
Fourth Plan (1969–74)	43.1	22.2	34.6
Fifth Plan (1974–79)	41.0	22.7	36.2
Sixth Plan (1980–85)	38.1	23.3	38.7
Seventh Plan (1985–90)	34.4	23.6	42.1
Eighth Plan (1992–97)	30.6	24.3	45.0
Ninth Plan (1997–2002)	26.3	24.1	49.6
Tenth Plan (2002–07)	21.7	25.1	53.2
Eleventh Plan (2007–12)	17.4	26.0	56.6

Note: The shares are based on the GDP estimates derived from 2004–05 as the base year. Figures are in percentage.

Source: Author's estimate based on data from 'Summary of Macro Economic Aggregates at Current Prices, 1950–51 to 2013–14', Statement 11, 27 March 2015. CSO, Ministry of Statistics and Programme Implementation, Government of India. Available at mospi.gov.in.

sector. The share of agriculture in GDP declined over the Five Year Plans. This decline was sharp from the Eighth Plan onwards, which coincides with the beginning of the economic reforms. On the other hand, the share of the services sector in GDP increased. The share of the services sector in GDP in the period of economic reform (the Eighth to the Eleventh Plan) was more than two and a half times of that witnessed in the pre-reform era (the First to the Seventh Plan).

The share of agriculture in GDP in the Eleventh Plan lowered to just one-third of that in the First Plan, while the share of the services sector in GDP nearly doubled. In the first four Five Year Plans (that is, the First Plan to the Fourth Plan), the share of industry in GDP increased by 7 percentage points whereas in the next seven Five Year Plans (that is, the Fifth Plan to the Eleventh Plan) the increase is only 3.8 percentage points.

Industrialization is synonymous with increase in the share of industry in the GDP. The story of India's industrialization that emerged with the above narrative pinpoints the fact that industrialization in the pre-reform days, in the true sense of the term, took place in the first three Five Year Plans, spanning over 1951–66. However, the higher industrial growth in this period (by 6.5 per cent per year) was largely aided by the thrust on industrialization in the Second Plan, and partly due to the base effect as the level of industrialization being low when the Five Year Plans were initiated in 1951. The industrial growth realized during the 10 years beginning from the Second Plan (that is, during the period 1955–56 to 1964–65) could not be maintained in the next 10 years (1965–66 to 1974–75). The annual average growth rate during the period 1955–65 was 7.5 per cent in industry and 4.2 per cent for the economy as a whole, whereas the same during the period 1965–75 was 3.2 per cent in industry and 2.6 per cent for the economy as a whole.

Though the share of industry in GDP increased somewhat faster in the latter years of economic reform (by merely a percentage point each in the Tenth and the Eleventh Plans), as the growth rate attained a higher trajectory, it put the scale of industrialization in considerable doubt. Indeed, the growth of industries, specifically its manufacturing segment, lagged way behind the services sector, causing such a measly rise in the share of industries in GDP after the Third Plan.

It is a different matter that part of the increase in the share of industry (in GDP) until the Third Plan may be due to the low base (of industry) in the initial years of planning.

The magnitude of the correlation coefficient between the annual growth rate of a specific sector (such as agriculture, industry, or services) and the growth rate of aggregate GDP can be treated as an indicator of the relative importance of the sector in the rate of aggregate income generation (measured by GDP growth rate). In the pre-reform years (1951–91), the correlation coefficient between the growth rate of aggregate GDP and agriculture was very high (0.95), whereas the correlation coefficient between the growth rate of aggregate GDP and the growth rate of industry (or services) was relatively low (0.57). This underlines the overwhelming dependence of the growth rate of aggregate GDP on agriculture in the pre-reform days. The scenario changed in the years of economic reform with the substantial lowering of the magnitude of the correlation coefficient between the rate of growth of agriculture and that of aggregate GDP. The dependence of the growth of aggregate GDP on that of agriculture waned considerably in the era of economic reform, demonstrating a reduced importance of agriculture in income generation. This should not, however, be confused with the primacy of agriculture in rural employment generation. The dependence of the rural populace on agriculture for employment and sustenance, either directly or indirectly, has not lowered. The correlation coefficient between the growth rate of aggregate GDP and that of industry or services increased in the era of economic reform, underlining their importance in increasing the GDP growth rate.

The isolation of agricultural growth from that of industry and services in the era of economic reform is corroborated by the near-zero magnitude of the correlation coefficient between rate of growth of agriculture with that of industry and services. The association between the rate of growth of agriculture and industry, and between agriculture and services, which was evident (though in small measure) in the pre-reform years (1951–91) did not exist whatsoever in the era of economic reform. This happened despite the low oscillation in the yearly growth rate of agriculture in the reform era. The association between the rate of growth of industry and the services sector was evident in the pre-reform as well as in the reform era.

Structure of Growth

The growth and development policies during the pre-reform years, and especially in the first three decades of planning, were tailored to generate a structure of growth that was more in conformity with the increase in income of the poor and the lower deciles of the population, and production of goods (basically wage goods) predominantly consumed by them. It has often been termed as pro-poor growth. It was not exactly a case of growth–equity trade-off but bears resemblance to it, since in this pursuit the planners did not hesitate to sacrifice a slice of the growth rate to yield its sectoral composition in the desired manner and form. In this process, the planners emphasized on the structure of growth as much as the rate of growth, though on the whole, they reconciled to a position of somewhat lower growth rate in order to keep the structure of growth pro-poor.

The strategy of pro-poor growth failed to make a dent on poverty as the realized growth rate was modest. And keeping in view the population growth, the increase in income in per capita terms in the initial four decades of planning, 1951–90, could be treated as dismal when compared with the growth performance of the low-income developing countries of the world. Even this modest growth was not distributed fairly or equally between persons or regions (rural and urban areas, different states). The interpersonal distribution of income remained highly unequal and never showed any sign of abating. While pursuing a pro-poor growth strategy, the income of the poorer section of the population did not increase faster in relation to the non-poor. The level of poverty, denoted by the percentage of poor in the total population, remained high throughout the first four decades of planning, and as a result of the increase in population, the number of poor increased in some years.

The overall rate of economic growth began to increase from the Eighth Plan onwards with the initiation of economic reform. As the growth path shifted on to a higher trajectory, the structure of growth got altered by way of a dominant services sector eclipsing traditional agriculture. This occurred without actively pursuing a pro-poor growth strategy in the Plans. Whether the resulting structure of growth in the years of economic reform can be termed as pro-poor, or has been able to benefit the poor and the lower deciles of the population proportionately more than others, can be debated. However, the high growth rate in the later years (2003–11) of the two decades of economic reform bears the evidence of percolation of the fruits of growth to the lower deciles of the population. As some of the reform programmes were believed to be detrimental to the interests of the poor and the marginalized group of the population in the short run, several measures were incorporated in the Plan to insulate these groups from the consequences of these programmes through inclusive policies. The policy of inclusive growth in the Eleventh Plan assisted a wide range of the population, predominantly belonging to the poor and the marginalized sections by enabling them to access a set of essential goods and services. In sum, the pro-poor growth strategy in the initial four decades of planning did not raise the growth rate of the economy to the desired level and, in the process, failed to increase the income of the poor commensurately. The structure of growth did not change ostensibly as the growth rate itself was low. Under economic reform, the growth rate attained a higher trajectory and even in the absence of an active pro-poor growth strategy, the income of the poor increased. It will be demonstrated in Chapter 7 that as a result of the relatively higher growth rate in the years of economic reform, poverty reduction was substantial. The moral of the story is that with pro-poor growth strategy, the average growth rate turned out to be lower and the structure of growth did not alter. The structure of growth changed when the growth rate attained a higher trajectory. And this happened in the period of economic reform without actively pursuing a pro-poor growth strategy.

Fluctuation of Growth Rate

The frequency distribution of annual growth rates in agriculture, industry, the services sector, and for the economy as a whole, that is, the growth rate of aggregate GDP, have been given in Table 3.3. The growth rates relate to the years 1951–52 to 2011–12.

Important in the Indian context are the peaks and troughs of the annual growth rate of GDP (that is, the overall rate of economic growth) encountered during 1951–2011. The annual growth rate of aggregate GDP during this period is characterized by three

Table 3.3 Frequency Distribution of Annual Growth Rates: 1951–52 to 2011–12 (Number of Years)

Growth Rate (Per Cent, Yearly)	Agriculture	Industry	Services	Total
Negative	15	4	0	4
0 to <1	8	2	0	0
1 to <3	8	4	5	12
3 to <5	7	13	16	10
5	6	2	14	9
6 to <8	6	19	14	15
8 to <10	7	9	5	10
10 +	4	8	7	1

Source: Estimated from the annual growth rates of GDP given in Table 3A.

modal values. These are: (*a*) 1 to less than 3 per cent; (*b*) 4 to less than 6 per cent; and (*c*) 6 to less than 8 per cent. Of these 61 years, the annual growth rates of 12 of the years range from 1 per cent to less than 3 per cent, of 16 years range from 4 per cent to less than 6 per cent, and of 15 years range from 6 per cent to less than 8 per cent. Therefore, 43 of these 61 years, that is, 7 out of every 10 years, were covered by these three modal values of the growth rate.

During the six decades of 1951–2011, agricultural growth rate declined in 15 years, that is, once every 4 years on an average. In about half of these 61 years, agricultural growth was less than 3 per cent (and that includes the years when the growth rate in agriculture declined). There are, of course, years with very high growth rate in agriculture, for example, when the growth rate exceeded 12 per cent. However, the high growth rate in agriculture in these years should be treated as notional and not real, as these happened at the back of a very low base, usually caused by unfavourable weather, such as drought or flood (as, for example: agricultural growth rate exceeded 12 per cent in 1967–68, 1975–76, 1980–81, and 1988–89, and declined by 1.2 per cent in both 1966–67 and 1974–75, by 11.9 per cent in 1979–80, and by 1.1 per cent in 1987–88). The growth rate in agriculture has clear cycles, which is evidenced in the first four decades of planning (1951–90), when agriculture was not quite insulated from aberrations of weather.

The industrial growth rate during 1951–2011 appears to have followed a bi-modal distribution. The two modes of the industrial growth rate are in the range of (*a*) 3 to less than 5 per cent; and (*b*) 6 to less than 8 per cent. The yearly industrial growth rate in more than half of these years (in 32 of the 61 years) was covered by these two modal values. The fluctuation of the annual growth rate in industry was less than in agriculture.

Of the three major sectors (agriculture, industry, and services), the fluctuation of annual growth rate was least in the services sector. In case of the services sector, the annual growth rate in 32 years lay in the range of 4 to less than 7 per cent, and that of 44 years lay in the range of 3 to less than 8 per cent. It shows that the growth rate of the services sector in more than half of the years between 1951 and 2011 fell within a range of 3 percentage points, and that in about three-fourth of the years fell within 5 percentage points.

The fluctuation of annual growth rates was highest in case of agriculture and lowest in the services sector. This is again evident from the range of the growth rate (defined as the difference between the maximum and the minimum rate of growth) between 1951–52 and 2011–12. The range of the growth rate in agriculture (27.6, which is the difference between 15.7 and –11.9, the highest and the lowest growth rate) is found to have been about three times of that in services and more than one and a half times of the industrial growth rate. The cycles of growth are found to be transient in nature, and do not manifest in the long run or even in the medium term. This is evident from the range calculated from the three-year moving average of growth rates. Using the three-year moving average, the range of growth rate in all the three sectors, namely agriculture, industry, and services, and that of the aggregate GDP turns out to be much lower than in case of yearly growth rate. For example, using the three-year moving average of the growth rates, the range in agriculture lowers to less than one-third (from 27.6 to 8.2) from that witnessed in case of annual growth rate. Similarly, the range of industrial growth becomes nearly half (from 16.3 to 9.6) in case of three-year moving average of growth rate.

The fluctuation of yearly growth rate tends to be more when the growth rate is low and less when the growth rate is high. It underlines a negative association between the variability of growth rate and the average rate of growth. Such an association, as the results indicate, cuts across major sectors, such as agriculture, industry, and services, besides the growth rate of aggregate GDP. This is noticeable from the fluctuation of yearly growth rate in the initial (1951–80) and the latter three decades (1981–2011) in the planning era. The average growth rate of GDP in the initial three decades of planning was 3.5 per cent per year. The growth rate increased in the latter three decades, 1981–2011, to 6.3 per cent per year. The fluctuation of yearly GDP growth rate, measured by the coefficient of variation, was significantly lower in the latter three decades of planning, when growth rate attained a higher trajectory, as compared with the initial three decades of planning, when the growth rate was less.

The relationship between the average growth rate and the fluctuation of annual growth rate may be expressed more precisely from the yearly growth rate in the pre- and post-reform period. The average growth rate during the pre-reform (1951–52 to 1991–92) and post-reform (1992–93 to 2011–12) period was 4 per cent per year and 7 per cent per year respectively. The variation in the annual growth rate is found to be less in the era of economic reform (when the growth rate was high) and more in the pre-reform years (when the growth rate was low). The fluctuation in the growth rate of aggregate GDP in the era of economic reform, measured by coefficient of variation, was about one-third of that in the pre-reform era. The relation between the growth rate and its variation that is evident in case of aggregate GDP is equally prominent in case of agriculture, industry, and the services sectors.

The fluctuation in the annual growth rate of agriculture was more than that in industry and services. Again, the fluctuation in the growth rate of industry was more than that in services. The features of the annual growth rate in agriculture may be probed so as to discover the underlying reasons behind its fluctuation. The fluctuation of annual growth rate in agriculture was more on account of its inability to withstand the impact of drought and flood, which until the 1980s, occurred almost in regular cycles. Agricultural output suffered as a result and the loss of output is noticeable. During the 37 years from 1951–52 to 1987–88, 12 years were affected by drought (or flood), as a result of which agricultural output suffered. The GDP in agriculture declined in these 12 years. In other words, in the first 37 years of planning, agricultural growth on an average declined every third year. The ability of the agriculture sector to withstand the vagaries of weather was noticeable since the late 1980s, and specifically from the severe drought that occurred in 1987–88. The drought in 1987–88 affected agricultural output in vast areas, and yet agricultural production declined by only 1.1 per cent. This is considered an imminent sign of change in the agriculture sector that is capable of withstanding the impact of drought. During the 24 years from 1988–89 to 2011–12, the agricultural growth rate declined in only three years (1991–92, 1997–98, and 2002–03). It implies that during the 24-year period of 1988–2011, the decline in agricultural growth rate occurred once every eight years (as compared to once every three years during the 37 years 1951–87). This was a remarkable turnaround by way of compensating for the loss of output in areas exposed to drought from the output in irrigated areas. It has been made possible largely by the expansion of irrigation facilities and partly by the introduction of drought-resistant crops.

The fluctuation of annual growth rates is a feature of developing countries. The fluctuation can be seen more in the low-income developing countries, like India for most of 1951–2011. In India's case, the aggregate GDP growth rate from 1951 to 2011 varied from a low of –5.2 per cent (in 1979–80) to a high of 10.2 per cent (in 1988–89). The range, that is, the difference between the lowest and the highest growth rate, therefore, was quite wide. The reason behind such a wide range can be traced to drought and its consequent impact on agricultural production. The decline in the GDP growth rate in 1979–80 was principally on account of the decline in agricultural output by an exorbitant 11.9 per cent. Industrial output in this year also declined and much of it was due to the agriculture–industry linkage. The high GDP growth rate in 1988–89 was largely the outcome of the low base, as the GDP growth rate in the previous year (1987–88) was only 3.5 per cent. The low growth rate of the economy in 1987–88 was primarily due to the decline in the GDP growth rate in agriculture by 1.1 per cent, caused principally by drought. The high GDP growth rate in 1988–89 (10.2 per cent) was aided by an exorbitantly high rate of growth in agriculture (15.7 per cent), which in itself is the outcome of a low base.

A counterfactual analysis shows that with agricultural growth being on the medium-term trend, the growth rate of aggregate GDP in 1988–89 returned to the trend level. Therefore, the low and the high growth rates of GDP occurring in 1979–80 and 1988–89 respectively were the outcomes of drought. From this angle, it would not be inappropriate to assign the fluctuation in GDP growth in the first four decades of planning, 1951–90, to vagaries in weather. As the aberrations of weather usually last for one agricultural season at a time, the fluctuation in the growth rate was transient. This is evident from the three-year moving average of the growth rates.

Investment Rate in Plans

The investment rate, defined as the ratio of investment to GDP (expressed as percentage), propels the GDP growth rate. The investment rate, along with the share of public and private sectors in total investment in the First to Eleventh Five Year Plan has been given in Table 3.4. The investment rate was low in the early 1950s (in the First Plan), and thereafter it increased in a near-secular fashion until the Eleventh Plan. Broadly, the investment rate between 1951 and 2011 has been observed as follows: (a) 10 to 15 per cent until the Fourth Plan; (b) close to 20 per cent in the Sixth and Seventh Plans; (c) around 25 per cent in the Eighth and Ninth Plans; (d) over 30 per cent in the Tenth Plan; and finally (e) 35 per cent in the Eleventh Plan, which was the highest ever in any of the Five Year Plans. The investment rate in the Eleventh Plan was three and a half times of the First Plan and two and a half times of the Second Plan, which had laid the foundation of a large industrial base in the country. In the era of economic reform, the investment rate increased by one and a half times between the Ninth and the Eleventh Plans. The increase in the investment rate between the Ninth and the Tenth Plans, and between the Tenth and the Eleventh Plans exceeds 5 percentage points each, and these are the highest between any two Plan periods within the six decades of planning. This increase in investment can be viewed as the outcome of the policies of economic reform, and can be said to be responsible for elevating the growth path of the economy onto a higher trajectory.

Table 3.4 Investment Rate in Five Year Plans

Plan	Investment Rate (% of GDP)			Share of Investment (%)	
	Public	Private	Total	Public	Private
First Plan (1951–56)	3.7	6.4	10.1	36.6	63.4
Second Plan (1956–61)	6.3	7.5	13.8	45.7	54.3
Third Plan (1961–66)	7.9	7.8	15.7	50.3	49.7
Fourth Plan (1969–74)	6.9	9.0	15.9	43.4	56.6
Fifth Plan (1974–79)	8.8	9.9	18.7	47.1	52.9
Sixth Plan (1980–85)	10.9	9.8	20.7	52.7	47.3
Seventh Plan (1985–90)	11.3	12.1	23.4	48.3	51.7
Eighth Plan (1992–97)	8.9	14.5	23.4	38.0	62.0
Ninth Plan (1997–2002)	7.3	17.6	24.9	29.3	70.7
Tenth Plan (2002–07)	7.4	23.8	31.2	23.7	76.3
Eleventh Plan (2007–12)	8.7	27.9	36.6	23.8	76.2

Notes:

1. The investment rates are based on NAS derived from 2004–05 as the base year.

2. Total investment has been adjusted after incorporating errors and omissions. *Source*: Author's estimate based on data from 'Summary of Macro Economic Aggregates at Current Prices, 1950–51 to 2013–14', Statement 11, 27 March 2015. CSO, Ministry of Statistics and Programme Implementation, Government of India. Available at mospi.gov.in.

Investment takes place in the private and public sectors. Amidst secular rise in the aggregate investment rate, the investment behaviour of the public and private sectors varied over time, and their nature and content varied as well. Setting aside the First Plan, in which there was no big-ticket investment, the increase in investment rate from an extremely low to a fairly high level during the six decades of planning can be encapsulated in three main phases as follows: (*a*) quarter century from 1956 to 1979, covering the Second to the Fifth Plan; (*b*) the 1980s, covering the Sixth and the Seventh Plans; and (*c*) the two decades of economic reform, 1992–2011, which cover the Eighth to the Eleventh Plan. The investment rate of the public and the private sector did not move in a similar fashion in these three phases. The investment rate in the public sector showed peaks and troughs whereas that in the private sector increased in a more or less uniform manner. The investment rate in the public sector averaged 7.5 per cent of GDP for the Second to the Fifth Plan, 1956–79. It increased in the 1980s (to be 11 per cent of GDP), but lowered under economic reforms (averaging 8.1 per cent of GDP in 1992–2011). Despite the decline, the investment rate in the public sector during the period of economic reform remained higher than the average investment rate of the public sector during the quarter century period of 1956–79, covering the Second to the Fifth Plan. On the other hand, the investment rate of the private sector increased in the 1980s to 11 per cent of GDP from 8.6 per cent (of GDP) in the quarter century covering the Second to the Fifth Plan, 1956–79. From the Sixth Plan onwards, the increase in the investment rate of the private sector was secular. The investment rate of the private sector in the Eleventh Plan was nearly three times that in the Sixth Plan. The private sector investment on an average increased to 21 per cent (of GDP) in the era of economic reforms (1992–2011) from 11 per cent in the 1980s. The increase in private investment in the years of economic reform can be termed as phenomenal.

In India, there is difference in the efficiency of utilization of capital in the public and private sectors. As a result, the relative level of investment in these two sectors becomes crucial to generate the growth momentum in the economy. The rate of economic growth and the pattern of investment in the public and private sectors show that in the three and a half decades of planning beginning from the Second Plan (that is, for the period 1956–90), the share of these two sectors in total investment was almost similar and the growth rate was relatively low. The share of the private sector in total investment increased under economic reform, surpassing that in the public sector, and the growth rate of the economy picked up. The nexus between the increase in investment rate of the private sector and the growth rate of the economy may be worth noting.

The three and a half decades from 1956 to 1990, which cover the Second to the Seventh Plan, by all means mark the heyday of planning, which, in theory, epitomized state control on economic activities. While pursuing such a policy, the government made no secret of its intention to encourage and allow the public sector to attain the commanding heights of the economy. The thought and the associated actions around this philosophy were publicized in great detail.

However, the state efforts to increase the investment in the public sector do not seem to be consistent with this policy. To be specific, the investment rate of the public sector in the period 1956–90, on average, is found to be about 1 percentage point lower than that of the private sector. It points out that public sector investment was not forthcoming to the extent it was desired.

The evidence points out that the state, instead of generating investment in the public sector, used the instrument of planning to control and regulate the activities of the private sector. The state efforts to canalize private sector investment to the desired areas and sectors of the economy fall in this category. In other words, the state, instead of making a foray into capital accumulation by itself, decided to control and regulate the capital that was being accumulated (that is, the investment generated) by the private sector. In such a situation, the private sector preferred to keep itself insulated from any serious effort to raise the level of investment on its own and depended almost solely on the government for financing the investment that it wanted to make. This fine point of fund management by the private sector at the height of the planning era is often missed. Planning in the three and a half decades of 1956–90 did not connote increased investment by the state. Instead, it is more of controlling and regulating the investment that has taken place in the private sector so as to suit the objectives set out in the Plan. It is a different matter that the state opened up the coffers of the financial institutions within its ambit to finance the investment of the private sector in a fairly liberal manner. But that is a different matter and the feasibility of such an approach can best be assessed from Plan outcomes.

The share of the public sector in total investment was only 36.6 per cent in the First Plan. The reasons behind such low rate of public investment have been mentioned earlier. Surprisingly, from the list of investments made in the public sector during 1956–90 (that is, beginning from the Second Plan and until the commencement of economic reform) what is not so easily discernible is the fact that the share of the public sector in total investment crossed the half-way mark (that is, exceeded 50 per cent of total investment) in only two of the six Five Year Plans (the Second to the Seventh) implemented during this period. The two Five Year Plans in which the share of the public sector in total investment crossed the half-way mark were the Third Plan (50.3 per cent) and the Sixth Plan (52.7 per cent). In the remaining four Five Year Plans implemented in the pre-reform era, the share of the public sector in total investment ranged from a high of 48.3 per cent (in the Seventh Plan) to a low of 43.4 per cent (in the Fourth Plan). Even in the Second Plan, which was a Plan aimed for industrial development led by the state, the public sector accounted for 45.7 per cent of the total investment. The genesis is that during the three-and-a-half-decade period of 1956–90 (in which six Five Year Plans, the Second to the Seventh, were implemented)—and, for that matter, in the first four decades of planning, 1951–90—the public sector could not marshal a greater part of the investment even as the planning and state control on economic activities were rigid.

The share of the public sector in total investment began to decline with the onset of the policies of economic reforms in 1991; the decline was by about 25 percentage points within three Five Year Plans, from the Seventh to the Tenth Plan. This decline in the share of public sector investment was natural as the state withdrew from most of the activities related to production and trade. The share of public sector became 23.7 per cent of the total investment in the Tenth Plan, and it stabilized around this level in the Eleventh Plan. In order to meet the expenditure on public administration and social welfare, it is necessary for the government to maintain a minimum level of investment. From this perspective, public investment may have reached a threshold level in the Tenth Plan, which was at the minimum possible level and could not lower further.

The role of planning, and by implication the role of the public sector, was distinct in the pre- and post-reform days. The decline in the share of the public sector in total investment in the years of economic reform was a natural corollary of the reform process. However, the inability of the public sector to marshal more than half of the total investment for three and a half decades (1956–90, the Second to the Seventh Plan) in the pre-reform era underlines that the state control on investment was not all-pervasive, besides raising considerable doubt about the ability, and even more the intention, of the government to control the means of production and distribution through planning. In pursuance of the socialistic policies adopted in the Second Plan, the government continued with the control and regulatory measures from 1956 to 1990. State control was introduced as early as in the Second Plan and internalized in the planning process, which was adopted then. However, the endorsement of the socialist policies cannot be noticed anywhere in the investment pattern. In plain terms, there is hardly any evidence of the state following social- ist policies in letter and spirit, if the relative investment rates in the public and the private sectors are any guide. A salient feature of the socialist economy is that the state engages itself in the accumulation of capital. This never happened in India beyond a point. In reality, the goals of socialism and the manner and method of attaining the social- ist targets were never made explicit in any Five Year Plan in terms of investment allocation between the public and the private sectors. The share of investment in the public sector throughout the three and a half decades in the pre-reform era fails to testify that the government had ever been serious in pursuing socialist policies. The fact is that the government professed socialist policies but did not pursue them. The moral of the story is that planning and state control on economic activities did not prevent the private sector from commanding a pro- portionately larger share of investment in the economy. It functioned in selected areas and sectors of the economy but with wider state control on their activities.

The emphasis on industrialization through planning in India in the mid-1950s has often been equated with the planning methodology practised in the Soviet Union in the 1930s and 1940s. In actuality, the methodology followed in Indian planning turned out to be very different from that in the Soviet Union. In the mid-1950s, or even afterwards, India did not follow the Soviet model of planning even as it embraced state control in several areas of economic activity. It is true that the Soviet Union earnestly desired that India should follow the planning model used by them in form and content. This inter alia means exclusive reliance on public sector and withering away of the private sector (this issue has been discussed in some detail in Chapter 5). But India did not agree with the Soviet proposition and adopted the 'mixed economy' approach. The concept of mixed econ- omy, in which the public and the private sector operated side-by-side, marks a substantial difference between the framework of planning in India and the central planning as practised in the Soviet Union. Thus, it was naive to wish that the public sector in India could have taken charge of the entire economy, even in the heyday of planning.

It would also have been unwise to expect socialism in the manner and form practised in the Soviet Union to be incorporated in the strategy of economic growth and development that India pursued in the pre-reform days.

Efficiency of Investment

The growth rate of the economy is contingent upon the level of investment and efficiency in the utilization of investment in the production process. How efficient the production process has been in generating the desired growth rate in the Five Year Plans can be indicated by the ICOR, which is conventionally treated as a summary expression for the existing technical conditions and structural configuration of the economy, capturing the relationship between investment and additional productive capacity. The ICOR within a Plan period can be quantified as the ratio of investment rate and GDP growth rate in the Plan and can be used as a measure of efficiency of capital use. In theory, low ICOR is an expression of efficient production process whereas high ICOR typically illustrates inefficiency in the production process. However, high ICOR may not always connote inefficiency (as can be found in some of the Five Year Plans). A longer gestation lag that usually accompanies large industry and infrastructure projects may be responsible for high ICOR in a Five Year Plan, when the investment made in the Plan does not yield output within the same Plan. With a long gestation lag, the output may yield in the next Five Year Plan or maybe even in the Plan that comes after that. In that case, the ICOR becomes high in the earlier Plan (when the investment actually took place) and low in the latter (when the project actually started yielding output). In addition, the difference in the value of the ICOR between any two Plans can be the outcome of a widely differing production process. While some of these factors may come in the way of a straightforward comparison of the ICOR, inter alia the efficiency in converting investment into output between Plan periods, it can convey a great deal about the operational efficiency associated with the production process. The ICOR in the First Plan was unusually low (2.6) in comparison with the other Five Year Plans, the Second to the Eleventh, implemented until 2011. The ICOR in the Second to the Eleventh Plan ranged from a low of 3.2 to a high of 5.6.

The reason behind the low ICOR in the First Plan was the absence of large-scale investment in industry, and preponderance of the investment in agricultural and rural areas. The projects in these areas are mostly labour intensive, in which the ICOR is usually lower. The low ICOR in the Second Plan (3.2) may be surprising since it was a Plan for industrialization and investment in industries indeed took place, which had implications on the value of the ICOR. In such a situation, there are reasons to believe that expenditure was efficient in the Second Plan and money was spent judiciously. These were the initial years of the planning era, aiming to take the country to a higher level of growth, and it seems some latent energy was at work. Among the 11 Five Year Plans in the six-decade period of 1951–2011, the ICOR was the highest in the Third Plan (5.6). This is mostly on account of drought in agriculture, when investment takes place but no output is accrued, rendering the incurred expenditure unproductive.

The ICOR in the Fifth and the Sixth Plans was relatively lower (3.8). In the Sixth Plan the ICOR became low even as the share of investment in the public sector (which is usually considered less efficient than the private sector in the matter of efficiency in capital utilization) rose. It may signify efficient utilization of capital and that the inefficiency in the Indian economy was not exclusively due to the perceived mismanagement of the public sector. The value of ICOR in these two Plans (the Fifth and the Sixth) is close to that in the Five Year Plans falling within the era of economic reform, which was around 4.0.

Savings Rate in Plans

Investment drives the rate of economic growth. Investment, in turn, is determined by savings, which is the amount of money that is set aside from disposable income for future use. Savings in India originate mainly from two sources: domestic and foreign. Domestic savings have been the principal determinant of investment in India; foreign savings usually constitute a small portion. Domestic savings in the economy originate from the public and the private sectors. The savings in the public sector originate from government administration and commercial undertakings (departmental and non-departmental); the latter includes public sector enterprises. In the private sector, savings originate from households and the corporate sector. The savings

Table 3.5 Savings Rate in Five Year Plans (Per Cent of GDP)

Plan	Private Sector		Public Sector	Total
	Household	Private Corporate		
First Plan (1951–56)	6.8	1.0	2.0	9.9
Second Plan (1956–61)	7.4	1.1	2.5	11.0
Third Plan (1961–66)	7.3	1.6	3.8	12.7
Fourth Plan (1969–74)	10.2	1.4	3.3	14.9
Fifth Plan (1974–79)	12.4	1.4	5.0	18.7
Sixth Plan (1980–85)	11.8	1.5	4.3	17.6
Seventh Plan (1985–90)	14.7	1.9	3.0	19.6
Eighth Plan (1992–97)	16.6	3.8	2.1	22.6
Ninth Plan (1997–2002)	20.9	3.8	−0.4	24.3
Tenth Plan (2002–07)	23.2	6.3	2.0	31.4
Eleventh Plan (2007–12)	23.4	8.0	1.9	33.4

Note: The savings rates are based on the NAS derived from 2004–05 as the base year.

Source: Author's estimates based on data from 'Summary of Macro Economic Aggregates at Current Prices, 1950–51 to 2013–14', Statement 11, 27 March 2015. CSO, Ministry of Statistics and Programme Implementation, Government of India. Available at mospi.gov.in

rate is defined as the ratio of gross domestic savings (GDS) to GDP, expressed as a percentage. The savings rate separately in the public and private sectors in each of the 11 Five Year Plans during 1951–2011 has been given in Table 3.5.

The savings rate, as in case of the investment rate, increased in a near-secular fashion during 1951–2011, which covers the 11 Five Year Plans. Again, as in the case of investment rate, the savings rate in the era of economic reform was more than that in the pre-reform years. The average savings rate in the era of economic reform, 1992–2011 (the Eighth to the Eleventh Plan), was nearly twice that of the first four decades of planning, 1951–90 (the First to the Seventh Plan).

The savings rate in the initial four decades of planning covering the First to the Seventh Plan (1951–90) was low—less than 20 per cent of GDP. The savings rate increased thereafter during the economic reforms, from 19.6 per cent in the Seventh Plan (that is, immediately before the beginning of the economic reforms) to 33.4 per cent in the

Eleventh Plan (2007–12). On average, the decadal increase in savings rate works out to 2.4 percentage points in the four decades of the pre-reform period as against 6.9 percentage points in the two decades of economic reform.

The movement of savings rate in the six decades of planning can be compartmentalized into three main phases: (*a*) the First to the Fourth Plan, covering about a quarter century, 1951–73; (*b*) the Fifth to the Seventh Plan, covering one and a half decades, 1974–89; and (*c*) the Eighth to the Eleventh Plan, which was the era of economic reforms, 1992–2011. It is worth mentioning that the savings behaviour in the two decades of economic reform was not uniform. The pattern of savings in the second decade of economic reform (2002–2011), which covers the Tenth and the Eleventh Plans, was different from that in the first decade (1992–2002), covering the Eighth and the Ninth Plans.

The savings rate in the early 1950s was low as the level of income was low. Savings were dominated by the household sector, which accounted for about two-thirds of the savings. Very little savings came from the private corporate sector in the 1950s.

The savings rate in the 1960s and 1970s increased but there was no structural change in the savings mobilization associated with this higher savings rate. The increase in savings in the 1960s and 1970s, as in the 1950s, was driven by the household sector.

The average savings rate increased in the 1980s. The increase took place across the board, namely, in the household sector, the private corporate sector, and the public sector. The increase in the savings rate, particularly of the public sector, marks financial discipline, a feature of the economy in the 1980s, especially the first half, coinciding with the Sixth Plan.

The private sector was the principal source of domestic savings during the six decades of planning, and specifically in the two decades of economic reform, that is, from the Eighth Plan to the Eleventh Plan. On the other hand, the savings of the public sector were traditionally low, and varied over the Five Year Plans. Plan-wise, the public sector savings ranged from a low of –0.4 per cent of GDP (that is, dis-savings) in the Ninth Plan to a high of 5.0 per cent in the Sixth Plan. Until the beginning of the economic reforms (that is, in the four decades of planning in the pre-reform days), the contribution of the public sector in total savings was proportionately higher, about one-fifth of the total domestic savings on average; it lowered to one-twentieth in the era of economic reform. The share of the public sector in domestic savings was relatively higher when the average savings rate was low, and it lowered when the average savings rate increased. The reasons behind the low savings rate of the public sector are multifaceted and these have not been discussed in detail here. The general inefficiency and mismanagement of resources has often been cited as the principal reason behind the low rate of savings or even the dis-savings of the public sector. However, much of the purported inefficiency of the public sector was due to the pricing of its products at lower than marginal cost. The public sector very rarely maintained the principle of marginal cost pricing in the initial four decades of planning (that is, in the pre-reform days). The withdrawal of the state from actively participating in production and trade was the key reason behind the drop in the share of public sector savings in the reform era. The drop was in absolute as well as in relative terms. The average savings rate of the public sector declined from 3.4 per cent in the pre-reform era to 1.4 per cent in reform era. This space in the period of economic reform were taken over by the private sector, especially the private corporate sector.

The first four decades of planning were synonymous with low savings, low investment, and low growth rate of the economy. The public sector savings in this period, as already mentioned, were proportionately higher. In tandem, the share of the private sector in domestic savings was high in the era of economic reforms. The public sector savings under economic reform were lower. This was an era of high rate of savings, high rate of investment, and high growth rate. This nexus is worth noting.

Within the private sector, households were the major source of savings. Indeed, the savings of the private sector, for the most part, were determined by the savings of the households. The savings rate of the private sector, and within it, the savings of the household sector, increased in a near-secular fashion over the six decades of planning. This was not so in case of savings of the private corporate sector. This constituted a relatively small part of the savings of the private sector until the beginning of economic reforms; it averaged 1.4 per cent of GDP in 1951–91. The savings of the private corporate sector began to rise from the Eighth Plan onwards as the economic reform measures were set into motion. It averaged 5.5 per cent of GDP in the two decades of economic reform, 1992–2011. The average savings rate of the private corporate sector in 1992–2011 was thus four times what it was in the first four decades of planning, 1951–90. Thus, the average savings rate of the household sector was more or less uniform over the six decades of planning; its average in the era of economic reform was twice that of the first four decades of planning.

The savings rate of the economy, as mentioned earlier, was driven largely by the savings of the private sector, which, in turn, was dominated by the savings of households. This is evident in the years before as well as after the initiation of economic reforms. The household savings on average constitute two-thirds of the total domestic savings in the initial four decades of planning, the First to the Seventh Plan, and three-fourths of the domestic savings in the two decades of economic reform (the Eighth to the Eleventh Plan). The major change in the pattern of savings that took place between the periods before and after the economic reform (that is, during the periods 1951–90 and 1991–2011) was associated with the savings of the private corporate sector.

It has been mentioned earlier that the contribution of the public sector in generation of domestic savings was relatively high (averaging about one-fifth of the total savings) in the first four decades of planning, 1951–90, covering the First to the Seventh Plan. This is true for each of the two phases (the First to the Fourth Plan, and the Fifth to the Seventh Plan) in these four decades. The average savings rate in these two phases and, for that matter, in the four decades of planning in the pre-reform years was low. The average savings rate in the first phase (1951–73), the First to the Fourth Plan, was about two-fifths of that in the Tenth and the Eleventh Plan (2002–12). Similarly, the average savings rate in the first four decades of planning 1951–90 (the First to the Seventh Plan) was about half of the average savings rate in the two decades of economic reforms. Incidentally, the savings rate of the public sector is found to be relatively high when the average savings rate is low. It may not be pure conjecture that the focus on savings generation in the public sector has been counterproductive to the savings generation for the entire economy.

The nationalization of commercial banks in 1969 is usually seen in the light of state control of the economy. What is often missed is its impact on the domestic savings rate and, in turn, on the investment and growth rate of the economy. The nationalization led to a significant rise in the number of bank branches, from about 8,000 in 1969 to 32,000 in 1980; many of these new bank branches were located in remote and unbanked areas. On the eve of banks' nationalization, India's savings rate was 12 per cent (1968–69). After a decade, it rose to 19.9 per cent (1979–80). The investment rate rose from 13.1 per cent to 20.4 per cent during the same period. The investment rate remained around 20 per cent in the 1980s and the growth rate of the economy exceeded 5 per cent per year in this period. This increase in savings rate has been attributed by several economists, notably Kaushik Basu, former chief economic adviser of the Government of India, to the increase in the number of bank branches and their spread in the wake of bank nationalization. By implication, the Indian economy's growth breaking the Hindu rate barrier owes at least in part to the nationalization of banks.

This sort of kink in the savings rate witnessed in the late 1970s, which is believed to be rooted primarily in the nationalization of commercial banks, tapered off in the early 1980s and the savings rate did not rise further until the late 1980s. The next phase of rising savings rate was evident from the late 1980s—a process that accelerated with the economic reforms taking shape. The domestic savings rate accelerated in the two decades of economic reform, and the acceleration was driven by the savings of the private sector. Within the private sector, the increase in savings was contributed by the household and the private corporate sector. The period of economic reform witnessed high average investment rate, and, in turn, high growth rate in the economy. The investment was induced by domestic savings, and hence the resulting increase in growth rate was the outcome of increased savings, clearly bringing out the simultaneity between income and savings.

The case of simultaneity between income and savings can be deliberated a little further. In the early years of planning, the level of income was low. As a result, the savings rate was low. Investment originates from savings. Simultaneously, investment yields income. Increase in the level of investment yields more income, which, in turn, generates higher savings. There is thus a simultaneity in (increase in) income and (generation of) savings. Until the beginning of economic reforms (that is, in the first four decades of planning), the share of the public sector in aggregate savings generation was proportionately higher. These were years of low investment and low growth rate. Under economic reform, the growth rate picked up and so did the savings of the private sector. The increase in growth rate generated income among households, which increased their savings propensity. The economic reforms eventually led to the corporatization of domestic savings. The profitability of the private corporate sector that came with the increase in the rate of economic growth eventually added to their savings. As the policies of economic reform took shape and spread across areas and sectors of the economy, the savings of the private corporate sector increased more relative to the household sector. This altered the composition of private sector savings in favour of the private corporate sector in the era of economic reform, and especially after the Ninth Plan. The share of the private corporate sector in the savings of the private sector rose faster in the Tenth and the Eleventh Plans. Its share crossed 20 per cent in the Tenth Plan and 25 per cent in the Eleventh Plan. It may be noted that this (share of the private corporate sector in the aggregate savings of the private sector) was about 10 per cent in the first four decades of planning (1951–90), and nearly doubled between the four decades of pre-reform period (1951–91) and the two decades of economic reform (1992–2011).

Annexure

Table 3A Annual Growth Rate of GDP by Sectors: 1951–52 to 2011–12 (Per Cent)

Year	Agriculture	Industry	Services	Total (GDP)
1951–52	1.9	4.6	2.7	2.3
1952–53	3.1	−0.4	3.1	2.8
1953–54	7.5	6.2	2.9	6.1
1954–55	3.0	8.8	4.7	4.2
1955–56	−0.8	11.7	5.0	2.6
1956–57	5.4	9.0	4.6	5.7
1957–58	−4.1	−1.8	3.8	−1.2
1958–59	9.8	7.4	4.1	7.6
1959–60	−0.8	7.0	5.0	2.2
1960–61	7.1	10.8	5.7	7.1

1961–62	0.3	6.9	5.4	3.1
1962–63	−1.4	6.2	5.6	2.1
1963–64	2.4	10.7	5.9	5.1
1964–65	8.8	7.4	5.8	7.6
1965–66	−9.9	3.2	2.8	−3.7
1966–67	−1.2	3.7	3.1	1.0
1967–68	14.1	3.3	3.8	8.1
1968–69	0.0	5.1	4.6	2.6
1969–70	6.3	7.8	5.2	6.5
1970–71	6.3	1.6	4.9	5.0
1971–72	−1.7	2.5	3.7	1.0
1972–73	−4.4	3.4	2.9	−0.3
1973–74	6.9	0.5	3.3	4.6
1974–75	−1.2	1.0	4.1	1.2
1975–76	12.8	6.5	6.6	9.0
1976–77	−5.2	9.3	4.6	1.2
1977–78	9.6	7.4	4.9	7.5
1978–79	2.3	7.3	6.7	5.5
1979–80	−11.9	−3.6	2.2	−5.2
1980–81	12.8	4.5	4.6	7.2
1981–82	5.2	7.4	5.2	5.6
1982–83	0.6	0.2	7.1	2.9
1983–84	9.5	8.5	5.7	7.9
1984–85	1.6	4.4	6.1	4.0
1985–86	0.7	4.3	7.7	4.2
1986–87	0.6	4.9	7.6	4.3
1987–88	−1.1	5.8	6.4	3.5
1988–89	15.7	8.2	6.9	10.2
1989–90	1.8	8.4	8.9	6.1
1990–91	4.7	6.9	5.2	5.3
1991–92	−1.4	−0.1	4.7	1.4
1992–93	6.0	3.6	5.7	5.4
1993–94	3.1	6.1	7.4	5.7
1994–95	5.2	9.1	5.8	6.4
1995–96	0.0	12.0	10.1	7.3
1996–97	8.9	7.2	7.5	8.0
1997–98	−1.3	3.3	8.9	4.3
1998–99	5.9	4.3	8.3	6.7
1999–00	2.8	6.2	12.1	8.0
2000–01	0.3	6.5	5.1	4.1

(Cont'd)

Table 3A *(Cont'd)*

Year	Agriculture	Industry	Services	Total (GDP)
2001–02	5.5	2.7	6.6	5.4
2002–03	−4.9	7.1	6.7	3.9
2003–04	8.2	7.9	7.9	8.0
2004–05	1.1	10.0	8.3	7.1
2005–06	4.6	10.7	10.9	9.5
2006–07	4.6	12.7	10.1	9.6
2007–08	5.5	10.3	10.3	9.3
2008–09	0.4	4.7	10.0	6.8
2009–10	1.5	9.5	10.5	8.6
2010–11	8.3	7.6	9.7	8.9
2011–12	4.4	8.5	6.6	6.7

Note: The growth rates are estimated from GDP at factor cost evaluated at 2004–05 prices by the CSO, Ministry of Statistics and Programme Implementation, Government of India.

Source: Author's estimate based on data from 'Summary of Macro Economic Aggregates at Constant (2004–05) Prices, 1950–51 to 2013–14', Statement 12, 27 March 2015. CSO, Ministry of Statistics and Programme Implementation, Government of India. Available at mospi.gov.in.

4

Growth and Development in Pre-reform Period

Planning in India commenced in 1951 when it was essentially a rural economy—an economy with hardly any industrialization and low level of income. After four decades of planned economic development based on state control and regulation of economic activities, economic reform and liberalization programmes were initiated in 1991. From the point of view of assessment of the rate of economic growth, the six decades of planning, 1951–2011, can be compartmentalized into (a) the four decades in the pre-reform era, 1951–90, when the rate of economic growth was definitely low (4 per cent per year); and (b) the two decades of economic reforms, 1991–2011, when the Indian economy positioned itself on a decidedly higher growth path (7 per cent per year). The growth rate within the four decades of the pre-reform era was not uniform. The manner and method of planning, and the administration of state control and regulation on economic activities associated with it were not similar throughout these four decades and neither were their outcomes. The economic growth rate in these four decades of planning was found to traverse three broad phases: (a) the 1950s, when the growth rate was recorded as 3.9 per cent per year, which cannot be termed as too low in the context of the situations prevailing then; (b) the 1960s and 1970s, when the growth rate can decisively be termed as low

(3.3 per cent per year); and (c) the 1980s, when the growth rate breached the 5 per cent mark for the first time since the inception of planning in 1951.

The four-decade period, 1951–90—and especially the first three decades, 1951–80—depicts a syndrome of low income, low savings, low investment, low growth. Within this, the average growth rate in the 1950s was more than in the 1960s and 1970s. Briefly, the low investment rate during the first three decades of planning resulted in the low rate of economic growth. The low investment is caused principally by low savings rate, which, in turn, is the outcome of low level of disposable income of the people. Several domestic as well as international experts consider the realized growth rate in the first four decades of planning (that is, in the pre-reform period) as far below the potential, and believe that India's growth rate could have been more. In view of this, it becomes necessary to take a look at the growth scenario in this period, 1951–90. The growth rate of aggregate GDP and by major sectors for these periods has been given in Table 4.1.

First Four Decades of Planning, 1951–90: A Synoptic View

The First to Seventh Five Year Plans were implemented in the first four decades of planning, 1951–90. Within 16 months of the constitution of the Planning Commission, the draft outline of the First Plan (1951–56) was finalized in July 1951. The Plan laid down the order of priorities as: (a) completion of projects and programmes which were

Table 4.1   Growth Rate of GDP: 1951–90 (Per Cent per Year)

Period	Agriculture	Industry	Services	Total
1950s (1951–52 to 1960–61)	3.2	6.3	4.2	3.9
1960s to 1970s (1961–62 to 1979–80)	1.7	4.7	4.5	3.3
1980s (1980–81 to 1989–90)	4.7	5.7	6.6	5.6
1950s to 1970s (1951–52 to 1979–80)	2.2	5.3	4.4	3.5
1950s to 1980s (1951–52 to 1989–90)	2.9	5.4	5.0	4.0

Note: The growth rates have been expressed in terms of GDP at factor cost and derived using 2004–05 as the base year.
Source: Author's estimates based on data in Table 3A.

initiated earlier at some stage; (*b*) implementation of projects and pro-grammes related to rehabilitation of displaced persons caused by the partition of the Indian subcontinent in 1947; (*c*) raising agricultural production through expansion of irrigation; (*d*) expansion of employ-ment opportunities; and (*e*) instituting a bunch of welfare services. The First Plan had set the target growth rate as 2.1 per cent per year (of national income). The realized growth rate was 3.6 per cent per year in terms of GDP.

Based on the array of proposals, the First Plan was divided into two components. The first component included projects and programmes initiated after Independence mostly by way of emergency measures. These included a number of developmental projects. The second component consisted of projects that were to be undertaken only after availability of external assistance. The Plan allocated 80 to 85 per cent of the total expenditure for the projects and programmes contained in the first component, that is, projects and programmes that were initiated after Independence and already in execution. The remaining 15 to 20 per cent of the total expenditure was devoted to the projects that figured in the second component of the Plan. It shows that the First Plan concentrated both on the present-day needs and on laying down the foundations for future—a task which began in earnest in the Second Plan. It would be interesting to mention that the First Plan turned out to be a voluminous document, so much so that I. G. Patel, a renowned economist and former governor of the RBI, wrote, albeit in a lighter vein, that 'there is nothing in the Indian economy which does not find a reflection in the Plan, and there is nothing in the Plan which is also not found in Indian reality'.[1] Patel himself offered plausible reasons for the document being bulky as he stated: 'It is natural that the first exercise in planned development should be a sort of reconnaissance trip—surveying and mapping out the entire terrain so as to understand it better.'

The task of building the foundation of an industrially developed nation was initiated in earnest in the Second Plan (1956–61). It was a Plan for industrialization that was formulated with great zeal and its implementation began with much fanfare. The focus of the Second Plan was on increasing output and wealth in the economy. The mathematical model behind the Plan was developed by Professor P. C. Mahalanobis at the ISI, Kolkata. The Plan was prepared by Indian experts, and in that way it can be termed as an entirely domestic endeavour. The implementation of the Second Plan, however, faced considerable roadblocks, mainly due to resource (especially foreign exchange) constraint. There was a balance of payments crisis when the Second Plan was midway. India desperately needed foreign assistance at this juncture to finance the ambitious capital goods–based industrial development programmes contained in the Plan. However, this was not forthcoming. In the 1950s, foreign assistance was rare as the developed countries in the West, known to be the main sources of assistance, were still in the grip of the financial strain created by the Second World War.

At the end of the Second Plan, it was time to take stock. Independence had generated huge expectations among the people, and particularly among the ordinary citizens and common men and women, who had been Mahatma Gandhi's foot soldiers in the freedom struggle. Within a decade, the latent energy was giving way. Problems of food supply, price inflation, and corruption turned out to be the major issues confronting the nation. Throughout the 1950s, the supply of foodgrains fell short of (market) demand, though, on the whole, agricultural growth rate in the Second Plan was higher than that in the First Plan, and also higher (though marginally) than population growth. The demand for food increased faster than the increase in production as a result of income growth, especially of the people in the lower deciles. This supply–demand gap in foodgrains put considerable pressure on prices. Price inflation was high and it was mostly triggered by food prices. As the government started spending huge sums of money for developmental projects, instances of corruption in both the public and the private sectors surfaced, and some of them even rocked the Parliament. It was a time when three issues, namely, food problem, price inflation, and corruption, usually figured in the customary addresses of the president of India made in the Joint Session of the Parliament, or on the eve of Republic Day and Independence Day.

The economic growth in the 1950s (the First and Second Plans) averaged 3.9 per cent per year. The increase in per capita income in this decade cannot be termed as meagre by the standards prevailing then, and particularly in view of the stagnancy in per capita income during the previous half a century or even a century. Despite the problems faced in the Second Plan, the fruits of economic growth and planned development were visible with people being better fed and better clothed. Many of them could build houses with bricks, which in those days was considered a sign of social mobility, moving from one class to another. It may sound strange today that around 1960, building the four walls of a room with bricks was recognized as a step forward in the pursuit of an improved living standard. The income of a section of the population increased, but at the same time many faced difficulties in making a living, and many more were just surviving. It was axiomatic that as a result of economic growth in the first 10 years of planning (1951–60), the income of every person did not increase by the same proportion. Some people benefited from the growth process more than others. Keeping this issue of income distribution at the centre, pertinent questions were raised about how the increase in national income, which was estimated to be 20 per cent in per capita terms during the first two Five Year Plans (1951–61), spread across different classes and groups of the population. In an attempt to get to the bottom of the situation, the Planning Commission constituted the Committee on Distribution of Income and Levels of Living under the chairmanship of Professor P. C. Mahalanobis in 1960.

The economic scenario at the end of the Second Plan was conducive to pitching for high growth in the immediate future despite food deficiency and price inflation adversely affecting the growth prospects of the economy and, to some extent, corruption making inroads into the different layers of the economic and political set-up. The big bang for economic upliftment was timed with the Third Plan (1961–66). The target growth rate in the Third Plan was fixed at a fairly high level of 5.6 per cent per year. It was an ambitious Plan, without doubt, much like the Second Plan, but it widely differed in its scope and content. The Third Plan incorporated solid measures to improve the standard of living and quality of life of the people in rural and urban areas, and dwelt on issues such as urbanization, demography, and regional equality in the sphere of growth. The sectoral growth targets of the Third Plan were built on the performance of the first two Five Year Plans. The size of the Plan was, however, debated in the context of resource availability.

It may be useful to mention here that unlike the Second Plan (which was formulated using the mathematical model developed by P. C. Mahalanobis, and was widely known as the Mahalanobis model), there was no specific mathematical model at the back of the determination of sectoral priorities in the Third Plan. Some of the parameters used to arrive at the macroeconomic projections in the Third Plan, according to several economists, prominent among them being Professor Sukhamoy Chakravarty, were treated as policy. Such a view was also echoed by Pitambar Pant, who was involved with the preparation of the Third Plan in the Planning Commission. From this angle, the Third Plan presents a marked departure from the Second Plan.

If the Second Plan was a move towards industrializing a poor, low-income developing country, then the Third Plan can be treated as a 'take-off' for a higher growth for future. This Plan can be viewed as an attempt to lay the foundation of a self-sustained economy so that the goal of a socialistic pattern of society and the welfare state (espoused in 1955 and adopted in the Second Plan) could take shape. The planners categorically mentioned that it was absolutely impossible to attain the goal of a welfare state and a socialistic economy in the absence of considerable increase in national income. Thus, the focus was on devising policies to maximize income at the first possible instance. Along with maximization of income, the emphasis was also on its equitable distribution. However, it is essential to note that the emphasis at the initial stage was on income generation, and the aspect of equity (in class distribution of income) only came later.

The Third Plan aimed at maximization of income even in the face of several odds, prominent among them being the foreign exchange crunch. Foreign assistance was needed and sought from the developed countries to meet several objectives of the Plan, important among them being the growth of large and capital goods industries. There was uncertainty of foreign exchange, but this never came in the way of preparing a bold and ambitious Plan. After all, no one wants to plan for a bleak future.

The targets fixed in the Third Plan went haywire as a result of major changes in the inter-sectoral allocation of resources warranted by the border conflict with China that occurred in October 1962. The change in sectoral allocation of resources (from what was envisaged while fixing the target growth rate of the Plan) had implications for growth rate. But the target growth rate of the Plan was never revised to factor in the changes in sectoral allocation of resources, though it is usual practice to make such revisions in the course of the mid-term appraisal of the Plan. The mid-term appraisal was not conducted during the Third Plan. Though the conflict with China was brief, its implications on the Indian economy and polity were widespread. In fact, the border conflict with China eventuated in a major overhauling of the sectoral allocation of resources from what was stipulated in the Third Plan, and more a significant change in the planning and development strategy, a la the future policies towards economic growth and development.

The strain on the Indian economy created by the border conflict with China was exacerbated by three successive years of drought (1964–66) in rural areas and a full-scale war with Pakistan in September 1965. The financial situation became precarious as a result of the two wars within the period of the Third Plan, and the war-induced sanctions imposed by the USA and several European countries. In view of this, it would not be appropriate to compare the realized growth rate in the Third Plan (2.8 per cent per year) with the target (5.6 per cent per year).

The 1960s were not a good a time for the Indian economy and yet the rate of economic growth was not that low. The overall rate of economic growth in the 1960s averaged 4 per cent per year, which is reasonably good. It occurred despite the GDP in agriculture declining or remaining stagnant in five of these ten years (as a result of drought). The loss of agricultural output led to recession in industries. Industrial output stagnated. Industry in the 1960s was dominated by farm-based industries such as cotton textiles, jute textiles, sugar, and edible oils, to name a few. The output of cotton, jute, sugarcane, and oilseeds stagnated or even declined as a result of drought. As the drought in agriculture prolonged, food production failed in successive years and, as a consequence, transport demand fell. The railways, the principal transporter of food, cancelled orders for railway wagons, triggering a recession in the engineering industry. Thus, industrial growth suffered as the decline in agricultural output prolonged.

Food shortage touched a new high due to shortfall in agricultural output eventuated by drought. The average per capita net availability of cereals in 1966 and 1967 (years affected by drought) was 14 per cent less than that in 1964 and 1965 (years with normal agricultural production) when the availability itself was not adequate to meet the market demand, which again was low due to lack of income and purchasing power. A large section of the population had to confront food shortage of such a great order that it was equated with a famine-like situation. There were large-scale food riots, leading to serious law and order problems in several states in 1966. However, the food crisis was successfully weathered by the late 1960s, so much so that India's status changed from a food-deficit to a food-surplus country, and food imports to meet consumption demand became a thing of the past. The manner in which this could be accomplished has been briefly spelt out in the section 'Weathering the Food Crisis in the Mid-1960s' later in this chapter.

In the 1960s, the Indian currency lost much of its value in the international market as a result of distortion in macroeconomic balance caused mainly by large trade deficit in the wake of the war against Pakistan in September 1965. The Indian rupee, which was then under the regime of a fixed exchange rate, had to be devalued in June 1966 by as much as 36 per cent against the major international currencies, such as the British pound and the US dollar. Although aimed at restoring the health of the economy, the devaluation was criticized by all the political parties, major or minor, in the opposition. These were difficult times for the Indian economy. The Five Year Plans were kept in abeyance for three years (1966–69) due to the position of resources, both domestic and foreign, being uncertain. Planning resumed in April 1969 with the Fourth Five Year Plan. The process now carried a somewhat altered set of priorities, emanating from a change in the strategy.

The Fourth Plan (1969–74) witnessed state management and control in wider areas of the economy through a series of measures which included nationalization of major commercial banks, insurance companies, coal mines, and a range of industries in the mining and manufacturing sectors, which were in private hands. The private commercial banks, which were nationalized in July 1969 (barely three months into the Fourth Plan) accounted for 85 to 90 per cent of the total bank deposits in the country and largely catered to the needs of their owners, who were among the leading industrialists of the time. This nationalization was driven by the desire to extend liberal financing to priority sectors, such as agriculture, and especially the small and marginal farmers engaged in agriculture. The mining and

manufacturing industries (coal, steel, copper, oil-refining, cotton textiles) were nationalized in the early 1970s to protect the employment
of organized labour. It may be mentioned here that nationalization
was not an agenda when planning was initiated in the 1950s as it
was limited to one commercial bank (the Imperial Bank of India), the
life insurance companies, and the private airlines. The nationalization of the Imperial Bank of India and the life insurance companies
was motivated by the urgency to marshal some amount of resources
essential to finance the expenditure on developmental activities. The
nationalization of the private airlines was prompted more by treacly
sentiments and less by economics.

Within the period of the Fourth Plan, along with nationalization,
efforts to bring the remaining private sector industries under stringent regulation and control of the state were in full swing. These measures can be viewed as a perpetuation of socialist policies conceived
of in the mid-1950s. Through the enactment of the Monopolies and
Restrictive Trade Practices (MRTP) Act, 1970, multifarious restrictions were imposed on the expansion of private enterprises in order
to curb concentration of economic power. It may be appropriate to
mention that the seeds of the MRTP Act were laid towards the end of
the Second Plan. Its enactment in the year 1970 can be viewed as a
follow-up measure of state control on economic activities associated
with the Second Plan and the socialist policies of the mid-1950s. On
the whole, state control in economic activities was strengthened in
the 1960s and 1970s, and planning became more watertight as the
public sector was encouraged to capture the commanding heights of
the economy. The origin of the measures related to strengthening of
state control that were witnessed throughout the 1960s and 1970s has
been chronicled in the section 'Strengthening State Control in the
Economy' in this chapter. It is interesting to see how these measures
were integrated with the overall growth and development strategy.

The allocation of central assistance to the states was based on a
schematic pattern until 1969. Such a method of resource allocation
was considered to be one of the prime reasons behind the unequal
spread of growth across the states. From the Fourth Plan, the central Plan assistance began to be allocated to the states based on the
Gadgil formula. The formula, carved out based on population, per
capita income, and tax effort of the states, ensured an objective basis

for allocation of central assistance for state plans. In order to reduce the inequality in the level of per capita income across states, the Gadgil formula entailed liberal financial assistance to economically backward states, some of which later came to be known as 'special category states'.

The actual growth rate in the Fourth Plan was about two-thirds of the target. Despite the shortfall in growth target, the Fourth Plan witnessed two major events. First, India became a food-surplus country, which is the dream of any developing country. India had been perennially short of foodgrains as domestic output was inadequate to meet the market demand, which itself was low due to lack of income and purchasing power of a large section of the population. The Green Revolution in agriculture in the late 1960s could solve the food problem in the sense that domestic production came to be in excess of market demand. Second, India earned a major military victory against Pakistan in 1971, heralding the birth of the new country Bangladesh in the Indian subcontinent. There was a third event which, though it did not occur right within the Fourth Plan period, had all its preparation and grounding there. This was the detonation of India's first nuclear device in May 1974, that is, two months after the termination of the Fourth Plan. These are important events that could not have taken place unless some solid strides were made in the development of a sound economy.

The late 1960s and the early 1970s witnessed major discontent about India's dependence on imports, especially food, fuel, fertilizer, or foreign exchange. In order to free the country from such dependencies, the desire for attainment of self-reliance almost reached a level of passion. Self-reliance was given definition and quantitative expression in the Fifth Plan (1974–79) and it was set as a strategic goal in the development perspective. Self-reliance was defined in terms of elimination of special forms of external assistance and it sought to reach a situation (by the end of the Fifth Plan) in which the foreign exchange receipts from exports, invisibles, and private capital transactions became adequate to meet import requirements and interest obligations on foreign debt. This, in effect, meant taking the economy to a level where it could meet the import requirements through exports, without undue dependence on foreign aid. It may be appropriate to mention that this is precisely the vision of self-reliance prophesied in the Third Plan when the country aimed at the big bang for growth. In pursuance of these policies, the consistency model developed by the Planning Commission to chart out the growth path of the Indian economy in the Fifth Plan provided for stringent control on input use. Imports were controlled by the state and tied to production. Industries were not permitted to produce more than the quantity for which they had been sanctioned licences. This model was developed by Professor Sukhamoy Chakravarty in the Planning Commission. The manner of setting the growth target in this model was different from the Mahalanobis model, which was used to formulate the Second Plan. However, in terms of state control on factors of production and distribution, the model developed by Professor Chakravarty aligned with the Mahalanobis model.

The 1970s were extraordinarily tough for the Indian economy. In 1971, India had to provide shelter to 20 million refugees from what was then known as East Pakistan, present-day Bangladesh, and faced a large-scale war with Pakistan that strained the economy. The economic growth in two successive years (1971–72 and 1972–73) took a beating due to both domestic and international events. Agricultural production in these two years declined due to drought. It impacted the food situation enormously. The rise in international price of crude oil in 1973 put tremendous pressure on domestic prices, and distorted the balance of payments. The annual price inflation (measured by the WPI) exceeded 20 per cent in two successive years, 1973–74 and 1974–75. The Indian economy has not witnessed such a high rate of inflation either before or after this. Then, there was the railway strike in May 1974, which lasted close to a month, disrupting the main channel of transport of goods. All these impacted the overall growth performance of the economy. The economic situation deteriorated in 1974–75 as the growth rate was only 1.2 per cent. There was discontent among the people on economic issues. From these economic problems, the country was thrown in the whirlpool of turbulence as a result of nationwide political agitation from mid-1974 to mid-1975. Originally started by a group of students in Gujarat in 1974 and centred basically on local issues, the agitation soon spread to Bihar, and finally reached the national capital, Delhi. It nearly paralysed the administrative authority of the government and eventually led to the imposition of internal Emergency in June 1975.

The Emergency lasted for 19 months, until January 1977. Within this period, the economy turned around as macroeconomic balance was restored and prices became stable. The growth rate picked up and became healthy. But, on the whole, the growth scenario in the 1970s was dismal. The growth rate in the 1970s (1970–71 to 1979–80) was only 3 per cent per year. This is lower than the growth rate recorded in the 1960s (1960–61 to 1969–70) which was 4 per cent per year. Both agricultural and industrial growth rate in the 1970s was about half of that in the 1960s.

The ICOR, a measure of the efficiency in capital use, turned out to be relatively higher in the 1960s and 1970s as compared to that in the 1950s, despite the 1950s witnessing large investment in the capital goods sector, where the gestation lag was high. However, while attributing the higher ICOR in the 1960s and 1970s to the deteriorating efficiency in the use of capital, it is essential to keep in mind the behaviour of the agriculture sector in this period. The high ICOR in the 1960s and 1970s, to a great extent, is on account of the loss of agricultural output in years of drought in addition to what might be the outcome of inefficient utilization of resources. Three years in the 1960s and five years in the 1970s, which means a total of eight years within these two decades, were affected by drought in agriculture. The drought created pressure on the economy via lowering in the agricultural output. It is well known that in a typical drought year, agricultural operations, such as sowing, and so on, take place, but the crop is lost in the end. In this process investment is made, some employment is generated, but there is absolutely no return on investment. Such a situation inflates the ICOR, and this is ostensibly one of the factors responsible for the high value of ICOR in the 1960s and 1970s. The increase in the ICOR was, therefore, not rooted so much in inefficient utilization of capital. This is notwithstanding the fact that the low ICOR in the 1950s, to a great extent, mirrored efficiency in the utilization of capital, especially in the industrial sector, as the higher growth rate (in the 1950s) owes to industry.

Briefly, in the first three decades of planning, 1951–80, state control on economic activities was treated as the most efficient way to maximize the rate of economic growth. It was believed that with growth maximization, the fruits of growth (income) would be distributed equally among the cross sections of the population and among the regions, and the living standard of the people would improve. But the consequences of these policies were not encouraging. The average growth rate in the 1960s and 1970s was less than that in the 1950s. Besides, the growth rate was not equitable between the states or between different regions within a state. As a result of the low growth rate and its unequal spread, historical inequalities could not be corrected. Regional inequality became more pronounced. Despite all these, the Indian economy witnessed several landmark events in the area of growth and development in the 1960s and 1970s. These include food self-sufficiency and development of a strong industrial base capable of propelling future growth.

The policy of state control on economic activities and bestowing a prominent place to the public sector pursued throughout the three decades 1951–80 was tweaked for the first time in the 1980s when a series of measures were taken to open up the Indian economy to the frontiers of market, and at the same time to concede greater space to the private sector for growth maximization. These include relaxation of several provisions of the MRTP Act in order to facilitate expansion of the private sector in wider sectors and areas of the economy. As a corollary, several changes were made in the industrial licensing policy. In 1984, a committee on trade policy chaired by Abid Hussain recommended shifting from import licensing to tariff-based protection. Then, in January 1985 a committee under the chairmanship of M. Narasimham recommended shifting from physical to financial control (for example, using financial instruments such as fiscal and credit measures, which are considered market-friendly and have the potential to stimulate growth), as a result of which import of capital goods was liberalized. These were indications of opening up of the economy to competition, at least in the domestic market. Then, corporate tax rate was lowered in order to incentivize the private sector; personal income tax was also lowered. These measures support the contention that the private sector and private initiative should be given a place of prominence in growth and development. The idea of placing the public sector at the commanding heights of the economy was not disbanded altogether, but at the same time, was not aggressively pursued.

Around this time, India started sending invitations to its citizens residing in the developed capitalist block (mostly in the USA and countries of Western Europe) to assist it to adopt modern and up-to-date technology. (It is worthwhile to mention that the association of Sam Pitroda with the information technology revolution in India in the 1980s–1990s was a culmination of this effort.) This invitation was marked by several administrative changes which helped the private sector to exploit economic opportunities and discharge its entrepreneurial role more smoothly and efficiently than ever before. Several public sector undertakings joined this drive to access modern technology.

That the policies related to growth and development in India were going to change became evident in several pronouncements the government made in the early 1980s. In February 1981, the prime minister, while seeking approval for the Sixth Plan by the NDC, stated that in socialist countries there was visible emphasis on giving up controls and rigid regulations in favour of incentives. In the same NDC meeting, the prime minister stated: 'Our socialism was a logical development of the concept of democracy, suiting the requirements of our system. It was built on the mobilisation of private initiative for the greatest good of our society. It was based on a mixed economy where the public sector played a dominant role. In our democracy, private sector was also allowed to grow fully to modernise our economy.'[2] These are clear enough indications of aligning with the market-led development and increased share of investment in the private sector—a trend which has strengthened since then. These indications may have driven the Government of West Bengal, led by the Communist Party of India (Marxist), to disagree with the Sixth Plan, which contained some of these market-friendly measures. How their consent was obtained makes for an interesting tale. This is chronicled in the section 'Arriving at Consensus in the Sixth Plan' in this chapter.

The growth strategy in the 1980s, no doubt, reflected some renewed attempts to incentivize the private sector so as to extend its area of operation in economic activities and make it an equal partner in the process of income generation. However, the emphasis on income generation through the private sector in India can in no way be aligned with the policies pursued in the 1980s by the political leaders in developed capitalist counties in the West, notable among them British Prime Minister Margaret Thatcher and US President Ronald Reagan. Thatcher's and Reagan's emphasis on income and wealth generation using the capitalist mode of production is legendary. The concern for the poor and marginalized sections of the population (who are not able to benefit adequately from the growth process) guided India to not rely exclusively on the private sector. Exclusive reliance on the private sector for income generation implies that the increase in income of the poor would have to depend on the percolation of the fruits of growth. Indian experience in this regard until 1980 was far from encouraging. Under the circumstances, it was not considered rational to make the poor or even the lower middle class wait for the percolation of the fruits of growth, which could be for too long a time, especially if the growth rate did not attain a reasonably high level in the near future. This led the strategy of 'growth with redistribution' to be embedded in the planning process in the 1980s so as to ensure that a component of growth could be used for the purpose of income redistribution in favour of the poor. As a sequel to it, for the first time in Indian planning, the concept of 'direct attack on poverty' was incorporated in the Sixth Plan (1980–85), marking a new chapter in the fight against poverty. It snowballed into a major policy shift in the development strategy with special measures to raise the income of the poor and the marginalized sections of the population. How the strategy of poverty alleviation evolved under quite a different development paradigm and was internalized in the Five Year Plan has been described in the section 'Internalizing Poverty Alleviation in the Plan' in this chapter.

The growth and development strategy in India in the 1950s was guided by the goal of maximization of income. The concept of equity at this time began and ended with the catchphrase (coined by Jawaharlal Nehru): 'India, being poor, there was no wealth for division among the people; there was only poverty to divide.' The concern, therefore, was about increasing the level of income; equity in income distribution came later. Growth maximization was treated and accepted as an essentiality in order to attain the living standard of wealthier countries. In the same breath there was a strong undercurrent which believed that the developed countries, in their bid to maximize economic growth, had committed some mistakes, many of which could have been avoided with a little care and attention to detail. Mindful of the fact that economic development in India should take an independent route, taking the best from the West and the East, there was perhaps an element of extra caution so that India did not commit similar mistakes. It is possible that such a mindset throughout the 1960s and 1970s, if not in the first four decades of planning, that is, until the beginning of economic reform, may have caused the planners to sacrifice a few basis points of the growth rate.

Weathering the Food Crisis in the Mid-1960s

The food situation in India at the time of Independence was precarious. It remained more or less same throughout the 1950s and the greater part of the 1960s. The growth rate in agriculture declined in 6 of the 12 years from the mid-1950s to the mid-1960s (1955–56 to 1966–67).[3] The average growth rate in agriculture in this 12-year period was only 1.3 per cent per year, which was nearly half of the rate of growth of population. Food production was always short of market demand and food had to be imported to meet the consumption requirement.

In the mid-1950s, India signed an agreement with the USA for importing food under the US Public Law 480 (PL 480). However, the import was not hassle free. It merits a short recounting of its history.

The PL 480 was born out of the Agricultural Trade Development and Assistance Act of 1954. The Act was signed into law by President Dwight D. Eisenhower in July 1954. The purpose of this Act in a broad sense was to expand international trade, promote economic stability of American agriculture, and make maximum use of its surplus agricultural commodities in the furtherance of foreign policy. The plan was to create a secondary foreign market by allowing food-deficient countries to pay for American food imports in their own currencies instead of in USD. It enabled export of American agricultural products while assisting the food-deficient, cash-strapped poor countries to tide over their food crisis. The import of food under PL 480 suited India for the liberal payment obligations, under which the food import bill could be paid fully with the Indian rupee. Ironically, for India, food import through PL 480 proved difficult in the mid-1960s when the food situation worsened as cereal output declined in successive years due to drought.

The problems for India began to surface as this law was revised, first in 1961 by John F. Kennedy, and then in 1966 by Lyndon B. Johnson. The amendments made in 1961 switched the focus of the law from disposal of surplus agricultural commodities to addressing humanitarian needs. India faced trouble since then, and particularly after the amendments in 1966, when the food importing countries were mandated to pay the bill in USD, and the quantum of imports was made contingent upon the importing country's plan of food self-sufficiency. It became difficult for India to import food under PL 480. India was starved of foreign exchange, restricting its ability to procure food from anywhere and at will.

The cereal output in 1965–66 was 20 per cent less than the previous year's output, which itself was not adequate to meet the demand. In the next year (1966–67), the food situation worsened further and the country was literally submerged in the crisis. The food shortage was so severe and penetrating that the government had to monitor the movement of the ships (carrying food from abroad) when they were in the high seas. The ships were directed to a specific port depending upon the food shortage in the region. It was as if the food was being transferred from the ship directly to the households, and the phrase 'from ship to mouth' was coined. It enabled the government to avert mass hunger and starvation in the country despite food import becoming expensive and uncertain.

Import of food cannot be a perpetual affair. The solution of the food problem lies in increasing cereal output. Its thread was picked up from the Intensive Agricultural Areas Programme (IAAP), which was formulated as a component of the agricultural strategy in 1964–65. It may be mentioned in this context that the idea of IAAP came from the Intensive Agricultural District Programme (IADP), formulated in 1960 as a component of the agricultural strategy under the umbrella of the Community Development Project (CDP). The IAAP was converted into a major package for agricultural production, based on the use of high yielding variety (HYV) of seeds (also known as 'modern variety') for wheat backed up by fertilizer, pesticides, and controlled water supply. The potentially developed districts (in terms of fertility of land and agricultural productivity) were chosen for the IAAP. It was a deliberate policy to select the developed districts and channelize agricultural investment there to maximize return. It may, in part, be a compulsion to choose the developed districts as application of HYV seeds needed assured irrigation, which the poorer districts lacked.

The diffusion of HYV seeds was remarkable. Cereal output in 1967–68 increased by more than 20 per cent, as compared with the previous year. This phenomenon of the application of HYV seeds contributing to substantial rise in cereal output was christened as the 'Green Revolution'. The areas which contributed to the additional cereal production extended over Punjab, Haryana, and the fertile districts of Uttar Pradesh, which are generally scattered over the western part of the state.

The Green Revolution of the 1960s could not be extended to other areas, even though foodgrain production in Andhra Pradesh, Odisha, Madhya Pradesh, and West Bengal increased subsequently (after about a quarter century) and they became food-surplus states. In the early 1980s, the Planning Commission made an effort to replicate the Green Revolution in the eastern region of the country comprising Assam, Bihar, Odisha, West Bengal, eastern Uttar Pradesh, and present-day Chhattisgarh. The process of formulating a new agricultural strategy in these areas to engineer a breakthrough in rice output was initiated in the Seventh Plan. There was some increase in rice output, as a result. But it was nowhere near the effects of the Green Revolution of the late 1960s.

The strategy in agriculture during the early years of the Green Revolution favoured developed areas, side-tracking the relatively poorer areas. The districts endowed with assured irrigation became the focus of agricultural production based on HYV seeds. Its benefit accrued largely to medium and large farmers. It had the potential of accentuating inequality in income and assets in rural areas—a phenomenon which was certain to come under flak in a democratic polity such as India where egalitarianism was usually treated as the password for progress. But this was a deliberate decision on the part of the state to concentrate on developed areas, though it could have been (and indeed was) questioned on grounds of equity. That it was a pragmatic decision was borne out by the fact that exactly at this time the government was pursuing the policy of ensuring equity at all costs and preventing concentration of economic power in industry—a policy exactly opposite to what was being practised in case of agriculture.

All said and done, it was a pragmatic decision to concentrate on developed areas as talk of equity in a situation of perennial food shortage leading to famine and starvation, and even international disgrace, hardly makes any sense. The country had to face humiliation for food import (cereals only) in the mid-1960s to stave off hunger and starvation. It forced adoption of policies that promote food production, irrespective of its potential impact on equity. After all, India could meet the food (cereal) needs of the individuals in general. This was not a mean achievement, judging the performance of countries with similar per capita income at that time.

The food crisis of the mid-1960s may have had some bearing on the decision of the Western economists to club India among a group of nations which would be in the grip of famine within the next decade 'because of overpopulation, agricultural insufficiency, or political ineptness'. A study conducted by the brothers William and Paul Paddock, published in the USA in 1967, concluded that the food deficiency in India would be so severe that any amount of aid could not rescue it from the crisis, and India would be a nation that could not be saved, and therefore, it would be best ignored and left to its fate. It would be a waste of effort to assist India with food aid. What is amusing is that they specified the year when India would reach such a situation. It was 1975.[4]

The message delivered in the Paddock brothers' study, in its usual wave, reached India. This was precisely the time when the nuts and bolts of a sustainable mechanism for food production under the canopy of Green Revolution were being put in place. Within a few years, food deficiency became a thing of the past, and India had a surplus of foodgrains, so much so that in 1977, it repaid a large amount of the old wheat credits (taken from the Soviet Union) through wheat. The timing of this repayment marks an important event. It is close to the year, 1975, which the Paddock brothers predicted would be the year when India would be in the grip of famine.

Strengthening State Control in the Economy

The MRTP Act was made into a law in 1970. The origin of this Act can be traced to the beginning of the 1960s. The circumstances leading to its enactment may be described so as to understand the reality of the situation, which brought about this whole event.

While moving the draft outline of the Third Five Year Plan in the Parliament (Lok Sabha) for consideration on 22 August 1960, the prime minister stated that at the end of a decade of sustained economic growth of the 1950s (First and Second Plans), the national income had increased by 42 per cent and the per capita income by 20 per cent. There was no precise information about the exact spread of this additional income across the income classes of the population. In order to enquire how exactly this additional income spread, the Planning Commission constituted the Committee on Distribution of Income and Levels of Living under the chairmanship of P. C. Mahalanobis in October 1960.[5] Widely referred to as the Mahalanobis Committee, its terms of reference were set as follows: (a) to review the changes in levels of living during the First and Second Five Year Plans; (b) to study recent trends in distribution of income and wealth; and (c) to ascertain the extent to which the operation of the economic system resulted in concentration of wealth and means of production. The terms of reference reflected quintessentially the anxiety of the government to place equity in the distribution of income and wealth at the forefront of the development strategy.

The Mahalanobis Committee submitted its first report in February 1964.[6] Acknowledging that they did not have the requisite data to draw valid conclusions concerning change in income distribution which might have taken place over the First and the Second Plans, the committee concluded: (a) income inequality was not higher in India than in some developed or underdeveloped countries; (b) the inequality in urban areas was more than that in rural; and (c) there was no clear indication of a significant change in income distribution over the 1950s, that is, during the First and Second Plans. The committee did not comment on the change in standards of living during these two Five Year Plans due to paucity of essential data to make such an assessment. They faced a similar problem with regard to the issue related to concentration of wealth and means of production. On concentration of economic power, the committee pronounced the verdict that despite all the countervailing measures taken by the government, concentration of economic power in the private sector was more than what could be justified as necessary on functional grounds. Unfortunately, it did not elaborate on this issue, or provide sufficient reason for such an assertion. On this particular verdict of the Mahalanobis Committee, the Federation of Indian Chambers of Commerce and Industry (FICCI) contended that it was not based on solid statistical or strong economic reasoning. The FICCI, in fact, had brought out a series of technical documents to demonstrate that the arguments of the Mahalanobis Committee were hollow.

The Mahalanobis Committee did not find it easy to suggest measures to contain, let alone reduce, the concentration of economic power in the context of a mixed economy, where the private sector has an important role to play in planned economic development. The committee stated in the same report:

> Industrialisation has its own logic, and neither the economies of scale nor that of full utilisation of scarce talent can be ignored with impunity. Economic development within a democratic framework remains a paramount objective of national policy. At the same time, the country is pledged to the realisation of a socialist pattern of society; and diminution and eventual elimination of concentration of economic power in private hands [p. 55].

It suggested that 'for devising adequate corrective measures in consonance with the economic growth objectives, more comprehensive and detailed information regarding the many aspects and ramifications of economic power and controls in the private sector is required'. On the back of it, the committee pointed out the necessity of a full-time agency with the requisite legal authority to facilitate the formulation of necessary policy that combines 'industrialisation with social justice' and 'economic development with dispersal of economic power'.

Within two months of receiving the report of the Mahalanobis Committee, the central government appointed (in April 1964) a five-member commission under the chairmanship of Justice K. C. Das Gupta to enquire into the concentration of economic power and suggest measures to regulate and control monopolistic and restrictive trade practices. Known as the Monopolies Inquiry Commission, its task was to enquire into the extent and effect of concentration of economic power in private hands and the prevalence of monopolistic and restrictive practices in important sectors of economic activity (other than agriculture) with special reference to the following: (*a*) the factors responsible for such concentration and monopolistic and restrictive practices; and (*b*) their social and economic consequences, and the extent to which they might work to the common detriment. In addition, the commission was asked to suggest legislative measures that might be considered necessary in light of the enquiry and the procedure and agency for the enforcement of such legislation. In a word, the commission was to enquire into the existence of concentration of economic power in the organized private sector and its effects on the Indian economy, and suggest remedial measures to contain it.

The Monopolies Inquiry Commission submitted its report in October 1965. It contains a draft of the MRTP Bill to check concentration of economic power and control monopolistic and restrictive trade practices. The principal objectives that were sought to be achieved through the MRTP Bill were (a) prevention of concentration of economic power; (b) control of monopolies; and (c) prohibition of monopolistic, restrictive, and unfair trade practices. Additionally, the commission recommended a separate legislation to deal with economic concentration and restrictive trade practices, and setting up of the Monopolies and Restrictive Trade Practices Commission. (The report of the commission was spread over 10 different subjects. One of the members, R.C. Dutt, did not agree with at least six of them and gave a dissent note.)

The MRTP Bill drafted by the Das Gupta Commission was made an Act and it came into operation from 1 June 1970. The law provides for the control of monopolies, and prohibits monopolistic and restrictive trade practices so that economic power is not concentrated in the hands of a few in the private sector. The MRTP Act has two specific aims in view: (a) the ownership and control of material resources of the community are so distributed as to best serve the common good; and (b) that the operation of the economic system does not result in concentration of wealth and means of production to the common detriment. As per the provisions of this Act, the Monopolies and Restrictive Trade Practices Commission was created with wide-ranging powers to control and regulate the activities of the private sector.

The MRTP Act spread its network throughout the 1970s and the 1980s. It was implemented in letter and spirit by an overzealous bureaucracy with the sole intention of establishing its supremacy in industry. The stringent control on private industries permitted by this Act made the development of industries in the private sector dependent on the whims and fancies of the government. There was an overwhelming emphasis on equity in the distribution of income and wealth arising from the growth of Indian industries. The concept of equity was taken at face value and imposed rigorously on the growth potential of the economy so as to generate an income profile which was egalitarian to the core. In the process, it overlooked the fact that there is a trade-off between growth and equity, and that talk of equity in a stagnant economy does not make sense. That the economy should attain a reasonable rate of income growth at the first instance, and then this income, as far as possible, should be distributed equally among the different cross sections of the population was not taken into consideration before pursuing the idea of equity so vehemently. In the end, industrial development was caught in the labyrinth of the growth–equity nexus.

Arriving at Consensus in the Sixth Plan

A Five Year Plan could be finalized only upon unanimous approval of the NDC in which the chief ministers of the states were members. In February 1981, consensus was almost going to elude the Sixth Plan and it was on the verge of being placed on the backburner because the Government of West Bengal decided not to give assent to the Plan. The West Bengal government wanted the Sixth Plan to address an array of issues related to fiscal policy, income distribution, price inflation, regional disparity, employment generation, choice of technology, regulation of subsidies, equity, and most of all improvement of living standard and quality of life of the people. These were mere intentions; how these could be achieved, was not revealed. As, for example, how equity in class distribution of income could be ensured, or how regional disparity in growth could be contained, was not specified. Similarly, the need for investment was mentioned, but it was not indicated how investment could be generated. Not a word was said on whether the resources for investment would be generated entirely from the domestic market or if there would be some dependence on foreign investment. There was no clue on how up-to-date technology could be procured to implement the projects and programmes in the Plan. Overall, what direction the growth path of the economy could take in the medium or long term was not mentioned.

More specifically, the litany of supposed infractions articulated by the West Bengal government did not clarify which of these issues were not factored in, either in the earlier Plans, or in the Sixth Plan. Likewise, how these could actually be used in the formulation of the Plan, or technically speaking, what the planning methodology would be, was not spelt out even remotely. Over and above, many of these issues were gradually becoming irrelevant in the contemporary economic scenario. Under the circumstances, these statements turned out to be mere rhetoric.

Upon persistence, the West Bengal government offered to accept the Plan if a chapter was added at the beginning (not at the end!), highlighting the failures (not the successes!) of the previous Five Year Plans (that is, the First to the Fifth Plan) spanning over 1951–80. The issue then came on the discussion table. There were ideas galore. The perception that planning during this period may not have yielded anticipated results is not new. However, the development effort was able to increase income and food availability, and eliminate hunger in its acute form; many people, though not all, could manage a roof over their head and sufficient clothing for their family members. This was certainly a situation better than what it was at the time of Independence; so, why not record these as well? It was then decided that the Sixth Plan document would begin with a chapter which would contain the successes and the failures of the first three decades of planning, 1951–80. Thus, the chapter titled 'Development Performance' chronicling the changes in the macroeconomic parameters and indicators relating to levels of living and quality of life of the people in 1951–80 was included. No one expected a rosy picture of the Indian economy from this exposition, however elegantly it might be presented. But in the end, it was not all so gloomy and depressing. In any case, it paved the way for the NDC's approval of the Sixth Plan, though the growth and development strategy did not change. The planning process remained the same as before.

Internalizing Poverty Alleviation in the Plan

The intellectual discourse around the measurement of poverty throughout the 1960s and 1970s was remarkable. Yet, the Third (1961–66) or the Fourth Plan (1969–74) did not explicitly use poverty as a parameter in Plan formulation. Until the mid-1970s, or to be precise, the Fourth Plan, the government actively pursued growth-oriented policies to tackle poverty. Acceleration in the rate of economic growth, reduction of disparities in income and wealth, and prevention of concentration of economic power were the basic premises on which the Five Year Plans had been framed until then. It was presumed that faster growth of income would yield a higher living standard for the people, including the poor, and for reduction of disparities in income and wealth, the scope of redistributive policies is severely limited.

The ideas began to change in the course of the Fourth Plan when it became apparent that the effectiveness of a growth-centric strategy for poverty reduction was limited and it was futile to wait for percolation of the fruits of economic growth for poverty alleviation in a tangible manner. This was probably the driving force behind the idea of poverty reduction through direct income generation for the poor using redistributive programmes. By crafting a cohesive policy to tackle the menace of poverty through these measures, the issue of poverty was placed at the forefront of the development debate.

After the attainment of food self-sufficiency in the late 1960s that came with the Green Revolution, the focus was on increasing the income of the poor in rural areas and improving their living standards through a series of state intervention measures in agriculture. The bulk of the rural poor are agricultural labourers (wage earners) or small and marginal farmers. (These two categories sometimes overlap since small and marginal farmers can work as agricultural labourers.) The incidence of poverty among them is higher than others. In order to induce the small and marginal farmers to adopt modern methods of cultivation, the emphasis shifted to area- and sector-based programmes, such as the Small Farmers Development Agency (SFDA) and Marginal Farmers and Agricultural Labourers (MFAL), which were incorporated into agricultural planning in the Fourth Plan. These were not poverty alleviation programmes per se. Their main plank was a kind of incentive to the poor for raising their income, and could be said to possess the elemental properties of anti-poverty programmes, which were taken up later in the Sixth Plan and labelled as 'direct attack on poverty'.

Poverty in India is concentrated in rural areas; increase in income of the rural population is the key to poverty removal. In the mid-1970s, the Ministry of Rural Development (MORD) was created in the central government with the purpose of administering growth-oriented programmes in agriculture so as to enthuse the state governments to undertake agricultural projects to foster income growth among the rural population on a sustainable basis. In course of time, the MORD became the focal point of administering a bunch of income redistributive programmes for increasing the incomes of the rural poor.

Towards the end of the Fourth Plan, the Planning Commission estimated that 40 to 50 per cent of the total population lived in abject poverty.[7] The technical exercises in the Planning Commission brought out that exclusive reliance on income growth would take another 30 to 50 years for the poor to reach the consumption level defined as the poverty line. The Fifth Plan found it too long a waiting period and decided, in principle, to launch a direct attack on poverty. Poverty being a predominantly rural phenomenon, the strategy was to attack rural poverty through pro-poor schemes. It was revealed that the growth momentum of four Five Year Plans in the previous quarter century (1951–74) could enable the economy to marshal adequate resources to finance these pro-poor schemes without substantially jeopardizing the growth prospects.

Inspired by some sustained thinking on the part of Indian economists, the strategy of development in the Fifth Plan was directly anchored to the objective of poverty removal. The concept was internalized in the Plan in terms of increase in consumption expenditure of the bottom (poorest) 30 per cent of the population to a minimum level. The target of the bottom 30 per cent of the population was considered optimal in the context of resource availability and long-term exigencies of growth, though the poverty ratio at this time was officially estimated as about twice this number.

It was not possible to raise the consumption of the bottom 30 per cent of the population to the desired minimum level (determined by the level of poverty line expenditure) depending solely on the growth of income targeted in the Plan. The prevailing inequality in income distribution came in the way. Since there was a limit to which the growth rate could be pushed up (due to resource and capacity constraint), the planners looked for ways and means to lower the level of inequality so that a larger share of the increased income reaches the bottom 30 per cent of the population. In effect, the growth rate fixed in the Fifth Plan could raise the consumption of the bottom 30 per cent of the population to the desired level if and only if there was reduction in inequality in income distribution. This brought about the idea of a redistributive growth process. Quantitative exercises in the Planning Commission revealed that equity across income classes of the population could not be ensured unless the pattern of production itself served the goal of redistribution of income and wealth by producing mass consumption goods such as food grains, edible oils, sugar, standard cloth, and cooking fuel. Increase in production of these goods, as a result, became essential to make an impact on poverty. In the Fifth Plan, such a measure to ensure equity was envisaged at the stage of income generation as well as allocation of income among different uses. It had a major thrust on policy, focusing on widening of employment opportunities in agriculture, especially for landless agricultural labourers and small and marginal farmers, who comprise the bulk of the poor.

At the end of the Fifth Plan, it was time to take stock. The economic growth realized during the first three decades of planning, 1951–80, was not sufficient to raise the income and consumption of the poor to a level that could make a major dent on poverty. The per capita income increased by an average of 1.1 per cent per year from 1950–51 to 1979–80, which was grossly inadequate to raise the standard of living to a decent level or to reduce the level of poverty in a sustainable manner. There was convincing evidence of limited effectiveness of the 'trickle down' effect of economic growth. The faith in the efficacy of growth-centric policies to yield a reasonable amount of income for the poor had been considerably dented by this time and the idea of benefiting the poor by allowing them a proportionately larger share of income through more equitable distribution gained ground. The political establishment and planners were also not comfortable with the idea that the poor should wait for percolation of the fruits of economic growth, ostensibly on the ground that its impact was not noticeable until then. Against this backdrop, there was a major tirade against poverty in the beginning of the 1980s, accepting that it cannot be removed by solely relying on economic growth, and equity in the distribution of the fruits of growth can be as critical as growth itself.

The level of poverty in 1980 was high as per the estimates of the Sixth Plan, which said that around half of the total population was poor. It identified three factors behind such a high level of poverty: (*a*) low rate of economic growth; (*b*) high inequality in income distribution; and (*c*) high rate of growth in population. In the first three decades of planning, the rate of economic growth remained low and the level of inequality did not lower. The high rate of growth of population is just a mirror image of poverty as poor people are compelled to keep their family size large for economic reasons. There was a renewed realization that poverty is the greatest curse and 'if the problem of poverty is solved, nothing else matters'. In addition to the growth-centric measures, the thought and action on poverty in the Sixth Plan focused on increasing the income of the poor through redistributive measures in tandem with maximization of the rate of economic growth. The approach is not very different from that of the Fifth Plan, except that it is much broader in scope and wider in content. It was christened as 'growth with redistribution'.

The income redistributive poverty alleviation programmes were framed in the areas of asset generation and wage employment. The asset generation programmes were designed for a section of the poor population who possessed the requisite skills so that state assistance combined with private entrepreneurship and skill produced a regular stream of income which, when added to the income originating from the general growth process, allowed them to cross the poverty line. The wage employment programmes were designed for the poor who had nothing but their raw labour power to sell. The wage income enabled the poor to cross the poverty line and join the non-poor group. This changeover from the poor to the non-poor group may not have been permanent. The wage employment programmes were often irregular. In the absence of employment, they may have rejoined the poor group.[8] The asset generation and wage employment programmes for the poor were introduced in 1980–81, that is, the first year of the Sixth Plan, and continued to be an integral component of the strategy of poverty alleviation in the next four decades.

It was not a minor decision to launch income redistributive poverty alleviation programmes in 1980, when available resources were inadequate to finance development programmes. India was still in the midst of low growth rate—a growth rate which could barely raise the level of income in per capita terms. Setting aside a part of the resources for redistribution means a compromise with the growth rate of the economy, and the bottom line is that the growth rate cannot be sacrificed in a major way. It is noteworthy that the planners did not wait for the economic growth rate to reach a higher trajectory to implement the income redistributive policies, and these were made a component of the Five Year Plans before the growth rate was healthy enough to be able to generate sufficient resources. However, the redistributive designs were kept within manageable limits. The financial situation in 1980 can in no way be compared with the profligacy of the state witnessed circa 2011. In the 1980s, the government was always starved of funds as it had to finance the investment in industry and infrastructure, which took the first charge on expenditure to keep up the growth momentum. Three decades later, almost the entire responsibility of investment in industry and infrastructure switched to the private sector. Besides, the increased growth rate could generate revenue in copious amounts, creating elbow room for the government to spend on income redistributive programmes.

In the beginning, the financing of these programmes was not easy, and no less easy was putting in place an effective institutional mechanism for their administration, which lay with the state governments. It took time for these programmes to be rooted and, as a result, there were instances of outright leakages through corruption and malpractice. Often the identification of beneficiaries was not fool proof. In plain terms, the non-poor were included as the beneficiaries of the programme and there were instances of the genuinely poor being left out. As it turned out, these problems persisted in the next three decades, though it may not have been in the same manner and form.

The 1980s: Signs of Take-off

The growth rate of the Indian economy in the first three decades of planning, was low (3.5 per cent per year). Within these three decades, the growth rate in the 1960s and 1970s was lower than that in the 1950s. The reason behind the low growth rate in the 1960s and 1970s lay squarely in agriculture. The agricultural growth rate declined during three years in the 1960s and five years in the 1970s. The decline in agricultural growth owed to natural calamity.

In sharp contrast to the events in the 1960s and 1970s, the Indian economy did not have to encounter major fire-fighting situations in the 1980s, though the decade did not begin on a promising note on the economic front either. There were serious problems on the table whose roots could be traced in international rather than domestic events. India in the early 1980s depended heavily on import of crude oil and finished petroleum products. There was a hefty increase in the international price of crude oil in 1979, which the Indian economy had to absorb. The inflated import bill on this account strained the balance of payments position. On the domestic side, the economy was not in excellent shape in 1980–81 as the growth rate in the previous year (1979–80) witnessed a massive decline. In 1979–80, the agricultural and industrial output declined by 11.9 per cent and 3.6 per cent respectively; consequently, the overall growth rate declined by a staggering 5.2 per cent. The price situation was not conducive either. The price inflation was high in 1979–80, and it was led by food and oil prices. The economy had to be steered out of the low growth rate and high inflationary situation. India borrowed from the International Monetary Fund (IMF) in 1980 to tide over the balance of payments crisis. It was an agreement of USD 5.8 billion credit under the IMF's 'Extended Fund Facility' programme. The loan was repaid on time. Importantly, India did not have to utilize the last instalment of the loan as the economic situation improved, and the growth rate exceeded the long-term trend. This was a remarkable turnaround from the late 1950s when several projects and programmes in the Second Plan failed to take off owing to inadequacy of foreign exchange. It was a different scenario from the foreign exchange crisis of the mid-1960s as well. To sum up, the domestic situation in the early 1980s was more conducive than in the 1960s or the 1970s. Expectedly, it was not as difficult a task as ushering in a new era of economic management. The manner in which India embarked on a new economic course in the 1980s has been discussed in this section.

The decade of the 1980s was coterminous with the Sixth and the Seventh Five Year Plans. The target growth rate in these two Plans were achieved. The average growth rate of the 1980s (5.6 per cent per year) was more than that in the first three decades of planning (3.5 per cent per year) but less than that in the two decades of economic reform (7.0 per cent per year). In view of the extremely low rate of GDP growth in the first three decades of planning and the high rate of growth in the two decades of economic reform, the 1980s can be considered as a 'buffer' between the years of low and high growth.

The growth target in the Seventh Plan (5 per cent per year) was fixed at a level less than the actual growth rate in the Sixth Plan (5.5 per cent per year). As things turned out, the realized growth rate in the Seventh Plan (5.7 per cent per year) exceeded both the target set for the Seventh Plan and the actual growth rate in the Sixth Plan. The decision to set the target growth rate at a relatively modest level in the Seventh Plan (that is, lower than the growth rate in the Sixth Plan) may have been guided by a typical base-effect syndrome. Besides, the planners may have been prejudiced against pitching the growth rate at a higher level since the long-term trend growth rate until the Sixth Plan barely breached the much ridiculed 'Hindu rate of growth' of 3.5 per cent a year. On the eve of the Seventh Plan, the long-term trend growth rate worked out to 3.8 per cent per year (for the period 1951–52 to 1984–85). This can be seen against the backdrop of the fact that the realized growth rate in the First to the Fifth Plan did not touch the 5 per cent mark. Even then, it can be said with some amount of confidence that while finalizing the growth target in the Seventh Plan the planners failed to read the true growth potential of the economy.

During the Sixth and Seventh Plans, the rate of economic growth during the two halves of the 1980s—or, in other words, in the Sixth and Seventh Plans—despite being pretty close, are structurally different. Agricultural growth in the Seventh Plan was disappointing with three of its five years recording a growth rate of less than 1 per cent. It may be interesting to note that with the agricultural growth rate in the Seventh Plan on the medium-term trend (for example, being at the level of the growth rate of the Sixth Plan) the overall rate of economic growth in the Plan would have exceeded 6.5 per cent per year. The structural shift in the growth rate during the Seventh Plan is evident from the performance of the non-agricultural sector as a whole (that is, industry and services taken together), which increased at a rate of 7 per cent per year as against 5.5 per cent per year in the Sixth Plan. The share of industry in the aggregate GDP did not increase much in the Seventh Plan, but the share of services increased. The increase in the share of the services sector in the aggregate GDP in the Seventh Plan was about twice that of any of the previous Five

Year Plans. Incidentally, the growth in the financial services was high in the Seventh Plan. This marked a new beginning for the Indian economy in the second half of the 1980s.

The Indian economy in the 1980s, on the whole, demonstrated certain features that can be viewed as a break from the practices of the previous three decades. It is believed, and is brought out by the evidence, that the decade of the 1980s indicates the first sign of the Indian economy coming out of the low growth rate of the previous three decades. The rate of economic growth in the 1980s (5.6 per cent per year) surpassed the long-term trend growth rate of the first three decades of planning, 1951–80 (3.5 per cent per year). The economy diversified in the 1980s as the industry and services sectors expanded. Agricultural growth in the 1980s was high, 4.7 per cent per year, which was twice the rate of population growth. This was in sharp contrast with the agricultural growth rate of 2.2 per cent per year realized during the first three decades of planning, which roughly equalled, or maybe was even less than, the rate of growth of population. It denotes stagnancy or possibly even decline in per capita agricultural output in the period of 1951–80 whereas it increased in the 1980s. The increase in per capita agricultural output contributed to hasten the pace of poverty alleviation, as the bulk of poverty is concentrated in rural areas and the rural people depend on agriculture for sustenance. Besides, a part of the benefits of high growth rate in the 1980s could be passed on to the lower deciles of the population, however small it may be, through income redistributive measures. The 1980s marked the introduction of income redistributive measures to assist the poorer sections of the population. These programmes were initiated in 1980–81, that is, the first year of the Sixth Plan, and expanded in scope and coverage in the Seventh Plan.

The high growth rate in the 1980s was the outcome of rising savings and investment rate in the domestic economy. Although the increase in savings rate in the 1980s was largely driven by the savings of the households sector, there was also an increase in the contribution of private corporate sector in domestic savings. The increase in investment rate was almost exclusively driven by the private sector. The household sector's orientation towards savings and the private sector's orientation towards investment in the 1980s can be viewed as an early sign of the intention of the government to allow additional space to individual initiative and to the private sector to shoulder responsibilities for growth.

The investment rate increased somewhat steadily in the 1980s. The increase in investment in the first half of the 1980s (Sixth Plan) was dominated by the public sector whereas in the second half (Seventh Plan) it was dominated by the private sector. Of the increase in investment that occurred between the Sixth and the Seventh Plans, four-fifths originated in the private sector. The share of the private sector in total investment in the Seventh Plan, as a result, became more than what it was in the Sixth Plan, and also crossed the halfway mark, or, in other words, exceeded public investment, pointing out that the Indian economy was receptive to the ideas of private investment.

The increase in private investment and the high growth rate of the economy in the second half of the 1980s signify a transition in the pattern of development. However, there was one issue that bothered some. In order to finance investment, especially in the Seventh Plan, the government resorted to increased borrowing from the international market. The growth rate of the economy increased as a result, but this specific process of financing investment eventually put pressure on the balance of payments situation. Its ultimate impact is not considered to have been favourable on the medium-term growth rate. Montek Singh Ahluwalia, who was the economic adviser to the prime minister when such borrowing was taking place, has suggested that the high growth in the latter half of the 1980s was partly due to the expansionary fiscal policy pursued by the government and to that extent, part of the growth could be called unsustainable.[9]

The actual growth rates in the Sixth and the Seventh Plans exceeded the target. Yet, two principal accompaniments of the Plan, namely, poverty reduction and employment generation, fell far short of their respective targets. The Sixth Plan had set an ambitious target for poverty reduction—20 percentage points within the five years of the Plan. The target of poverty reduction in the Seventh Plan was lowered to exactly half of that in the Sixth Plan, that is, 10 percentage points. The poverty estimates are not available for the base and terminal years of the Five Year Plans so as to enable an assessment on the performance of poverty reduction within the Plan period. The poverty ratios estimated for the years around the Plan periods (given in Table 7.1 in Chapter 7) bring out the fact that poverty reduction in the Sixth and Seventh Plans was nowhere near their respective targets.

The target of employment generation in the Sixth Plan was 34 million standard person years, which was close to the estimated increase in labour force in the five years of the Plan. It implied that if all the new jobs were created on a full-time basis, then the total jobs created in the five years of the Sixth Plan could accommodate the entire increase in labour force. In a similar way, employment potential of 40 million standard person years was considered adequate to meet the employment demand originated within the five years of the Seventh Plan, but insufficient to wipe out the backlog of unemployment created until then. Like the poverty estimates, the estimates of employment are also not available for the base and terminal years of the Sixth and the Seventh Plans, preventing any assessment of the employment generation in these two Plans. The estimates of employment generation for the years around the Plan periods indicate that poverty reduction in the Sixth and Seventh Plans was nowhere near the respective target.

In several ways the strategy of growth and development pursued in the 1980s was different from that in the first three decades of planning. In the 1980s, the private sector was accommodated in the areas of investment and growth rather than blanket encouragement being given to state monopolies and the public sector. This was backed by concerted attempts towards incentivizing individual efforts and, in tandem, private enterprises. These policies could be viewed as attempts to usher in a sort of new era of openness in economic areas, without deviating much from the beaten track. There was a growing concern about the failure of the mechanism of state control and regulation on economic activities to exploit the inherent capacities in a large number of areas and sectors of the economy, with the result that the overall rate of economic growth was far below the potential. In order to come out of the low-growth trap, India desperately tried to weave its policies to conform to the developments in the international arena, in particular with its neighbour–competitor, China. Noting that countries with much less state interference in the management of their economies than China were able to attain a higher level of growth rate, the Third Plenary Session of the Eleventh Central Committee of the Chinese Communist Party (held in December 1978) decided to reform the country's economic system. By the early 1980s, China ended its tryst with planning and, in order to spur growth, settled for market mechanism guided by the state. It dismantled the central planning apparatus in the process, which they had so assiduously consolidated since the liberation in 1949 and loosened the state control on economic activities. China welcomed foreign technology and investment, and invited multinational corporations to invest in their country. This was an exceptional move by a country professing communism as its ideal and control on economic activities as the basis for growth and development. The wisdom of the Chinese perhaps echoed in India, inducing it to relax some of the state control and regulation on economic activities, and, at the same time, focus on market-based economic policies and lean on the private sector for growth maximization. However, the policy shifts during the 1980s were so feeble that they could not transform the country's economic juggernaut even ephemerally. It had to wait a few more years to witness a real shift in the economic policies. That happened in 1991 when the economic reform measures were initiated.

However ephemeral the changes in the 1980s were, it cannot be denied that these marked the process of rolling back the frontiers of state intervention and reformulating the planning and development strategy. Although these measures might pale in the face of the policies of economic reform and liberalization initiated in 1991, they were able to raise the growth rate of the economy to a level of more than 5 per cent per year, which eluded the country for a long period of the three decades of 1951–80. Given the fact that the growth rate of the economy in 1951–80 symbolized low growth syndrome, and that the economy moved onto a higher growth trajectory in the two decades of economic reforms and liberalization, 1992–2011, the 1980s can be treated as the transition from one growth path to another, signalling the signs of advancing to a higher growth path. The 1980s, for this reason, can be viewed as a 'buffer' between the low growth of the first three decades of planning and the high growth of the two decades of economic reform and liberalization. From this angle, the signs of change in the management of the Indian economy that were witnessed in the 1980s may be treated as the precursor of the economic reforms and liberalization in the 1990s.

A Judgement on the Growth Rate in 1951–90

State control and regulation of economic activities tailored to place the public sector at the commanding heights of the economy were the centrepiece of planning for economic growth and development during the period of 1951–90, which coincides with the first four decades of planning in independent India. By the 1970s, the planners and policymakers began to question the efficacy of state control and regulation, the essential prerequisite of planning, precisely as it became apparent that the Indian economy lacked efficiency and competitiveness, and mainly as a result of this was growing at a rate much below its potential. The growth rate of GDP in the first three decades of planning did not merely fail to attain a reasonably high level but was pronounced to be low. The low rate of economic growth in 1951–80 became a paramount issue in the 1980s, and there were doubts on the performance of the Indian economy. By implication, the effectiveness of the growth and development strategy in general, and planning in particular, to raise the rate of economic growth and improve the living standard of the people came under the scanner.

The low rate of economic growth in the first three decades of planning is a fact. However, this growth rate, as subsequent events revealed, contributed to sustainable development of the Indian economy. Otherwise, India could not, within three years of the military reverses faced at the northern borders (in 1962), fight a major war with Pakistan (in 1965) and in less than a decade defeat Pakistan in another large-scale war (in 1971). Planning in this period (1951–80) cannot be termed as a total failure, if the fundamentals of the economy at the end of the Second Plan are any guide. The growth rate in the first two Five Year Plans (1951–61) averaged 3.9 per cent per year, and this connotes no mean achievement for a newly independent nation emerging from two centuries of colonial rule and a decaying socio-economic condition. The foundation of a strong industrial base initiated in the Second Plan was able to propel future growth.

What can be argued is how far the growth and development strategy based on planning and the accompanying state control and regulation on economic activities can be held responsible for the growth rate to be low or, to put it in a different way, less than the potential. An assessment of the impact of the policies to maximize the rate of economic growth and ensure overall development in the initial four decades of planning may be futile in the absence of a benchmark. Some estimates of growth rate of the Indian economy in the pre-Independence days are available. But the comparison of the growth rate in 1951–90 with that of the pre-Independence days may be invalid for two reasons. First, the growth rates in the pre- and post-Independence years were derived using different methodologies, and hence these two cannot be compared. Second, the efforts to increase the economic growth rate by an independent nation with the purpose of improving the living standard of its people cannot be treated at an equal footing with the growth rate that is planned or achieved under foreign occupation. The British government always had a different view on the growth strategy that had to be pursued for the Indian economy. In any case, the available estimates in the pre-Independence years indicate very low rate of growth—around 1 per cent per year or even less. As the rate of growth of population in the pre-Independence days was similar to that of income, it is obvious why the per capita income remained static.

As an alternative, the growth performance of the Indian economy in 1951–90 may be compared with that of the neighbouring countries, as most of them gained independence after the Second World War, and like India, began their journey of economic growth and development. However, a comparison of the performance of economic growth rate of India with its neighbouring countries may not be straightforward and in actuality is beset with complications. None of India's neighbours except China can be used for a comparison on account of their small populations, and areas as well. The comparison between India and China can be meaningful as the area and population of these two countries are not very different, and also because planning, though different in form and content, is the common numeraire in these two countries. Both India and China made their foray into planned economic development around the same time (India in 1951 and China in 1953). Both the countries devoted the initial three years (India after Independence in 1947 and China after liberation in 1949) to prepare the groundwork for planning. From 1947 to 1950, India took a series of measures to unify the country and tackle the problems arising from the Partition, which led to widespread violence and dislocation of millions of families.

At the time of Independence, the two main entities that India consisted of—British India, which was the area under direct rule of the British government, and the Indian States, which were the Princely States—were unified. Then, the Constitution was finalized in November 1949 and the country was proclaimed as a Republic in January 1950. With this, India began its journey towards a democratic nation state, and the planning process was initiated in 1951. On the other hand, the Chinese economy was essentially disjointed and fragmented in 1949 when the country was proclaimed as a People's Republic. The country was in the grip of runaway inflation and its industry lay in the doldrums. China implemented a series of measures from 1949 to 1952 under the codename 'restoration' so as to enable the economy to gather momentum. Despite these similarities, the comparison between India and China may be somewhat blurred by the different historical perspectives of these two countries.

India was under colonial subjugation for nearly 200 years from 1757 to 1947. It began with the East India Company in 1757, and then continued from 1858 under the direct rule of the British government (Queen Victoria). Indian wealth was systematically transferred to England throughout this period. When India entered into the era of planned economic development in 1951, its economy was stagnant and poverty and destitution were at their peak. In comparison, China had not been under colonial subjugation, at least for the 300 years before the proclamation of the People's Republic by the Communist Party of China in 1949. It had been an independent country ever since the establishment of the Qing dynasty in 1644. The Qing dynasty ended in 1912, when Sun Yat-Sen founded the Chinese Republic. Such contrasting backgrounds of India and China naturally come in the way of a fair comparison of the economic growth and development that has taken place in these two countries since the 1950s.

China's First Five Year Plan started in 1953. It conforms to the Soviet model of planning. China's First Plan attempted to lay the foundation of heavy industry, and it has been regarded as enormously successful. The economy attained a high growth rate. At the end of the First Plan, the macroeconomic indicators emerged strongly and the indicators that comprehensively define the standards of living and quality of life of the people improved.

The success of China's First Plan, to a large extent, can be attributed to the generous assistance from the Soviet Union under a bilateral treaty signed between the two countries in 1950. A number of economic and technical cooperation projects flowed to China under this treaty. These projects formed the core of China's First Plan. However, towards the closing years of the First Plan, China decided to abandon the Soviet model of planning, lock, stock, and barrel. In some way, the Chinese were convinced that efficient utilization of domestic resources, coupled with latent energy, could yield faster growth rates for industry and agriculture at the same time. The strategy was nicknamed the 'Great Leap Forward' and was announced at the Second Session of the Eighth Party Congress of the Chinese Communist Party in May 1958.

It appears that the Great Leap Forward was born out of fear and faith. The fear originated from the long-term implications of Soviet assistance on the Chinese economy. The faith was in the fact that the growth rate of the economy could be raised without foreign assistance and using domestic resources alone. The exercise involved an enormous amount of experimentation. As it had no detailed blueprint except a few underlying strategic principles, it is not surprising that the Great Leap Forward pushed the Chinese economy into a turbulent atmosphere. By the late 1950s, the rate of economic growth in China stagnated and under its impact, the standard of living of the people deteriorated. China faced acute food shortage, culminating in widespread hunger and famine in 1959–61, in which an estimated 30 million people perished in the countryside. Mao Zedong, the architect of the Great Leap Forward, accepted moral responsibility for the disaster and resigned from the position of the chairman of the People's Republic of China in April 1959, though he remained the chairman of the Chinese Communist Party.

Considering the industrialization programme, India's Second Plan (1956–61) bore considerable resemblance to China's First Plan (1953–57). The development strategy in these two plans (India's Second Plan and China's First Plan) was nearly similar for both the countries, but the manner and method of implementation of the Plans differed substantially. The private sector in China, as in the case of the Soviet Union, withered before the initiation of planning. It was subsumed under the state. In contrast, India relied on a mixed economy approach in which the public and the private sectors operated side by side. A more substantial issue is that China could implement the Plan through generous technological and financial assistance from other countries, notably the Soviet Union and the East European countries, which were then under the umbrella of the Warsaw Pact whereas India had to trade for these, and yet showed the courage and determination for industrialization.

In the beginning of the 1960s, China was in the midst of a severe economic crisis. This was precisely the time when the Indian economy saw an average growth rate of about 4 per cent per year for a decade (the 1950s). This sustained growth of the economy for a decade enabled India to prepare a bold and ambitious Third Five Year Plan.

The GDP growth rate in India and China in aggregate as well as per capita terms did not differ much until the 1980s. From the 1990s onwards, the GDP growth rate in India fell behind China. Its impact was evident in the level and change in poverty in these two countries. The World Bank estimates show that the poverty ratio (percentage of people living below the poverty line) in China was much higher than in India until the 1980s. With increase in income, the poverty ratio in China declined faster, and it became lower than that of India from the 1990s.[10]

There is a subtle point which makes the comparison of growth rates in India and China somewhat misty. Planning is known to be synonymous with state control in economic activities. The difference in the application of planning in the two countries lay in the degree of state control or, in other words, the areas and sectors of the economy covered under state control. In China, the state control was absolute and extended to each and every sphere of the economy. On the other hand, the state control in India was not all-pervasive as in China because of the simultaneous existence of public and private sector in a mixed economy framework.

The economic management in China is conducted in the environs of a totalitarian form of government. There is a centralized decision-making authority, which can enable implementation of the projects and programmes in the Plan at a faster pace. In contrast, India's democratic decision-making process is time-consuming and needs a lot of persuasion across the range of stakeholders. In the natural course, the process yields results rather slowly. The quick decisions in China did not help them in the long run or even in the medium term; in many cases growth faltered because the decisions taken ran contrary to popular perception. In the case of India, the decisions may have taken little more time but they were durable.

India and China adopted different routes to growth and development, even under the nomenclature of planning. The planning in China, as mentioned earlier, began with the Soviet model. However, the bonhomie with the Soviet Union did not last long and the Chinese soon abandoned the Soviet model and adopted an indigenous method; this, however, failed initially. The Soviet Union earnestly desired India to adopt the path they had charted in pursuit of economic growth and development. But India did not concede and assiduously avoided straightforward application of the Soviet model, despite a lot of cajoling from the Soviet Union. The planning methodology employed in India in the mid-1950s (in the Second Plan) was different from what was practised in the Soviet Union then, or even earlier in the 1930s and 1940s. The ingenuity lies in the adaption of planning in a democratic framework, in which the public sector is not made the sole agent of the economy and there is space for the private sector. The public sector in India was assigned a role, and a fairly important one, in the development of basic and capital goods industries. While performing this role, the public sector operated side by side with the private sector. The operations of these two sectors took place through planning under the canopy of a democratic set-up. It was indeed a risk that India took, because the decision to use such a form of planning was taken at a time when its efficacy in maximizing the rate of economic growth and ensuring development was not clearly established in a democratic framework.

There may still remain some questions around the growth rate of the Indian economy during the first four decades of planning. First, could the growth rate have been more if an alternative policy (such as market-led growth espoused by the developed capitalist world) was pursued? Second, by how much would the growth rate in the first four decades of planning have increased with the altered policies? These are interesting questions but unfortunately cannot be provided with a reliable answer simply because it is not possible to make a counterfactual analysis of historical events. It cannot be denied that the events of the Indian economy pertaining to the first four decades of planning have entered into history.

Notes

1. I. G. Patel, *Glimpses of India's Economic Policy: An Insider's View*, Oxford University Press, 2002, p. 38.

2. Thirty-Fifth Meeting of the National Development Council, 13–14 February 1981, 'Summary Record of Discussions of the National Development Council (NDC) Meetings: Five Decades of Nation Building (Fifty NDC Meetings)', Vol. III, page 458, Government of India, Planning Commission, 2005.

3. The six years when the GDP growth rate in agriculture declined are: 1955–56 (0.8 per cent), 1957–58 (4.1 per cent), 1959–60 (0.8 per cent), 1962–63 (1.4 per cent), 1965–66 (9.9 per cent), and 1966–67 (1.2 per cent). The figures in brackets denote the rate of decline.

4. While predicting global famine by 1975, the Paddock brothers suggested that the food surpluses of the West should be utilized for countries capable of being saved, while countries incapable of being saved should be left to starve for the greater good of humanity. They clubbed India in the latter group. For details, see William Paddock and Paul Paddock, *Famine 1975! America's Decision: Who Will Survive?* Little, Brown and Co., USA, 1967.

5. Other members of this Committee were V. K. R. V. Rao, P. S. Lokanathan, B. N. Ganguli, Vishnu Sahay, D. L. Mazumdar, B. K. Madan, B. N. Datar, and P. C. Mathew.

6. Report of 'The Committee on Distribution of Income and Levels of Living', Part I, *Distribution of Income and Wealth and Concentration of Economic Power*, Government of India, Planning Commission, February 1964.

7. It is not clear why this is called abject poverty instead of simply poverty as it is the conventional poverty ratio. The poverty estimates are derived from the Working Group (1962) poverty line with appropriate adjustment for price inflation, and the class distribution of NSS consumer expenditure. For details, see 'Towards an Approach to the Fifth Five Year Plan', circulated in the 28th meeting of the National Development Council, 30–1 May 1972.

8. The idea of wage employment originally came from the National Commission on Labour in 1969. It suggested rural works programmes,

such as road building, minor irrigation, soil conservation, area development programmes, irrigation, and so on, to engage the underemployed workers in rural areas.

9. Montek S. Ahluwalia, 'The 1991 Reforms: How Home-Grown Were They?' *Economic and Political Weekly*, Vol. 51, No. 29, 16 July 2016, pp. 39–46.

10. The poverty estimates for India and China have been derived using the poverty line of 1 USD a day. The details can be found in Shaohua Chen and Martin Ravallion, *The Developing World Is Poorer Than We Thought, But No Less Successful in the Fight against Poverty*, Policy Research Working Paper 4703, Development Research Group, World Bank, August 2008.

5

Planning, Mixed Economy, and Jawaharlal Nehru

In the 1930s and 1940s, the Soviet Union mesmerized the world with central planning. That comprehensive planning is indispensable for economic growth and development of countries which are afflicted with extreme poverty and inequality was suggested by economists as varied as Gunnar Myrdal, Joan Robinson, Ian Little, Nicholas Kaldor, Thomas Balogh, Paul Streeten, and Oscar Lange, to name a few. It echoed throughout the developing countries, both resource-rich and resource-starved, and they gravitated towards planning. After the Second World War, besides the Warsaw Pact countries in Eastern Europe, many developing countries belonging to the market economy used planning for economic growth and development. The People's Republic of China adopted the Soviet model of planned development in the early 1950s. It is true that it abandoned the Soviet model in a few years, but in its place it adopted a planning process in which state control on economic activities—the basic tenets of central planning—was kept firmly in place. The concept of planning gained ground in India to maximize the rate of economic growth and ensure faster percolation of the fruits of growth to the poor and the lower deciles of the population so that the standard of living could be improved within the shortest possible time.

Shaping the Course of Planning

India gained Independence after nearly two centuries of colonial rule, which epitomized loot and plunder of its resources—first by Robert Clive and the East India Company, when wealth in the form of gold was physically transported from India to England, and later by the British government through policies that systematically exploited India. The advent of the British in India and the Industrial Revolution in England began around the same time. Robert Clive established his supremacy in India after winning the Battle of Plassey in 1757, and according to economic historian Arnold Toynbee, the Industrial Revolution in England began in 1760.

Industry is an expensive venture. It requires a substantial amount of investment, and it is essential to mention that in the initial years these investments do not yield returns because of high gestation lag in industries. Clive's victory in Plassey opened the floodgate of money from India, which at that time was more developed than England in the field of both industry and agriculture. This money, at that point of time, greatly helped England to finance the investment in industries. England was extraordinarily fortunate in getting these vast sums of money from India (routed through the East India Company) just when it needed to develop its industries. The activities of the East India Company, although officially known to be based on trade, in reality was plunder. Clive plundered so much and in such a brazen manner that at a later stage he was probed by the authorities in England. Perhaps, as a result, he committed suicide.

The policies of the British government after the departure of Robert Clive were no less harmful to India. Through industrial and trade policies, Indian industries were destroyed in a planned way. The British took away raw materials from India to England, processed them in their factories and sent their manufactured goods to India for sale. Thus, the British used India as a source of raw materials for their industries, and as a destination for finished products. As a result, India, which had been renowned for its manufactured products, was reduced to being a supplier of raw materials for the British industries and a market for their manufactured goods. As Indian industries were destroyed, its artisans, craftsmen, and weavers, who then were more efficient than their counterparts in England, were forced to abandon their age-old occupations and flock to agriculture for their livelihoods. This initiated a kind of ruralization of the Indian economy, which continued for two centuries. Its consequence was disastrous. Agriculture became overburdened with population, and the return from land was not adequate to support even the bare necessities of the farming families. The process of ruralization increased the pressure on land. The holdings of the peasantry shrunk and most of them became uneconomic as they were unable to yield sufficient income.

Agriculture was dependent on weather, and was frequently affected by regular cycles of natural calamities, affecting crop output. Crop loss resulted in famines in the countryside, which in the nineteenth and the twentieth centuries occurred at almost regular intervals of 10 to 15 years. It was quite common for famine and natural calamities to wipe out large sections of the population in the rural areas, even as much as one-third in some areas. And yet, the British government took pride in their administrative efficiency by exacting full rent from these hapless peasants. The oppression on peasants was inhuman.

The land policy of the British government worsened the condition of the peasants. As there was not enough land, a class of landless labourers developed in rural areas. In the zamindari areas, the landlords took advantage of this situation and raised the rent in an arbitrary manner, knowing fully well that the peasantry would be unable to bear the burden. The peasants had no other option than to borrow from the village moneylender (or bania) and, in the process, were thrown in the cycle of debt. Soon, the situation became such that Indian peasants were born in debt, lived in debt, and died in debt. This, according to economic historians, is the 'foundation and basis of India's problem of poverty'.

Two-fifths of India's population were subjugated by the Princely States. This intensified rural destitution. With the exception of a few isolated spots, there was no administration worth mentioning in these states, and feudalism was at its peak. The British government appointed 'Residents' to assist the administration in these states. In practice, the Residents looked after the interests of the British government rather than the interests of the people, let alone the poor. Development in the Princely States was far removed from their agenda.

The political leaders who liberated the country from foreign sub-jugation were passionate about taking it out of the morass of poverty and destitution, and placing it at the pinnacle of prosperity and influ-ence. They looked for ways and means to maximize the rate of eco-nomic growth, and to ensure that the benefits of growth percolated equally to all sections of the population, if not proportionately more to the lower deciles. The issue basically boiled down to this: how was the rate of economic growth to be maximized in a low-income capital starved country so that the income of the people could be increased faster, and within the shortest possible time?

By the end of the Second World War, the capitalist path of growth and development laid out by the classical economists had fallen out of favour. The new ideas in this regard radiated from the Soviet Union, which used planning to transform a feudal country (which it was at the time of the 1917 revolution) to an advanced industrial nation. Planning in the Soviet Union had begun in 1928. By 1950, it had implemented four Five Year Plans and was able to raise the income and standard of living of its people. The quality of life of the people, notably those at the lower end of the pyramid of the income distribu-tion, improved. The economists in the West, who generally viewed state control on economic activities as obstructing development and retarding the growth process, did not deny the growth and develop-ment that had taken place in the Soviet Union after years of economic stagnation. They, however, hastened to note that the development was achieved at the expense of wastage of resources. The Soviet Union, indeed, is endowed with huge resources.

Before the 1917 revolution, the Soviet economy was predominantly agricultural, and the country was afflicted with enormous poverty and illiteracy. The situation in India at the time of Independence appeared to be somewhat similar. It is plausible that such resemblance (for example, a predominantly agricultural economy, with lack of industri-alization, widespread illiteracy, and poverty) induced India's political leadership to rely on planning.

Initiation of Planning

India's per capita income was abysmally low in 1950, and its class dis-tribution was highly unequal. The economy was predominantly rural, and poverty and deprivation were widespread. The prime need at that stage, as contemporary economists believed, was to develop necessary infrastructure to maximize the rate of economic growth. That state intervention was necessary to maximize the rate of economic growth and that it is an essential prerequisite to transform a resource-scarce economy into a high-income country with a developed industrial base were not disputed. In order to eliminate India's age-old social and economic inequalities, it was necessary to initiate a process of development that would be capable of raising the standards of living of the people and opening up for them 'new opportunities for a richer and more varied life'. The task was not easy. India then faced insurmountable problems in its bid to maximize the rate of economic growth. A few of them are mentioned here so as to underline their spread and seriousness.

(a) There was lack of coordination between different regions in economic administration, and it was not possible to have a precise idea about availability of domestic resources.

(b) The integration of former Indian states resulted in the emergence of new geographical and economic facts, calling for fresh assessment of resources, both physical and financial, and of essential conditions of progress.

(c) There were inflationary pressures inherited from India's involvement in the Second World War.

(d) There were balance of payments difficulties, which were rooted in the exploitative nature of the policy of the British government.

(e) As a result of the partition of the Indian subcontinent, there was an influx of several million persons into India after being displaced from their homes, and by implication, occupations; supplies of several essential raw materials were severely disrupted and food shortage was aggravated.

It is against this backdrop that India decided to repose its faith in planning. The First Five Year Plan was launched in April 1951. The first major effort to develop a strong industrial base and take the economy into a developed stage was made in the Second Plan.

In the Second Plan, the growth and development of the Indian economy was given a strategic dimension with the use of the 'growth model' formulated by Professor P. C. Mahalanobis at the ISI, Kolkata, which, as a hotspot of intellectual activities, had acquired international recognition and fame. Mahalanobis developed the scientific basis for the Second Plan and made it explicit in a two-sector, and later four-sector, model for charting a feasible growth path for the Indian economy. The model mirrored the dominant views of development economics in the West. The four-sector model was used to indicate investment allocations to achieve the target growth rate and employment level in the Second Plan.

The Mahalanobis model set the foundation of planning with its ramifications of state control on economic activities. The features of the Mahalanobis model have been described in Chapter 2. The mathematical consistency of the model was discussed and debated thoroughly from several angles and in different forums before it was used to formulate the Second Plan. The technical issues related to the Mahalanobis model were published in *Sankhya*, the house journal of the ISI, which enjoyed international repute. The Planning Commission discussed the nitty-gritty of the Mahalanobis model in an expert committee before deciding to use it. The expert committee was constituted in 1955 under the chairmanship of G. D. Deshmukh, then finance minister of the Government of India, and consisted of 24 members who were experts in the area of planning and development. All the members of the expert committee, excepting one, supported the use of the Mahalanobis model for development planning in India. The sole exception was B. R. Shenoy, who opposed several propositions associated with the model. Specifically, Shenoy disagreed with the scale of money creation, the degree of state control, and the scope of nationalization associated with the Second Plan. Terming the Second Plan as too ambitious, he argued that money creation on the scale envisaged in the Plan would result in inflation or balance of payments crisis, or both. Such an observation may not be unusual from the monetarist point of view, which Shenoy was passionate about.

Opposition to the Second Plan also came from the Planning Commission. One of its members, K. C. Neogy, in a note mentioned in the Appendix 1 of the Plan, expressed alternative views, which are nothing but straightforward arguments of dissent to the planks on which the Second Plan was founded. He branded the calculation of financial resources for the public sector in the Plan as 'wishful thinking rather than reasonable expectations' and questioned the estimate of revenue generation, foreign aid, and deficit financing. The sum and substance of his view was that the Plan was unrealistic, too ambitious, and needed to be curtailed to make it practicable. The reply to Neogy came from Morarji Desai, chief minister of Bombay (present-day Maharashtra), who, in a meeting of the NDC said that these views (Neogy's views on the Second Plan) had come from pessimism rather than from a realistic view of things.[1] Desai went on to suggest: 'A pessimistic view was dangerous and would not enable anything to be done. The essence of planning was that it should be possible to raise resources and income to a greater extent than could have been done without planning.'[2] He was firm that some risk had to be taken and the Plan should not be scaled down. Hopes were raised among the people by the First Plan; and if it was not possible to fulfil these in the Second Plan, there would be greater demoralization than what was feared by Neogy. In this, Desai was basically suggesting that Plans should be prepared to scale new heights. As a matter of fact, the best of the social scientists and mathematical minds do not plan for a bleak future.

The opposition to planning and specifically state control on economic activities came from members of the Congress Party. C. Rajagopalachari, who was a minister in the interim government and later served as the country's governor general, differed with the growth and development strategy adopted by Nehru so much that he resigned from the Congress Party and subsequently founded the Swatantra Party in 1959 to pursue a liberal approach to development.

Several chief ministers of the states had alternate views on planning, which bordered on straightforward disagreement. But, in the end, they acquiesced and supported planning. A few instances may underline the profundity of their thoughts. On the importance accorded to heavy industry in the Second Plan, B. C. Roy, then chief minister of West Bengal, pointed out its lower employment intensity. In addition, Roy maintained that the state governments did not have the necessary capacity and wherewithal to control and regulate the activities of the private sector that come with the industrialization policies. Roy was extremely concerned about the capability and efficiency of the administrative apparatus of the state governments to oversee the functioning of private enterprises, and more so of the private sector. Roy feared this could result in red-tapism and delay the implementation of the projects and programmes embodied in the Plan. He mentioned that the frequent interface between government officials (state or centre) and the private sector, which was the lineament of industrial policy associated with the Plan, could be the epicentre of corruption. With this, Roy was expressing his anxiety about the efficacy of state control, and particularly how effective the control would be in the real sense of the term. However, Roy's wholehearted support of the planning strategy rendered these issues ephemeral. In conformity with the industrialization policy of the Plan, Roy himself took the initiative to set up an integrated steel plant in his home state. The emphasis on basic and heavy industry led to the construction of three integrated steel plants (Rourkela in Odisha, Bhilai in Chhattisgarh, and Durgapur in West Bengal) and the heavy machine–making industries in the Second Plan. It was a courageous effort by a newly independent nation. The capital goods and basic industries, such as fertilizers, oil, and power, gave India a strong and diversified industrial base in the years to come.

Morarji Desai had been an ardent supporter of planning throughout. His assiduous support (in 1956) for the Second Plan has been mentioned earlier. In 1968, as the deputy prime minister, Desai dismissed the feeling of disillusionment on planning.[3] He stated that

the target set out in the First and Second Plans had been largely achieved; it was only in the Third Plan that some difficulties had come up. It was of great importance that a wrong feeling should not be created in the country as emphasizing only the failures and not referring to our achievements would lead to general despondency. There had been outside factors not within our control which were largely responsible for many of the difficulties in the third plan.[4]

Then, in 1978, as the prime minister of India, Desai stated that planning was introduced by Pandit Jawaharlal Nehru with great foresight and imagination. Plans were essential and but for them the advance that had been made could not have occurred.[5] Regarding its inadequacies, he said that the introduction of planning was a new exercise, and therefore, everything could not have been foreseen. It is, indeed, a very clear and straightforward observation. In the early years of planning, even the Soviet Union was embroiled with the mismatch between demand and supply in several critical sectors.

Wage Goods Model: A Digression

C. N. Vakil and P. R. Brahmananda, both professors of the University of Bombay, developed a wage goods model as an alternative to the Mahalanobis model. The model was presented to a panel of economists of the Planning Commission in 1955.

In contrast to the Mahalanobis model, which laid emphasis on the capital goods sector, the wage goods model accorded priority to the wage goods industries in the matter of allocation of investment. It listed the wage goods, important among them being foodgrains; other items in the list of wage goods include edible oil, milk, fish, eggs and meat, sugar, fruits and vegetables, tea, coffee, cloth, soap, kerosene, and so on. The model was founded on the premise that it is necessary to expand the supply of wage goods so as to solve the problem of unemployment and poverty. This made it necessary to increase the investment in wage goods or, in other words, there had to be enough capital stock for the production of wage goods. This approach was quite in contrast to the path laid down by the Mahalanobis model, which focused on capital goods industries and investment.

Most experts on development planning did not find the wage goods model appropriate for Indian conditions, even though the model was modified later, as, for example, by introducing poverty. The assertion of Vakil and Brahmananda that employment growth depends solely on the production of wage goods and, more importantly, that capital goods do not have an important role in employment generation was also doubted, for example, by Professor M. L. Dantwala, as asserted by a number of works and scholars.

The wage goods model gained some currency in India due to the seminal work of Piero Sraffa, a professor of the University of Cambridge, *Production of Commodities by Means of Commodities*, which was published in 1958. Sraffa made a distinction between wage goods and non-wage goods, and specifically mentioned that the consumption of wage goods increases workers' productivity. This somewhat strengthened the logic of the wage goods model developed by Vakil–Brahmananda. However, the basic concerns remained.

Sraffa noticed that 'at low levels of consumption, the productivity of workers depended on how much they consumed'. He began with consumer goods, but in the process found it necessary to make a distinction between wage-goods and non-wage-goods within consumer goods, and suggested that the initial emphasis (with regard to investment) should be on the wage-goods sectors so as to increase productivity of workers. The emphasis will change to investment in the capital goods sector when the supply of wage goods is sufficient to meet the needs of the workers. In plain terms, the initial emphasis should be on the production of wage goods, especially foodgrains, and it should then shift to the capital goods sector when more of wage goods are not necessary to increase workers' productivity. By this logic, the wage goods model became superfluous with the advent of the Green Revolution in the 1960s.

Economists, in general, favoured the Mahalanobis model in the mid-1950s for its elegance of form. The issue, to begin with, was not the model as such but rather if India would use planning as an instrument of policy or not. When this issue was resolved, the choice of the Mahalanobis model came naturally. The international community was all in favour of a capital goods–oriented model. There was hardly any support from contemporary planners and policymakers for the wage goods model, and Jawaharlal Nehru went by the ideas of a cross section of experts in the field of economics and statistics and, of course, politicians and social workers to adopt the Mahalanobis model. Concurring with them, Nehru, in all likelihood, was merely obeying the conventional wisdom of his time. He is not known to have held a dogmatic approach on planning.

Planning in a Mixed Economy

The form of planning adopted in India after Independence entails state control and regulation of economic activities. State control is rooted in the concern that economic power should not be concentrated in the hands of a few in the private sector. The political leaders associated with framing of the growth and development strategy were guided by the perception that private ownership is concomitant with the prosperity of only a few (who own industries) and the exploitation of a vast majority of the population. They held the view that the private sector and, for that matter, capitalists operated exclusively for profit maximization, and in the process there could be waste of resources (which were limited) through competition between classes of capitalists and businessmen. The private sector was not considered as the only or the principal option for its propensity to perpetuate economic inequality, which could have made India an unequal society. It was believed that if the state could own and control at least the principal means of production, such as the land and the key and basic industries, then the exploitation of the masses could be prevented and inequality in the class distribution of income and wealth could be contained. The public sector had a redistributive element in income generation and hence could contain inequality. It induced the political leaders to prefer the public sector.

It may be worthwhile to mention in this context that the idea of state ownership of means of production and distribution was not born after Independence. It dates back to the freedom struggle. Inspired by the notion 'the class that controls the means of production is the class that rules', the Indian National Congress in its Karachi Session held in 1931 adopted a resolution that 'the key and basic industries and services should be state-controlled', and this was considered necessary to tackle the 'real issue', which was 'ending poverty and exploitation of the masses'. Thus, the decision to give primacy to the public sector under the aegis of planning was rooted in the resolution of the Karachi Congress. The emphasis on the public sector (largely in pursuance of the Karachi Resolution) is ideologically motivated and indicated in the Indian Constitution, which spells out clearly the arguments against concentration of money and economic power in private hands.

Independence generated high expectations among the people and, in the process, thrust upon the state a long list of responsibilities. Improvement in living standards of the people was at the top of this list. On this issue, the people expected the state to perform, and their overwhelming expectation made it incumbent for the state to engage in economic activities so as to raise the rate of economic growth and position itself at the forefront of delivery of goods and services, which are essential for an improved living standard. This, at the initial stage of development was not possible without associating the public sector in the growth process, which, in turn, was feasible only through planning.

Industrialization was believed to be the key to come out of the centuries-old economic stagnation. Based on this premise, the government embarked on a massive industrialization programme in the Second Plan, which placed the state and the public sector at the forefront of the growth strategy. The basic and heavy industries are highly capital-intensive. The private sector did not have the capacity to finance the investment in these industries. Moreover, it did not have the technology to produce most of the capital goods. In lay terms, the private sector did not have the requisite capacity or the wherewithal to handle these responsibilities.

At the time of Independence, India had a reasonably developed private sector and its entrepreneurial abilities were sufficiently recognized. By virtue of its fairly long engagement with the development of industry, trade, and commerce, the private sector possessed enough expertise and a talent pool, which could be harnessed by the state. Keeping this in view, in the conceptual framework of mixed economy, the private sector was made a partner in the growth and developmental activities, but it was ensured that it did not reach the strategic points of the economy that could result in the concentration of economic power. Unlike in the Soviet Union or China, the private sector was not subsumed by the state. It maintained its identity and operated within the framework of planning and state control. This simultaneous existence and operation of the public and the private sectors is known as the 'mixed economy'. India adopted the mixed economy within the framework of planning. The private sector operated under the aegis of planning and played an active role in economic development.

Tracing the Origin of Mixed Economy

The decision to embrace a mixed economy in the framework of planning can be traced to several interrelated factors. India was subjugated by foreign rulers for nearly two centuries. There is no dearth of accounts of the pitiable condition of the country and the miserable life of its people during this period of colonial rule. They sum up the poverty and destitution of the entire range of population, barring a microscopic section who could position themselves close to or around the power structure. They were the zamindars and *talukdars* (landholders with administrative powers) in rural areas, and the English-speaking people who were the backbone of the British administration in urban areas. Even these people, who could barely escape poverty and deprivation, had no power or position in the society, let alone authority. They were just different from the rest of the population for being able to make both ends meet.

With Independence, the politically subjugated and economically deprived people could dream of a better situation in the days ahead. First and foremost was that they wanted instant improvement in their living standards. This was not possible without increase in income, for which it was essential that the rate of economic growth was maximized. For maximizing the growth rate, the prevailing opinion in those days (that is, in the years immediately following the Second World War) was to engage the state in economic activities through planning. The idea, no doubt, came from the Soviet Union, which, by the time India embarked on planned economic development in 1951, had completed four Five Year Plans, and was able to turn a primarily feudal economy into an industrially developed one, with considerable improvement in the living standard of its population. The Marshall Plan for post-war reconstruction, a major investment programme for war-torn countries in Europe, brought the role of the state in economic development on the surface. Several countries of the Western block decided to rely on planning within the framework of the market economy. In the early 1950s, the United Kingdom accepted the theme of the state controlling the commanding heights of the economy.

An alternative view was to leave a major part of the task of growth maximization to the private sector. That India's private sector was reasonably developed at the time of Independence has been mentioned earlier. Between the two World Wars, the growth of Indian industries was somewhat rapid. Indian industrialists were associated with the development of textiles and mining industries. The iron and steel industry got a boost, aided by the discovery of large deposits of iron ore in the part of Bihar which is now known as Jharkhand. Along with manufacturing, there was growth of trade and commerce. The financial sector developed with a network of banking and insurance companies. It is a different matter that the growth of industry and trade did not change the condition of workers as they lived a pitiable life, with long hours of work, miserable wages, and insanitary living conditions.

The choice before India ranged from complete state control on economic activities institutionalized through straightforward nationalization of industries and services falling in the private sector (as happened in the Soviet Union after 1917 and in the People's Republic of China after 1949), to depending fully on the private sector for growth and development. In the first case, the industries and services in the private sector can be brought under direct control and supervision of the state and the entire responsibility of growth and development falls on it. In the latter situation (that is, fully depending on the private sector), the state would have been at the mercy of the private industrialists and entrepreneurs for production and delivery of goods and services. The nationalization route was not a crowning success in the Soviet Union, where it was applied. Its outcome in China was yet to be ascertained in 1950 when India was debating this issue. The idea of depending on private industrialists and entrepreneurs to meet the consumption demand of the people or to raise their living standard never gained much currency in India, as there was a perception that the private industrialists operate exclusively for profit maximization. After a scrutiny of events from the economic histories of Europe, and specifically England during the Industrial Revolution, many Indian leaders, primary among them being Jawaharlal Nehru, questioned the capability, if not the earnestness, of the private sector to improve the living standard of the masses.

Such doubts about the efficacy of leaving the entire or even a greater part of the responsibility of economic growth and development to the private sector were also aired by M. N. Roy, a founder–member of the Mexican Communist Party and a blue-eyed boy of Vladimir Lenin.[6] Roy, known to be critical of Mahatma Gandhi and his policies, but being familiar with Nehru's ideas as well, prepared a plan for India in 1941. This is known as the 'People's Plan', in which Roy recommended that the public sector be charged with the responsibility of industrial development, and that industrial investment be financed exclusively from domestic resources.

At the same time, India's private sector was not too enthusiastic to take up the task of growth maximization in its entirety. In the mid-1940s, leading Indian industrialists, notably J. R. D. Tata and G. D. Birla, formulated the 'Bombay Plan'.[7] It dealt with the growth strategy to be adopted after attainment of Independence. In this, Indian industrialists made a public pronouncement that in independent India, the state has to intervene in, and control the economy. The Bombay Plan gave assent to the state ownership and control of key industries, and suggested a direct role of the state in the production of capital goods. It floated the idea of a central authority to ensure successful implementation of economic plans, conceding that the private sector would function under the directions laid out by the state. In essence, the private entrepreneurs desired the state to take over the responsibility of investment in industry and infrastructure. The basic and heavy industries are highly capital-intensive. The private sector did not have the capacity to finance the investment in these industries. Most importantly, they did not have the technology to produce most of the capital goods.

India refrained from the two polar options as mentioned previously (complete state control on economic activities or depending fully on the private sector for growth) and instead decided to marry the two, enabling the public and the private sectors to operate side by side under the conceptual framework of mixed economy. This way, the private sector was made a partner in the growth and development effort. The entrepreneurial abilities of the private sector were utilized through the mixed economy route. The nationalization of existing private sector industries was not on the cards. A few instances of nationalization indeed took place in the 1950s, but these happened before the adoption of the mixed economy in 1956. For example, the Imperial Bank of India, the leading commercial bank in the private sector, was nationalized in 1953 to become the State Bank of India, and later the life insurance business was taken over by the government and named the Life Insurance Corporation of India. These measures were prompted by the urgency to marshal some amount of resources to finance developmental activities. Another notable nationalization, though not necessarily for financial reasons, relates to the civil aviation companies then operating in the private sector, leading among them being Air India owned by J. R. D. Tata. The domestic airlines were nationalized in 1953 and renamed as Indian Airlines for domestic operations, and Air India for international operations. After all, a newly independent country cannot be blamed if it prides itself on having its own airlines.

It is probable that while zeroing in on a mixed economy in the framework of planning, India was influenced by the conditions prevailing in Europe and especially in England during the Industrial Revolution as well as the economic development that unfolded in the then Soviet Union after the 1917 revolution. These two events, though, had opposite impacts.

In Europe, the increase in income and wealth during the Industrial Revolution accrued to a small group of the population that owned industries. The living standard of only a minuscule portion of the population improved while the masses remained poor. The income inequality increased and 'the difference between the luxury of the very rich and the poverty of the poor became even greater than it was in the past'.[8] The living standard of the workers improved very slowly. They had to work for long hours (sometimes as long as 18 hours a day, until the factory legislation came into place in the 1830s) in stifling conditions with low wages. Women were paid less than men for the same amount of work; the wages for children were still lower. Such inequity and impecuniousness for the labour class is the bleak side of the Industrial Revolution. It is the end result of capitalism. The economic development in Europe in the eighteenth and nineteenth centuries was spearheaded by capitalism. It placed private ownership and control of industry at the pinnacle, and was never designed to promote welfare of workers. Rather, aided by the private ownership of industries, workers were exploited. The exploitation of workers was rooted in capitalism.

That industrial development is a prerequisite for growth and progress and that the supremacy of England and the European countries came primarily through development of industries was never in doubt. The aim was to make India an industrially developed nation. However, the benefit of the capitalist mode of production was doubted, and that induced India to eschew private ownership and lean towards the public sector for industrial development. After this, the decision about who would own large and heavy industries, and how the owners of these industries would treat the workers came naturally. The welfare of workers—an issue that was thoroughly ignored in the European countries during the Industrial Revolution—was a major concern. The facilities and services provided to the workers of the public sector undertakings in India during industrialization in the 1950s and 1960s are shining examples of their improved living conditions.

The events that unfolded from planning in the Soviet Union filled certain critical gaps in the development of European society. The process of income generation in the Soviet Union allowed for direct accrual of income to the workers in the form of wages, and a part of the increased income flowed as social welfare activities, such as workers' housing, education of their children, sanitation facilities, and so on. There was visible improvement in the quality of life of workers and the living standard of the people.

India's decision to rely on planning is found to be rooted in two somewhat contrasting events. The development stories of the Soviet Union in the aftermath of the 1917 revolution may have encouraged India to adopt planning. There was yet another set of events that followed from the working of capitalism and the private sector during the Industrial Revolution in England and Europe; it was the coexistence of mass poverty along with increase in income and wealth of a very small group of population who owned industries. This induced India to eschew capitalism. These two events shaped India's decision to rely on planning and the antecedent role it gave to the state and the public sector. Apart from this, the efforts, in actuality, were concentrated on devising an approach which was consistent with India's own thinking. It culminated in the adoption of the mixed economy.

India adopted a mixed economy at a time when the social elements in development discourse were gaining ground at a tremendous pace even in countries which are capitalistic in structure. The decision on the role that was to be earmarked for the public and the private sectors in the mixed economy framework was taken by planners. The role of the public sector and its expansion in India was guided by three main factors: (a) for augmenting resources; (b) to make income distribution egalitarian; and (c) to facilitate generation of trained manpower, which was necessary for implementation of projects and programmes contained in the Plan. India suffered greatly from all these. It was resource-constrained. The inequality in income distribution was stark and a largely non-literate population was unable to meet the manpower requirement. The state of these three factors appeared to be similar in India and in the Soviet Union when these two countries began their forays into planned economic development. The degree of income inequality in the Soviet Union in 1917 was considerable, though it may have been less than what it was in India in 1950. The availability of trained manpower was an issue in the early days of planning in the Soviet Union. Even with its vast resources, the Soviet Union had to face problems in resource generation. The similarities between the two countries (India and the Soviet Union) might have induced India to give a prime position to the public sector in the course of economic development. At the same time, these did not motivate India to adopt the planning mechanism of the Soviet Union in its entirety. Evidently, the similarity and contrast between these two countries was carefully analysed by the planners and policymakers in India before treading an independent and innovative path, that of the mixed economy.

The concept of a mixed economy, which was the pole star of India's industrial growth in the planning era, in a way rules out the hypothesis that the model of growth and development employed by the Soviet Union or the Soviet planning superstructure (Gosplan) was followed straightforwardly in India. It is true that the Mahalanobis model (which was the basis for India's Second Plan) bore some similarity to the Feldman model (employed by the Gosplan). Again, it is true that industrialization was considered as the ultimate answer to all the ills of underdevelopment and, in an alignment with the Soviet approach, the public sector was singled out for industrialization. Heavy industry was considered as the fountainhead of industrialization; if heavy machine–making industries could be built, then everything else would come in as a balancing factor. In this entire approach, India consciously avoided the Soviet model of relying exclusively on the public sector, and left considerable space for the private sector in the conceptual framework of mixed economy. The idea of the mixed economy as embedded in Indian planning made a great difference.

India's inclination on heavy industry–based industrialization in the mid-1950s induced the leadership in the Soviet Union to believe that India would follow them. The Soviet Union earnestly desired that India would follow their model, and the 'public sector only' approach. They were disappointed with India adopting the mixed economy approach.

Evolution of the Mixed Economy

The mixed economy was adopted in the Second Plan (1956). The circumstances that led to the adoption of a mixed economy have been mentioned earlier. How the mixed economy evolved within the planning framework has been described here.

In November 1954, barely a year and a half before the adoption of mixed economy in the framework of planning, the prime minister, while reviewing the progress made in the first three years (1951–54) of the First Five Year Plan, stated in the third meeting of the NDC that 'private enterprise is undoubtedly useful so far as our country is concerned; we wish to encourage it, but the dominance which the private enterprises had throughout the world during a certain period is no more'.[9] Then he stated that a system based on acquisitiveness of society was out of date, and basing society purely on acquisitive instinct is immoral. Two months later, at the 60th session of the Indian National Congress (held at Avadi, Tamil Nadu) in January 1955, a 'socialistic pattern of society' was declared as a goal. Known as the Avadi Resolution, it was founded on the premise of social ownership of means of production. It centred on the theme that basic and key industries should be either owned or controlled by the state. This was subsequently construed as the public sector occupying the commanding heights of the economy. The political leadership had a genuine predilection for the public sector, but at the same time they were not averse to the private sector. This was apparent when they stated that there will be enough space for the private sector in the context of a socialistic pattern of society, but the private sector has to accept the objective of the national plan and fit into the general pattern of the planned economy and not run on lines which might create monopolies. These laid the contours of the mixed economy, which India was to adopt the next year in its Second Five Year Plan.

The private sector in India operated in the environs of planning. In the planning for industrial development (in the Second Plan), the role of the private sector was circumscribed by the industrial policy resolution (IPR) of 1956. In fact, the industrialization policy embedded in the Second Plan was implemented through the IPR, 1956, in which industries were classified in three categories: (*a*) industries which would be owned only by the state; (*b*) industries where existing private sector units could continue and operate but could start a new unit; and (*c*) industries which were to remain in the domain of the private sector. In case of industries which remained in the domain of the private sector, their activities were regulated by the state through the industrial licensing mechanism and a host of control and regulatory measures. It is a different matter that the licensing mechanism and the accompanying regulatory measures stymied entrepreneurial capabilities and restricted expansion of industries in the private sector.

The relative role of the public and the private sectors in investment evolved over the successive Five Year Plans. At the outset (for example, in the First Plan), these two sectors of the economy were not treated as separate entities insofar as investment was concerned, and were considered part of the same process. The mixed economy was adopted in the Second Plan. This Plan (1956–61), aided and abetted by the IPR, 1956, prevented the private sector from operating in most of the key and basic industries, as these were kept in the exclusive domain of the public sector. The idea was that operation of the public sector in basic and heavy industries could yield large surpluses, which could be used for further investment so that the rate of economic growth was maximized in future. The Third Plan (1961–66) confirmed the supremacy of the public sector to prevent the growth of monopolistic tendencies, and to curb concentration of economic power. The process of endowing the public sector with additional responsibilities and areas of operation continued with great enthusiasm in the Fourth Plan (1969–74) when they were encouraged to scale the commanding heights of the economy. As a part of this process, which continued for two decades from the Second to the Fourth Plan, the public sector expanded in the mining, metallurgical, chemical, petro-chemical, and fertilizer industries. These industries provided the basic impetus to India's growth in later years, though there is very little doubt that they came with substantial curbs on the activities of the private sector, which was believed to be the principal reason behind the low rate of economic growth in the 1960s and 1970s.

The industrial licensing mechanism was devised as an instrument to guide industrial production, keeping in view the medium- and long-term objectives of planning. In effect, it controlled and regulated industrial production, which in the process adversely affected industrial growth. A close look at the determinants of industrial growth until the 1980s reveals that the licensing mechanism per se may not have created so many obstacles for expansion and growth of industries in the private sector. What mattered most in this case was the associated control and regulation spread around the activities of the private sector. These were numerous and covered almost every single aspect of industrial activity. The regulatory measures did not affect industrial growth in the 1950s in a major way. However, its after effects impacted growth in the 1960s and the 1970s, and continued until the economic reform measures were initiated. The regulatory measures introduced during the Fourth Plan (aiming to ensure equality) stifled the business environment. The enactment of the MRTP Act, 1970, and increase in marginal rate of personal income tax to as high a level as 97 per cent in the early 1970s can be cited as examples. Many of these regulatory measures extraordinarily empowered the bureaucracy, causing proliferation of corrupt means and practices. The regulatory measures initiated at this time were often more stringent than the original policies (licensing mechanism) for the sake of which these were brought in.

The decision to rely on the public sector and prioritize it over the private sector originated from the anxiety to curb monopolies and lower the inequality in income distribution. Beyond this, the state did not follow a doctrainaire approach in the trade-off between the public and the private sectors. The state actions related to planning and the mixed economy were not rigid or stereotyped; rather they were found to be pragmatic as the private sector was permitted to operate in suitable areas, where it could prosper and grow. The real challenge of indutrialization lay in the production of heavy machinery, which is called 'machine-making-machine' or, equivalently, basic and heavy (capital) goods industry. The public sector was charged with the responsibility to build these industries. The setting up of heavy industries is a complex job in terms of technical expertise, and its investment requirement is high. Besides, the whole process of industrialization is taxing for the people. The high gestation lag of heavy industry led to tremendous suffering of the people in the early days of development (industrialization), when incomes were low and people were starved of almost the entire range of wage goods. In the initial years of planning it may have been necessary for the country to sacrifice the present consumption of basic necessities in order to build the heavy industry base. In India, in the Second Plan, one-third of the total investment was devoted to the capital goods sector or, equivalently, to basic and heavy industries, and there was a simultaneous provision for the production of wage goods. The Mahalanobis model found this (one-third of the investment devoted to capital goods sector) the appropriate choice for maximizing inter-temporal growth.

With self-sufficiency in capital goods, it becomes possible for the private sector to shoulder the responsibility of producing the items of mass consumption (consumer goods and wage goods). This is precisely the approach that India followed in the Second Plan.

Between the IPR, 1956 (through which the industrialization programme in the Second Plan was implemented), and the initiation of economic reforms (in 1991), the industrial policy was tweaked twice, first in 1977 and then in 1980. The change in 1977 was marginal and certainly not in a planned manner. The change in 1980 allowed for a wider scope and greater opportunity for the private sector. In all likelihood, the motivation to dislodge the public sector from the monopoly in the market, and allow greater space to the private sector came from the events in India's neighbourhood (with China deciding to abandon central planning and embrace market economy). The question of equity was not brushed under the carpet. It was tackled in a different manner than in the 1960s or the 1970s. This marked a new beginning for the private sector in the 1980s, and, for that matter, for the mixed economy principle.

The mixed economy framework is meant to be an ideal mix of the public sector and the private sector in terms of investment, and, in its due turn, income generation. The relative shares of these two sectors in mobilization of investment and generation of income mirror the degree of openness or, from an opposite angle, the intensity of state engagement in the economy. Here, the moot question relates to the ideal mix. An equal sharing of the aggregate investment by the public and the private sectors may connote an ideal mix from this angle.

The mixed economy was adopted in the Second Plan. The share of the public sector in total investment became more than half of the total investment (and that too marginally) in only two of the six Plans, the Second to the Seventh, implemented during the period 1956–90, when state control on economic activities was the norm. These demonstrate that the economy was truly mixed.

Some of the areas and sectors of the economy with preponderance of private sector activities may be cited to underline the real content of the policy of mixed economy that was pursued during the three and a half decades of 1956–90. India's agriculture, small and medium industries, services industries (except external trade), and a large part of the large-scale industries have been in the private sector throughout. The production decisions in agriculture are taken by millions of farmers in the countryside. The state can, at the most, influence farmers' decision through prices, and fiscal and other signals. The financial sector, barring the life insurance business, was in the private sector until the late 1960s. The aggregate investment in the economy, as mentioned, was shared almost equally by the public and the private sectors. The growth of the private sector in India, to a great extent, owes to the liberal state support. The public sector commercial banks and financial institutions have been generous in financing the investment needs of the private sector. The governance of the public and the private sectors is based on similar rules and there is no discrimination. True, there are some restrictions on the private sector with respect to location, pricing of product, and so on, but these are present in varying degrees even in countries where economic development is market-led.

In the era of economic reform, the responsibility of growth shifted from the public sector to the private sector. In tandem, the share of the public sector in total investment lowered. The public sector accounted for 48.3 per cent of the total investment in the Seventh Plan (1985–90), that is, immediately before the beginning of economic reform. It lowered to 23.7 per cent in the Tenth Plan (2002–07) and remained around this level till the Eleventh Plan (2007–12). Under economic reform, the public sector enterprises had to operate under the auspices of the market, just like the private sector. With this, the mixed economy, which started with great fanfare in 1956, was given a quiet burial after three and a half decades.

On the Role of Jawaharlal Nehru

Known as the architect of planning in India, Jawaharlal Nehru steered the growth and development of the Indian economy for 17 years (1947–64) at a stretch. Nehru is also credited with the concept of mixed economy that was introduced in the framework of planning. In course of time, the reliance on planning and associated state control on economic activities became a contentious issue mainly as the realized growth rate in the first four decades of planning was low and fell short of the expected level. Overall, the policy initiatives of Nehru in the areas of economic growth and development came under the scanner, notwithstanding the fact that most of the experts in the late 1940s and early 1950s supported such policy initiatives.

It is often said that the economic growth and development in the Soviet Union in the wake of the November 1917 revolution induced Nehru to be inclined towards planning. There may be some truth in it. However, tracing the course of planning and the conceptualization of the mixed economy within the framework of planning may suggest that it is not the whole truth.

Nehru visited the Soviet Union in 1927 to attend the tenth anniversary of the November 1917 revolution. On reaching India, he prepared a booklet (in 1928) titled 'Soviet Russia, some random sketches and impressions', summarizing his ideas on economic and social development that had taken place in the Soviet Union during the 10-year period of 1917–27. Going by this account, there is no doubt that he was impressed with the development of the Soviet Union in this short period of ten years. But it would be a stretch of the imagination to relate Nehru's interest on planning (in the Indian context) to these developments because what the Soviet Union experimented with in this 10-year period is War Communism (1918 to 1921) and the New Economic Policy (NEP, 1921 to 1928).[10] Planning in the Soviet Union commenced in 1928, a year after Nehru's visit.

Ten years later, in 1938, Nehru documented his assessment on the key areas of the First (1928–32) and the Second Five Year Plans (1933–37) of the Soviet Union.[11] Though created a decade before Indian Independence, it is plausible that his ideas on planning in the context of Indian economic development might have been sourced from this assessment. Nehru was convinced that the first two Five Year Plans were able to transform the Soviet Union from a feudal country (which it was at the time of the 1917 revolution) to an advanced industrial nation, and there was tremendous improvement in the quality of life of the people, notably those at the lower end of the pyramid of income distribution.

The pattern of growth and development in Europe during the Industrial Revolution may have crystallized Nehru's ideas on capitalism. That capitalism is an inefficient mode of production despite being able to generate wealth and increase output was ingrained in his mind. The inefficiency originated from the nature of the production process, in which all the activities were left to individual initiative and chance. A large part of the wealth generated was used to finance competition among industrial capitalists, often resulting in waste. Noting the futility of such competition, Nehru harped that 'this acquisitive economy, this policy of individual grab, with no planning, with its waste and conflicts and periodical crises, must go'.[12] Controlling the different industries through a single coordinated Plan can prevent wastage of resources, both material and human. The idea of state control on economic activities under planning in India originated from the premise that it would be able to eliminate wastage of resources.

Nehru seemed to be happy with the success of planning to meet the basic needs of the people in the Soviet Union, while as a practising democrat, he was utterly dismayed with the Stalinist purges that began with the exile of Leon Trotsky and his supporters, first to Siberia, and then outside the Soviet Union. This induced Nehru to view planning in the framework of democracy instead of a totalitarian form of government. This apart, the concept of the mixed economy is at variance with the planning in the Soviet Union. Planning in India, much to the dismay of the Soviet Union, allowed space for the private sector, and assigned it specific areas of activities. In contrast, the private sector in the Soviet Union withered before planning began; it was nationalized (without compensation) and subsumed by the state.

In India, the policies related to economic growth and development were discussed and debated threadbare. Nehru discussed and debated these issues with his party colleagues and the chief ministers of all the states. His reliance on theoreticians brought about an intellectual element into this debate. He endorsed the idea that the fallout of the policies at almost every stage of development may necessitate brainstorming a debate within as well as outside the government. The experts on growth models and development regularly visited the Planning Commission. Quite often, Nehru himself called upon national and international experts for debate on these issues.[13] The press was used as a forum for discussion and debate. The ideas of a cross section of experts in the field of economics and statistics as well as politicians and social workers may have induced Nehru to adopt planning for economic development in 1950. Concurring with them, Nehru, in all likelihood, was merely obeying the conventional wisdom of his time. He never held a dogmatic approach on planning. He was well aware about its fault lines. When the First Plan was under preparation, he observed that 'it is not good to have a theoretical plan and not implement it'.

Was the introduction of Five Year Plans a mistake? It is natural that the state takes the responsibility to ensure food, clothing, shelter, education, and health care services to people at large. When the country is mired in poverty and hunger, the state ideally has to take a lead role in meeting these essential needs of the people because the private sector lacks the requisite resources (mainly investment) and capacity (technological know-how) to deliver these services. The state can perform this job by directly engaging in economic activities. It makes state intervention through planning an essential prerequisite for improving the living standard of the population.

The importance of planning in India fluctuated with the capability and seriousness of the members of the Planning Commission. There is no doubt that Nehru took his position as chairman of the Planning Commission seriously, and devoted adequate time and energy for planning. If the Planning Commission insiders are to be believed, Nehru timed the big bang for economic upliftment in the Third Plan and drafted its 'introduction'. It shows how deeply he was engrossed with the task of planning.

Rural Development

When planning for economic development began in 1951, the quality of life in villages was poor, and the villagers faced poverty and starvation even at the best of times. The near-primitive state of the rural economy could be visualized from the fact that even until the early 1970s, hunting was officially counted as one of the means of income generation.

It was Nehru's view that unless enough attention was paid to the rural areas, and they were brought up to a certain level of development, the urban and semi-urban areas would be weighed down by them. The ideas of rural development conceptualized by Mahatma Gandhi were integrated into the planning model so as to transform a largely traditional population into modern agricultural and industrial community. It would, however, be naive to suggest that Nehru totally followed the ideas of Mahatma Gandhi in this regard.[14] Nehru considered Mahatma Gandhi as the leading light but held his own views in the affairs of economics and politics, even if it was at the risk of crossing the perimeters delineated by Gandhian ideas and thoughts.

The rural development strategy in the 1950s relied squarely on increasing agricultural production and productivity. The centrepiece of this strategy was to end the isolation of the countryside—a legacy of the colonial rule—and to bring it to the level of cities and towns, to a single coherent economy. The strategy had three main foundations: (a) restructuring of land ownership by an extensive programme of land reforms; (b) improvement of economic and social life of rural population through the CDP; and (c) implementation of rural development programmes through the Panchayati Raj Institutions (PRIs).

Land is a major asset in rural areas. Its distribution was lopsided and highly unequal. A large section of the rural population was landless. A long chain of intermediaries existed between peasant producers and big landlords. The idea of changing the face of the rural economy depended a great deal on redistribution of land from the landed to the landless through land reforms. Land reform was necessary to create the requisite economic, social, and institutional framework essential for agricultural development.

Providing ownership rights of land (through land reform) could empower the landless agricultural workers, among whom the incidence of poverty is far greater than in other occupations. Land reform is necessary to empower the socially disadvantaged classes, such as the Scheduled Castes and the Scheduled Tribes, who, being landless, are among the poorest and survive typically by selling their labour. The redistribution of land from the landed to the landless, as many studies suggest, can raise agricultural production and productivity, and thereby contribute to increase in income and reduction in absolute poverty in rural areas.

In order to ensure an equitable distribution of land, the land reform legislations were taken up with great earnestness after Independence. The federal structure of the administration makes land a state subject and, as a result, the laws related to land reform are to be enacted and implemented by the state governments. The policy directions came from the central government. The legislations were framed in the

1950s with a focus on: (*a*) abolition of intermediaries; (*b*) transferring ownership rights to farmers; (*c*) consolidation of holdings; (*d*) rights and security of tenure of tenants; (*e*) providing minimum wages to agricultural labourers; and (*f*) imposing ceiling on land ownership.

It is axiomatic that land reform destroys the economic and social might of the rural elite who wield their authority and power in society through possession of agricultural land. The land reform in India relied on democratic rules of governance, which had been established by then. The lands were taken away from the landlords after paying appropriate compensation.

Unfortunately, in the prevailing social and political circumstances, the landlords were able to circumvent the land reform laws and retained ownership or effective control on most of the land, relinquishing largely the unproductive or inferior land tracts. The administrative apparatus of the state governments was not equipped to handle large-scale operations involving identification of the excess land and allotting them to the landless. In many cases, land acquisitions were disputed, with cases piled up in courts. The land reform of the 1950s and 1960s could not correct the polarization of land ownership in any substantial manner and was unable to transform the land–peasant relationship that used to exist in the British period. The state failed to redistribute land to the landless in the manner and form it was expected. In consequence, the labourer, as before, remained alienated from the land and, in turn, from the process of cultivation.

The CDP was initiated in 1952 to improve the socio-economic conditions in rural areas. It focused on small-scale and cottage industries so that agricultural work force could be shifted to industry. It embodied a broad-based strategy to meet the basic welfare needs of the people, enshrined in the Karachi Resolution of 1931.

By the mid-1950s, there was widespread apprehension about the usefulness of the CDP. The prime reason was agriculture, and specifically food production. The increase in agricultural production in the 1950s was not satisfactory. Although weather was unfavourable, the failure of agriculture to meet the growing consumption demand was taken to be synonymous with the failure of the CDP. Four evaluation reports in a row, the third to the sixth, prepared by the Programme Evaluation Organization (PEO) of the Planning Commission made this clear by 1955, when the people were in search of a mark of the CDP in agriculture. Quite naturally, the CDP came under scrutiny. Nehru was not spared either. His approach to rural development came up for censure essentially because of his anglicized upbringing and origin in the top echelons of the society whose ideas about the hard realities of daily life faced by the rural folk could at best be ephemeral. It was forgotten that he spent considerable time among the peasants in the heat and dust of Indian villages.

In order to review the workings of the CDP, the central government appointed a committee in January 1957 under the chairmanship of Balwantrai Mehta, a noted Gandhian renowned for his scholarly attributes. The committee singled out excessive reliance on bureaucracy to implement rural development programmes as the principal reason behind the failure of the CDP. It suggested a three-tier local self-government at the village, block, and district levels elected on the basis of universal adult franchise under the Panchayati Raj so as to make the villages self-sufficient. Panchayati Raj was inaugurated by Nehru on 2 October 1959. It became a typical Western liberal democratic solution to India's local government problem, under which the administrative authorities are made accountable to elected representatives of the people in the village. It endured for the next three decades until the government decided to redefine the role and function of the Panchayati Raj in the late 1980s.

Political Views

Was Nehru a communist, a socialist, or a nationalist? Can there be a definite answer? As the president of the Indian National Congress in 1929 (Lahore Congress) and again in 1936 (Lucknow session of the Congress), Nehru stated that he did not love communism in any shape or form. He did not believe in communism as an ideal of society and had fundamental ideological differences with the communists, whether they are from home or abroad.

Nehru's idea of socialism is not an extension of, or drawn from, communism. It is different from the Marxian concept of socialism or the kind of socialism advocated or preached by the Marxists in the 1920s and 1930s. At the Lucknow session of the Congress (1936), Nehru stated: 'I am convinced that the only key to the solution of the world's problems and of India's problems lies in socialism, and when I use this word I do so not in a vague humanitarian way but in the scientific, economic sense.' The persecution of political leaders in the Soviet Union by Joseph Stalin in the early 1930s did not seem to interfere with Nehru's idea on socialism as he stated in Lucknow: 'Much has happened in the Soviet Union which has pained me greatly and with which I disagree.' But he does not seem to be disenchanted with the economic policies pursued in the Soviet Union, as he said: 'I look upon that great and fascinating unfolding of a new order and a new civilization as the most promising feature of our dismal age. If the future is full of hope it is largely because of Soviet Russia and what it has done, and I am convinced that, if some world catastrophe does not intervene, this new civilization will spread to other lands and put an end to wars and conflicts which capitalism feeds.'[15]

Socialism, according to Nehru, is something even more than an economic doctrine. He looked at socialism as an inevitable step to social and economic change when he said: 'I see no way of ending the poverty, the vast unemployment, the degradation and subjection of the Indian people except through socialism. That involves vast and revolutionary changes in our political and social structure, the ending of vested interests in land and industry, as well as the feudal and autocratic Indian States system.'[16]

The bottom line is that Nehru was never a communist. He never regarded Marxism as a holy doctrine. He was a socialist only up to a point as he cherished the idea of equity. Over and above, he was a nationalist, being involved with a nationalist organization like the Indian National Congress.

In his prime ministerial years, Nehru was often found to enunciate certain aspects of economic theories of socialism as the solution to India's problem of unemployment and poverty, more or less in line with the ideas he conceived of in the mid-1930s. Before launching the Second Five Year Plan, the government pledged for a socialistic pattern of society. However, it cannot be even remotely equated with the Marxian concept of socialism practised in the Soviet Union. That Nehru did not want to follow and indeed did not follow the socialist lines of the Soviet Union is clear from the institutionalization of democracy based on adult franchise in India. Besides, the application of the mixed economy principle to reach the goal of a socialistic pattern of society is quite different from the kind of socialism espoused in the Soviet Union. Socialism in the Marxian sense was never an option in India after Independence. It is by design, and not incidental, that the word 'socialist' (and secular) was not included in the Indian Constitution in 1950. These two phrases were inserted in the Preamble to the Constitution a quarter of a century later, in 1976, through the 42nd amendment.

On Democracy

Democracy is at the heart of India's political philosophy. Since Independence, India has been gifted with a functioning democracy. A few countries in Asia and Africa gained independence after the Second World War and began their journey with democracy, but faltered at some point and came under authoritarian rule or military dictatorship. India remained the sole exception.

India's vibrant democracy with its parliamentary form of government was supported by a well-organized bureaucracy. These bind the economy and the country into one unit. The institutions to support the democratic system were created under the watchful eyes of Jawaharlal Nehru. His theoretic clarity and passionate commitment to democracy made it possible to accomplish this job despite insufficient resources and lack of technically qualified manpower. That many of these institutions are still playing a formidable role in the democratic process gives an idea about his foresight.

The relationship between the armed forces and civil administration has plagued the developing countries in Asia and Africa. In India, a section of the population wanted an active role for the army in economic development, mostly citing reasons of efficiency and discipline. Nehru differed from this idea completely, and developed an administrative structure insulating the civil administration from the armed forces. The army was placed under overall supervision of civil authorities.

As early as 1931, Mahatma Gandhi wrote: 'I am wedded to adult suffrage. Adult suffrage is necessary for more reasons than one.'[17] Then, immediately before Independence, he again harped on the issue: 'I swear by the franchise of all adults, males and females, above the age of twenty-one or even eighteen.'[18] Going by Gandhi's decision, India accepted universal adult franchise when a large number of people were illiterate and very little to no information on political or economic issues reached them (as per the 1951 Census, the literacy rate was 27.2 per cent for males and 8.9 per cent for females). India accepted universal adult franchise as a tool to ensure political equality, and also to ensure economic and social equality.[19] The idea that people cannot be made party to the democratic process in the absence of voting rights lies at the root of universal adult suffrage in India.

The election to the Parliament (Lok Sabha) and the State Legislative Assemblies is central to the democratic governance. The first general election was conducted from October 1951 to February 1952. It was an arduous task. Gathering the names of the electors with their age, sex, and address—an essential job to prepare electoral rolls—proved to be formidable. An example would suffice. Women had no identity except being the wife or mother of someone. They were known through their husbands or children rather than their first names. Unmarried women en bloc were reluctant to enter their name in the electoral roll, for their age would be disclosed. The minimum age of voting was 21 years at that time. It was a social stigma for the women (more than for her family) to remain unmarried until 21. However, the Election Commission showed determination and prepared the electoral rolls.

In the run-up to the first general election, the government was virtually clueless about the manner in which a largely rural and illiterate electorate would exercise their franchise. The anxiety was: would the people show interest in the election and turn up to the polling station to cast their vote? There were no precedents or yardsticks available then.

As it turned out, people took an interest in the election. More than half of the 173.2 million electorate turned up to vote. Contrary to general expectations, the turnout in rural areas exceeded that in urban. Nehru termed the high turnout as a visible expression of people's interest in the electoral process. It shaped the politics of the country.[20]

Nehru stayed at the centre-point of the country's democratic ideals and values. Nirad C. Chaudhuri, an eminent intellectual, has written (in the second part of his autobiography)[21] presciently about the inculcation of ideals and values maintained by Nehru, which was required at the formative stage of India's democratic polity. It comes from a person who is well-recognized at the international level, and yet not espoused in the same way by his fellow Indians ostensibly as his writings are full of scorn for India and what is Indian, and eulogize the British. Chaudhuri is eloquent in his praise for Nehru. He says that Nehru possessed some of the sterling qualities which were essential to lay the foundations of democracy when the economy was exclusively rural and the population was largely illiterate. He also mentions Nehru's unwavering support for free press, which has been a maxim for India's democratic polity. Nehru frequently mentioned that in olden days India enjoyed a tremendous amount of freedom of thought and writing, and there was freedom of conscience. In Europe, however, such freedom is only of recent origin. It is probable that the idea of the free press in India is a logical extension of its past heritage.

The finalization of the Constitution of India is a mark of Nehru's democratic credentials. Dipankar Gupta, a renowned sociologist and former professor of New Delhi's Jawaharlal Nehru University, despite finding a thousand faults with Nehru, acknowledges the role he played in keeping India together in the most critical years after Independence. Citing Nehru's tirade against the practice of untouchability, the support for minority rights, and the abolition of feudal privileges, Gupta states that India was a young Republic in 1950, but it looked, talked and walked like a seasoned democratic nation-state. True, he was not alone in this, but as prime minister it was Nehru, more than anybody else, who fleshed out the most singular aspects of our Constitution. It would have been the easiest thing to renege on them given the tensions and uncertainties India faced in the early post-Independence years, but Nehru remained firm.

The idea that a totalitarian form of government could speed up the pace of growth and development was aired in the early days of Independence. However, Nehru was never in doubt about the essentiality of democracy. He was aware that in a democratic set-up, changes in economic and social arena may take a little more time, but in the long run it becomes lasting.

On Religion

Nehru was a Hindu by birth and never renounced his religion. As the prime minister of India, he assiduously separated religion from the functioning of the state. He tried to dissuade political leaders holding high offices from publicly displaying their association with religious faiths and institutions. When Rajendra Prasad, the president of India, went to inaugurate the newly built Somnath Temple in Gujarat in 1951, Nehru opposed vehemently.

It appears that Nehru's views on religion were influenced by the practice of Christianity in Europe. It was not out of choice but due to differences in the Church that a section of the believers left England to settle in America. The journey in those days was perilous and the people resorted to such an adventurous path only to escape from the orthodoxy of the manner in which religion was being pursued in England. On matters related to application of science, the Church in Europe often behaved in a regressive manner. Nehru was deeply moved by the ignorance of the Church about many new and novel ideas and its refusal to accept new knowledge and information that came its way.

Nehru recognized and accepted the immense power of religion to influence the masses. In his autobiography, he was candid about the demonstration of the power of religion citing the example of the Kumbh Mela, where millions of devotees converge once every 12 years for a holy bath in the Sangam, which is the confluence of three rivers— the Ganga, the Yamuna, and the mythical Saraswati. He discovered with astonishment, and reverence, that there was no announcement, no advertisement, and no publicity campaign to attend this event, except that there is a mention in the almanac, and that drives millions of people from all over the country to converge to the Sangam. There must be some power in religion which makes people flock towards the Sangam. This was his impression of the Kumbh Mela in the 1930s. Throughout the 1920s, Nehru toured the rural areas of Uttar Pradesh to organize the hapless peasants, who literally had nothing but the miseries of poverty and hunger. It was extremely difficult to bring them to a meeting, far more difficult to engage them in a discussion about the hardship they faced. The same people would attend the religious rituals voluntarily. This is the power of religion.

The Indian social structure, on the whole, was graded along caste lines. It was common for the people at the bottom of the caste hierarchy to be exploited and as Nehru said, '[T]hey had to bear the weight of all those at the top.'[22] The people at the top took care to perpetuate the caste system, which, in turn, was perpetuated by religion. Nehru firmly believed that religion was used as a tool to keep the people at the bottom of the caste hierarchy in perpetual poverty. Religion seemed to give a permanent and even an honoured place to poverty and misery.

Secularism, according to Nehru, was not something that was opposed to religion. The state should honour all faiths equally and give them equal opportunities. The state should not allow itself to be attached to one faith or religion, which then becomes the state religion. In his famous 'Tryst with Destiny' speech delivered on the midnight of 14–15 August 1947, Nehru made it clear: 'All of us, to whatever religion we may belong are equally the children of India with equal rights, privileges and obligations.' He stated in unequivocal terms that religion cannot be the basis on which the state can be founded. Though the idea that independent India would not be a Hindu state and that the government would be elected by the people's representative rather than any religious groups or communities originally goes to Mahatma Gandhi, to bring this into fruition was not a small issue after Partition in 1947, and particularly the communal violence and bloodbath that preceded and followed it.

On Education

Nehru faced loud protests for some of his ideas on education. Several institutions of international excellence created at his initiative after Independence were drubbed as elitist. The Indian Institute of Technology (IIT) is a prominent example.

It may sound strange that India's first IIT (IIT Kharagpur) was born in a gaol—the Hijli Detention Camp in Midnapore district of West Bengal. Nehru delivered the first convocation address of IIT Kharagpur in April 1956. There he stated: 'Here in the place of that Hijli Detention Camp stands this fine monument of India today representing India's urges, India's future in the making. This picture seems to me symbolical of the changes that are coming to India.'[23]

The central universities created after Independence were the result of a courageous decision in view of the financial stringency faced at that time by the government. Nehru associated himself with the programmes of these universities and used to spend considerable time and energy in their development. The case of Viswa-Bharati University at Santiniketan can be an example. Rabindranath Tagore, the Noble Laureate, had built the Viswa-Bharati University brick by brick. In February 1940, an ageing Tagore, unable to arrange the sinews required to run the Viswa-Bharati requested Mahatma Gandhi to accept the institution under his protection. In the early 1950s, Viswa-Bharati was converted into a central university. As the chancellor of the university, Nehru never missed its convocation. This is worth mentioning because the journey from Delhi to Santiniketan (located in the Birbhum district of West Bengal) was not smooth in the 1950s.

***

Indian political leaders while reconstructing the country after Independence were, as Nehru said, 'functioning on the edge of history' and at the same time engaged in 'the processes of making history'. Precisely for this reason, it is all the more necessary to take a look at the measures taken by Nehru in the context of the socio-economic situation prevailing then, rather than through the yardsticks of the present day.

In a speech at the meeting of the All India Congress Committee (AICC) in Wardha on 15 January 1942, Mahatma Gandhi announced that Jawaharlal Nehru would be his political heir. This sealed the doubts about Nehru's ascendency to the post of prime minister in the event of India gaining independence. Nehru was an undisputed leader throughout the 17 years of his prime ministership. In the late 1950s and early 1960s, a series of studies were conducted on a single issue: who would be the prime minister after Nehru. Welles Hangen, an American journalist (then posted in India), wrote a book titled *After Nehru, Who?*. Assessing their professional competence and a few other factors, Hangen zeroed in on eight persons as Nehru's potential heir. Nehru's successor, Lal Bahadur Shastri, and Shastri's successor, Indira Gandhi, were among these eight persons. Morarji

Desai, among these eight, became prime minister in 1977. Another person in this list also came close to the post of prime minister but could not make it finally. Y.B. Chavan was invited by the president to form the government in 1979. Being unable to muster necessary support, he declined the offer.

Nehru's first Cabinet had 14 members. Five of them were not from the Indian National Congress. They are: B. R. Ambedkar, S. P. Mookerjee, John Mathai, C. H. Bhabha, and Shanmukham Chetty. All of them, particularly Ambedkar and Mookerjee, were fierce critics of the policies of the Congress Party. Yet, they carried on well with Nehru. It is an eloquent exposition of Nehru's multifaceted personality and gentle dignity which proved quite useful to create an environment of cooperation at that nascent stage of development.

Mookerjee resigned from Nehru's Cabinet in April 1950 and Ambedkar in September 1951. These resignations were on account of their differences on specific policy issues and in no way connected with the day-to-day functioning of the government. Mookerjee resigned in protest against the Nehru–Liaquat Pact signed by the prime ministers of India and Pakistan on issues related to minority populations in the two countries. Frustrated by his failed attempts to legislate the Hindu Code Bill, Ambedkar resigned with the full knowledge that the subject was debatable and Nehru needed some more time to convince his colleagues in the Indian National Congress.

Mookerjee's resignation had a wider canvas, based on the shaping of the Hindu–Muslim equation in independent India. Nehru was not specifically responsible for this, but he has often been blamed for the resignation of Ambedkar.

It is no secret that for at least two decades (the 1930s and 1940s) Ambedkar had been a bitter critic of the Indian National Congress, and especially of Mahatma Gandhi. In spite of this, Gandhi persuaded the Congress to invite Ambedkar to join Nehru's Cabinet so that he himself could frame the rules for the abolition of untouchability and decide the ways and means for the upliftment of those described till then as Untouchables. Thus, Ambedkar became the law minister of India and performed this job. The practice of untouchability was abolished in 1950, and the Untouchables came to be known as Scheduled Castes. A set of positive discriminatory stances, such as reservation of seats in the Parliament and State Legislative Assemblies and jobs in the central and state governments were introduced for their empowerment.

After working in close association with Nehru for more than four years, Ambedkar resigned on 27 September 1951. Then, in a 'personal statement in explanation of his resignation' in the Parliament on 10 October 1951, he presented a list of complaints, which showed that the Hindu Code Bill was not the only issue that triggered his resignation from the Cabinet. It is true that some of the complaints were against the government, and one of them indeed related to Nehru. Ambedkar felt that the law ministry was too small a world for him and wanted additional responsibilities. This would not have been unusual for a brilliant and hard-working person like him. Nehru had promised him the planning ministry. That did not materialize until his resignation as the concept of planning for industrialization was still in its embryonic stage.

Ambedkar perhaps overlooked Nehru's assurance that he would ensure the passage of the Hindu Code Bill after the elections to Parliament and State Legislative Assemblies were over. Subsequently, the Hindu Code Bill originally drafted by Ambedkar as the law minister was decomposed into four bills separating the issues related to (*a*) marriage; (*b*) succession; (*c*) minority and guardianship; and (*d*) adoptions and maintenance, and passed by the Parliament in 1955 and 1956.

That Nehru imposed his ideas of growth and development on the state governments is more of a myth than reality. The chief ministers of the states, such as Srikrishna Sinha in Bihar, Morarji Desai in Bombay, Ravi Shankar Shukla in Madhya Pradesh, Nabakrushna Chaudhuri in Odisha, Bhimsen Sachar in Punjab (Patiala and East Punjab States Union), Govind Ballabh Pant in Uttar Pradesh (United Provinces), K. Hanumanthaiah in Mysore (Karnataka), and B. C. Roy in West Bengal, to name a few, were men of great virtue and impeccable integrity, had their own minds, and were capable of pronouncing judgements without fear or favour, keeping the interest of the nation uppermost in mind. They depended on Nehru as much as Nehru depended on them. That was a different time, when the home minister of a state would not hesitate to confront the prime minister on issues of Constitutional propriety.[24]

As the growth rate of the Indian economy moved on to a higher trajectory in the years of economic reform (1992–2011), Nehru again came into the news, though for all the wrong reasons. The high growth rate in these years brought out the memories of low growth of the first four decades of planning (1951–90), the reasons for which are believed to be rooted in state control on economic activities. The low growth rate in 1951–90 is treated as the necessary condition and the high growth rate in 1992–2011 as the sufficient condition to demonstrate that the policies of growth and development pursued by Nehru through planning were not suitable, if not outright erroneous. Much has been written and talked about in denunciation of the policies pursued by Nehru, largely by comparing the economic growth during the first four decades of planning (1951–90) with that of the two decades of economic reforms (1992–2011). This has dominated the way, ignoring the well-known dictum that it is not wise to judge the past from the standards of the present. It would be inappropriate to judge Nehru from the prism of the market-led development of recent times. The suitability and appropriateness of planning in India's economic growth and development have to be judged from the circumstances prevailing in the late 1940s and the early 1950s.

Notes

1. Seventh Meeting of the NDC, 1–2 May 1956, 'Summary Record of Discussions of the National Development Council (NDC) Meetings: Five Decades of Nation Building (Fifty NDC Meetings)', Vol. I, p. 145, Government of India, Planning Commission, 2005.
2. Seventh Meeting of the NDC, 1–2 May 1956, 'Summary Record of Discussions of the National Development Council (NDC) Meetings: Five Decades of Nation Building (Fifty NDC Meetings)', Vol. I, p. 145, Government of India, Planning Commission, 2005.
3. The disillusionment came primarily from the low growth rate of 2.8 per cent per year realized in the Third Plan and 3.4 per cent per year in the Fourth Plan. In comparison, the average growth rate of the three years of annual plans of 1966–67 to 1968–69 was 3.9 per cent per year. As the growth rate in the Third and Fourth Plans turned out to be lower than that in the annual plans, some, though in a lighter vein, doubted the efficacy of planning in maximizing growth rate. The insinuation is that as the growth rate without planning (that is, in the annual plan years)

becomes higher than under planning (for example in Third and Fourth Plans) there is perhaps little justification for planning if a higher growth rate is the objective to achieve.

4. Twenty-Fifth Meeting of the NDC, 17–18 May 1968, 'Summary Record of Discussions of the National Development Council (NDC) Meetings: Five Decades of Nation Building (Fifty NDC Meetings)', Vol. II, page 531. Government of India, Planning Commission, 2005.

5. Thirty-Second Meeting of the NDC, 18–19 March 1978, 'Summary Record of Discussions of the National Development Council (NDC) Meetings: Five Decades of Nation Building (Fifty NDC Meetings)', Vol. III, page 235. Government of India, Planning Commission, 2005.

6. M. N. Roy, or Manabendra Nath Roy, an acclaimed intellectual and a founder-member of the First International, was named Narendra Nath Bhattacharyya by his parents. He used more than a dozen pseudonyms, the last being M. N. Roy. Impressed with Roy's ideas and abilities, Lenin engaged him for organizing communist parties in several countries. However, Joseph Stalin did not like Roy and expelled him from the International. In direct consequence, Roy was expelled from the Communist Party of India, despite claiming to be its founder. Soon after, Roy became disillusioned with communism and branched out to a philosophy known as radical humanism, which too represents leftist forces.

7. The Bombay Plan was titled 'A Brief Memorandum Outlining a Plan of Economic Development for India'. It was prepared by J. R. D. Tata, G. D. Birla, Purushottamdas Thakurdas, Lala Shri Ram, Ardeshir Dalal, A. D. Shroff, and Kasturbhai Lalbhai.

8. Jawaharlal Nehru, *Glimpses of World History*, Letter No. 97, 26 September 1932, Penguin Books India, 2004, p. 401.

9. Third Meeting of the NDC, 9–10 November 1954, 'Summary Record of Discussions of the National Development Council (NDC) Meetings: Five Decades of Nation Building (Fifty NDC Meetings)', Vol. 1, p. 23, Government of India, Planning Commission, 2005.

10. War Communism was principally founded on the policy of withering away of the private enterprises by nationalizing industries which were in private hands and requisitioning food grain from the peasantry, wielding brute state power. In order to come out of the economic maelstrom triggered by the policies of War Communism, the NEP outlined several measures to associate farmers and businessmen in the management of the economy.

11. Nehru's assessment of the first two Five Year Plans of the Soviet Union can be summed up as follows. The First Plan, in general, was a success,

though it failed in particular aspects, such as in regard to the quality of goods produced. There was emphasis on heavy industry, but also a shortage of consumption goods. However, planning laid the foundations of future progress by industrializing Russia and collectivizing its agriculture. The Second Plan changed the emphasis from heavy to light industry. It intended to produce more of consumers goods and made concerted efforts to get rid of the deficiencies of the First Plan. Though planning was not a smooth affair, the face of the Soviet Union changed within a decade, 1928–37, which covers the first two Five Year Plans ('Postscript', dated 14 November 1938, *Glimpses of World History*, Jawaharlal Nehru, Penguin Books India, 2004, pp. 1122–3).

12. Jawaharlal Nehru, *Glimpses of World History*, Letter No. 193, August 6, 1933, Jawaharlal Nehru Memorial Fund and Oxford University Press, 1998, p. 933.

13. Bibek Debroy mentions how such mass-scale invitation created embarrassment for the government. Nehru once requested the president of the USA to send an expert. The president sent Milton Friedman, an outright champion of market economy internationally recognized for his strong views against planning and state control. Obviously, the Planning Commission officials were not comfortable with his suggestions and brought the matter to Nehru's notice. Nehru then wrote a letter to the US president saying that he wanted an expert to help India for planning, and the person the president had sent wanted India to abandon planning!

14. Mahatma Gandhi recorded his ideas on development in a booklet titled 'Hind Swaraj' (1910). In this, Gandhi raised development issues in the form of questions and answered himself. On the development of villages, he said that arrangements had to be made for the villagers to stay in the villages, and not in the cities. It was not possible to accommodate the villagers in the cities. Even if it was, it would not have been possible for them to live peacefully.

15. Jawaharlal Nehru, 'Presidential Address to the Indian National Congress', Lucknow, 1936, in *Report of the 49th Session of the Indian National Congress Held at Lucknow in April 1936*, published by The General Secretary, All India Congress Committee, Allahabad. Printed at the Oudh Printing Works, Lucknow, by Dr. Murari Lal, General Secretary, Reception Committee of the 49th Session of the Indian National Congress, p. 20.

16. Jawaharlal Nehru, 'Presidential Address to the Indian National Congress', Lucknow, 1936.

17. *Young India*, 8 October 1931.

18. *Harijan*, 2 March 1947.

19. A comparison of the Indian situation with England may be worthwhile here. The Parliament in England was constituted after the Glorious Revolution in 1688. For a long time it was used by aristocrats, the landowning class, rich merchants, and bishops. The laws were made to protect the rights and privileges for them. Seats in the Parliament were traded and there was a great deal of bribery. Until 1800 AD, pocket boroughs (that is, constituencies with just a few electors and which are under someone's control) were in plenty. Throughout the eighteenth and the nineteenth centuries, a vast majority of the population in England did not have voting rights. In contrast, all Indians—men and women, literate and illiterate—were granted voting rights very soon after Independence. The women in England were granted voting rights 240 years after their Parliament was established and the women in the USA 144 years after it became independent.

20. In the first general election, the Indian National Congress secured an absolute majority in the Lok Sabha but failed to get the majority in the Legislative Assemblies of three states, namely PEPSU (Patiala and East Punjab States Union), Madras, and Travancore–Cochin. The election threw surprises with the defeat of incumbent chief ministers in Madras, Rajasthan, and Madhya Bharat.

21. *Thy Hand, Great Anarch! India, 1921–1952*, Addison-Wesley Publishing Company, INC, Reading, PA, 1987.

22. Jawaharlal Nehru, *Glimpses of World History*, Letter No. 45, May 14, 1932, Jawaharlal Nehru Memorial Fund and Oxford University Press, 1998, p. 132.

23. Quoted in the 57th Annual Convocation Address delivered by Manmohan Singh, Prime Minister of India at IIT Kharagpur on 22 August 2011.

24. The Government of West Bengal banned the Communist Party of India in the state in the wake of its failed armed rebellion in 1948 and took a number of its members into custody. On the modalities of tackling the insurgency, Nehru maintained that communism is a faith and it cannot be resisted by arms. The imprisoned should rather be released. Kiran Shankar Roy, then home minister of West Bengal, held his ground and the communist party members were not released from detention.

6

Economic Reform and Inclusive Growth

I ndia's tryst with planning placing the state at the helm of economic activities virtually ended in July 1991 when the economic reform and liberalization measures were initiated. It proved to be a seismic change in economic policies with the opening up of the Indian economy to the world, heralding in a new strategy of growth and development. The reform measures changed India's economic landscape forever.

Four Five Year Plans, the Eighth to the Eleventh, were implemented during the two decades of economic reform, 1991–2011. The successive governments in these two decades pursued policies of economic reform and liberalization.

Road to Crisis: November 1989 to June 1991

In several ways the Seventh Plan (1985–90) can be termed as excellent for the Indian economy. (This has been discussed in some detail in the second section of Chapter 4.) The economic growth rate in the Plan (5.7 per cent per year) was impressive by contemporary standards. It was higher than any of the previous Five Year Plans implemented during the three and a half decades, 1951–85. Towards the closing months of the Seventh Plan, India witnessed a general election (in November 1989). The performance of the economy rarely has a bearing on the election results in India, and non-economic issues usually take precedence. Towards the latter half of the Seventh Plan surfaced what is known as the 'Bofors case', which is about an alleged financial impropriety in the procurement of Howitzer guns for the Indian Army from a Swedish firm (Bofors). The Swedish Radio reported that Bofors paid an illegal commission to Indian politicians and defence officials to finalize the deal. The opposition political parties in India, aided by the print and electronic media, launched a case of corruption against the government. The results of the Parliamentary elections in November 1989, in all probability, were swayed by the sustained campaign on the Bofors issue. Riding on this wave a new government came to power in the wake of this election.[1]

The months following the general election in 1989 were not particularly good for the Indian economy. There was a minority government in power, supported by an array of political parties ranging from the extreme right to the extreme left. Thus, it is no wonder that the government lasted less than a year. Another general election was held in May–June 1991. The Indian economy by then had entered into a trouble zone. The economic crisis was triggered by a variety of factors.

In August 1990, Iraq invaded Kuwait. It had a twin impact on the Indian economy. First, the inflow of remittances from countries in the Persian Gulf was affected as the Indians working there either lost their jobs or returned home for safety and security. Second, the international price of crude oil increased drastically, intensifying the strains on an already weak fiscal situation. India was in the midst of a severe fiscal crisis, and was on the verge of defaulting on international debt repayment, which was a rare situation as the country's reputation as a reliable debtor was never at stake despite its abject poverty and low level of income.

The economic problems were exacerbated as the minority government decided to implement the recommendations of the Mandal Commission, which related to the reservation of government jobs and seats in educational institutions to some of the backward classes of the population, known as Other Backward Classes (OBCs). This commission was constituted in 1978 under the chairmanship of B. P. Mandal, and was mandated to identify the socially or educationally backward sections of the population. The commission used literacy rate, size of landholding, and access to drinking water to determine backwardness, and submitted its report in December 1980. Due to the inappropriate choice of indicators, and possibly due to its political impact, governments with a strong majority in the Parliament throughout the 1980s did not take a decision on this issue. Yet, a minority government, against the express wishes of several political parties that supported it, decided to accept the recommendations of the Mandal Commission in August 1990. It led to large-scale violence and created a law and order problem.

A weak economy and the troubled political atmosphere shook international confidence in India's economic viability. The IMF ignored India's request for a loan to tide over the fiscal crisis. India was compelled to pledge its gold stocks at the Bank of England and the Union Bank of Switzerland to borrow so as to avoid default in payment of international loans.[2]

In June–July 1991, the economic situation turned bleak. Price inflation, which began to accelerate in 1990, was high, with headline inflation (measured through the WPI) hitting a peak level of 16.7 per cent in August 1991. The balance of payments reached rock bottom with the foreign currency assets at the end of June 1991 barely proving to be enough to finance two weeks of imports. Foreign commercial banks had stopped lending to India. Non-resident Indians began to withdraw their deposits. Industrial growth was affected by a massive import squeeze, forced by scarcity of foreign exchange. The growth rate of the economy decelerated sharply to 1.4 per cent in 1991–92 from 5.3 per cent in the previous year. Industrial growth declined by 0.1 per cent in 1991–92.

It was at the height of this major economic and political crisis that the process of economic reform and liberalization was initiated by a newly elected government, which came to power in the wake of the general election in May–June 1991.

Approach to Economic Reform

In June 1991, the government announced its intention to pursue economic reform and liberalization measures. This carried the message that India was ready to swim with the waves of the international economy. In July 1991, the finance minister spelt out the reform measures in the annual budget (of the central government) to the Parliament (Lok Sabha). It was an attempt to free the Indian economy from the shackles of state control and regimentation, and allow economic forces to play their role in growth and development. This changed the language and approach of management of the Indian economy forever.

Two specific features of the reform process in India may be noted to understand its acceptability and application in the Indian economy. First, in the two decades of economic reform, political parties with widely differing ideologies governed the country. Their views were not similar on many economic and political issues and they professed diverse faiths. Despite this, the successive governments carried on with the reform measures. The moot point is that the changes in governments in no way affected the economic policymaking during the two decades of economic reform, though it should be accepted in all fairness that the process of carrying out the reform programmes often varied. Second, when in opposition, the political parties opposed the reform tooth and nail; yet, they carried on with the same reform measures when in power. Such a dual approach of the political parties to reform measures was generally guided by two factors. First, the reform programmes were essential to accelerate the pace of growth and development. This compelled the political parties to pursue the reform measures when in power. Second, in the short run, many of the measures pertaining to economic reform appeared to be, and some of them indeed were, detrimental to the interests of a specific section of the society or a particular income class of the population. In a democratic set-up such as India, the opinions of the disadvantaged group mattered, whether they were located in the organized or the unorganized sector. No political party can risk a measure that has the potential to alienate it from the people. This made the implementation of the reform programmes in India somewhat measured.

It is believed that Prime Minister Narasimha Rao, who decided to launch the economic reform measures, did not have a policy of his own either to preach or practice. He was neither a protagonist of the IMF–World Bank theme of market-driven growth nor a votary of state control on economic activities that is associated with socialism as preached and practised by the Indian National Congress since the mid-1950s. The prime minister wanted a technical expert outside the political arena to fill the post of finance minister to execute the reform programmes. Manmohan Singh, a rank economist of the government and former secretary of the Ministry of Finance, was identified for this challenging and prestigious assignment.

There was no confusion about the agenda of reform, as these were well laid out. The areas to be covered were systematically defined by the IMF and the World Bank. It may be worthwhile to mention that initially the IMF was not very insistent about the strategy of economic development that its member countries would pursue. The World Bank was largely overseeing the activities of the developing countries and devising strategies for economic growth and development that they might like to pursue. By the early 1980s, the financial position of the less developed countries, and also several middle-income countries (as defined by the World Bank, based on per capita income), became precarious for a variety of reasons. The IMF, which was observing the activities of the World Bank located just across the road (the headquarters of the World Bank are at 1818 H Street and the IMF at 1900 Pennsylvania Avenue, Washington DC), entered the scene as the custodian of the international monetary system. The IMF formulated its own package of economic reform and liberalization measures for developing countries worldwide.

In India, the task of dismantling state control and administering the policies of economic reform, whose hallmark was market mechanism, and replacing the different agents of the government as dominant decision-makers was left to the finance minister. Two issues became relevant in this context: (*a*) the content of the programmes in terms of its dimensions and depth; and (*b*) their sequencing and strategizing at the ground level. These were handled by the administrators in India, keeping in view the ground realities. It required a tremendous effort on the part of Indian officials (administering the reform programmes) to adjust to the reform process so that its impact on the poor and the lower deciles of the population could be contained to a tolerable level, without impinging on the rate of economic growth. The measures were decided in-house at the level of the central ministries, the RBI, and the Planning Commission.

The Reform Measures

The economic reform and liberalization measures initiated in July 1991 can be classified under two principal categories as short-term stabilization policy and long-term economic reforms. The stabilization policy addresses the balance of payments disequilibrium through devaluation, improvement of macroeconomic balance through curtailment of government expenditure, reining in price inflation through management of monetary liquidity, and market liberalization (mainly by way of eliminating subsidies on goods and services, and price control). The long-term economic reform measures were related with deregulation of industry, trade liberalization, removing the protective tariff barrier, privatization of financial institutions and public sector enterprises, privatization of social programmes, and rationalization of the tax system.

The reform measures were synonymous with relaxation or even removal of state control in economic activities, allowing a greater play for market. It set in motion the process of decontrolling and de-bureaucratizing the Indian economy. As the economy gets deregulated and decisions become based on the market, the government no longer remains a silent spectator to the emerging vulnerabilities of the market but intervenes in the market. The intervention is rare, and the aim is to get the most effective result with the least intervention.

The reform process was initiated with the downward adjustment in the exchange rate of the rupee in 1991, a la devaluation of the rupee, first on 1 July and then on 3 July. The adjustment of exchange rate of the Indian rupee on these two days effectively translated into devaluation of little less than 20 per cent against major international currencies. (From 1975 onwards, the rupee was linked with a basket of currencies of the major trading partners, and the terminology 'downward adjustment of the exchange rate of rupee' was coined in place of devaluation.)

There might have been initial inertia for devaluation as it was carried out not in one stroke but in two stages, separated only by a day. In reality, the devaluation of the rupee was a few points more than what was needed, judging the extent of its appreciation vis-à-vis major international currencies, most importantly the US dollar. The devaluation was the first step associated with reform measures, and the quantum of devaluation was enough to instil international confidence in the Indian rupee. It served as a signal to the international community on India's willingness to tread the path of reform. After that, the industrial licensing mechanism, which was a feature of planning since Independence, was dismantled a few hours before the presentation of the annual budget on 24 July 1991, which, as mentioned before, unfolded the reform package.

The abolition of the industrial licensing system is the handiwork of the Ministry of Industry. This is well known. But few would remember that the Ministry of Industry in July 1991 was under the charge of the prime minister. It may not be off the mark to state that the announcement of abolition of industrial licensing from the prime minister helped to gain international confidence about India's commitment to reform. It is perceived that the prime minister retained the industries portfolio with himself so that the industrial licensing policy, which lays down the broad contours of the strategy of industrial development, could be altered in tune with the ideas of exposing the domestic industries to international competition and technology.

The RBI is responsible for exchange rate management. It monitors the development in the financial markets at home and abroad and coordinates its market operations with suitable monetary, regulatory, and other measures. It intervenes in the foreign exchange market and adopts appropriate measures to counter speculative pressure on the Indian rupee and to smooth excessive volatility in exchange rate. The exchange rate management is conducted in such a way that it remains consistent with the macroeconomic fundamentals of the economy. A pragmatic and flexible exchange rate policy based on monetary management, control of fiscal deficit, and short-term external indebtedness have been the key priorities for a sound macroeconomic policy in the Indian context.

Within a few years of the beginning of the process of economic reform, the Indian rupee was made convertible on current account. The move towards convertibility has been gradual and cautious, keeping an eye on a number of factors which include fiscal deficit, money supply, and inflationary situation. It began with partial convertibility (in March 1992), in which all foreign exchange remittances (earned through export of goods and services, or transfer by migrants from their earnings abroad) were converted into rupees using a dual exchange rate. The dual exchange rate stipulated that 40 per cent of the export earnings were evaluated at the official exchange rate and the remaining 60 per cent could be sold freely in the open market or used for import under what was termed as liberalized exchange rate management system (LERMS). Then, in March 1993, the dual exchange rate was changed to a unified exchange rate (INR 31.37 for USD 1). It was market-determined. With this, convertibility of the rupee in current account could be achieved. Thus, the rupee was made freely convertible for trading, but not for investment purposes. It can be treated as a testimony of strength and self-reliance of the Indian economy born out of reform measures.

In 1991, India's customs tariff rates were high in relation to its competitor countries, where the tariffs operated at moderate levels. As part of the reform measures, the general level of customs tariff was lowered and the dispersion of rates reduced. The tariff structure was rationalized by abolishing numerous end-use exemptions and concessions, which were introduced over a period of time with the intention to incentivize certain sectors and areas of the economy to use specific technology in the production process and to ensure an element of equity in income distribution. As a matter of strategy, the tariff rates were lowered gradually over five years so as to allow sufficient time to the domestic industry to be exposed to external competition. The peak level of import duty was lowered from 300 per cent to 150 per cent in the annual budget of 1991. The peak rate was further lowered to 110 per cent in the next year and to 50 per cent within the next five years. Simultaneously, the rates of indirect taxes (central excise duties) on commodities were lowered.

In case of direct taxation, the rates of personal income tax and corporate tax were moderated. The marginal rate of personal income tax was as high as 97.5 per cent in 1973–74 with as many as 11 layers of rates. The rate was lowered to 50 per cent in the mid-1980s and remained unchanged with a four-tier tax structure, when the economic reforms were initiated in 1991. The marginal rate of income tax was lowered to 40 per cent in 1993–94 with a three-tier tax structure. The rates were further lowered in 1998–99 with the marginal rate at 30 per cent. At the same time, the rates of corporate tax were rationalized and rules were laid down to liberalize foreign investment.

A well-developed and efficient financial sector can ensure mobilization of savings and its allocation to productive users as investment funds. This is one of the prerequisites to accelerate the rate of economic growth. It is, therefore, essential that reform in the real sector is matched by financial sector reform. When economic reforms were initiated in 1991, the financial health of the economy was far from being sound. The reform of the financial sector began somewhat later and has been half-hearted, being often plagued by controversies. In actuality, India has not been able to respond to the challenges associated with the development of institutional and regulatory architecture that has to act as a canopy of the financial system.

The reform of the economic system entails restructuring of sectoral interrelations. A number of developing countries which were practising some form of planning earlier pursued the economic reform programmes at one go. In contrast, the reform programmes in India were implemented in a phased manner so that it would be possible for the economy and the people to absorb the shocks and so that they were not forced into a difficult situation.

Impact of Reform Measures

The implementation of the policies of economic reform and liberalization in India has been watched with great interest both within and outside the country. Its outcome at almost every stage has been evaluated by a wide range of organizations and political parties. The Eighth to the Eleventh Plan was formulated and implemented in the two decades of economic reform (1991–2011). The Eighth Plan was formulated under a consistency planning framework with state control on economic activities, but implemented under the aegis of economic reforms. As the reform process was not instantaneous in most cases, the Eighth Plan could be tuned to fit into the overall scheme of reform programmes as they unfolded over time. Several economic parameters in the Eighth Plan were adjusted quickly as the reform process began. The Plan was tailored to these changes though the originally fixed targets were not altered until the mid-term exercises (which usually took place halfway through the Plan), in which the five-yearly targets of the Plan were tweaked on the basis of the performance of the first two years and the assessment of economic and social parameters for the next three years. The three subsequent Five Year Plans under the economic reforms (the Ninth to the Eleventh Plan, covering the years 1997–2012) were formulated and implemented in the environs of a liberalized economy.

The formulation of the Five Year Plans depended on the degree of India's fusion with the international economy. Often this was not instantaneous and straightforward. India had to fit itself into the reform programmes. This required adaption of many of the reform policies to Indian circumstances and realities in the economic and social sectors. India's agriculture is known for its predominance of small and marginal farmers, and its high dependence for employment and income. In agricultural operations, the state is responsible for creation of infrastructure, subsidizing farm inputs, and regulating prices, while the production decisions are taken by millions of farmers in the countryside. The farmers produce in the private sector picking up price and fiscal signals from the state. The state intervenes in the market during bumper years by mopping up surplus farm produce to prevent fall in its prices so that farmers are able to market their produce at remunerative prices. The state takes care of the interest of consumers by pumping in farm products in the market to contain prices at affordable levels. The state assists and possibly guides agriculture, but the agricultural operation takes place entirely within the private sector under a market system. Agriculture thus operates under a market system which is free, but the state has a say in the development of the market. Through this modus operandi, agriculture, for quite a long time, has been generating surplus production of foodgrain over market demand without any proven evidence of increase in inequality in the distribution of income. The average growth rate of agriculture in the two decades of economic reform, 1992–2011, was faster (3.5 per cent per year) as compared to that in the four decades of the pre-reform era, 1951–91 (2.8 per cent per year).

Administrative price mechanism was a feature of Indian planning in the pre-reform era. Under this, the state used to fix the price of a product with a specific objective in view. The objective often was social rather than purely economic. This created dual (in some cases, even multiple) pricing of a product. The dual price mechanism has been viewed as a means to ensure equity and social justice despite its potentially adverse impact on efficiency and growth. It covered a large number of items, including wage goods and critical industrial raw materials. The price of input used for intermediate use and the price of a product meant for final consumption were also covered by it. As a part of the economic reform programme, the administered price mechanism was abandoned and prices were allowed to be determined in the market.

The economic reform measures, in the course of reaching a new equilibrium, reset the product prices of several items, and that includes some of the daily necessities whose weight in the consumption basket of the poor and the marginalized sections of the population is fairly large. In the absence of a commensurate increase in income, these people may not be able to pay the market prices for these products. First and foremost in this list comes food (essentially foodgrains), for which the state subsidy is increased as more people are brought within the ambit of the public distribution system. Similar measures are initiated in respect of some of the social services, such as education, housing, health care, drinking water, and sanitation facilities, which are offered to these people either free or at a nominal price. In the initial years of reform, it was a kind of tightrope walk for the government to manage sufficient funds for these programmes. In the course of the reform process, as the growth rate increased, it became less difficult to meet expenditure on this count. In reality, two events occurred simultaneously in the reform era that enabled the government to embark on food distribution, wage employment (for those who have nothing but their raw labour power), and the vast expanse of social sector programmes, whose major beneficiaries were the poor and the marginalized sections of the population, and in addition, individuals and families who were adversely affected by the reform-related measures in terms of income and employment losses. These two events were: (*a*) the increase in revenue realization of the government as the growth rate attained a higher trajectory; and (*b*) much of the responsibility of investment in material production sector (notably large industry and infrastructure projects) shifting from the government to the private sector. The increased revenue earnings and the reduced investment in industry and infrastructure by the government provided it with elbow room to spend more on income redistributive poverty alleviation and social sector programmes, and most of all, on heavily subsidizing foodgrain. These provided the much-needed safety net for a large section of the population, including the poor.

The reform process did not move with similar pace in all the sectors and areas of the economy. Also, its impact was not uniform, either at the sectoral level or for the income classes of the population. Mainly as a result of this, the rate of economic growth in the reform era was not uniform. In the initial years, the growth rate picked up slowly. This may have been largely due to the staggering of the reform process. The reforms began with the measures initiated by the central government. In India, the state governments have a matching role in economic growth and development, as they are endowed with the responsibility to implement many of the growth-oriented projects contained in the Five Year Plans and also a range of social welfare programmes. As a rule, much of the realization of the targets fixed in Five Year Plans depended on the state governments underlining quintessentially the criticality and importance of the implementation of reform programmes at the level of states. However, the reform process at the state level was neither uniform nor did it take place at the same pace. Many of the rules and regulations which fell in the domain of the states could not be changed as they dithered, ultimately impacting on the growth rate.

The Indian economy, as a result of the reform policies, did not reduce itself to a pure market economy. Structurally, it resembles the mixed economy set-up of the planning era, characterized by the simultaneous existence of the public and private sectors, with the important exception that both these sectors are now exposed to market forces. The private sector in the era of economic reform does not have to operate under state guidance or follow the direction laid down by the state. Similarly, the public sector enjoys complete autonomy and operates in the market just like the private sector. The economic situation in India after two decades of reform and liberalization resembles a mixed economy, where the public and the private sectors coexist, with the difference of an altered share in investment and output from that in the pre-reform years.

Under globalization, there is a tendency for relatively advanced regions within the developing countries growing faster than the backward regions. Such a tendency is evident in India with the foreign investment being concentrated in the developed regions of the country. Private investment is known for generating income inequality at interpersonal as well as inter-regional levels. As such, the economic growth between the states and between different regions (say districts) within a state has been uneven. Foreign investment reinforces this tendency. Therefore, the emerging pattern of growth may not be so conducive for a large section of the population, as inequality between regions and between persons may widen. Of course, income inequality has increased more in the emerging economies. However, that cannot be a solace.

Economic Growth under Reform: 1991–2011

The growth rate of the Indian economy moved onto a higher trajectory of 7 per cent per year in the two decades of economic reform from an average of 4 per cent per year in the four decades of the pre-reform years. A comparison of the macroeconomic parameters in the 20 years of economic reform with the 40 years of the pre-reform period could help us decipher the impact of the reform measures on the Indian economy. The values of the macroeconomic parameters in · these periods have been given in Table 6.1.

A feature of the growth process in the reform era was that it was not uniform across the period. The growth rate in the initial 11 years of the reform 1992–2002 (5.9 per cent per year) was pretty much the same as realized in the 1980s (5.6 per cent per year). Therefore, the reform measures did not have much of an impact on the growth rate in the 1990s. The growth rate accelerated to 8.3 per cent per year in the last nine years of reform, 2003–11. As mentioned earlier, the manner and method of implementation of the economic reform programmes in these two decades was not uniform, and that may have been the reason behind the lack of uniformity in the growth rate in this period. The difference in the growth rate between these two periods (1992–2002 and 2003–11) should not, however, gloss over the fact that in the initial eleven years (1992–2002), there were four agriculturally bad years (1997–98, 2002–03, 1995–96, and 2000–01), whereas during the last nine years (2003–11) agricultural output suffered in only

Table 6.1 Macro Parameters in the Pre- and Post-reform Periods

	1951–52 to 1991–92	1992–93 to 2002–03	2003–04 to 2011–12	1992–93 to 2011–12
1. GDP Growth Rate by Sector	Per Cent per Year			
a. Agriculture	2.8	2.9	4.3	3.5
b. Industry	5.3	6.2	9.1	7.5
c. Services	5.0	7.7	9.3	8.4
d. GDP: Total	4.0	5.9	8.3	7.0
2. Increase in GDP Share	Per Cent of Total GDP			
a. Agriculture	−21.2	−9.2	−6.6	−15.8
b. Industry	8.7	1.0	1.7	2.7
c. Services	14.5	8.5	4.9	13.4
3. Investment Rate	Per Cent of GDP			
a. Public	9.0	7.8	8.3	8.1
b. Private	10.0	16.6	26.8	22.9
c. Total	19.0	24.4	35.1	31.0
4. Investment Share	Per Cent of Total Investment			
a. Public	47.4	32.0	23.6	26.1
b. Private	52.6	68.0	76.4	73.9
5. Gross Domestic Savings	Per Cent of Total GDP			
a. Household Sector	11.7	19.4	23.4	21.9
b. Private Corporate Sector	1.6	3.8	7.6	6.1
c. Public Sector	3.4	0.5	2.1	1.5
d. Total	16.8	23.8	33.1	29.5
6. ICOR	4.8	4.1	4.2	4.4

Notes: Agriculture includes forestry, fishing, mining, and quarrying. Industry includes manufacturing, construction, electricity, gas, and water supply. The GDP growth rates have been measured here in terms of factor cost, and at 2004–05 prices. ICOR is implicit, estimated as the ratio between the investment rate and the growth rate of GDP.

Source: Estimated from 'Summary of Macro Economic Aggregates at Current Prices, 1950–51 to 2013–14', Statement 11, and 'Summary of Macro Economic Aggregates at Constant (2004–05) Prices, 1950–51 to 2013–14', Statement 12, CSO, Ministry of Statistics and Programme Implementation, Government of India, 27 March 2015. Available at mospi.gov.in.

one year (2008–09). Therefore, lower growth rate in 1992–2002 was partly due to depressed agriculture whereas the higher growth rate in 2003–11 cut across major sectors, namely agriculture, industry, and services. The average growth rate in agriculture in 2003–11 was high (4.3 per cent per year) as compared with that in the initial 11 years (2.9 per cent per year in 1992–2002). This should be kept in mind while evaluating the average growth rates in these two periods in the reform era, and at the same time, its impact on the standards of living of the population, because agricultural growth is the main driver of rural income and consumption.

Agricultural production under economic reforms was characterized by increase in the production of the crop sector and the newly emerging items, such as floriculture, horticulture, and so on. The industrial growth in the reform era cut across sub-sectors such as manufacturing and non-manufacturing. The structure of growth within the manufacturing was broadly similar in pre- and post-reform years. The structure of growth within the services sector altered marginally under economic reform, with the relatively higher growth rate in trade and financial services, especially as the aggregate growth rate attained a higher growth trajectory.

The high growth rate in the reform era eventuated change in the structure of the economy. The share of agriculture in GDP declined on average by about 1 percentage point per year during economic reform as compared to 0.5 percentage point per year in the four decades (1951–90) until the reform. It implies that the decline in the share of agriculture in the reform era was nearly four times as compared to that in the four decades 1951–90. The share of the services sector in the reform era increased at twice the rate as compared to the pre-reform era. The share of industry in the aggregate GDP increased at a slower pace under economic reforms, pointing to a major blot in the pattern of growth.

Peaking of Growth Rate

The impact of the economic reform measures on the growth momentum of the 1990s cannot be termed as phenomenal as the rate of economic growth attained a healthy mark of 8 per cent only during two years (1996–97 and 1999–2000). In the remaining seven years of the 1990s, the growth rate averaged 5.3 per cent per year, which is less than the growth rate realized in the 1980s (5.6 per cent per year).

The twenty-first century did not begin with high hopes on the growth front either. The growth rate in the first year of the new millennium (2000–01) dipped to 4.1 per cent, from 8 per cent in the previous year (1999–2000). However, within the next two years the growth rate attained a higher trajectory of 8 per cent. The rate of economic growth in 2003–04 touched 8 per cent and remained around the same level for the next four years (2004–05 to 2007–08) in a row. The average growth rate in the five years from 2003–04 to 2007–08 was 8.7 per cent per year. It signified a structural shift of the growth curve from the long-term as well as the medium-term trend. Again, within these five years, the growth rate in three years from 2005–06 to 2007–08 averaged 9.5 per cent per year—a peak by any reckoning. The high growth rate during the period 2003–04 to 2007–08 cut across major sectors as it averaged 4.8 per cent per year in agriculture, 10.3 per cent per year in industry, and 9.5 per cent per year in services.[3] The average growth rate in agriculture in these five years was higher than any of the three-year (moving) averages since the initiation of economic reform in 1991. The average growth rate in industry and services sectors in these five years far exceeded the three-year (moving) averages since the beginning of the planning era in 1951.

The medium- and long-term growth rates of the Indian economy since the inception of planning demonstrate that the growth rate indeed picked up in the first decade of the new millennium (that is, the 2000s). The high growth rate underlined strong macroeconomic fundamentals and matched the expectations of a fast expanding economy.

The economic growth rate of more than 9 per cent realized during the three-year period of 2005–06 to 2007–08 became a rallying point for charting out the growth path in the Eleventh Plan (2007–12). The growth rate in the Eleventh Plan was fixed at 9 per cent per year. Though such a high growth rate had not been targeted in any Five Year Plan earlier, it was perfectly in tune with the economic scenario prevailing then. Indeed, the Indian economy in 2007–08 was at its high point, as can be observed from the state of the macroeconomic parameters concomitant with the growth surge.

The growth rate during the five-year period of 2003–04 to 2007–08 averaged 8.7 per cent per year. The agricultural growth rate in this period averaged more than 4 per cent per year and the growth rate in industry and services sectors was around 10 per cent per year. The growth surge in this five-year period was characterized by acceleration of savings and investment rate. The savings rate increased from 26.4 per cent of GDP in 2002–03 to 37.7 per cent in 2007–08, and the investment rate went up from 25.2 per cent to 39.1 per cent. The increase in investment rate was faster than that in savings rate. The growth was triggered by domestic investment. The increase in domestic investment was caused principally by increase in domestic savings, which, in turn, was the result of high rate of economic growth. Evidently, the simultaneity of income and savings was at work.

The growth rate increased in the environs of rising share of investment in the private sector. With the onset of economic reform in the 1990s, the share of the private sector in total investment began to increase. From around half of the total investment at the time of commencement of economic reform in 1991, the share of the private sector in total investment increased to three-fourths in the Tenth Plan (2002–07).

The economic growth from 2003–04 to 2007–08 was driven to a great extent by industry. The average growth of industries exceeded 10 per cent per year. The production of capital goods, basic and intermediate goods, as well as consumer goods increased by more than 10 per cent per year. The growth of automobiles production, which included passenger cars, utility vehicles, and two and three wheelers was around 15 per cent per year.

Industry was not all about the large ones. The micro and small enterprises (MSE) performed well and its 12.8 million units in 2006–07 accounted for about 40 per cent of the industrial production and 6 per cent of GDP. The MSEs increased by 12 per cent per year. The employment intensity of the MSEs being more than in the other segments of industry, it was conducive to employment generation.

The growth of the infrastructure sector, though less than average industrial growth, was high. Electricity generation, rail freight, and ports cargo increased and so did wireless and telephone connections. The road connectivity projects of the National Highway Authority of

India (NHAI) were in full swing. This pointed towards the interest of foreign investors (and domestic investors, too) in India.

The growth in the services sector was broad-based. The export in services increased. It was basically driven by software, business, financial, and communication services. Rising flow of invisibles led to rapid accretion of foreign exchange reserves, which exceeded USD 300 billion.

The trade–GDP ratio in 2006–07 increased to 34.8 per cent from 22.5 per cent in 2000–01. With trade of services included, the trade–GDP ratio is observed to have increased from 29.2 per cent to 48 per cent of GDP in this period.

The business sentiments are reflected in high inward FDI spread across financial services, manufacturing, information technology, and construction. At the same time, outward investment surged, mirroring domestic industrial and entrepreneurial capabilities. It is a sort of globalization of Indian enterprises as outward investment from India reached USD 14.4 billion in 2006–07, from less than USD 2 billion in 2003–04.

The Indian economy at this point of time was characterized by robust macroeconomic fundamentals with high growth, relative price stability, a healthy financial sector, and high return on investment. All these made India an ideal investment destination. Keeping these factors in mind, the target growth in the Eleventh Plan was fixed as 9 per cent per year—the highest ever in any Plan since Independence.

The Economy in the Doldrums: 2008–09

The state of affairs in the Indian economy in 2007–08, the first year of the Eleventh Plan, as described in the previous section, was certainly bright and promising. The next year, 2008–09, did not begin on an unpleasant note either, as the growth rate in the first half of the year (April–September 2008) was 7.5 per cent. However, in the beginning of the second half (October 2008–March 2009) two incidents occurred which affected the growth prospects of the Indian economy in a major way. Importantly, neither of these two incidents originated in India.

First, the international prices of a few commodities, which include energy and energy-intensive products, metals, food, and so on, began rising towards the closing months of the year 2007, and this continued in 2008–09. Mainly as a consequence, the prices of coal, iron ore, iron and steel products, and petroleum products not covered by the administered price mechanism began to rise in the domestic market from December 2007. The international price of crude oil firmed up in 2008–09 and peaked at USD 145 per barrel in the beginning of July 2008, whereas the Eleventh Plan projections had been calibrated at the price of USD 80 per barrel. The price rise in the international market had a ripple effect on domestic price inflation, which far exceeded the annual inflation rate of 5 per cent built into the growth projections in the Eleventh Plan. The fiscal situation, as a result, was considerably strained.

Second, a major international financial and economic crisis erupted in September 2008. It originated from the sub-prime crisis in the USA. The sub-prime crisis was rooted in financial inclusion, to achieve which rules and regulations covering the control of mortgage banks in the USA were considerably relaxed. The encouragement to financial inclusion had come from the excess liquidity in the international economic system, led by the financial architecture of the USA. Financial inclusion brought families with low levels of income and assets into the credit market, known as sub-prime market. The practice of lending money to borrowers who do not qualify for the market interest rate because of their deficient credit history is known as sub-prime lending. The term 'sub-prime' refers to the credit status of the borrower (being less than ideal), rather than the interest rate on the loan itself. The interest rate on sub-prime loan is higher due to increased risk. The high interest rate, poor credit history, and adverse financial condition of the borrower rendered sub-prime lending risky for both lender and borrower. Such lending led to massive capital erosion in the financial system in the USA. It resulted in a slowdown of the US economy, and the global economic situation deteriorated as industrially developed countries of Europe and Japan entered into recession.

The Indian economy could not escape from the after-effects of the global economic crisis because the policies of economic reform and liberalization pursued since 1991 had integrated India with the global economy more than ever before. However, there are differences of opinion about the depth and intensity with which different areas and sectors of the economy and the people were affected by the crisis. Under these circumstances, the government's perception of the crisis and an assessment of the measures taken by it to contain the fallout from the crisis for the domestic economy is of paramount interest.

Growth Implication of Global Economic Crisis: Real Sector

All the sectors of the economy were not equally affected by the global economic crisis. The sectors with strong linkages to the international economy are likely to be affected most in such a crisis, and in that way the impact of the crisis on sectoral income generation becomes a matter of degree.

The agricultural operation in India is labour-intensive and its low share in income generation (around 18 per cent of GDP in 2008–09, when the global crisis struck) obscures the essential role it plays in providing sustenance and livelihood to more than half of the work-force (54.6 per cent as per the decennial population census of 2011) in the country. Besides, agricultural growth has a strong spillover effect on the economy in terms of forward and backward linkages, and hence its multiplier effect on the overall rate of economic growth is large. It generates consumption demand, an essential prerequisite to maintain the growth momentum of the economy.

The growth rate of agriculture in the five years preceding the global crisis (2003–04 to 2007–08) averaged 4.8 per cent per year. It is much better in comparison with the previous five years (1998–99 to 2002–03, when the growth rate of agriculture was a measly 1.9 per cent per year) and is a sign of resilience in income and consumption in rural areas. This, coupled with the minimum external trade, kept Indian agriculture insulated from the global economic crisis.

A downturn of the global economy can potentially impinge upon the operating parameters of industrial firms in India in four major ways. First, industries producing globally traded products can be affected via low demand, low price, and, in consequence, low revenue. Second, decline in global commodity prices can adversely affect income and output of some sectors. Third, depreciation of the rupee arising from disequilibrium in the foreign exchange market can help exporters; at the same time, it can adversely affect the sectors whose import intensity is relatively high. Fourth, overseas acquisition of assets and enterprises can face difficulty.

The growth rate of industrial production lowered in the aftermath of the global economic crisis. The decline in industrial growth was widespread, covering basic, capital, and intermediate goods.

The impact of the global economic crisis on the mining and quarrying sector was negligible as nearly 90 per cent of mining consists of coal and crude oil, which are used in the domestic market; about 5 per cent of the output produced in the mining sector is exposed to external trade.

The manufacturing sector has two distinct components, registered and unregistered, and they accounted for two-thirds and one-third of the manufacturing GDP respectively in the 2000s. By and large, the impact of the global economic crisis on the manufacturing sector was not uniform on these two components (registered and unregistered) and they were affected by the crisis in different ways. The registered manufacturing was affected due to slowdown of exports and by liquidity squeeze due to its excessive dependence on borrowing. As a result, the impact of the global crisis on registered manufacturing was moderate to large, whereas the impact on unregistered manufacturing was moderate rather than large owing to its lower dependence on institutional credit. Recognized for its labour intensity, loss of output in unregistered manufacturing was sine qua non with loss of employment, affecting the low paid unskilled and semi-skilled sections of the labour force.

Electricity generation remained indifferent to the global economic crisis as operation and maintenance of power plants were done domestically.

The impact of the global economic crisis on the growth of the construction sector could be felt via credit crunch, even as the government tried to counter this problem through fiscal stimulus measures by arranging concessional finance for housing construction.

Within the services sector, trade as well as hotels and restaurants remained neutral to the global economic crisis though high-end hotels faced excess capacity. Rail transport was not affected, but road transport faced some problem in acquiring vehicles because of credit crunch. The crisis left considerable impact on air transport.

Communication remained largely neutral to the global economic crisis.

It was feared that the slowdown of domestic economic activities caused by the global economic crisis would affect the banking sector. However, its impact turned out to be only marginal as credit and bank deposits remained buoyant. Margins were never under pressure. There was the fear of increase in non-performing assets (NPAs) of the commercial banks. The insurance sector was much more exposed to the global crisis, but due to its small size, the impact, on the whole, was minimal.

The impact of the slowing world economy was felt on business services. The real estate sector remained subdued throughout.

The increase in expenditure on account of implementation of the recommendations of the Sixth Pay Commission for the central government employees increased the salaries of government employees and, in turn, their disposable income. India's defence expenditure is more weaved with strategic factors, and hence not so strongly correlated with the growth rate of the economy. The expenditures on income redistributive programmes and social services were increased. It insulated the growth of community and the social services sectors from the global economic crisis.

The services sector as a whole tends to be less affected by cyclical downturns than other sectors, such as manufacturing. This is notwithstanding the fact that the growth of the services sector is inextricably linked with the manufacturing sector by way of forward and backward linkages. The high share of the services sector in aggregate GDP (more than half of the GDP) was able to moderate the adverse effect of the global economic crisis on the rate of growth of aggregate GDP.

Implication of Global Economic Crisis: Financial Sector

The global economic crisis could have affected India's financial sector through exposure to stressed global assets and linkages with money and the foreign exchange market in the USA and countries in Western Europe. The exposure of the Indian banking system to these countries, and especially to the failed and stressed financial institutions, either directly or through derivatives, was limited. In fact, none of the Indian or foreign banks operating in India were directly exposed to the sub-prime market in the USA or Europe. The commercial banks in India were well-capitalized and financially sound. However, the deepening of the crisis and subsequent de-leveraging and risk aversion in the global market affected Indian equity and the foreign exchange market. The crisis impacted domestic money, debt, and the credit market indirectly through forward and backward linkages. In this way, the global economic crisis disrupted the growth and development of the Indian financial market, more by way of moderating the capital flows.

In the equity market, all the major world stock indices, such as Dow Jones (USA), DAX (German), Nikkei (Japan), the Brazilian stock index, Hang Seng (Hong Kong), and Jakarta composite (Indonesia) suffered losses. The sensitive index of the Bombay Stock Exchange (Sensex) followed suit, being impacted largely from outflows by foreign institutional investors. The state of the Indian securities market in September 2008 was in line with the major indices world over. The market remained subdued for the next five months (until February 2009) despite the monetary and fiscal measures set in motion by the government to tackle the crisis.

A large part of the decline in the Indian securities market owes to the outflow of funds emanating from a withdrawal of deposits by foreign institutional investors. The problem was aggravated by dipping domestic sentiments. About one-third of India's security market melted in 2008, in terms of overall market capitalization. Banking, realty, and capital goods stocks topped the list of losers. The brighter side of the picture is the foreign institutional investors' flow of funds. Though negative on a net basis, the gross flows on both sides were sufficiently large, indicating that investor views on India were not unilateral.

The contours of the global economic crisis can be described as follows: (*a*) reduced private debt and equity flows to developing countries; (*b*) shrinking of international credit and bond markets; (*c*) freezing of the US money market; (*d*) moderation of cross-border capital flows; and (*e*) curtailment of cross-border banks lending to developing countries. The impact of these factors on Indian equity and the foreign exchange market was not severe as compared to most of the developing countries, though it impacted business sentiments.

The impact of the global economic crisis transmitted through capital flows and financial markets had enough power to moderate the rate of growth of the Indian economy.

Implication of Global Economic Crisis: External Sector

The degree of integration of the Indian economy with the rest of the world is mirrored in its share of trade in GDP. The share of (merchandise) trade in GDP was about 14 per cent when the economic reforms were initiated in 1991. After a decade, the (merchandise) trade–GDP ratio increased to 21.2 per cent in 2000–01. It further increased to 36.5 per cent in 2007–08. Including trade in services, the trade–GDP ratio increased from 29.2 per cent in 2000–01 to 48 per cent in 2006–07. This increase is considered phenomenal when compared with the past, and was largely due to the inflow of invisibles comprising international trade in services, income from financial assets, labour and property, and cross-border transfers (mainly workers' remittances), which are the after-effects of economic reform measures.

India's external sector remained robust until the global economic crisis erupted in September 2008. The crisis impacted both exports and imports. The merchandise trade deficit increased, but it was greatly eliminated by the surplus (net) in the flow of invisibles, mainly driven by increase in private transfers and non-factor services. The export of services is the major contributor to invisibles receipts, which is dominated by software and business services and private transfers. Invisibles payments are mainly driven by dividends and profits paid on foreign investment and interest payment on external debt and technology and business services. Both receipts and payments are large in case of travel, transportation, business services, and investment income account whereas inflows are nearly unidirectional in case of software services and private transfers.

The major sources of capital inflow are FDI, short-term credit, portfolio investment, and external commercial borrowing. A liberal (small negative list and most of it being allowed on automatic route) and transparent policy (moderate and stable tax regime) on FDI initiated under economic reform programmes made India a favourable destination for international investors. India remained a viable investment destination even in the midst of the global economic crisis.

Before the eruption of the global economic crisis, the exchange rate of the Indian rupee against the US dollar was driven primarily by capital flows. The rupee began to depreciate against the US dollar before the global crisis surfaced, and the rate of depreciation started accelerating from August 2008 in keeping with the worsening global economy. As the global economic crisis surfaced, the US dollar began to appreciate against major world currencies from September 2008 onwards. The rupee depreciated in consequence. The movement of the rupee against the US dollar at this time was in sync with the movement of the other major currencies in the world vis-á-vis the US dollar.

The appreciation of the US dollar against the euro and pound sterling essentially owes to, and reflects, the liquidation of foreign assets by US residents and institutional investors to cover their domestic sub-prime losses. Its ripple effect was felt in India, and the RBI found it prudent to intervene in the market by selling foreign exchange in order to protect the exchange rate of the Indian rupee against excessive volatility.

State Response to Global Economic Crisis

Governments the world over did not leave the problems arising from the global economic crisis for the market forces to tackle alone. They intervened. The USA set in motion a near trillion dollar stimulus package to bail out its economy. The state intervention was so deep and widespread that some countries even went to the extent of pursuing protectionist policies, expecting that the bailout process would be simpler and the time taken to come out of the crisis would be short. India followed suit, and resorted to fiscal and monetary policies in order to tackle the crisis.

The global economic crisis was triggered by the malfunctioning of the financial sector of the developed industrial world. It eroded people's faith on the basis of which the financial architecture of the industrially developed countries, especially the USA, are founded and flourished for a long time. The first priority at this juncture was to reassure the people of the stability of the financial system in general and safety of the bank deposits in particular. In India, policy initiatives of the government came from the central government as well as the country's central bank, the RBI. The central government formulated two back-to-back stimulus packages to counter the slack in demand and generate investment to promote economic growth. These were backed up by a slew of monetary measures initiated by the RBI to restore business confidence, which was essential to keep the nuts and bolts of the economy moving.

Stimulus Package

The government announced two stimulus packages, first on 7 December 2008 and then on 2 January 2009. The first stimulus package provided the basis for a contra-cyclical policy stance through increase in expenditure and reduction of excise duty rates on a range of items to bring down prices of manufactured goods so as to push consumption demand. The package contained specific measures to boost the growth momentum in several areas of industry and earmarked a substantial amount of expenditure on social welfare programmes, which had the potential of generating consumption demand to ensure that the economy bounced back to a higher growth path.

The second stimulus package (January 2009) had a wider spread and contained measures to promote public investment, particularly in the infrastructure sector, and aimed to ease credit delivery to sectors and areas of the economy that were considered to be affected most by the global crisis. It also contained sector-specific measures for labour-intensive and export-oriented industries.

As the growth rate of the Indian economy lowered with the eruption of the global economic crisis, the finances of the state governments came under strain. The states faced constraints in financing developmental expenditure because of slower revenue growth. In order to maintain the momentum of expenditure, the states were permitted to raise additional market borrowings amounting to half a per cent of their gross state domestic product (GSDP) in 2008–09.

This was not the end. A set of proposals aimed at boosting the consumption demand was announced further in February 2009. These can well be termed as the third dose of stimulus. The proposals included reduction in service tax by 2 percentage points, from 12 per cent to 10 per cent. Service tax was levied on about 150 broad services and became one of the front runners of revenue mobilization in the central government. The service sector was least affected by the economic slowdown, and, as a result, the revenue sacrifice was real and had the potential of increasing the disposable income.

Excise duty rates were lowered by 4 percentage points in the first stimulus package (December 2008). In February 2009, the excise duty rate on items attracting 10 per cent was reduced by 2 percentage points. As 96 per cent of all the items then attracted 10 per cent excise duty, this particular case (of 2 percentage points reduction) in effect represent a case of 'across-the-board' reduction. The countervailing duty on imported goods was levied in lieu of excise duty on the domestic product. The lowering of the excise duty rate, therefore, meant a corresponding lowering of the countervailing duty levied on imports, which meant further loss of state revenue. It was a huge tax concession presumed to benefit consumers in the form of lowering of prices, so that it could boost consumption. These tax reductions, in the end, had serious implications for the fiscal scenario.

The thrust of public expenditure in the stimulus packages lay centred in the revenue expenditure. The expenditure on social welfare programmes falls in this category. In tune with the inclusive growth espoused in the Eleventh Plan (2007–12), the government began to spend large sums of money in education, health care, drinking water, sanitation, urban infrastructure development programmes, and so on, through several flagship programmes so as to assist the poor and a segment of the non-poor population who are unable to pay market prices for these services. Additional spending on these flagship programmes was the hallmark of the stimulus packages. The expenditure on most of these programmes instantaneously translated into income and consumption demand.

In order to spur economic growth as a part of a contra-cyclical fiscal policy stance, total expenditure of the central government in 2008–09 was increased by 20 per cent. Its consequence on the macroeconomic scene was perhaps never considered seriously at that time. The stimulus measures resulted in the contraction of revenue and increase in expenditure. The revenue receipts lowered on two counts: (*a*) due to lowering of the economic growth rate; and (*b*) due to the lowering of tax rates. The contra-cyclical policy stance was continued for two years, and with the same intensity. This eventually sowed the seeds of macroeconomic disequilibrium. With high fiscal deficit, inflation raised its head and the growth rate of the economy plummeted. That is, however, a different story.

Monetary Measure

Before the onset of the global economic crisis in September 2008, the RBI had been pursuing a tight monetary policy to counter the upward rise in domestic prices, largely caused by increase in the price of crude oil and energy-intensive commodities in the international market. The domestic inflation rate spiked to double digits in August 2008. The RBI used conventional measures such as the cash reserve ratio (CRR) and open market operations (OMO) to ensure that excess liquidity conditions did not turn into credit to fuel further inflationary pressure in the domestic market. The measures also included market stabilization scheme (MSS) and liquidity adjustment facility (LAF).

There is considerable doubt about the necessity and, by implication, the efficacy of the tight monetary policy measures pursued by the RBI to tackle domestic inflation when the prime cause of inflation is believed to be rooted in the developments in the international market. This was evident from the easing of global commodity prices, which brought the domestic inflation rate down to single-digit level by the beginning of November 2008. However, by then, the global economic crisis had taken over.

The moderation of prices began with the contraction of demand internationally as the fallout of global economic crisis. This process began in October 2008, that is, within a month of the onset of the global crisis. Prices of food, metal, and oil, which led the price inflation at the international level, came under control by this time. Crude oil prices reduced to around USD 40 per barrel in November 2008 from its peak level of USD 145 per barrel barely four months before in July. Since August 2008 the decline in global commodity prices was sharp, led by the decline in the price of crude oil, and by way of moderating the prices of products that use crude oil or its products as inputs, such as fertilizers, chemicals, man-made fibres, and so on. The prices of energy-intensive products, such as metals, reduced. The reasons for the decline in prices of these commodities were different and it is not necessary to recount them here. It is sufficient to state that the decline in prices was due to a sharp decline in demand in the USA and Europe, and the expectation of slowing demand in the developing countries. Simultaneously, supply factors played an almost equal role in moderating the price level. Grain prices fell by about 25 per cent in two months between September and October 2008, mainly due to weakening of demand and improved supply prospects, the latter being largely led by India, with its bumper crop.

The domestic price inflation remained in the range of 3 to 4 per cent from December 2008 to February 2009. It made room for easing the monetary policy, considered essential to raise the growth rate. It was perceived that the economy was growing below its potential due to the tightening of credit supply by the RBI, which led to increase in the cost of credit. The moderation in the GDP growth rate at this time was largely considered to be the outcome of the tight monetary policy pursued by the RBI. The global economic crisis made it obligatory for the RBI to ensure that the tight liquidity condition did not restrict credit availability in the domestic market. Sufficient liquidity in the market is an essential prerequisite to maintain the growth momentum of the economy.

At this point, the RBI initiated a series of measures to ease the flow of credit. These included reduction in the CRR and signalling interest rate reduction through lowering of repo and reverse repo rates. The CRR, that is, the proportion of deposits banks set aside with the RBI, was reduced in phases, from a high of 9 per cent. The benchmark lending rate, the repo rate, which is the interest that the RBI charges from banks for lending money, was reduced by 350 basis points in a near regular fashion (five times within five months) from 8.5 per cent in mid-September 2008 to 5 per cent in the first week of March 2009. The reduction in the repo rate lowers the cost of credit and raises the volume of credit availability in the economy. The reverse repo rate is the rate at which the RBI borrows cash from the commercial banks. It can be viewed as the rate at which the commercial banks park their surplus cash with the RBI for a short time. An increase in reverse repo rate can cause the banks to transfer more funds to the RBI due to attractive interest rates. It can cause the money to be drawn out of the banking system. The banks are generally inclined to lend money to the RBI for reasons of safe investment and remunerative return. The interest rate offered by the RBI is usually considered attractive. The reverse repo rate under the LAF window was lowered by 250 basis points in four instalments within five months, from 6 per cent in mid-September 2008 to 3.5 per cent in the first week of March 2009. The lowering of reverse repo rate discourages commercial banks from parking their surplus funds with the RBI through the LAF and encourages them to boost lending to the commercial sector. Other measures initiated by the RBI to pump liquidity into the system included lowering of the statutory liquidity ratio (SLR), enhancing interest rate ceilings on foreign account deposits, relaxing norms for external commercial borrowings, and opening a foreign currency swap window for banks.

The lowering of the benchmark policy rates by the RBI, signalling lower interest rate regime, induces the banking system to lend more at a lower interest rate. In addition, easing the monetary policy is necessary to offset the global increase in demand for money that is usually transmitted to India. These measures are intended to help a wide range of industry and infrastructure, which are considered to be affected by a global economic slowdown.

Growth Rate in the Aftermath of the Global Crisis

In 2008–09, the streak of high growth rate of the Indian economy during the preceding five years (2003–07) ended as the global economic crisis surfaced. The global crisis unfolded in September 2008. Therefore, the growth rate for the first half of 2008–09 (April–September 2008) could not have been affected by the crisis; it turned out to be 7.5 per cent. The growth rate in the first half of 2008–09 did not fluctuate between its two quarters (7.6 per cent in April–June 2008 and 7.5 per cent in July–September 2008). The pertinent issue is to find out the magnitude of the growth rate in the second half of 2008–09 (October 2008–March 2009), when the global economy was thick into the crisis.

In December 2008 and January 2009, more than a dozen domestic and international research institutions made forecasts of growth rate of the Indian economy for 2008–09 using a variety of short-term forecasting models. These are: the World Bank, the IMF, the Credit Rating Information Services of India Limited (CRISIL), the Institute of Economic Growth, the Centre for Monitoring Indian Economy

(CMIE), Merrill Lynch, Citigroup, Asian Development Bank, the Economic Advisory Council to the Prime Minister, the Associated Chamber of Commerce, the National Council of Applied Economic Research, the United Nations Council for Trade and Development, and the Confederation of Indian Industries. The median growth rate from these forecasts is 7 per cent. The forecasts were made under broad aggregative assumptions and, as a result, are often unable to capture adequately the micro-level factors impacting specific sectors of the economy and their inter-linkages with other variables. Besides, the rigidities of the economic systems are known to restrict the ability of mathematical models to portray the process of real income generation in the very short run. These may render the forecast estimates less precise. The uncertainties prevailing in the international economic scenario compounded the problem.

In the end, the Indian economy clocked a growth rate of 6.8 per cent in 2008–09, which was not very different from most of these forecast estimates. The global economic crisis impacted the growth rate of the second half of 2008–09 (October 2008–March 2009) as it dipped to 6 per cent from 7.5 per cent in the first half. As the crisis took time to penetrate into different areas and sectors of the economy, the growth rate in the fourth quarter of the year (January–March 2009) was 5.8 per cent, lower than that in the third quarter (October–December 2008), 6.2 per cent.

In order to find out the impact of the global economic crisis on the rate of growth of the Indian economy, it is appropriate to dissect the reasons behind the decline in the growth rate in 2008–09. The growth rate in the first half of 2008–09 (7.5 per cent), which was not affected by the crisis, is found to be 2 percentage points lower than the average growth rate during the previous three years (9.5 per cent per year from 2005–06 to 2007–08). This reduction in the growth rate cannot be attributed to the global crisis. It points out that the Indian economy had failed to sustain the high growth rate of 9 per cent per year before the eruption of the global economic crisis. Domestic factors obviously come under suspicion for this.

Ideally, the difference between the actual growth rate of the first half (7.5 per cent) and the second half (6.0 per cent) of the year 2008–09 should be treated as the impact of the global economic crisis on the growth rate of the Indian economy. In that case, the impact of the global crisis translates to a loss of growth rate by 1.5 percentage points. Of course, such an assertion is valid under the presumption that the entire decline in the growth rate between the two halves of 2008–09 was exclusively on account of global factors. If there were domestic factors interfering with the growth possibilities, then the impact of the global crisis would have been lesser. It is, however, difficult to decompose the influence of domestic and global factors in pushing the growth rate of the Indian economy down.

The lower GDP growth rate in the second half of 2008–09 is a fait accompli. India could not remain immune to the incidents in the international arena, and the impact of recession in the industrially developed countries was felt in both the real and financial sectors of the economy. The real sector was affected as a result of its interaction with the developed industrialized countries through trade. Indian exports were affected as industrially developed countries entered into recessionary stage. The slowdown of the global economy impacted the domestic financial sector. The decline in capital inflow triggered by foreign investors' need for liquidity impacted domestic stock market. The ability of domestic investors to raise resources for investment became restricted, hurting the growth rate. The bright spot in this otherwise gloomy scenario was that the Indian economy's acceleration to a higher growth path until 2008–09 was largely domestically driven or, in other words, due to the predominantly domestic nature of financing of investment. As a result, the impact of the global financial turmoil on India's economic growth turned out to be less severe than anticipated.

The growth rate of the Indian economy in 2008–09 (6.8 per cent) cannot be termed as appalling in view of (*a*) the degree of integration that the Indian economy enjoyed with the international economy as a result of the policies of economic reforms and liberalization; and (*b*) major economies posting very low and even negative growth rates. India's economic growth rate in 2008–09 made it the second fastest growing developing economy in the world.

In the middle of this growth downturn, India stood out on yet another issue. The incidence of low growth and consequent loss of income (as a result of the decline in growth rate) did not fall disproportionately on the poor and the marginalized sections of the population. The Indira Gandhi Institute of Development Research (IGIDR),

Mumbai, regularly prepared growth scenarios for the Indian economy on behalf of the Planning Commission. Using a CGE model, which is a useful tool for providing an indication of economy-wide impact of specific policies, it assessed the impact of the global economic crisis on class distribution of income and found that the incidence of low growth (in 2008–09) impacted different income classes in a near equal manner. The essence is that the bottom deciles of the population (in which the poor and the marginalized groups are located) were not disproportionately affected by the income loss arising from the global crisis.

The global economic crisis was in full bloom in 2009–10 and spread over the 12 months of the year (as compared with six months in 2008–09). The fear that the Indian economy would plunge into a serious crisis was widespread. The impact of the crisis on the growth rate of the Indian economy was likely to be more in 2009–10 as compared to 2008–09. The message in its subtle form was that the growth rate in 2009–10 would be less than 6.8 per cent, which was the growth rate realized in 2008–09, or maybe even less than 6 per cent, which was the growth rate in the second half of the year. A similar message was conveyed by the short-term forecasting of growth rates from the institutions which had earlier predicted the growth rate for the year 2008–09. The Planning Commission carefully avoided offering short-term growth forecasts of the Indian economy citing rules of business of the government which make it responsible for preparing medium- and long-term growth prospects of the country; the short-term growth forecasts fall in the domain of the finance ministry.

Defying all prophecies, the growth rate of the Indian economy in 2009–10 (8.6 per cent) became higher than in 2008–09 and, remarkably, by a wide margin. The growth rate in the next year (8.9 per cent), that is, in 2010–11, was high too. The growth rate thus recovered from a low of 6.8 per cent in 2008–09 to average 8.8 per cent per year for the next two years, 2009–10 and 2010–11. This is even higher (though only marginally) than the average growth rate of the five years preceding the global crisis (8.7 per cent per year during the period 2003–04 to 2007–08). The increase in growth rate in 2009–10 and 2010–11 cut across the major sectors of the economy, averaging 4.9 per cent per year in agriculture, 8.6 per cent per year in industry, and 10.1 per cent per year in services. These are comparable with the growth rate of 4.8 per cent per year in agriculture, 10.3 per cent per year in industry, and 9.5 per cent per year in services during the five-year period from 2003–04 to 2007–08. The economic growth in 2009–10 and 2010–11 therefore returned to a higher trajectory, and it would be a travesty of truth if such high growth rate for two consecutive years is not treated as a withering of the impact of the global economic crisis on the Indian economy. In actuality, the initial idea that the impact of the global economic crisis on the growth rate of the Indian economy would be widespread in the end turned out to be false.

The growth rate in 2011–12, the terminal year of the Eleventh Plan, was relatively lower, at 6.7 per cent. Still, the average growth rate in the Eleventh Plan was 8.1 per cent per year. Though less than the target of 9 per cent per year, it is the highest ever growth rate realized in any Five Year Plan. The growth rate in the Eleventh Plan was spread across sectors, averaging 4 per cent per year in agriculture, 8.1 per cent per year in industry, and 9.4 per cent per year in services. Thus, the growth rate of the Indian economy in the first decade of the new millennium did not end on a sour note despite the global economic crisis.

Drivers of Growth: 1991–2011

The investment rate, defined as the ratio of investment to GDP, is the principal determinant of the rate of economic growth. The average investment rate in the two decades of economic reform (1992–2011) was higher than that in the four decades of the pre-reform period (1951–91). The increase in investment rate during the period of economic reform was accompanied by a significantly altered composition (of investment) between the public and the private sectors. In the pre-reform years, aggregate investment in the economy was shared by the public and the private sectors in a near-equal manner. These shares underwent substantial change in the reform era when the private sector accounted for three-fourths of the total investment. The increase in investment of the private sector was a direct consequence of the policies of economic reform entailing withdrawal of the state from trade and production activities, leaving the space to the private sector.

In the reform era, the rate of economic growth accelerated in the latter nine years (2003–11). The acceleration in growth rate was caused by the surge in investment, especially domestic investment. The average investment rate in 2003–11 was 10.1 percentage points more as compared with the initial 11 years of reform, 1992–2002. Increase in investment of this order propelled the growth rate to a higher level. The share of the private sector in total investment in 2003–11, as mentioned here, was about three-fourths of the total. The dominance of private sector investment was believed to be an extremely important factor behind the acceleration of growth rate in 2003–11.

Investment is composed of domestic savings and foreign savings. Out of the two, foreign savings constitute an essential but a much smaller proportion of aggregate savings. The share of foreign savings in total savings reduced in the years of economic reform. In the pre-reform days, foreign savings rate averaged 2.2 per cent of GDP; it lowered to 1.5 per cent of GDP in the reform era. A larger proportion of savings under economic reform originated from the domestic sector, leading to a situation where domestic savings became the principal determinant of investment. The increase in savings rate was substantial in the reform era. The savings rate averaged 29.5 per cent of GDP in the two decades of economic reform as compared with 16.8 per cent in the previous four decades. A feature of savings generation under economic reform was the increase in savings of households and the private corporate sector. The average savings rate of the household sector in the reform era was nearly double that of the pre-reform years. The savings rate of the private corporate sector was very low in the pre-reform years, averaging 1.6 per cent of GDP; it increased significantly to 6.1 per cent in the reform era. The increase in savings rate of the private sector impacted favourably on investment. Under economic reform, the increase in the rate of economic growth altered the savings behaviour, which, in turn, changed the investment pattern.

Again, the average savings rate rose significantly between the initial eleven years (1992–2002) and the latter nine years (2003–11) of economic reform, and importantly, the increase in savings in the latter nine years occurred across sectors, namely households, private corporate, and public sector—a clear sign of the efficacy of the policies of economic reform after 2003–04. The foreign savings rate rose, from an average of 0.6 per cent of GDP in 1992–2002 to 2 per cent in 2003–11, implying an increase of more than three times. It mirrored the sound fundamentals of the Indian economy in the later nine years of economic reform.

The surge in the growth rate witnessed in 2003–11 was driven by the acceleration in domestic investment rate, which, in turn, was the result of a high domestic savings rate, indicating a domestic savings–investment driven growth. In the reform era, the average investment rate in 2003–11 was 10.1 percentage points more and the savings rate was 9 percentage points more than in 1992–2002. This sharp increase in savings and investment rates was a notable feature of the spurt in GDP growth in the latter nine years of economic reform.

It is not denied that the momentum of growth may have its own compulsion. The realized growth rate of the economy may be functionally related to the dimension and spread of the reform process. While tracing the differential impact of economic reform in the years 1992–2002 and 2003–11, it should be acknowledged that the outcome of some of the policies taken during 1992–2002 may have been reflected in the growth rate of 2003–11. This is more likely in view of the long gestation lag of investment, particularly of the infrastructure and capital goods industries, which were the focal points of the reform process. This should not be overlooked while drawing inferences from these results.

Redistribution in the Reform Era: 1991–2011

The policy of economic reform and liberalization changed the approach to planning as the state refrained from directly participating in the production of goods and services in large segments of the economy, allowing space to the private sector. The emphasis in the period of economic reforms was on maximization of the rate of economic growth, and the growth was led by the private sector. While reposing faith on the private sector–led growth, there was apprehension that the income generation for the poor and the marginalized sections of the population could be relegated to the back seat. The empirics, however, show that growth maximization under economic reform, despite being led by the private sector, was not a case of 'growth at all costs', or in other words, the high growth rate in the reform era did not take place at the cost of the well-being of the poor and the marginalized. In actuality, income in rural areas expanded faster under economic reform, thus benefiting the people who are subjected to hardcore poverty.

The improvement in the standards of living and quality of life of the people happens primarily through increase in income. As the growth of income is not distribution-neutral, the share of income is smaller for the lower deciles of the population as compared to the upper deciles. In order to increase the income of the people in the lower deciles, in which the poor and the marginalized groups are located, several income-redistributive poverty alleviation programmes were incorporated into the Five Year Plans. Such programmes were initiated in the 1980s and strengthened in the reform era; important among them being the asset generation and wage employment programmes. Then, within a year of commencement of economic reform, a scheme was initiated to provide highly subsidized food to the poor and marginalized section of the population. It became an essential component of the redistributive programmes.

As the growth rate of the economy moved on to a higher trajectory in the Tenth Plan, the financial situation became somewhat comfortable, permitting the government to extend the benefits of some of the service-oriented programmes to the people who usually remain within the realm of transient poverty and are unable to pay for the market prices for these services. Also included in this group are the people who are vulnerable to poverty that may result from changes in economic, social, or political actions.

Enabler of Redistribution: Self-Employment

As a component of the income-redistributive poverty alleviation programmes in rural areas, the Integrated Rural Development Programme (IRDP) was introduced as a self-employment programme in 1980. Its basic objective was to assist poor families by providing them income-generating assets through a mix of state subsidy and institutional (bank) credit so as to generate a regular stream of income, which in conjunction with income from other sources (general growth process), enabled them to cross the poverty line. The idea was to employ productively the available workforce (who have limited skill or expertise) using the resource endowment and potentialities that are available at the local level. This way, the measure of poverty reduction was linked with growth-centric policies.

Income generation from the IRDP has been marginal throughout. A scan of the micro as well as comprehensive studies quantifying the percentage of beneficiaries in an area or of a class being able to cross the poverty line indicates that about 30 per cent of them, on average, could cross the poverty line in the best of circumstances. The impact of IRDP has been different in low and high income regions, in regions with low and high poverty, and in regions with low and high resource endowments. By the time economic reforms commenced in 1991, the IRDP had about half a dozen programmes appended to it.[4]

There is one factor which may be responsible for the percentage of beneficiary families crossing the poverty line being so modest. In the beginning, the IRDP followed the *antodaya* approach, in which the poorest of the poor were chosen as the beneficiaries. The initial income of these families was so low that the income accrued from IRDP did not enable them to cross the poverty line. They shifted from a position of too low to nearer the poverty line. This does not lower the poverty ratio, but reduces the depth and severity of poverty. The percentage of beneficiary families crossing the poverty line increased in later years when the antodaya approach was abandoned and the beneficiaries were picked from the poor group, but not necessarily the poorest.

In 1999, the IRDP was restructured into the Swarnjayanti Gram Swarozgar Yojana (SGSY). The SGSY moved away from the individual (or family) beneficiary–oriented approach (practised in the IRDP) to a group approach (groups of individuals or families) to provide livelihood opportunities to the poor in rural areas. The beneficiaries of the SGSY are known as *swarozgaris* (self-employed) and the groups are called self-help groups (SHG). The aim of the SGSY remained the same as in the IRDP: to enhance the income of the rural poor through creation of self-employment opportunities using a mix of state subsidy and institutional credit. Like IRDP, the SGSY espouses the interests of weaker sections of the society, such as the Scheduled Castes and the Scheduled Tribes by specifically earmarking a portion of investment to them.

The SGSY works its way through social mobilization of the poor people in rural areas. The state identifies livelihood projects in each district and assists in capacity-building and training. It is credit-driven and the subsidy is back-ended; credit is its critical component, subsidy being an enabling element. The emphasis is on formation of SHGs of the poor and assists them with subsidy and credit to take up income-generating schemes. As in case of the IRDP, a portion of investment of the SGSY is earmarked for the weaker sections of the society.

The SHGs move through four stages: (*a*) first: social mobilization of the beneficiaries and formation of groups; (*b*) second: savings and internal lending among the members of the group on their own and augmented by grants from the government and financial institutions; (*c*) third: obtaining micro-finance; (*d*) fourth: setting up of micro-enterprises. This is a long process and groups require time to mature as cohesive units.

The SGSY operated for 10 years, 1999–2009, in which 3.9 million SHGs were formed. As mentioned earlier, the SHGs have to pass through different stages to obtain credit and subsidy for undertaking economic activities. The attrition rate in each stage has been high. Only 768,000 SHGs, that is, one-fifth of all the SHGs, could obtain credit and subsidy to undertake economic activities. This falls far short of the expectation. The social composition of the beneficiaries, however, indicates inclusiveness of SGSY. Scheduled Tribes and Scheduled Castes account for 52 per cent of the beneficiaries and women account for 72 per cent.

The SGSY became the monopoly of relatively developed areas. The small number of SHGs formed in the poverty pockets is quite typical of the feature of the growth-oriented programmes, which usually benefit the relatively developed areas, bypassing the back-ward areas. India's northern and eastern states account for more than 60 per cent of the rural poor whereas 40 per cent of total SHGs are located in these states. On the contrary, the southern states account for about 10 per cent of the rural poor but more than 30 per cent of the SHGs.

Relying on the experiences of the SGSY, the self-employment pro-gramme was re-structured into the National Rural Livelihood Mission (NRLM) in 2011, trying to give poverty alleviation a target-oriented strategic framework. It is designed to tap the opportunities arising from rapid economic growth. The idea is to reach out to the poor households in rural areas and stay engaged with them till they come out of poverty. It concentrates on poverty pockets and vulnerable groups among the rural poor.

The impact of self-employment programmes on the income generation of the poor seems to have been ephemeral in the reform era. The reason could be that the state desired the skill and expertise of the beneficiaries of these programme to be used in growth areas. The state was more concerned about landless labourers, who possess nothing but their raw labour power, and are unable to participate in the growth process. As a result, there were serious efforts to generate wage employment in the reform era.

Enabler of Redistribution: Wage Employment

The wage employment programme, as part of the strategy of income redistribution, had been operating since the beginning of the Sixth Plan. It began with the National Rural Employment Programme (NREP) in 1980. Then, in order to mitigate unemployment among landless agricultural labourers in specific poor and backward areas, the Rural Landless Employment Guarantee Programme (RLEGP) was introduced in 1983. The NREP and RLEGP were merged into the Jawahar Rozgar Yojana (JRY) in 1989 and it was the sole wage employment programme in rural areas when economic reform was initiated in 1991.

The employment generation through JRY, as such, was not adequate in the context of the intensity and spread of unemployment in rural areas. The evaluation studies on the JRY made by the Planning Commission in the early 1990s revealed that the employment generation was inadequate and the resources were thinly spread in an effort to increase the number of beneficiaries at the expense of duration of employment. The JRY focused more on asset-building and creation of economic and social infrastructure, rather than generation of wage employment.

The wage employment programmes increased the income of the poorest of the poor, especially in lean agricultural season, when they have no other sources to fall back upon. Its operation, as evident from the NSS of consumer expenditure, shows that it could contain acute hunger in the countryside, particularly in the areas where poverty is deep and widespread. The incidence of hunger, measured by the percentage of households unable to get two square meals a day in some months of the year, was high in rural areas in the early 1980s. As per the NSS consumer expenditure data (38th Round), the incidence of hunger in rural areas was 18.6 per cent in 1983. Thus, nearly one in every five rural households remained hungry in some months of the year. The incidence of hunger was widespread in Bihar (including Jharkhand), Odisha, and West Bengal where 35 to 40 per cent of the rural households were unable to get two square meals a day in 1983. In 1993–94, the incidence of hunger in rural areas lowered to 5.1 per cent (NSS 50th Round). This decline, in all likelihood, owed to the wage employment programmes.[5]

The initiative to increase the quantum of wage employment in the reform era came first in 1993 with the launching of the Employment Assurance Scheme (EAS) in 1,778 economically backward rural development blocks scattered over 261 districts. These blocks were located in drought-prone, desert, tribal, and hill areas, and were already covered under the Revamped Public Distribution System (RPDS), which was a food distribution programme initiated in 1992. The EAS was universalized in 1997–98, that is, extended to all the rural development blocks. It is designed to provide 100 days of casual manual employment per family in a year at statutory minimum wages.

The EAS started as a demand-driven scheme, in which money is allocated among the states in response to demand for employment. Traditionally, such schemes have been found to benefit the states endowed with better infrastructure, more than others, resulting in a kind of skewed distribution of resources as the developed states made a proportionately larger draft on earmarked funds. The demand-driven programmes have not been conducive to the interests of the relatively poorer states as they are unable to claim a fair slice of the pie. In order to rectify this anomaly, the central government began to allocate funds (under EAS) among the states based on their level of poverty. This change was effected from April 1999, that is, six years after its launch and two years after universalization. Simultaneously, the contents of the EAS were changed, and the JRY was restructured as the Jawahar Gram Samriddhi Yojana (JGSY). The JGSY retained the features of the JRY. The EAS continued to be the main wage employment programme for the rural poor.

In 2001, the Food for Work Programme (FFWP) was introduced in backward and drought-affected areas known for hardcore poverty. As a result, three wage employment programmes—EAS, JGSY, and FFWP—operated simultaneously in rural areas. In some areas (rural development blocks), all the three programmes operated simultaneously with substantial degree of complementarities.

In September 2001, the Sampoorna Grameen Rozgar Yojana (SGRY) was introduced as a wage employment programme, when three such programmes (JGSY, EAS, and FFWP) were already in operation. In April 2002 the SGRY was made the sole wage employment programme, subsuming the other three. The objectives of the SGRY and its operational features remained quintessentially similar.

The FFWP was merged with the SGRY in April 2002. With this, the task of employment generation in backward and drought-affected areas was subsumed in the SGRY. However, the resource allocation for SGRY was not adequate. It took two years to realize that due to the thin spread of resources (which has been a perennial feature of wage employment programmes), the SGRY was unable to generate sufficient employment in the backward areas, which customarily needed supplementary wage employment the most. The situation resembled the proverbial 'back to square one'. The demand for employment in backward areas, where wages are low and poverty is high, re-surfaced. The National Food for Work Programme (NFFWP) was launched in November 2004 to ensure a minimum level of employment and income to the poor in backward areas. The expenditure of the NFFWP is borne entirely by the central government so that the employment generation in these areas does not have to rely on the financial solvency of state governments. The NFFWP covered 150 economically backward districts identified by the Planning Commission using the following criteria: (*a*) agricultural productivity per worker; (*b*) agricultural wage rate; and (*c*) proportion of Scheduled Caste and Scheduled Tribe population.

In 2004, there were two wage employment programmes operating simultaneously in rural areas: the SGRY covering all the districts and the NFFWP operated in 150 backward districts.

The economic growth rate started picking up from 2003–04, enabling the government to sharpen its focus on wage employment and making it a statutory right through the National Rural Employment Guarantee Act (NREGA). The NREGA was launched in 2006–07 with 200 backward districts, which included the 150 districts where NFFWP was then in operation. The NREGA was extended to 330 districts in 2007–08 and universalized in the next year, replacing the SGRY. In October 2009, the programme was renamed as Mahatma Gandhi NREGA (MGNREGA).

The MGNREGA differs from the earlier approach to wage employment on three major counts. First, employment under MGNREGA is statutorily guaranteed. Second, one member of all families, poor and non-poor, is provided employment in MGNREGA whereas earlier only the poor were entitled to employment. Third, MGNREGA is structured as demand-driven whereas earlier wage employment programmes were mostly allocative.

The accomplishment of MGNREGA in making inroads into the standards of living of the rural poor can be judged from employment generation and inclusiveness (employment of the poor and marginalized sections of the population). In the first four years of universalization, 2008–09 to 2011–12, which incidentally coincided with the last four years of the Eleventh Plan, shows that like any other demand-driven employment generation programmes in the past, the distribution of benefits from MGNREGA has been skewed. At the state level, there is hardly any association between employment generation and preponderance of the poor. The incidence of rural poverty in five states, namely, Chhattisgarh, Madhya Pradesh, Odisha, Jharkhand, and Bihar is high. These states have a fairly large concentration of Scheduled Caste or Scheduled Tribe populations, among whom the incidence of poverty is far greater than others. Employment generation in these states does not resonate well with the incidence of poverty.

The MGNREGA, as planned and expected, has been inclusive. The employment share of the socially backward section of the population comprising the Scheduled Castes and the Scheduled Tribes, who epitomize the hard core of rural poverty, exceeded 50 per cent. This is twice their share in total population and number of poor. The programme demonstrates gender-friendliness; about 40 per cent of the total employment generation accrued to women. It is less than their share of population, but close to their share in working population.

The wage employment programme ideally should be used as an emergency measure to generate employment when agricultural employment dries up and people who depend on earnings from wage labour have nothing to fall back upon for a living. Instead, it is being treated as a substitute (and a superior substitute from the angle of wage rate), with disastrous consequences for agriculture in many areas of the country.

In addition, the gainfully employed productive workers in the industries in the informal and unorganized sectors may like to switch to MGNREGA if the employment, as statutorily promised, is provided closer to home. Industrial employment may often require either migration from rural to urban areas or to some other state.

The fundamental principles behind MGNREGA are that employment must be provided on demand and it is a statutory right. The employment (100 days in a year) is to be provided within 15 days of applying for the job, failing which the applicant is entitled to unemployment allowance. The work should be arranged within 5 kilometres of the applicant's residence and there should be basic worksite facilities. The wages have to be reimbursed within 15 days of the completion of work and there should be no gender discrimination in wages. Implemented in letter and spirit, MGNREGA can script a systemic intervention to transform the geography of poverty. However, the success in these areas is not unalloyed. It has often faltered by delaying employment and payment of wages. The litany of infractions can be expanded.

During the two-decade period of economic reform, the wage employment programme was changed as many as 10 times, that is on average once in two years, whereas the self-employment programme was altered only twice (in 1999 and 2011). In this context, a chronology of the change in the wage employment programme may have been in order. The JRY was the only wage employment programme when economic reforms were initiated in 1991. The EAS was introduced in specific areas in 1993, and extended to all rural areas of the country in 1997. In April 1999, the content of the EAS was changed and the JRY was restructured as the JGSY. In early 2001, the FFWP was initiated in several drought-affected areas. In September 2001, a new wage employment programme, the SGRY was introduced. In April 2002, the EAS, JGSY, and FFWP were merged into the SGRY. In November 2004, the NFFWP was initiated in 150 backward districts. Finally, the NREGA was introduced in 2006–07. The change in the wage employment programme at regular intervals may have been driven by the desire to make it more result-oriented. It may also reflect quintessentially the indecisiveness of the government. The reality may never be known. A safe guess is that the truth lies somewhere in between.

The effectiveness of the wage employment programmes in increasing the income of the beneficiaries and enabling them to cross the poverty line remains open to debate. A scan of the micro-studies conducted in the first decade of economic reform indicates that 10 to 15 per cent of the beneficiaries, on average, could cross the poverty line in the best of circumstances. The increase in the income of the beneficiaries living way below the poverty line may not be enough to lower the level of poverty, but it may be sufficient to reduce the depth and intensity of poverty.

Enabler of Redistribution: Food Security

That there was considerable apprehension, if not fear, that the economic reform might not be able to increase the income of the poorer sections of the population in proportion to others has been noted earlier. The government was worried that paucity of income might prevent a section of the population, especially the poor, in accessing food from the market, leading to hunger and starvation. In order to meet the exigencies arising from such a situation, the PDS was strengthened. In 1992, that is, within a year of the commencement of the economic reforms, the RPDS was introduced in backward and drought-prone areas, and areas that remain inaccessible for a considerable period of the year. This was in addition to the existing PDS.

Five years later, in 1997, the RPDS was replaced by the Targeted Public Distribution System (TPDS) with the purpose of providing foodgrain to the poor (officially recognized by the government) at half of the minimum support price (MSP).[6] Foodgrain was also distributed to some of the non-poor through the PDS chain at a higher price, but still a great deal lower than the market price. In view of its low cost (half of the MSP), larger quantity, and regular availability, the TPDS became a major instrument to ensure food supply to the poor and the vulnerable, who are victims of poverty and malnutrition as a result of low income and purchasing power.

The TPDS brought in antecedent problems too that were not so uncommon in the context of the low income and lack of purchasing power of a large section of the population which bordered on the poverty line and were often subjected to transient poverty. The entitlement of TPDS was restricted to the poor, as defined and measured by the Planning Commission. The poor at the ground level were identified by the state governments (in association with the Ministry of Rural Development in rural areas and the Ministry of Housing and Urban Poverty Alleviation in urban areas) using a set of visible indicators of poverty and deprivation. The beneficiaries of poverty alleviation programmes (and food) were selected from this list. The number of poor families identified by the state governments differed from that of the Planning Commission, and importantly, the former would invariably surpass the latter by a wide margin. This had implications on food subsidy. The finances of the government were not in excellent shape and meeting the huge cost of subsidy for TPDS could have bordered on profligacy. All these could have rendered the TPDS in jeopardy.

In the meantime, the TPDS had a domino effect. The state governments, saddled with an inflated number of poor (as compared to the Planning Commission estimate), brought more people under the food subsidy scheme. The central government did not allow the quota of food to exceed the amount stipulated by the poverty estimate of the Planning Commission. Around this time, many states began producing foodgrains well in excess of market demand. (The growth rate in agriculture exceeded 4 per cent per year for a fairly long period of one and a half decades from 1980 to the mid-1990s. It can be termed as pretty good in view of the rate of population growth and the increase in demand.) The increased foodgrain production provided elbow room to meet the food needs of the TPDS. The states accepted the food offered by the central government (as per the Planning Commission norm) and in order to maintain the number of beneficiaries at a higher level, they arranged the remainder on their own. Against this backdrop, social activists joined the fray, demanding a broader coverage under the TPDS—as much as 90 per cent of the rural and 50 per cent of the urban population, whereas the class distribution of consumer expenditure (in 2004–05, revealed from the NSS consumer expenditure data of 61st Round) brought out that at the most, only the bottom 40 per cent of the population may need food support.

After implementing the TPDS for nearly a decade, the government toyed with the idea of food security in 2009. A wide range of consultations conducted through the labyrinth of bureaucracy and civil society organizations over a period of five years, 2009–14, culminated in the enactment of the National Food Security Act (NFSA), somewhat hurriedly, in 2014 by a government which was on the verge of completing its tenure. The NFSA covered three-fourths of the rural and half of the urban population.

The state subsidy on foodgrain expanded over time to reach gigantic proportions. It has been a contentious issue in the context of economic reform. However, in a country such as India, with its billion-plus population and mouths to feed every day, and a vast majority of them without the adequate purchasing power, the opportunity cost of withdrawing the food subsidy may be enormous. Not surprisingly, the ambit of food subsidy widened in the reform era. That it can at most be targeted to specific groups has been the accepted paradigm.

Notes

1. Even after investigation and litigation over the next quarter of a century, it is yet to be established that there was indeed a case of corruption in the procurement of these guns. This is a statement of fact made by none other than the president of India in 2016.

2. The IMF insisted that India should put in its resources, such as gold, to demonstrate its earnestness to tide over the crisis. The government pleaded that India, being a depository of gold reserves for the IMF, should be entitled to keep within the country the gold required to be pledged. The IMF did not agree and the RBI had to transport the gold physically to pledge it with the Bank of England and some to the Union Bank of Switzerland. This entire operation was conducted almost in James Bond style by C. Rangarajan, then deputy governor of the RBI. India pledged 67 tonnes of gold to receive a loan of little more than USD 600 million. Essentially there is nothing wrong with pledging or

selling gold, but it is an emotive issue in India. The pledged gold was redeemed by November 1991. In a remarkable turnaround, the RBI in 2009 surprised the IMF by buying 200 tonnes of gold for USD 6.7 billion from it. This is half the total quantity of 400 tonnes of gold that the IMF sold then to raise resources for lending to poorer countries.

3. In comparison, the sectoral growth rates from 1991–92 to 1999–2000 were 3.2 per cent per year in agriculture, 5.7 per cent per year in industry, and 7.8 per cent per year in services. These are close to the growth rates realized from 1980–81 to 1989–90, which were 4.7 per cent per year in agriculture, 5.7 per cent per year in industry, and 6.6 per cent per year in services.

4. Important among these programmes are: (*a*) Training of Rural Youth for Self-Employment (TRYSEM) to provide technical and entrepreneurial skills to rural youths so as to enable them to take up income-generating schemes; (*b*) Supply of Improved Toolkits to Rural Artisans (SITRA) to provide suitable hand tools to rural artisans to enhance quality of products; (*c*) Development of Women and Children in Rural Areas (DWCRA) to empower women belonging to families living below the poverty line; (*d*) Million Wells Scheme (MWS) to construct open irrigation wells for small and marginal farmers belonging to the Scheduled Castes and Scheduled Tribes; and (*e*) Ganga Kalyan Yojana (GKY) to provide irrigation facilities through exploitation of ground water using bore wells and tube wells.

5. It is not an objective measurement of food inadequacy; rather it is based on the perception of the household. This information is obtained from the household by asking a direct question (in the consumer expenditure survey) only if the investigator suspects that the household may have faced inadequacy of food.

6. The MSP is the benchmark price guaranteed by the state to the farmers for their agricultural produce, and can be viewed as a form of market intervention and support system by way of a safety net for the producer. It is fixed keeping in view the overall economic situation, taking into account the interests of producers and consumers.

7

Poverty under Planning
Levels and Change

The Indian economy was stagnant when the planning era began in 1951. The per capita income was abysmally low and its class distribution was highly unequal. The prime need at that stage was to build the necessary infrastructure to generate sufficient income. The first two Five Year Plans (1951–56, 1956–61) focused on this theme, though the Second Plan made provision for production of wage goods through labour-intensive techniques of production so as to meet the consumption demand of the poor and the lower deciles of the population. In the 1950s, a distinction between the poor and the non-poor was not that relevant for planning because the entire population, barring a few landed gentry and the English-speaking people who were the mainstay of the British administration, could be termed as poor not only by the present yardsticks but also by the standards prevailing in those days, which were minimal. Any measure of income generation then would have benefited the poor.

The rate of economic growth recorded was about 4 per cent per year during the first 10 years of planning. Per capita income increased over time, but the growth in per capita income was not distribution-neutral. Some people benefited from the growth process more than others. In essence, a large part of the incremental income bypassed the poor and the lower deciles of the population. In order to plan for a proportionately greater flow of fruits of growth to the poor, it was necessary to first identify them. This made it essential to develop a methodology to locate the poor, find out who they were, where they lived, and what they did; thus, determination of the poverty line and measurement of poverty turned out to be important. In tandem, the level of poverty and the pace of poverty reduction came to be treated as an acid test for India's planning and development strategy.

An assessment of the level and change in the incidence of poverty depends upon availability of comparable poverty estimates. The Planning Commission was the nodal agency of the Government of India for measurement of poverty at the national and state levels. The available estimates from the Planning Commission enabled assessment of the poverty situation for the years 1973–74 to 1993–94 in the pre-reform days, and from 1993–94 to 2011–12 in the era of economic reform.

Poverty in the Pre-reform Period

The poverty estimates from 1973–74 have been used here to assess the poverty situation in the pre-reform years. The analysis of poverty in the pre-reform era would be incomplete without mentioning the theoretical and empirical exercises throughout the 1960s and 1970s, which attained great heights as a galaxy of economists, statisticians, and nutritionists estimated poverty ratio at the national and state levels. These originated from the use of the poverty line determined by a Working Group constituted by the Planning Commission in 1962. Based on the norm of the balanced diet recommended by the ICMR in 1958, the Working Group determined the rural poverty line as per capita monthly consumption expenditure of INR 20 (at 1960–61 prices) at the national level. In view of the higher cost of living, the amount was increased slightly for urban areas. The poverty ratio (that is, the percentage of total population living below the poverty line, also known as headcount ratio) is estimated from the poverty line and the class distribution of persons obtained from the NSS data on consumer expenditure. The number of poor is estimated from the poverty ratio and the total population.

This national poverty line worked out by the Working Group was decomposed into state-wise poverty lines (using state-specific price indices) to estimate state-wise poverty. The studies concentrated on factors affecting poverty and the impact of income and prices on changes in poverty. These were path-breaking exercises on poverty, opening new vistas for its causalities.

Estimate of Poverty: 1973–93

In 1979, the Planning Commission adopted the Task Force methodology to estimate poverty (the Task Force methodology has been described in Chapter 2). Based on this methodology, it estimated the poverty ratio for several years in the 1970s and the 1980s. After nearly two decades, in March 1997 the Planning Commission replaced the Task Force methodology of poverty estimation by the Expert Group (Lakdawala) methodology, and estimated poverty for a number of years from 1973–74 to 1993–94. These are used to assess the performance of poverty reduction in the pre-reform years. Before deliberating on the poverty estimates, it would be useful to take a look at the incidents that propelled the Planning Commission to switch over from the Task Force to the Expert Group (Lakdawala) methodology.

The Task Force methodology of poverty estimation ordains pro rata adjustment of NSS consumption to NAS across different expenditure groups of the population. (The possible reason behind such an adjustment has been discussed in Chapter 2 in the context of the mathematical model used in the Sixth Plan.) The Task Force method yielded the poverty ratio in 1993–94 as 12 per cent. It was considered unimaginably low, and not consistent with the values of major macroeconomic variables. The reason behind such low level of poverty (12 per cent) in 1993–94 could be traced to the large discrepancy between NSS and NAS consumption because the poverty ratio in 1993–94 following the Task Force method but without adjusting NSS consumption (to NAS consumption) became 36 per cent. There was no evidence that the discrepancy between the two consumptions was same for lower and upper deciles of the population. Hence, the poverty ratio in 1993–94 estimated from the Task Force method was perceived more to be an artefact than real.

The state governments feared that such a low level of poverty, if used in the poverty-based central allocation of food and fund, may spell doom for them. The low level of poverty might not have significantly altered the relative position of the states, thereby leaving the structure of interstate allocation of the central (government) funds unaffected. However, it was a time when the poverty ratio was also being used as a yardstick to allocate central assistance to states under various developmental and social security programmes. A lower level of poverty connotes lesser allocation in anti-poverty programmes, and also in developmental programmes, as the latter uses poverty as one of the criteria in the allocation of these funds, both inter- and intra-state. This prompted the state governments to voice their anxiety over the Task Force method. Academicians and theoreticians joined the fray as they regarded the Task Force methodology as inappropriate in giving a representative picture of the incidence of poverty on grounds of (a) the manner and method of adjusting NSS consumption to NAS level; (b) the choice of deflator to represent price change in the poverty line; (c) application of the same poverty line in all the states, which meant ignoring interstate price differentials; (d) use of a fixed consumption basket for the poor over time; and (e) identical consumption basket of the poor in all states. With academicians joining the politicians, the issue of poverty crossed the threshold of economics and statistics. The Planning Commission, being caught in a quagmire, constituted the Expert Group on Estimation of Proportion and Number of Poor in September 1989 (henceforth, Expert Group) with Professor D. T. Lakdawala as the chairman. It was mandated to 'look into the methodology for estimation of poverty and to re-define the poverty line, if necessary'.

It has been mentioned earlier (in Chapter 2) that the Task Force estimated the average calorie norm as 2,400 kcal per capita per day for rural population and 2,100 kcal for urban population. Then, it worked out the consumption basket (at national level, separately for rural and urban population), which is able to meet the calorie norm along with other non-food necessities (such as clothing, shelter, transport, education, health care, and so on). The monetary expenditure needed to attain the consumption basket is termed as the poverty line. These consumption baskets (at national level, separately for rural/ urban population) worked out by the Task Force were adopted by the

Expert Group (Lakdawala) as the poverty line (in rural/urban areas). The Expert Group (Lakdawala) anchored these (rural/urban) poverty lines in the respective calorie norm determined by the Task Force. The state-specific poverty lines were worked out by evaluating these rural and urban consumption baskets (determined by the Task Force) at the state's prices. This was done from state-specific price indices and interstate price differentials. The state-specific price indices were constructed from the CPIAL in rural areas and CPIIW in urban areas. The interstate price differential was measured by Fisher's Index, which computed the cost of a fixed consumption basket for the states from the quantity and value of consumption of each item. Thus, the commodity composition of the (national consumption) basket remained invariant across states and differed only to the extent of prices. The state-wise poverty lines represented the amount of consumption expenditure necessary in the state, at the states' prices, in order to acquire the national consumption basket.

The state-specific poverty ratios in rural and urban areas were calculated from the state-specific poverty lines and state-specific distribution of persons by expenditure groups obtained from the large sample survey of consumer expenditure, which is available from the NSSO (National Sample Survey Office) once in approximately five years. The aggregate poverty ratio of the state was worked out by combining its rural and urban poverty ratios. The national poverty ratio is computed as an average of state-wise poverty ratios.

The national poverty line (separately in rural and urban areas) was worked out as an interpolated value from the national consumption distribution obtained from NSS consumer expenditure data and the national poverty ratio. Hence, estimate of the national poverty line in this method was implicit.

Three factors largely distinguish the Expert Group (Lakdawala) methodology of poverty estimation from those of the Task Force. First, the Expert Group used state-specific poverty lines as against national poverty line for estimation of poverty in the states. It thereby captured the cost of living in the states more accurately as compared to the Task Force method. Second, it relied exclusively on NSS consumption and, by implication, did not adjust the NSS consumption to NAS consumption. It may be noted that exclusive use of NSS consumption assumed that only the non-poor are responsible for the discrepancy between the two consumptions (NSS and NAS), which eventually overstated the poverty estimates. Third, the Expert Group method used state-specific cost of living indices to update the poverty line in rural and urban areas. The Task Force used only one all-India index which was the same for rural and urban areas.

The Planning Commission accepted the Expert Group (Lakdawala) methodology in March 1997 and this became the basis of poverty estimation at the national and state levels for the next one and a half decades. The poverty estimates at the national level (separately in rural and urban areas) derived from this method are given in Table 7.1.

The poverty ratio in 1993–94 was two-thirds of the level in 1973–74. It makes the rate of decline in poverty ratio during this two-decade 1973–93 less than a percentage point per year. Due to faster increase in population, the number of people in poverty remained stationary at about 320 million in this period 1973–93.

The change in poverty has its rural–urban ramification. The decline in poverty ratio in rural and urban areas was not that different in this period. However, the number of poor in rural areas declined while it increased in urban areas. Higher population growth in urban areas caused largely by rural to urban migration (mainly of the poor) was responsible for the increase in the number of poor in urban areas.

A feature of poverty reduction in 1973–93 was that the decline in poverty ratio took place in an environment of lower growth rate

Table 7.1   Poverty Ratio and Number of Poor: 1973–74 to 1993–94

Year	Poverty Ratio (%)			Number of Poor (in Million)		
	Rural	Urban	Total	Rural	Urban	Total
1973–74	56.4	49.0	54.9	261.3	60.0	321.3
1977–78	53.1	45.2	51.3	264.3	64.6	328.9
1983	45.7	40.8	44.5	252.0	70.9	322.9
1987–88	39.1	38.2	38.9	231.9	75.2	307.1
1993–94	37.3	32.4	36.0	244.0	76.3	320.3

Note: The poverty ratios are derived from the Expert Group (Lakdawala) methodology.
Source: 'Estimates of Poverty', Press Information Bureau, Government of India, 11 March, 1997.

of per capita GDP. The elasticity of poverty ratio with respect to per capita GDP was more in the initial 10 years (1973–83) as compared to the latter 10 years (1983–93). It implies that higher income growth was required to yield a similar decline in poverty ratio in the latter 10 years. The elasticity is an expression of the impact of the growth momentum on the rate of reduction in poverty. The elasticity of poverty ratio with respect to per capita consumption was found to be more in the latter 10 years as compared to the initial 10 years. It shows that a lower rate of growth of consumption yielded similar decline in poverty ratio in the latter period. The reason may lie in the generation of income (consumption) from anti-poverty programmes, which were rooted in the development strategy from 1980 and continued thereafter.

The poverty estimates were available from the Planning Commission once every five years. However, these estimates did not synchronize with the five years of the Plan, and as a result it was not possible to determine exactly how much of the target of poverty reduction (set in a Five Year Plan) could be achieved. The two-decade period of 1973–93 covers three Five Year Plans (Fifth, Sixth, and Seventh). The periodicity of the Fifth Plan was 1974–79. The two closest years for which the poverty ratios can be compared are 1973–74 and 1977–78. The poverty ratio declined by 0.9 percentage points per year in 1973–77. There was no official target for poverty reduction in the Fifth Plan.

The periodicity of the Sixth Plan was 1980–85. There are three points of time (1977–78, 1983, and 1987–88) around the Sixth Plan for which the poverty ratios are available. Between any two of these three years, the decline in poverty ratio was 1.2 percentage points per year. Similarly, the periodicity of the Seventh Plan was 1985–90 and there are three points of time (1983, 1987–88, and 1993–94) around the Seventh Plan for which the poverty ratios are available. The poverty ratio declined by: (a) 1.2 percentage points per year in 1983–87; (b) 0.5 percentage points per year in 1987–93; and (c) 0.8 percentage points per year in 1983–93. The target for poverty reduction was set at 4 percentage points per year in the Sixth Plan and 2 percentage points per year in the Seventh Plan. Clearly, the decline in poverty ratio in these two Plans was way behind the targets.

Economic Reform and Poverty

When economic reform measures were initiated in 1991, there was considerable apprehension, if not fear, among the planners that the process of income generation could be iniquitous, making the class distribution of output and income unfavourable to the lower deciles of the population, resulting in rise in the level of poverty and even immiserization. Prominent among those who created such a suspicion were intellectuals and policymakers reposing exclusive faith on the state for growth maximization and for steering economic development. Some of them even cautioned that the opening up of the economy through reform measures would provide an opportunity to multinational companies to capture the Indian market for goods, in the way that the East India Company did earlier in the seventeenth century, which led to India's colonization for the next two hundred years. It is no wonder that the impact of economic growth on the level of poverty and the rate of its decline became a central issue in the era of economic reform.

The rate of economic growth, to a large extent, determines the standards of living of the population. The impact is felt primarily by way of increase in income. The state efforts to increase the income of the poor and the lower deciles of the population in the era of economic reform were weaved into three specific areas. First, acceleration of the rate of economic growth was expected to result in increase in income of all the sections of the population, including the poor and the lower deciles of the population, in a near-equal manner. The idea was that the growth-oriented measures should result in increase in incomes of the poor, at least as much as others, if not more, by making the income distribution more equitable. Second, as the growth process may take a longer time to raise the income of the poor to the level of the poverty line, the state envisaged several income redistributive programmes. It is a component of the policy of direct attack on poverty which was already being pursued since 1980 (in the Sixth Plan). Moreover, there were pensions for the old, disabled, and widows, and subsidized food for the poorest of the poor. There was an added emphasis on food distribution to the poor, who mainly due to lack of sufficient income were unable to access adequate food for the family. The PDS was strengthened and food was supplied to the poor at a token price. Third, human and social development programmes were formulated by the state in order to elevate the economic status of the poor and the weaker sections of the society. It included literacy, education, health care, nutrition, housing, and service-oriented programmes such as drinking water supply and sanitation. The benefits of these programmes also accrued to a section of the population who were unable to pay for the market price of these services. This three-pronged measure marked a paradigm shift in the approach to poverty alleviation during the period of economic reform. All of these programmes may not have added directly to the income of the poor but enhanced their capability and welfare, and to a great extent served as a safety net.

Poverty in the 1990s: Initial Estimates

The issue of poverty took centre stage in the development debate throughout the two decades of economic reform. The debate was fierce because the level and change in poverty ratio was treated as a direct outcome of the policies of economic reform. Whether the economic reform measures were able to make a dent in poverty is the prime question.

The economic reform measures were initiated in 1991. In March 1997, the Planning Commission adopted the Expert Group (Lakdawala) methodology for measurement of poverty, and using this method they estimated the poverty ratio for earlier years, and that includes 1987–88 and 1993–94. Obviously, the poverty estimates of 1993–94 cannot be treated as a referendum on economic reform, for the simple reason that the reforms began just two years ago. At best, it could be compared with 1987–88 to have an idea about the direction of change in poverty. The poverty ratio in 1993–94 (36 per cent) was lower than that in 1987–88 (38.9 per cent), and that cleared the litmus test that the reform measure had not increased the level of poverty.

The Expert Group (Lakdawala) method ordains estimation of poverty from a large sample survey of consumer expenditure, which is available from the NSSO once in approximately five years. After 1993–94, the large survey of consumer expenditure data was available for 1999–2000 (NSS 55th Round). This data was eagerly awaited so that an assessment of the policy shift associated with economic reform and liberalization measures on standards of living of the population, and specifically on the poor, could be made. Using this (NSS 55th Round) data, the Planning Commission (in February 2001) estimated the poverty ratio for 1999–2000 as 26.1 per cent.[1] It had earlier estimated the poverty ratio in 1993–94 as 36 per cent. On this basis, the decline in poverty ratio within a span of six years, 1993–94 to 1999–2000, is found to be 9.9 percentage points, and the decline in the number of poor is 60.1 million—considered a remarkable feat in view of the fact that the number of poor remained stagnant for two decades, from 1973–74 to 1993–94.

The manner and method of collection of consumer expenditure data in 1999–2000 (NSS 55th Round) have been different from that in 1993–94 (NSS 50th Round). It is argued that this change rendered the consumer expenditure data of these two years non-comparable. In direct consequence, the poverty estimates in these two years becomes non-comparable.

In 1999–2000, the NSSO changed the recall period (also known as reference period) in respect of food items and a few non-food items. The apprehension is that the change in the recall period overstated consumption, especially of food. In such an eventuality, the poverty ratio in 1999–2000 estimated by the Planning Commission becomes understated. Hence, it is not possible to arrive at a concrete decision about the magnitude of decline in poverty from 1993–94 to 1999–2000.

In order to arrive at a decision about the impact of economic reform measures on the poverty situation, it is essential to derive the poverty ratio in 1999–2000 which is comparable with 1993–94. Researchers at home and abroad tried to devise ways and means to make the NSS consumer expenditure data of 1993–94 and 1999–2000 comparable, and then work out the poverty ratio in these two years so that a fair assessment of the change in poverty situation in six years of economic reform from 1993 to 1999 could be made. The poverty estimates made by Angus Deaton, K. Sundaram and S. D. Tendulkar, and Abhijit Sen and Himanshu have been mentioned here for their elegance in technicalities.

Deaton deduced that the food consumption in 1999–2000 had been overstated. He corrected the food consumption using a complex yet elegant mathematical model, and estimated the decline in poverty ratio from 1993–94 to 1999–2000 as 7.5 percentage points.[2] The decline in poverty ratio estimated by Deaton is thus three-fourths of that of the Planning Commission.

Sundaram–Tendulkar concluded that the food consumption data in 1999–2000 had not been overestimated. Using the same data but an alternate method (than the Planning Commission), they estimated the magnitude of decline in poverty ratio from 1993–94 to 1999–2000 as 8.2 percentage points and the decline in the number of poor as 42.8 million.[3] After some time, they revised these estimates to 4.9 percentage points and 13.1 million respectively.[4]

Using a somewhat rigorous method, Sen–Himanshu arrived at the conclusion that the per capita food consumption of 1999–2000 had been overestimated by 3.4 per cent in rural areas and 4.4 per cent in urban areas. After correcting the food consumption of 1999–2000, they estimated the decline in the poverty ratio from 1993–94 to 1999–2000 as 2.8 percentage points, which is around one-fourth of that estimated by the Planning Commission.[5]

The estimated decline in poverty ratio in the six years from 1993 to 1999 made from these three methodologies yielded a wide range—from 2.8 percentage points in Sen–Himanshu's estimate to 7.5 percentage points in Deaton's. Sen–Himanshu's estimate of the decline in poverty ratio was so little that it was not enough to reduce the number of poor, and hence their natural conclusion: India's growth revival after 1992 largely bypassed the poor.[6]

The impact of economic reform programmes on the poor was not as transparent as Sen–Himanshu try to depict. Following the methodology adopted by the Planning Commission, it can be found that there were at least two points of time in the 1990s (1994–95 and 2000–01) between which poverty reduction is exactly 10 percentage points.[7] This estimate of decline in poverty ratio was not clouded with comparability problems of the kind that impinged on the poverty estimate of 1993–94 and 1999–2000. The poverty ratios in 1994–95 and 2000–01 have been derived from NSS consumer expenditure data of the 51st and 56th Rounds respectively. These are thin sample surveys of the NSS with a one-year survey period (agricultural year, July–June) and identical to the large sample survey. Ironically, the Planning Commission did not endorse the poverty estimates based on thin samples, even though, as Deaton says, the sample sizes were large enough to support accurate poverty estimates at the national level. The comparability of poverty ratios from the thin NSS samples could be compromised if these have different subjects of enquiry. The principal subject of enquiry in NSS 51st and 56th Rounds is similar, namely unorganized manufacturing, and therefore, there is little reason for the national trends for these two mutually comparable rounds to be less valid than from the large samples.

The discussion on the poverty estimates for the years 1993–94 and 1999–2000 made earlier enable tracking the nature and intensity of the debate on poverty in the era of economic reforms. It can throw some light on the weight of the poverty estimates to decide the course, if not the fate, of economic reforms.

Poverty: 1993–94 to 2011–12

In 1997, the TPDS was introduced to provide food to the poor groups of the population at a token price. While formulating the Tenth Plan (2002–2007), the government noted instances of the non-poor availing of this benefit. In view of the huge financial implication, it reiterated that the benefits of the TPDS would be restricted strictly to the poor as officially measured by the Planning Commission.

The TPDS, as in the case of income redistributive poverty alleviation programmes, was implemented by the state governments. The number of beneficiaries identified by the state governments for these programmes always exceeded the number of poor estimated by the Planning Commission. The state governments did not find the idea of containing the number of beneficiaries to the level determined by the Planning Commission tenable. Social activists joined the fray and clamoured for a change in the methodology of poverty estimation so that the level of poverty could be raised. It was not a debate on the poverty line or the level of poverty as such, because there was no serious issue with the Expert Group (Lakdawala) methodology, which the Planning Commission was using then. It was a clear-cut call to raise the level of poverty, to which the Planning Commission meekly gave in by constituting an Expert Group in December 2005, under the chairmanship of Professor Suresh D. Tendulkar, with the mandate to construct a new poverty line.

The Expert Group (Tendulkar) deliberated for four eventful years, 2005–2009. In this period, the Indian economy went through a phase of transformation, triggered by the high rate of economic growth (averaging 7.9 per cent per year in three years, 2005–06 to 2007–08). This resulted in increase in income and consumption, and in the overwhelming improvement in the living standards of the people, which fuelled the expectations of better standards of living among the poor and the lower middle class. This may have warranted a revision of the poverty line. There was an analogous reason as well. The poverty line then used by the Planning Commission was originally based on the consumption expenditure pattern of 1973–74. The increase in per capita income since then has been four to five times, and evidences point out changes in the consumption behaviour as a result. These needed to be factored in the construction of the new poverty line. The Expert Group (Tendulkar), while suggesting a methodology for measurement of poverty, bypassed these issues. They did not construct a new poverty line. Instead, they endorsed the urban poverty line of 2004–05 then being used by the Planning Commission for the entire country. The urban poverty line (owing to higher cost of living) is higher than the rural poverty line. Use of the urban poverty line in rural areas increased the rural poverty ratio in 2004–05 to about one and a half times from the existing level. However, it was not enough to assuage the middle class, or even the lower middle class, that emerged following the growth surge in the era of economic reform. These were people with high aspirations, trying to reach a higher strata of the society as quickly as possible. Until then, they wanted to access the benefits that the government was offering to the poor.

The Expert Group (Tendulkar) submitted its report in November 2009.[8] The Planning Commission was caught in a Hobson's choice. It was a repeat of the situation in 2005 that led to its constitution. In April 2012, the Planning Commission constituted another Expert Group. This time, it was under the chairmanship of C. Rangarajan, then chairman of the Prime Minister's Economic Advisory Council.

Rangarajan suggested a methodology of measurement of poverty in the same mould as the previous ones, specifically the Task Force, and submitted it to the Planning Commission in June 2014. In August 2014, the Planning Commission was disbanded. Its replacement, the

NITI Aayog, decided in September 2016 not to accept this methodology. The poverty estimates derived from the Expert Group (Tendulkar) method continue to be the official measure of poverty. These will be used here to assess the performance of poverty reduction in the era of economic reform. Before analysing the poverty estimates, the methodology recommended by the Expert Group (Tendulkar) may be looked into.

The methodology of measurement of poverty suggested by Expert Group (Tendulkar) is built upon the Expert Group (Lakdawala) method. It uses the urban poverty line and poverty ratio derived from the Expert Group (Lakdawala) method as the starting point to develop the methodology of poverty estimation. The estimation of the poverty line in rural and urban areas in the Expert Group (Tendulkar) method can be described in three steps.

First, the national urban poverty line (in 2004–05) derived by Expert Group (Lakdawala) method, which is uniform recall period (URP) consumption–based, is converted into mixed recall period (MRP) consumption.[9] The MRP consumption–based urban poverty line is worked out as the level of per capita consumption expenditure in the MRP consumption distribution that corresponds to the bottom 25.7 per cent of the population (which is the urban poverty ratio derived from the poverty line and the class distribution of consumption based on URP consumption, 2004–05). This is the starting point.

Second, state-specific urban poverty lines are derived from (MRP consumption–based) national urban poverty line (estimated in the first step) using 'state-relative-to-all-India' price index numbers. The price index numbers are constructed from a variety of price data, most of which are implicit.

Third, state-specific rural poverty lines are worked out from state-specific urban poverty lines (as estimated in the second step) by applying state-specific urban-to-rural price relatives. The state relative to the all-India price index and the state-specific urban-to-rural price relatives are computed from the implicit price indices derived from the quantity and value of different items gathered in the NSS consumer expenditure survey.

The state-specific poverty ratios are estimated from state-specific class distribution of persons obtained from MRP consumption distribution of NSS consumer expenditure and the state-specific poverty line. The national poverty ratio is estimated as an average of state-wise poverty ratios.

The outcome of the Expert Group (Tendulkar) methodology is as follows: the national urban poverty ratio in 2004–05 remained the same as the existing estimate of the Planning Commission (25.7 per cent). The national rural poverty ratio in 2004–05 increased from 28.3 per cent from the existing estimate to 41.8 per cent.

There are at least two salient inconsistencies in the basic presumptions on which the Expert Group (Tendulkar) methodology is founded. First, it presumes that the urban poverty ratio derived from the Expert Group (Lakdawala) method is less controversial and has general acceptance while the rural prices are understated, leading to low rural poverty line and, in consequence, low rural poverty ratio. These contentions are just the opposite of the facts in this regard. In actuality, it is the urban poverty line and poverty ratio from the Expert Group (Lakdawala) method which can be disputed and not the rural poverty lines or poverty ratios as these are not low by any reckoning. Second, the Expert Group (Tendulkar) methodology entails estimation of state-specific rural poverty lines from state-specific urban poverty lines using urban-to-rural price relatives derived from Fisher's price indices, which are computed from quantity and value of purchases of different items in NSS data on consumer expenditure. This is not a cohesive approach, especially in an expanding economy where peoples' incomes change fast with consequential change in the composition of the consumption basket, as was the case in India between 2004–05 and 2011–12. In such a situation, Fisher's index is unlikely to reflect the actual price rise encountered by the poor, impacting on the precision of the state-specific poverty lines, and eventually the state-specific poverty ratios. Fisher's index should not have been calculated from the implicit prices obtained from the quantity and value of purchases made by households, especially because the consumption basket of the poor can alter significantly within a short period of time. Equivalently, when computed from implicit prices of NSS consumer expenditure data, Fisher's index is not ideally suited to capture the real price inflation in an expanding economy characterized by fast changes in income and consumption of a large section of the population. The Expert Group (Tendulkar) either overlooked the theoretical complexities inherent in working out Fisher's index or could not anticipate the kind of expansion that the Indian economy witnessed in terms of income and consumption of the people in such a short time of seven years, 2004–11.

Using the Expert Group (Tendulkar) methodology, the Planning Commission estimated poverty for the years 1993–94, 2004–05, 2009–10, and 2011–12. On account of being derived from a uniform methodology, these estimates can be used to assess the poverty situation in the era of economic reform. The poverty estimate in 2009–10 has not been used here as it is not regarded as a normal year because drought in agriculture in large areas resulted in loss of output and income, and income generation from a wide range of activities was adversely affected as a result of the global economic crisis that erupted in September 2008. In view of this, the poverty estimates of 1993–94, 2004–05, and 2011–12 have been used to assess the poverty situation in the era of economic reform. The poverty ratio and number of poor for these three years have been given in Table 7.2. The decline of poverty ratio since 1993–94 has been given in Table 7.3.

In the two decades of economic reform, the level of poverty reduced to less than half (from 45.3 per cent in 1993–94 to 21.9 per cent in

Table 7.2 Poverty Ratio and Number of Poor: 1993–94 to 2011–12

Year	Poverty Ratio (Per cent)			Number of Poor (in Million)		
	Rural	Urban	Total	Rural	Urban	Total
1993–94	50.1	31.8	45.3	328.6	74.5	403.7
2004–05	41.8	25.7	37.2	326.3	80.8	407.1
2011–12	25.7	13.7	21.9	216.7	53.1	269.8

Sources: (1) The poverty ratios for 1993–94 are available in 'Poverty Estimates and Poverty Lines for 1993–94', Annexure B, p. 18; the poverty ratios for 2004–05 are available in 'Final Poverty Lines and Poverty Head Count Ratio for 2004–05', Annexure A, p. 17, *Report of the Expert Group to Review the Methodology for Estimation of Poverty*, Government of India, Planning Commission, November 2009. The number of poor in these two years is author's estimate.

(2) The poverty ratio and number of poor for 2011–12 are available in *Press Note on Poverty Estimates, 2011–12*, Government of India, Planning Commission, July 2013.

Table 7.3   Decline in Poverty Ratio: 1993–94 to 2011–12

	Rural	Urban	Total
A. Decline in Poverty Ratio (Percentage Points per Year)			
1993–94 to 2004–05	0.75	0.55	0.74
2004–05 to 2011–12	2.32	1.69	2.18
1993–94 to 2011–12	1.36	1.01	1.30
B. Rate of Decline in Poverty Ratio (Per Cent per Year, Compound)			
1993–94 to 2004–05	1.6	1.9	1.8
2004–05 to 2011–12	6.7	8.6	7.3
1993–94 to 2011–12	3.6	4.6	4.0

Source: Author's estimate using the data in Table 7.2.

2011–12). The decline was higher in the later part of the reform (15.3 percentage points in seven years, 2004–11) as compared to the earlier years (8.1 percentage points in eleven years 1993–2004). The annual average decline in poverty ratio in 2004–11 was nearly three times of that in 1993–2004. The compounded rate of decline in poverty ratio accelerated to 7.3 per cent per year in 2004–11, from 1.8 per cent per year in 1993–2004.

The increase in income and consumption in 1993–2004 reduced the poverty ratio, but not the number of poor, which remained unchanged at around 400 million. As income and consumption increased faster in 2004–11, the number of people in poverty declined by 137 million in this period.

The faster decline in poverty ratio and number of poor in 2004–11 was the logical outcome of increase in growth rate of per capita GDP by 7.1 per cent per year and per capita net national income (NNI) by 6.7 per cent per year. The poverty reduction was facilitated by expansion of wage employment and food distribution programmes. Additional government revenue generated from high growth rate of the economy provided elbow room for financing the expenditure on these programmes.

The higher growth rate of the economy in 2004–11 was reflected in the growth of per capita consumption. In 1993–2004, real per capita consumption increased by 1 per cent per year in rural areas and

1.8 per cent per year in urban areas. These became 2.9 per cent per year in rural areas and 3.4 per cent per year in urban areas in 2004–11.[10] Therefore, the annual increase in per capita consumption in 2004–11 was about three times of that in 1993–2004 in rural areas and twice of that in urban areas. In view of the high rate of increase in per capita consumption, it is not surprising that the poverty ratio as well as the number of poor declined in 2011–12.

The poverty reduction from 2004–05 to 2011–12 can said to have taken place due to increase in income and consumption, eventuated by a high rate of economic growth because inequality in class distribution of consumption did not decline; rather, it increased marginally. The inequality in consumption distribution is measured by the Lorenz ratio, whose value lies between zero and unity. The closer the value of the Lorenz ratio to zero, the more egalitarian is the consumption distribution. Conversely, the closer the value of Lorenz ratio to unity, the more unequal is the distribution. A higher value of the Lorenz ratio, therefore, represents greater inequality. The value of the Lorenz ratio estimated from NSS consumer expenditure data is found to increase from 0.266 in 2004–05 to 0.280 in 2011–12 in rural areas and from 0.348 to 0.367 in urban areas. The changes in per capita consumption and inequality in its distribution point out that poverty reduction in 2004–11 was the result of growth in income or, in other words, the outcome of growth effect.

Poverty reduction in 2004–11 was accompanied by a change in the consumption pattern by way of decline in the share of food in total consumption, the share of foodgrains within food, and the share of cereals within foodgrains. The consumption of food items such as milk and milk products, egg, fish and meat, edible oil, and sugar, which were earlier the prerogative of the non-poor, now entered into the consumption basket of the lower deciles of the population. The taste and preference of a large section of the population changed in response to change in income eventuated by rapid economic growth and growth-induced change in the socio-economic condition. The demographic and societal changes along with the diversification of the food industry are considered to be the important catalysts of this change.

As the growth rate of the economy moved on to a higher trajectory, along with the poverty ratio, the distribution-sensitive measures of poverty—such as the poverty gap ratio, which is a measure of the depth of poverty, and the squared poverty gap, which is a measure of the severity of poverty—reduced. The poverty gap ratio indicates the magnitude of the effort required to shift the consumption of all persons below the poverty line to the level of the poverty line. The squared poverty gap indicates the higher intensity of efforts required to address the people who are progressively further below the poverty line in order to bring them out of poverty.

Even after the huge decline in poverty, 270 million persons remained poor in 2011–12. This constituted a fifth of the total population, and hence is not a small number. Moreover, they have been counted against a poverty line, which is viewed as a bare subsistence level of living, a level below which they are under severe stress and their survival is threatened. It underlines that poverty remains a major challenge.

The media, social activists, and even some academicians have attributed the poverty line, and in turn the poverty ratio, as too low. Relying on this, they have denounced the extent of poverty reduction that took place in the period of economic reform. It may be true that the low magnitude of the poverty line impacts the estimate of the poverty ratio. However, the rate of reduction in poverty does not depend at all on the magnitude of the poverty line. It is true that the poverty ratio will be higher if the poverty line is raised. It is equally true that in the event of a rise in the poverty line, the rate of decline in poverty ratio would remain unchanged. The rate of poverty reduction remains unaltered with poverty lines fixed at higher or lower levels. The conclusion on poverty reduction in the period 2004–11 does not alter if the poverty line is raised or lowered. The absolute level of poverty would be high or low depending upon whether the poverty line is fixed at a higher or lower level. However, the rate of decline would be more or less the same.

There is a lack of consensus on sufficiency of the amount of consumption expenditure denoting the poverty line. It is argued that the poverty ratio derived from a consumption expenditure–based poverty line may not be able to determine the 'true' poverty. It is also not denied that poverty ratios over a period of time can serve the purpose of tracking the impact of economic growth on poverty by way of a check on the number of people living below the poverty line. It gives an idea about the efficacy of planning and development strategy and denotes the impact of growth on poverty. The moot question is whether the number of people below the poverty line is rising or falling. This is answered by the poverty ratio, despite the arbitrariness of the poverty line. The poverty ratio can be treated as the primary indicator to judge whether economic growth has resulted in improvement of levels of living of the population as a whole.

The estimates of poverty have been used in planning and policymaking in India in two major ways: first, to formulate an effective plan for poverty alleviation, and then, to track the progress of development over time and space. It is mainly three groups of people that are concerned with poverty-related issues: (a) theoreticians and academicians; (b) administrators and civil servants; and (c) civil society and non-governmental organizations. On the measurement of poverty, theoreticians in general have been consistent in their support of the consumption-based approach followed by the Planning Commission. This is not unusual as the World Bank also used the Indian method and poverty line (in the early 1980s) to estimate poverty in its member countries. Academicians are a mixed lot as some of them often critique the precise estimates, terming the poverty line as inadequate. Administrators and civil servants are less interested in the technical complexities of measurement of poverty; they are more concerned with the implementation of poverty alleviation programmes, which became a feature of the poverty reduction strategy since the 1980s, and gathered momentum in the period of economic reform. They would prefer a transparent, straightforward, and unequivocal approach to identify the poor, rooted in the ground realities of the countryside and in the urban peripheries. The civil society organizations and social activists representing non-governmental organizations, undoubtedly, are passionate about poverty. Their emotional bonding with the poor overlooks the complex theoretical (and empirical) issues related to measurement of poverty and identification of poor. The 'white noise' around poverty estimates made by social activists cannot be ignored in a democratic society with a vibrant press, and more so when poverty alleviation is no longer viewed as fulfilling the demand for coarse cereal and cloth, which was the case in 1951 when planning began.

State-wise Poverty under Economic Reform

Beneath the high rate of poverty reduction in the later years of economic reform (2004–11) lies a regional picture, which brings out more or less the same message as in the earlier years of the economic reform (1993–2004) when the growth rate was low to moderate, and the poverty reduction was negligible to marginal. As the rate of economic growth attained a new high in the later years of economic reform, the level of poverty lowered at the state level. But the pattern of poverty reduction across the states remained more or less the same as before, when the growth rate was low or moderate. The disparity among the states in respect of poverty reduction that existed in 1993–2004 remained unchanged in 2004–11. These are evident from the state-wise poverty ratios for major states in 1993–94, 2004–05, and 2011–12 given in Table 7.4 and the rate of decline in state-wise poverty ratios in Table 7.5.

The rate of decline in the poverty ratio accelerated from 1.8 per cent per year in 1993–2004 to 7.3 per cent per year in 2004–11. The acceleration took place in both rural and urban areas. The decline in poverty in 2004–11 can be called widespread in the sense that it occurred across the states. The rate of decline in poverty ratio (rural and urban combined) in the states was significantly higher in 2004–11 as compared to 1993–2004. This is evident from the following: (*a*) the rate of decline in poverty in only two states was more than 4 per cent per year in 1993–2004 whereas 17 states experienced similar rate of decline in 2004–11; and (*b*) the rate of decline in poverty in 1993–2004 was less than 2 per cent per year in 11 states as against 1 state in 2004–11. The pattern was similar in rural and urban areas. In rural and urban areas of 11 states, the poverty ratio declined by more than 8 per cent per year in 2004–11.

In 10 states, the poverty ratio declined by more than 10 per cent per year in 2004–11. Among these were the states with relatively low poverty rate, such as Punjab, Haryana, and Himachal Pradesh, and the three southern states (Andhra Pradesh, Kerala, and Tamil Nadu), which have been successful in reducing poverty earlier. The rate of decline in the poverty ratio in Uttarakhand and Tripura was high against the background of their relatively lower per capita consumption, indicating possibly the inclusive nature of economic growth.

Table 7.4 State-wise Poverty Ratio in the Era of Economic Reform (Per Cent)

No.	State	Poverty Ratio: 1993–94			Poverty Ratio: 2004–05			Poverty Ratio: 2011–12		
		Rural	Urban	Total	Rural	Urban	Total	Rural	Urban	Total
1	Andhra Pradesh	48.1	35.2	44.6	32.3	23.4	29.9	11.0	5.8	9.2
2	Assam	54.9	27.7	51.8	36.4	21.8	34.4	33.9	20.5	32.0
3	Bihar	62.3	44.7	60.5	55.7	43.7	54.4	34.1	31.2	33.7
4	Chhattisgarh	55.9	28.1	50.9	55.1	28.4	49.4	44.6	24.8	39.9
5	Gujarat	43.1	28.0	37.8	39.1	20.1	31.8	21.5	10.1	16.6
6	Haryana	40.0	24.2	35.9	24.8	22.4	24.1	11.6	10.3	11.2
7	Himachal Pradesh	36.7	13.6	34.6	25.0	4.6	22.9	8.5	4.3	8.1
8	Jammu & Kashmir	32.5	6.9	26.3	14.1	10.4	13.2	11.5	7.2	10.3
9	Jharkhand	65.9	41.8	60.7	51.6	23.8	45.3	40.8	24.8	37.0
10	Karnataka	56.6	34.2	49.5	37.5	25.9	33.4	24.5	15.3	20.9
11	Kerala	33.9	23.9	31.3	20.2	18.4	19.7	9.1	5.0	7.0
12	Madhya Pradesh	49.0	31.8	44.6	53.6	35.1	48.6	35.7	21.0	31.6
13	Maharashtra	59.3	30.3	47.8	47.9	25.6	38.1	24.2	9.1	17.3
14	Odisha	63.0	34.5	59.1	60.8	37.6	57.2	35.7	17.3	32.6
15	Punjab	20.3	27.2	22.4	22.1	18.7	20.9	7.7	9.2	8.3
16	Rajasthan	40.8	29.9	38.3	35.8	29.7	34.4	16.1	10.7	14.7
17	Tamil Nadu	51.0	33.7	44.6	37.5	19.7	28.9	15.8	6.5	11.3
18	Tripura	34.3	25.4	32.9	44.5	22.5	40.6	16.5	7.4	14.1

(*Cont'd*)

Table 7.4 (Cont'd)

No.	State	Poverty Ratio: 1993–94			Poverty Ratio: 2004–05			Poverty Ratio: 2011–12		
		Rural	Urban	Total	Rural	Urban	Total	Rural	Urban	Total
19	Uttar Pradesh	50.9	38.3	48.4	42.7	34.1	40.9	30.4	26.1	29.4
20	Uttarakhand	36.7	18.7	32.0	35.1	26.2	32.7	11.6	10.5	11.3
21	West Bengal	42.5	31.2	39.4	38.2	24.4	34.3	22.5	14.7	20.0
22	All India	50.1	31.8	45.3	41.8	25.7	37.2	25.7	13.7	21.9

Note: The estimates in 1993–94 and 2004–05 are from Expert Group (Tendulkar). The estimates of 2011–12 have been made by the Planning Commission using the Expert Group (Tendulkar) method.

Sources: (1) The poverty ratios for 1993–94 are available in 'Poverty Estimates and Poverty Lines for 1993–94', Annexure B, p. 18; the poverty ratios for 2004–05 are available in 'Final Poverty Lines and Poverty Head Count Ratio for 2004–05', Annexure A, p. 17, *Report of the Expert Group to Review the Methodology for Estimation of Poverty*, Government of India, Planning Commission, November 2009.

(2) The poverty ratio for 2011–12 are available in *Press Note on Poverty Estimates, 2011–12*, Government of India, Planning Commission, July 2013.

Table 7.5 Rate of Decline in State-wise Poverty Ratio in the Era of Economic Reform (Per Cent per Year, Compounded)

No.	State	1993–94 to 2004–05			2004–05 to 2011–12		
		Rural	Urban	Total	Rural	Urban	Total
1	Andhra Pradesh	3.6	3.6	3.6	14.3	18.0	15.5
2	Assam	3.7	2.2	3.7	1.0	0.9	1.0
3	Bihar	1.0	0.2	1.0	6.8	4.7	6.6
4	Chhattisgarh	0.1	−0.1	0.3	3.0	1.9	3.0
5	Gujarat	0.9	3.0	1.6	8.2	9.3	8.8
6	Haryana	4.3	0.7	3.6	10.2	10.5	10.4
7	Himachal Pradesh	3.4	9.4	3.7	14.3	0.9	13.9
8	Jammu & Kashmir	7.3	−3.8	6.1	2.8	5.1	3.4
9	Jharkhand	2.2	5.0	2.6	3.3	−0.6	2.9
10	Karnataka	3.7	2.5	3.5	5.9	7.3	6.5
11	Kerala	4.6	2.3	4.1	10.7	17.1	13.7
12	Madhya Pradesh	−0.8	−0.9	−0.8	5.6	7.1	5.9
13	Maharashtra	1.9	1.5	2.0	9.3	13.7	10.6
14	Odisha	0.3	−0.8	0.3	7.3	10.5	7.7
15	Punjab	−0.8	3.3	0.6	14.0	9.6	12.4
16	Rajasthan	1.2	0.1	1.0	10.8	13.6	11.4
17	Tamil Nadu	2.8	4.8	3.9	11.6	14.6	12.6
18	Tripura	−2.4	1.1	−1.9	13.2	14.7	14.1
19	Uttar Pradesh	1.6	1.1	1.5	4.7	3.8	4.6
20	Uttarakhand	0.4	−3.1	−0.2	14.6	12.3	14.1
21	West Bengal	1.0	2.2	1.3	7.3	7.0	7.4
22	All India	1.6	1.9	1.8	6.7	8.6	7.3

Source: Author's estimate using the data in Table 7.4.

The states experiencing a high rate of decline in rural poverty had a high rate of decline in urban poverty. The reverse was also true as the states with a low rate of decline in rural poverty had a low rate of decline in urban poverty. However, the situation was not similar in case of per capita consumption. At the level of the states, the rate of growth of per capita consumption was not similar in rural and urban areas. The correlation coefficient between the rate of decline in rural and urban poverty ratio (across the states) was high (0.67) while that between the rate of growth of rural and urban per capita consumption was low (0.32).

The rate of poverty reduction was relatively high in the states with low poverty rate. At the same time, poverty reduction was low in the states where the poverty ratio was high. This was a feature of poverty reduction in 1993–2004 when the growth rate was low to moderate. It was a similar situation in 2004–11 when the growth rate touched a new high. The level of poverty and the rate of poverty reduction in two groups of states, namely five states with high level of poverty and four southern states with low level of poverty, bear evidence in support of this hypothesis. Bihar, Jharkhand, Madhya Pradesh, Chhattisgarh, and Odisha were the five states with a high level of poverty. The poverty ratio in these five states was higher than the national average (irrespective of the methodology employed to measure poverty) for a pretty long time. In the era of economic reforms, the poverty ratio in these five states lowered but at a rate much slower than in others. As a result, their relative position in terms of poverty ratio remained unchanged. These five states ranked among the poorest states in 2004–05 and remained so in 2011–12.

On the other hand, the poverty ratio in four southern states, namely, Andhra Pradesh, Karnataka, Kerala, and Tamil Nadu, was consistently lower in the years before as well as after the commencement of economic reform. The rate of decline in poverty ratio in these four low-poverty states was about twice of that in the five high-poverty states, as mentioned earlier. The difference in the average poverty ratio between these five high-poverty states and the four low-poverty states that was evident in 2004–05 continued to remain so in 2011–12, albeit at a lower average level of poverty in both. The high growth in 2004–11 did not alter the relative position of these states.

The top five states in terms of rate of poverty reduction in 2004–11 were Andhra Pradesh, Tripura, Uttarakhand, Himachal Pradesh, and Kerala. On the other hand, the five states with the lowest rate of poverty reduction were Assam, Jharkhand, Jammu and Kashmir, Chhattisgarh, and Uttar Pradesh. The difference in the average poverty ratio between these two groups of states nearly doubled from 2004–05 to 2011–12, despite lowering in the poverty ratio in both. It once again underlines that the pattern of poverty reduction in the states did not change even as the rate of economic growth became high. The population in these two groups of states, however, differed. The population in the five states with the lowest poverty reduction was about two and a half times of that in the five states with highest poverty reduction.

In 2004–11, the annual rate of decline in poverty ratio in 21 major states ranged from 1 per cent to 15.5 per cent, when poverty in general declined significantly. The interstate variation in the rate of decline in poverty ratio measured from standard deviation (of state-wise rate of decline in poverty ratio) in 2004–11 is found to be twice of that in 1993–2004. The large interstate variation in the rate of decline in poverty ratio in 2004–11 underlines the dissimilarity in the performance of poverty reduction across states in the environs of high growth. As a result, some states had a poverty rate which was higher than even the most deprived countries of Africa while some are close to the prosperity levels of middle-income Latin American countries.

The disparity in the level of poverty existed between different states, between different districts within a state, and between different blocks within the district. It was the result of the initial conditions mainly arising from historical inequalities and also because the fruits of economic growth were not shared equally by all the regions. The pattern of development in some cases was asymmetric—leading to existence of pockets of poverty even within the developed areas of the state.

The way poverty is defined and measured makes increase in per capita consumption important for poverty reduction. The per capita consumer expenditure in rural and urban areas at the level of states for the years 2004–05 and 2011–12 are available from the NSS of consumer expenditure in nominal terms, that is, at the prices prevailing in the year in which these have been gathered. The per capita consumer expenditure in nominal terms has been converted into real terms by applying the price inflation implicit in the consumption basket of the poor derived from the Expert Group 2009 (Tendulkar) method. The state-wise growth rates of nominal and real per capita consumption during the period 2004–05 to 2011–12 have been given in Table 7.6. This table also gives the price inflation of the consumption basket of the poor during this period. These are given for 21 major states. These states account for 98.8 per cent of the rural population, 94 per cent of the urban population, and 97.3 per cent of the population for the country as a whole. At the national level, the real rate of growth of per capita consumption during the seven-year period of 2004–05 to

Table 7.6 Rate of Growth of Per Capita Consumption: 2004–05 to 2011–12 (Per Cent per Year, Compound)

No.	State	Nominal Consumption		Price Inflation		Real Consumption	
		Rural	Urban	Rural	Urban	Rural	Urban
1	Andhra Pradesh	14.6	12.9	10.3	8.7	3.9	3.9
2	Assam	9.0	9.2	8.2	7.7	0.8	1.4
3	Bihar	11.8	9.7	8.7	8.4	2.8	1.3
4	Chhattisgarh	10.7	9.1	9.2	7.4	1.4	1.6
5	Gujarat	12.1	10.8	9.3	8.3	2.6	2.3
6	Haryana	11.4	16.0	9.7	9.3	1.5	6.1
7	Himachal Pradesh	11.6	12.1	8.4	8.4	3.0	3.5
8	Jammu & Kashmir	10.3	11.0	7.9	7.3	2.2	3.5
9	Jharkhand	11.1	9.3	9.2	9.0	1.8	0.2
10	Karnataka	14.4	14.3	11.6	9.2	2.5	4.7
11	Kerala	12.5	12.3	9.6	7.8	2.7	4.2
12	Madhya Pradesh	12.1	10.9	9.5	7.7	2.4	2.9
13	Maharashtra	13.5	13.3	10.4	8.6	2.8	4.3
14	Odisha	11.5	12.8	7.9	8.2	3.3	4.3
15	Punjab	13.1	11.2	9.9	8.7	2.8	2.2
16	Rajasthan	13.4	12.9	9.5	8.4	3.5	4.1
17	Tamil Nadu	14.7	11.7	10.3	7.6	3.9	3.8
18	Tripura	12.9	10.5	8.5	7.5	4.0	2.8

19	Uttar Pradesh	10.3	12.0	8.5	8.5	1.7	3.2
20	Uttarakhand	13.3	13.2	8.8	8.7	4.1	4.1
21	West Bengal	10.7	11.5	8.4	8.0	2.1	3.3
22	All India	12.1	12.2	9.0	8.1	2.8	3.8

Note: The consumption relates to the mixed recall period. The rate of growth of per capita nominal and real consumption at the state level is the author's calculation using the state-wise per capita consumption in 2004–05 and 2011–12 obtained from the NSS consumer expenditure data and the price inflation implicit in the state-wise consumption basket of the poor, estimated from the increase in the magnitude of the poverty line between 2004–05 and 2011–12.

Sources: 1. The state-wise nominal consumption in rural and urban areas in 2004–05 is obtained from *Level and Pattern of Consumer Expenditure, 2004–05*, NSS 61st Round (July 2004–June 2005), Report No. 508 (61/1.0/1), National Sample Survey Organisation, Ministry of Statistics and Programme Implementation, Government of India, December 2006, Table 5R, pp. A-205 to A-240, and Table 5U, pp. A-241 to A-276.

2. The state-wise nominal consumption in rural and urban areas in 2011–12 is obtained from *Key Indicators of Household Consumer Expenditure in India*, NSS 68th Round (July 2011–June 2012), Government of India, Ministry of Statistics and Programme Implementation, National Sample Survey Organisation, June 2013, Table 1.1b-R, pp. A-5 and A-6, and Table 1.1b-U, pp. A-7 and A-8.

3. The state-wise poverty lines in rural and urban areas in 2004–05 are available from 'Final Poverty Lines and Poverty Head Count Ratio for 2004–05', Annexure A, p. 17, *Report of the Expert Group to Review the Methodology for Estimation of Poverty*, Government of India, Planning Commission, November 2009.

4. The state-wise poverty lines in rural and urban areas in 2011–12 are available from *Press Note on Poverty Estimates, 2011–12*, Government of India, Planning Commission, July 2013.

2011–12 works out to 2.8 per cent per year in rural areas and 3.8 per cent per year in urban areas. These are much higher in comparison with the growth in per capita consumption during the initial 11 years of economic reform, 1993–2004. The annual rate of increase in per capita consumption during the period 2004–11 is three times of that in the period 1993–2004 in rural areas, and twice in urban areas.

The increase in per capita consumption in 2004–11 was not same for all the states. A huge gap existed between the top and the bottom five states. In rural areas, the search for the bottom five states in terms of per capita consumption ended with the five high-poverty states (Bihar, Jharkhand, Madhya Pradesh, Chhattisgarh, and Odisha). On the other side, Punjab, Haryana, Himachal Pradesh, Jammu and Kashmir, and Kerala were the top five states in terms of per capita consumption. The poverty ratio in these five states with high per capita consumption was low. This was true in both 2004–05 and 2011–12. The position of the top and bottom five states did not change even as the per capita consumption in 2004–2011, on the whole, increased at a faster rate.

The poverty ratio in the low consumption states (Bihar, Jharkhand, Madhya Pradesh, Chhattisgarh, and Odisha) was high. In tandem with this, the poverty ratio was low in the high consumption states (Kerala, Punjab, Haryana, Himachal Pradesh, and Jammu and Kashmir). The rate of decline in poverty ratio is positively associated with the rate of growth of per capita consumption. The five high-poverty and low-consumption states accounted for one-third of India's population. Jharkhand and Odisha are contiguous and are located in the east while Chhattisgarh shares its borders with Odisha and Jharkhand. The five high-consumption states account for less than 10 per cent of India's total population. Among these five states, only Kerala was from the south and the other four states were from the north and contiguous. It is evident that economic growth has not been regionally balanced.

The association between rate of growth of per capita consumption and rate of decline in poverty ratio was strong in the states with low rate of poverty reduction, and weak in the states with high rate of poverty reduction. In 10 of the 21 states the rate of decline in poverty ratio during the period of 2004–05 to 2011–12 was high (ranging from 10.4 per cent per year to 15.5 per cent per year). The correlation coefficient between the rate of growth of per capita consumption and the rate of decline in poverty ratio for this group of states was low. In the remaining 11 states, the rate of decline in poverty ratio was low (being less than 8.8 per cent per year). For this group of 11 states, the correlation coefficient between the rate of growth of per capita consumption and the rate of decline in poverty ratio was high (the correlation coefficient being 0.82 in rural areas and 0.75 in urban).

In a similar way, the association between the rate of growth of per capita consumption and the rate of decline in poverty ratio is found to be strong in the states with high level of poverty, where the rate of poverty reduction was low. The level of poverty was high in Bihar, Jharkhand, Madhya Pradesh, Chhattisgarh, and Odisha; the rate of poverty reduction in these states was low. For these five high-poverty states, the correlation coefficient between the rate of decline in poverty ratio and the rate of growth of per capita consumption is 0.98 in rural areas and 0.95 in urban. The correlation coefficients being close to unity underline that poverty reduction in these high-poverty states prima facie depend on increase in consumption. The poverty reduction in these five states is not found to be sensitive to income (as the correlation coefficient between the rate of poverty reduction and growth in per capita net state domestic product in these five states is only 0.28). It is apparent that increase in per capita consumption can be a major instrument of poverty reduction in the states with high level of poverty. The increased consumption from poverty alleviation programmes and food subsidies can make a solid impact on the poverty situation.

Such reliance on consumption is not evident in the states where the average level of poverty is low, or the rate of reduction in poverty is high. It is plausible that the poverty alleviation programmes may have benefited the poorer states more than others.

The high growth rate during the period 2004–11 was not able to alter the pattern of development, if the state of poverty and the rate of poverty reduction are a guide. The per capita consumption in the poorer states increased, but this was a part of the global process as it increased in other states too, leaving the relative position of the poorer states completely unaffected. The gap that used to exist between the poor and the less poor states in per capita consumption in the pre-reform years or even during the initial 11 years of economic reform, 1993–2004, did not change despite the GDP growth rate rising to a new high in 2004–2011. The level of poverty in the states reduced but their relative position did not change. Perhaps seven years is too short a time to bring about a change. It is essential to sustain the high growth rate of income and consumption for a longer time to affect the desired change.

Inclusive Growth and Poverty

The level of poverty among several marginalized groups of the population was found to be higher than others. This, in large part, was caused by a lack of inclusiveness in economic development. The concept of inclusiveness espoused in the Eleventh Plan (2007–12) encompasses a number of affirmative actions for the marginalized groups of the population, such as the Scheduled Castes, the Scheduled Tribes, OBCs, minorities, and women. These actions did not connote a shift in emphasis from higher growth to more equitable distribution, or imply a trade-off between growth and distribution. Inclusive development is characterized by economic growth that reduces poverty, creates employment opportunities, and provides access to essential services for the poor and the marginalized groups. It is a development process that ensures a broad-based improvement in the quality of life of the poor and the marginalized sections of the population who are often unable to participate in, and benefit from, the growth process.

The level and change in per capita consumption and poverty among the social groups estimated from NSS consumer expenditure data can provide a fair idea about the efficacy of inclusive measures. The social groups considered here are (a) the Scheduled Castes; (b) the Scheduled Tribes; and (c) OBCs.[11]

Consumption by Social Group

A comparison of per capita consumption across the social groups in 2011–12 (estimated from the NSS consumer expenditure data of the 68th Round) shows that in rural areas (a) per capita consumption of the OBCs was more than that of the Scheduled Castes and the Scheduled Tribes, and is similar to the national average; (b) per capita consumption of the Scheduled Castes was 12 per cent lower than the national average (and of the OBCs), and 30 per cent lower than the general category population; (c) per capita consumption of the Scheduled Tribes was 75 per cent of the national average and 10 per cent less than the Scheduled Castes.

The consumption pattern of the social groups in urban areas was somewhat different. In 2011–12, (a) per capita consumption of the OBCs was 14 per cent lower than the national average; (b) per capita consumption of the Scheduled Castes was about 75 per cent of the national average and 60 per cent of that of the general category population; and (c) per capita consumption of the Scheduled Tribes was 8 per cent more than the Scheduled Castes and 67 per cent of that of the general category population. The higher average consumption of the Scheduled Tribes in urban areas should be viewed in the context of their limited numbers and migration. The census authorities do not count the Scheduled Tribes in urban areas. However, the NSS does not follow the census line and it counts the Scheduled Tribe families located in urban areas. The higher per capita consumption of the Scheduled Tribes, as compared to the Scheduled Castes, is significant in the context of their entry into the mainstream of the economy.

The general standard of consumption among the above-mentioned social groups can be summed up as follows: the consumption standard of OBCs is better than that of the Scheduled Castes and Scheduled Tribes. The consumption standard of Scheduled Castes is better than that of the Scheduled Tribes in rural areas, but not in urban ares. In both rural and urban areas, the per capita consumption of the Scheduled Castes and Scheduled Tribes is less than that of all population. However, the disparity in per capita consumption between these two groups reduced in the era of economic reform.

Poverty by Social Group

The poverty ratio among the social groups in rural and urban areas has been estimated for the years 2004–05 and 2011–12 using the consumption distribution of the social groups as obtained from the NSS consumer expenditure data (NSS 61st Round and NSS 68th Round) and the national poverty line (that is, the poverty line applied to all population), derived from the Expert Group (Tendulkar)

Table 7.7 Poverty Ratio by Social Group: 2004–05 and 2011–12

Population Group	Rural		Urban		Total	
	2004–05	2011–12	2004–05	2011–12	2004–05	2011–12
Scheduled Tribes	62.3	45.3	35.5	24.1	59.4	43.0
Scheduled Castes	53.5	31.5	40.6	21.7	51.0	29.3
OBCs	39.8	22.6	30.6	15.4	37.6	20.7
Others	27.1	15.5	16.1	8.2	22.8	12.5
All Population	41.8	25.7	25.7	13.7	37.2	21.9

Note: Others represent the general category population.
Source: Planning Commission estimates.

methodology. The poverty ratios in rural and urban areas are combined (using the NSS population proportion in the two areas as weights) to obtain an estimate for the country as a whole. These have been given in Table 7.7.

The level of poverty ratio across social groups exposes the dominance of the age-old caste system on the economic scene. The poverty ratio among the most disadvantaged social group is highest; it declines as the group rises in the ladder of caste structure. The poverty ratio among the Scheduled Tribes is more than among the Scheduled Castes. Again, the poverty ratio among these two groups is more than that of the OBCs, which, in turn, is more than that of 'others', that is, the general category population.

The decline in poverty ratio among the social groups in the seven years 2004–2011 has been given in Table 7.8. The decline was most

Table 7.8 Decline in Poverty Ratio by Social Group: 2004–05 to 2011–12 (Percentage Points)

Population Group	Rural	Urban	Total
Scheduled Tribes	17.0	11.4	16.4
Scheduled Castes	22.0	18.9	21.7
OBCs	17.2	15.2	16.9
Others	11.6	7.9	10.3
All Population	16.1	12.0	15.3

Source: Author's estimate based on the poverty ratios in Table 7.7.

in case of the Scheduled Castes, underlining the inclusive nature of development.

The social groups are not homogenous. There is multiplicity of classes within each social group. The phenomenon of 'castes within a caste' is not new. Among the Scheduled Tribes, there are primitive tribal groups, and among the Scheduled Castes there are Dalits and Mahadalits, whose levels of living are even worse. The OBCs are also not a homogenous group. The disparity in terms of either income, consumption, and living standards between broad groups of OBCs is perhaps more pronounced than other social groups.

The Scheduled Castes and Scheduled Tribes together accounted for about 25 per cent of the total population and 33 per cent of the poor population in 2004–05. Despite the higher rate of decline in poverty ratio, the share of the Scheduled Castes and Scheduled Tribes among the total number of poor remained around the same level in 2011–12 due to higher population growth.

The inclusiveness of development in 2004–2011 is evident from the faster decline in poverty ratio among the Scheduled Castes and Scheduled Tribes as compared to others. The average poverty ratio among the Scheduled Castes and Scheduled Tribes declined by 20 percentage points in 2004–2011 (from 54 per cent in 2004–05 to 34 per cent in 2011–12) as compared to 15 percentage points for the entire population (from 37 per cent in 2004–05 to 22 per cent in 2011–12) and 10 percentage points for the general category population (from 23 per cent in 2004–05 to 13 per cent in 2011–12). Much of the decline in poverty took place as a result of increase in income arising from general growth process as the class distribution of consumption remained more or less unchanged. The income redistributive measures contributed only ephemerally to lift people out of poverty, but they were able to lower the intensity of poverty.

State of the Scheduled Castes

In the era of economic reform, the decline in poverty ratio among the Scheduled Castes was more than that of all population. This is also the case with the persons whose per capita consumption expenditure was less than three-fourths of the poverty line, and who were known to be living under crippling poverty. These underline the reduction in the average level of poverty as well as the intensity of poverty among the Scheduled Castes.

The poverty ratio across the social groups in 2004–05 and 2011–12 given in Table 7.7 has been derived using the Expert Group (Tendulkar) methodology. The decline in poverty ratio in the seven years 2004–2011 was 21.7 percentage points among the Scheduled Castes as compared to 15.3 percentage points for all population. It has not been possible to estimate the poverty ratio for the social groups in earlier years (before 2004–05) using the Expert Group (Tendulkar) methodology. However, the Planning Commission in the past estimated the poverty ratio by social groups for the years 1993–94 and 2004–05 using the Expert Group (Lakdawala) methodology. Based on this, it is found that in 1993–2004, the poverty ratio among the Scheduled Castes declined by 11.5 percentage points as against 8.5 percentage points for the entire population. It is true that the declines in poverty ratio in 1993–2004 and 2004–2011 calculated based on two different methodologies are not comparable. But their directional change can be used for inference. The estimate of the decline in poverty ratio in the two periods 1993–2004 and 2004–2011 (though derived from two different methodologies) points to faster decline (in poverty ratio) among the Scheduled Castes as compared to all population. It mirrors inclusive development in the era of economic reform.

Between 2004–05 and 2011–12, for the Scheduled Castes, the rate of decline in the percentage of persons with per capita consumption expenditure less than three-fourths of the poverty line was more than that of the poverty ratio. It is a sign of percolation of increased consumption to the poorest of the poor. The increase in consumption among the Scheduled Caste population took place in such a manner that it has produced a kind of cascading effect. This is again visible from the increase in the percentage of Scheduled Caste population whose per capita consumption is more than one and a half times of the poverty line. The people with per capita consumption exceeding one and a half times of the poverty line can be said to have benefited from the growth and development process, and this can be treated as a measure of the progress in poverty reduction. In 2011–12, the percentage of persons with per capita consumption expenditure exceeding one and a half times of the poverty line among the Scheduled Castes and all population was as follows: (*a*) 30.9 per cent and 39.2 per cent in rural areas; (*b*) 51.7 per cent and 64.1 per cent in urban areas; and (*c*) 35.5 per cent and 46.3 per cent for the country as a whole (that is, rural and urban areas combined). A section among the Scheduled Castes, estimated as 30 per cent in rural areas and 50 per cent in urban areas, can be termed as well-off as their per capita consumption exceeds the poverty line by one and a half times. This adequately substantiates that the Scheduled Castes have ceased to be a homogenous group. In view of this, the Scheduled Caste population whose per capita consumption exceeds the poverty line by one and a half times may be kept outside the purview of the positive discriminatory stance of the state. The space vacated by this group (Scheduled Caste population with per capita consumption more than one and a half times of the poverty line) can be covered by those who survive on per capita consumption of less than three-fourths of the poverty line. These people (who survive on per capita consumption of less than three-fourths of the poverty line) lead a miserable life as a result of low income, and more due to lack of opportunities. Such a measure may not lower the average poverty ratio of the Scheduled Caste population per se, but will lower the intensity of poverty of a much larger section. The principles of equity and natural justice solicit precise targeting of the population, even when the distribution is viewed as intra-class.

Calorie Deficiency as Poverty

The poverty line is quantified as the monetary expenditure to attain the calorie requirement of persons along with a minimum expenditure of non-food items, such as clothing, shelter, education, health care, transport, and so on. The calorie requirement was estimated in 1979 by the Task Force (Alagh) as 2,400 kcal per capita per day for the rural population and 2,100 kcal for the urban. These are derived from age–sex–activity distribution of the population and calorie norms recommended by the ICMR. The poverty line calculated this way presumes that each person would allocate his/her total consumption on food and non-food items in such a manner that the expenditure on food items enables him/her to attain the calorie requirement.

The poverty ratio is estimated from the consumption expenditure distribution and the poverty line. The percentage of the calorie deficient population is worked out from the distribution of calorie intake and calorie norm. The consumption expenditure distribution and the distribution of calorie intake is obtained from the NSS consumer expenditure data.

The Task Force quantified the poverty line from the consumption expenditure distribution for the year 1973–74. By definition, the poverty ratio and the percentage of calorie-deficient population were identical in this year. In later years, the poverty lines were updated for price inflation to estimate poverty ratio. It turned out that the poverty ratio derived from the price-adjusted poverty line was consistently lower than the percentage of the calorie-deficient population. In 2004–05, about 75 per cent of the population was estimated as being calorie-deficient whereas the poverty ratio was 40 per cent. In a similar way, in 2011–12, the poverty ratio was 22 per cent whereas 80 per cent of the population was calorie-deficient.

In the context of the difference between the poverty ratio and the percentage of calorie-deficient population, suggestions have often been made (for example, by Utsa Patnaik) to use the latter as the true incidence of poverty in place of the poverty ratio.[12] In that case, it is obvious that the level of poverty is high and it has increased over time. This is in contrast with the poverty ratio measured by the Planning Commission which showed substantially lower levels of poverty and its significant decline over time, particularly in the years of economic reform.

In view of the difference between poverty ratio and calorie-deficient population, the Expert Group (Lakdawala) decided that the poverty line should be anchored on the norm of calorie requirement (2,400 kcal per capita per day in rural areas and 2,100 in urban areas). It explicitly stated that the poverty line, while being anchored in the calorie norm, does not seek to measure the nutritional status, and more specifically, the incidence of malnourishment or under-nourishment in the population.[13]

Subsequently, on the relationship between poverty and malnutrition, the Expert Group (Tendulkar) stated that the fact that the poverty line is anchored in a norm of calorie requirement does not mean that those below the poverty line can be considered as malnourished or uniformly undernourished everywhere or all the time. They also observed that the level of calorie consumption (as yielding from the NSS consumer expenditure data) is not well correlated with the nutritional outcomes either over time or across space (that is, between states or rural and urban areas).[14]

There is nothing unusual in viewing poverty as a lack of energy requirement, such as calorie intake of the individuals. In fact, the poverty line of the Task Force (Alagh) was founded on this premise. However, equating poverty with calorie deficiency can be misleading when incomes are rising, consumer behaviour of the people is changing, and people are voluntarily choosing to consume fewer calories.

The reasons behind the mismatch between the poverty ratio (estimated from the price-adjusted poverty line) and the percentage of the calorie-deficient population can be traced back to two factors. These are: (*a*) change in the consumer behaviour of households; and (*b*) lowering of the calorie norm over time.

The changes in consumer behaviour have resulted in the decline in calorie intake, especially for the lower deciles of the population. The NSS consumer expenditure data of 2004–05 and 2011–12 unravels a different consumption basket from that in the 1970s, when the poverty line was originally constructed. There has been a decline in consumption of cereals (in quantity) along with a change in the composition of the cereals basket. This, in large measure, is the outcome of diversification of food intake, caused by rise in aggregate consumption. People are no longer consuming inferior varieties of cereal, such as jowar and bajra, whose unit cost of calories is lower, and instead opting for rice and wheat. There is a change in the pattern of consumption arising from dietary diversification towards more consumption of animal products, such as milk, meat, fish, poultry, and of fruits and vegetables, eventuating reduced cereal consumption.

Many individuals now prefer a low-calorie diet. The NSS consumer expenditure data shows that it is a voluntary choice of individuals (particularly among those around the poverty line class) not to consume more calories. Analysing the pattern of calorie intake and per capita consumption, Pronab Sen observed that over time, with rising standards of living, the food habits of people have changed in such a way that people in the poverty line expenditure class are no longer consuming the normative levels of calories despite it being within their means.[15]

The calorie norms specific to age–sex–activity recommended by the ICMR in 2010 were lower than those in 1968 (based on which the poverty line was constructed by the Task Force in 1979). As, for example, the recommended calorie norm of male workers engaged in heavy activities was lowered to 3,490 kcal per capita per day in 2010, from 3,900 kcal in 1968.

The change in lifestyle of the population and technological innovations sweeping the economy and the lives of the people are considered to be responsible for the decline in overall requirement of calories. The lifestyle change has occurred for even the poorest of the poor. For example, earlier people used to walk several miles to their workplace whereas today they take a bus or ride a bicycle. The occupational structure of the population has altered over time, resulting in the lowering of the calorie norm. The calorie requirement of moderate or sedentary workers is less than that of heavy workers. The proportion of the population engaged as heavy workers has lowered over time, while that of moderate or sedentary workers has increased.

Following a method akin to the Task Force (Alagh), the Expert Group (Rangarajan) constituted by the Planning Commission in 2012 estimated the average calorie requirement of the population taking into account the age–sex–activity distribution of the population in 2011 and the calorie norm as recommended by the ICMR in 2010. The average calorie requirement on this basis worked out to 2,155 kcal per capita per day in rural areas and 2,090 in urban areas. The calorie norm for rural areas was considerably lower than that estimated by the Task Force. The decline was marginal in urban areas 'due to a more pronounced shift in the age-distribution towards adults with higher calorie requirements'.[16]

The average calorie norm lowered due to changes in the occupational structure of the population and lowering of the calorie requirements of individuals. The change in occupational structure is part of the emerging demographic pattern. The lowering of calorie requirement of individuals is due to changes in lifestyle of all sections of the society.[17] These point out the inappropriateness of equating the phenomenon of decline in calorie intake of the population with rising poverty. The poverty ratio is a measure of incidence of poverty. The percentage of the calorie-deficient population is a measure of nutritional status of the population. The estimate of poverty ratio is different from calorie deficiency as the latter, by definition, is more related to under-nutrition than poverty, and for several well-known reasons, poverty reduction may not be reflected in the nutritional status of the population.

Treating calorie deficiency as 'true' poverty can stir up confusion between poverty which is an absolute concept and under-nutrition which is a relative concept. The jury is still out on whether one measure is more superior than the other.[18] The issues in this regard may be summed up as follows: (*a*) poverty and under-nutrition are different; (*b*) the calorie requirement for leading a healthy and active life has lowered over time; and (*c*) the disparity between poverty ratio and percentage of the calorie-deficient population is natural. As a result, the anxiety over the difference between the two should not be relevant in the measurement of poverty.

Notes

1. 'Poverty Estimates for 1999–2000', Government of India, Press Information Bureau, New Delhi, 22 February 2001.
2. Angus Deaton, 'Adjusted Indian Poverty Estimates for 1999–2000', *Economic and Political Weekly*, Vol. 38, Issue No. 4, 25 January 2003, pp. 322–26.
3. K. Sundaram and Suresh D. Tendulkar, 'Poverty Has Declined in the 1990s: A Resolution of Comparability Problems in NSS Consumer Expenditure Data', *Economic and Political Weekly*, Vol. 38, Issue No. 4, 25 January 2003, pp. 327–37.
4. K. Sundaram and Suresh D. Tendulkar, 'Poverty in India in the 1900s: Revised Results for All-India and 15 Major States for 1993–94', *Economic and Political Weekly*, Vol. 38, Issue No. 46, 15 November 2003, pp. 4865–72.
5. Abhijit Sen and Himanshu, 'Poverty and Inequality in India–I', *Economic and Political Weekly*, Vol. 39, Issue No. 38, 18 September 2004, pp. 4247–63; and Abhijit Sen and Himanshu, 'Poverty and Inequality in India–II: Widening Disparities during the 1990s', *Economic and Political Weekly*, Vol. 39, Issue No. 39, 25 September 2004, pp. 4361–75.
6. Sen and Himanshu, 'Poverty and Inequality in India– II', p. 4372.
7. These are estimated in Sen and Himanshu, 'Poverty and Inequality in India– II', p. 4366, Table 12.

8. *Report of the Expert Group to Review the Methodology for Estimation of Poverty*, Planning Commission, Government of India, November 2009.

9. In URP, the consumer expenditure data is gathered from the households using a 30-day recall period (reference period) for all the items. In MRP, the consumer expenditure data for five infrequently purchased non-food items (clothing, footwear, education, institutional medical care, and durable goods) are collected from a 365-day recall period, and 30-day recall period is used for the remaining items.

10. The growth rates are derived from MRP consumption of the NSS consumer expenditure data. The consumption expenditure at current prices has been converted into real terms by applying the rate of growth of cost of living index of the poor, estimated by the Planning Commission and used to update the poverty line.

11. Two points need be mentioned about the statistics on social groups gathered in the NSS data on consumer expenditure. First, the social group reported by the informant (in response to NSS questionnaire) relates to the head of the household and this is taken to be the same for all the members of the household. Second, the status of the social group of the household is a faithful recording of the information provided by the head of the household and its authenticity is not verified or cross-checked from the official orders notified by the government.

12. Utsa Patnaik estimated the percentage of the calorie-deficient population based on the calorie norm of 2,200 kcal per capita per day, and treated these as the actual incidence of poverty (Utsa Patnaik, 'Poverty Trends in India 2004–05 to 2009–10: Updating Poverty Estimates and Comparing Official Figures', *Economic and Political Weekly*, Vol. 48, Issue No. 40, 5 October 2013, pp. 43–58).

13. *Report of the Expert Group on Estimation of Proportion and Number of Poor*, Perspective Planning Division, Planning Commission, Government of India, New Delhi, July 1993, p. 11, para 2.11.

14. *Report of the Expert Group to Review the Methodology for Estimation of Poverty*, Planning Commission, Government of India, November 2009, p. 8.

15. Pronab Sen, 'Of Calories and Things: Reflections on Nutritional Norms, Poverty Lines and Consumption Behaviour in India', *Economic and Political Weekly*, Vol. 40, Issue No. 43, 22 October 2005, p. 4611–18.

16. *Report of the Expert Group to Review the Methodology for Measurement of Poverty*, Government of India, Planning Commission, June 2014, pp. 56–7, Table 4.1 and para 4.15.

17. Angus Deaton and Jean Dreze, 'Food and Nutrition in India: Facts and Interpretations', *Economic and Political Weekly*, Vol. 44, Issue No. 7, 14 February 2009, pp. 42–65.

18. The relationship between poverty and under-nutrition was the subject matter of serious and thought-provoking intellectual debate among economists and statisticians in the early 1980s, important among them being two eminent personalities in this area, P. V. Sukhatme and V. M. Dandekar. These debates were chronicled in the *Economic and Political Weekly* and can be found in: V. M. Dandekar, 'On Measurement of Poverty', *Economic and Political Weekly,* Vol. 16, Issue No. 30, 25 July 1981, pp. 1241–50; V. M. Dandekar, 'On Measurement of Undernutrition', *Economic and Political Weekly,* Vol. 17, Issue No. 6, 6 February 1982, pp. 203–12; P. V. Sukhatme, 'On Measurement of Poverty', *Economic and Political Weekly*, Vol. 16, Issue No. 32, 8 August 1981, pp 1318–24; and P. V. Sukhatme, 'Measurement of Undernutrition', *Economic and Political Weekly*, Vol. 17, Issue No. 50, 11 December 1982, pp. 2000–16.

8

Indian Economy in the 2010s

The state of the Indian economy and its growth performance in the first six decades of planning, 1951–2011, assessed in the preceding chapters, is based on the macroeconomic aggregates derived by the CSO of the Government of India using 2004–05 as the base year. These estimates were used for policymaking until January 2015, when the CSO changed the base year from 2004–05 to 2011–12, and in the process incorporated some changes in the measurement of national accounting statistics, both in terms of methodology and coverage of data. On the basis of this changed methodology and data, along with 2011–12 as the base year, the CSO estimated the macroeconomic aggregates from the year 2004–05. In this chapter, the growth performance of the Indian economy in the 2010s will be assessed on the basis of the macroeconomic aggregates derived by the CSO using 2011–12 as the base year.[1] Since the change in methodology and data coverage is marginal, these macroeconomic estimates will be referred to here as the data from the new base year 2011–12.

Before using the macroeconomic aggregates from the CSO with the new base year 2011–12, it may be pertinent to note that as a result of the change in the methodology, the focus of growth shifted from GDP to gross value added (GVA), precisely because in the new method, the GDP estimates are available at market prices, and the GVA is measured at basic prices. The GVA at basic prices can be termed as an improved and more precise version of the earlier estimates at factor cost. On the nature of the change in the methodology and its ramifications on the estimates of macro-aggregates, a note has been appended in Annexure 8.1 at the end of this chapter. On the features of the new estimates, that is, the estimates derived from the changed methodology and database, coupled with the base year 2011–12, it may be sufficient to mention here that the size of the economy increases and there is evidence of structural change from the earlier estimates.[2]

The annual growth rate of GVA at basic prices, aggregate and by major sectors from 2005–06 to 2019–20, as per the new estimates have been given in Table 8.1. The domestic savings and investment rates for the years 2004–05 to 2017–18 have been given in Table 8.2. These estimates of GVA and savings and investment rates will be used here to analyse the economic situation and make an assessment of the performance of the Indian economy in the 2010s.

The economic growth rate (measured by the GVA at basic price) in the 2010s (2010–11 to 2019–20) is estimated at 6.4 per cent per year. This is lower than the average growth rate of 7 per cent per year attained in the second half of the 2000s (2005–06 to 2009–10). And there is structural difference in the growth rate between these two periods. The growth rate of industry and manufacturing in the 2010s is substantially lower by 3.6 percentage points than that in the second half of the 2000s.

In the 2010s, the growth rate in the two halves were almost identical (averaging 6.4 per cent per year in the first half, 2010–11 to 2014–15, and 6.5 per cent per year in the second half, 2015–16 to 2019–20) and less than the growth rate during the second half of the 2000s (7 per cent per year).

In the two halves of the 2010s, though the aggregate growth rate is almost identical, the pattern of growth varies widely. The first half of the 2010s began and ended on a high note on the growth front, tracing a U-shaped growth curve. In contrast, the growth rate in the second half was on a downward slope; the growth rate began to decline steadily from 2016–17.

Table 8.1 Growth Rate of GVA: 2005–06 to 2019–20 (Per Cent)

Year	Agriculture	Mining and Quarrying	Manufac-turing	Industry	Services	Total
2005–06	4.8	6.1	9.3	10.2	9.1	8.3
2006–07	2.9	4.7	17.8	14.7	7.0	8.1
2007–08	5.5	4.6	7.0	8.6	7.8	7.4
2008–09	−0.2	−2.5	4.7	5.0	6.5	4.3
2009–10	−0.9	6.0	11.0	9.2	8.7	6.9
2010–11	8.8	13.5	7.7	7.1	7.8	8.0
2011–12	6.4	−17.5	3.1	6.6	5.9	5.2
2012–13	1.5	0.6	5.5	3.6	8.4	5.4
2013–14	5.6	0.2	5.0	4.2	7.8	6.1
2014–15	−0.2	9.7	7.9	6.7	9.8	7.2
2015–16	0.6	10.1	13.1	9.7	9.5	8.0
2016–17	6.8	9.8	7.9	7.5	8.5	8.0
2017–18	5.9	4.9	6.6	6.5	7.0	6.6
2018–19	2.4	−5.8	5.7	6.0	7.8	6.0
2019–20	4.0	3.1	0.03	0.7	5.6	3.9

Notes: 1. The growth rates are derived from the GVA estimates at basic prices using 2011–12 as the base year.
2. Agriculture includes crop sector, animal husbandry, forestry, and fishing.
3. Industry covers manufacturing, construction, electricity, gas, and water supply.
4. Services sector covers trade, hotels, transport and communications, finance, banking, insurance, real estate, business services, community, social and personal services, public administration, and defence.
5. The GVA in 2016–17 is Third Revised Estimate.
6. The GVA in 2017–18 is Second Revised Estimate.
7. The GVA in 2018–19 is First Revised Estimate.
8. The GVA in 2019–20 is Provisional Estimate.
Source: NSO, Ministry of Statistics and Programme Implementation, Government of India.

Economic Growth in the 2010s: 2010–14

The decade of the 2010s began on a promising note on the growth front. The growth rate in 2010–11 was high, at 8 per cent. This high growth rate in 2010–11 may be viewed against the relatively lower

Table 8.2   Savings and Investment Rate: 2004–05 to 2017–18 (Per Cent)

Year	Savings Rate	Investment Rate
2004–05	34.0	35.2
2005–06	34.4	36.4
2006–07	34.1	36.0
2007–08	36.7	39.1
2008–09	34.9	38.4
2009–10	34.9	38.9
2010–11	36.2	39.8
2011–12	33.8	39.0
2012–13	33.1	38.7
2013–14	31.4	33.8
2014–15	31.6	33.5
2015–16	30.5	32.1
2016–17	29.9	30.9
2017–18	30.1	32.3

Note: The savings rates are expressed as the ratio of savings to gross national disposable income and the investment rates are expressed as the ratio of investment to GDP.
Source: NSO, Ministry of Statistics and Programme Implementation, Government of India.

growth rate averaging 5.6 per cent per year in the previous two years (2008–09 and 2009–10), believed to have been impacted by the global economic crisis that erupted in September 2008. When the growth rate reverted to the higher trajectory of 8 per cent in 2010–11, there were enough reasons to presume that the Indian economy had been able to withstand the fallout of the global economic crisis. The growth performance in the previous five-year period (2005–06 to 2009–10), which coincided with the second half of the decade 2000s, was excellent as the aggregate growth rate, measured by the GVA, averaged 7 per cent per year, despite two of these five years falling under the period of the global economic crisis. This high growth rate in the second half of the 2000s was driven by domestic investment (38 per cent of GDP), which, in turn, was driven by domestic savings (35 per cent of gross national disposable income). Economic growth is led by industry, and industrial growth is triggered by manufacturing. The growth rate of both industry and manufacturing sectors in the second half of the

2000s was about 10 per cent per year. More than half of the income (GVA) originated from merchandise trade and services, but its growth hinged on the manufacturing sector as well. This underlines the circularity of the process of income generation in the economy that renders the role of industry, and within it, the manufacturing sector, critical in maximizing the overall rate of economic growth, that is, the growth rate of aggregate GVA.

The high growth rate in the second half of the 2000s was inclusive too. The socio-economic indicators, which are known to determine the levels of living and quality of life of the people, registered the highest-ever growth in this period. In real terms, the increase in per capita consumption, as estimated from the NSS data on consumer expenditure, in the seven-year period from 2004–05 to 2011–12 was about three times of that realized in the previous 11-year period, 1993–94 to 2004–05. While analysing the nature and pattern of per capita consumption in Chapter 7, it has been brought out that the incidence of poverty declined, and 137 million people crossed over the poverty line during the seven-year period of 2004–2011. This was the highest-ever decline in the number of poor in the planning era, and was the outcome of the high growth rate.

What happened after the high growth in 2010–11 (8 per cent) was something which could not have been anticipated. Betraying such a bright picture, the growth rate lowered in the next three years (2011–12 to 2013–14) and averaged 5.6 per cent per year, which is exactly the average growth rate of the two years (2008–09 and 2009–10) when economic growth was affected by the global economic crisis. The slide in the growth rate could be arrested from 2014–15 when it exceeded 7 per cent and remained around this level for the next two years, 2015–16 and 2016–17. The reasons behind the slump in the growth rate in the intervening years, 2011–12 to 2013–14, remained a kind of mystery that needed to be unravelled.

The global economic crisis was not entirely over in 2009–10 or 2010–11. It dragged on for some more time and its effect on the growth rate of the international economy was noticeable. Even in 2011–12, the growth rate of the USA and several countries of the Eurozone did not return to the trend level. Resting on this, the low growth rate of the Indian economy in 2011–12 was largely, if not entirely, attributed to the prolonging of the global economic crisis. Was the lowering of the growth rate after 2011–12 caused by the global economic crisis? Or, was it induced by domestic factors? That is the moot question. Before making an attempt to explore the factors that are likely to be responsible for the lowering of the growth rate, it would be worthwhile to mention that the size of the Indian GDP on the basis of purchasing power parity (PPP) increased to USD 5.75 trillion in 2011. What is more important is that India's position was elevated to the world's third-largest economy (after the USA and China) in 2011 from tenth in 2005. Therefore, in just six years, from 2005 to 2011, India notched up seven ranks, which is not a mean achievement.[3]

Slowdown of Growth Rate, 2011–13: Cause and Effect

There are mainly two views on the reasons behind the low growth rate of the Indian economy witnessed between 2011–12 and 2013–14. The first view is that the high growth rate in the second half of the 2000s (2005–06 to 2009–10) occurred in the absence of structural reforms. As such, the reforms were long overdue. The reform in the financial sector did not take place, and as a result, the flow of funds from the corporate sector was not available for investment. In such an eventuality, the growth rate had to slow down, sooner or later, and that had happened.

The other view pins the blame almost squarely on the stimulus measures implemented by the government from December 2008 to contain the adverse impact of the global economic crisis on the growth rate of the Indian economy. It terms the stimulus measures as overdosed and extended as these went on even after the growth rate reverted to the high level of 8 per cent in 2010–11. It is believed that before prolonging the stimulus measures, its implication on the macroeconomic scenario was not meticulously assessed. The contracyclical fiscal policy stance, a major component of the stimulus measures, carried with it the risk of inflating the fiscal deficit. How far the increased fiscal deficit could impact the growth rate in later years was not evaluated. A section of the policymakers were of the view that the stimulus measures were not needed for such a long time and its spread could have been restricted, if not discontinued outright, after 2010–11. The increase in expenditure and, at the same time, the revenue sacrifice concomitant with the stimulus measures was not possible to bear without distorting the macroeconomic fundamentals. And that had happened as the fiscal deficit and the current account deficit went out of control. In plain terms, the stimulus measures devised to diffuse the adverse impact of global economic crisis were responsible for setting in motion the macroeconomic disequilibrium.

Where can the truth possibly lie? Is it the lack of reform, or over-dosed and prolonged stimulus measures? The search for an answer makes it necessary to trace the course of some of the events in the two decades of economic reform and liberalization, 1991–2011, that shaped the Indian economy when the stimulus measures were extended to maintain the medium-term trend growth rate.

The growth rate increased in the two-decade period of economic reform, and there are cycles of highs and lows, eventuated by either domestic or international factors, and often even both. The growth rate is primarily driven by domestic investment. Consumption rather than export is the major catalyst of growth. As a result of the high growth, the structure of the economy changed but the change was confined to the agriculture and services sectors as the share of industry, and especially manufacturing, in the GVA remained almost unchanged in the period of economic reform. Income generation witnessed a shift from agriculture to services. These happened against the backdrop of two significant changes in the area of investment.

First, the public investment earmarked for growth maximization lowered in a secular fashion as the state refrained from directly participating in production and trade. The share of the private sector in total investment increased in the period of economic reform and, in consequence, the responsibility of growth fell squarely on it. The private sector investment took place in a range of basic and capital goods industries, and in a large segment of the infrastructure sector, which earlier were the forte of the public sector. The role of the private sector became prominent in growth maximization.

Second, and mainly as a consequence of the first, the government was able to divert expenditure on redistribution of income in favour of the poor and raise the bar of social spending to extend benefits to a section of the non-poor who are often subjected to transient poverty. In this process, the expenditure of the government moved away from growth to non-growth. If implemented properly, these social welfare and redistributive expenditures can improve the levels of living and quality of life of the people. However, the possibility that such expenditure can raise the rate of economic growth is remote. Income redistributive measures are hugely popular in the multi-party frame of Indian democracy. The government fell in line and progressively increased such expenditure, often at the expense of growth. This is true for the central government, and equally, if not more, for the state governments.

The income- and consumption-enhancing redistributive and social welfare programmes became a major component of inclusive growth espoused in the Eleventh Plan (2007–12). In order to counter the fallout of the global economic crisis on the growth rate of the Indian economy, these programmes were strengthened in the stimulus packages from the beginning of 2009. It opened the floodgates of consumption, which was already booming as a result of the high growth rate in the preceding three years, 2005–06 to 2007–08; the economic growth rate in this three-year period measured by GVA at basic prices averaged 7.9 per cent per year, with the industry and manufacturing sectors each registering a growth rate of 11 per cent per year. The consumption of the lower deciles of the population increased as a result of public spending on the income- and consumption-enhancing programmes. It created a ripple effect on demand, particularly of wage goods. This fuelled food inflation, mainly by way of raising the prices of wage goods. The expenditure on these programmes often bordered on profligacy, impacting the fiscal deficit. In this whole process, the fiscal deficit was used to generate additional demand, which the government thought would fall in consequence of the global economic crisis.

The fiscal deficit became unsustainable when the growth rate faltered. The rise in public expenditure in the absence of commensurate rise in income, mainly due to lowering of the growth rate, raised the fiscal deficit of the central government to more than 6 per cent of GDP in 2009–10; it lowered to the range of 4.9–5.9 per cent in the next three years, 2010–11 to 2012–13. It was high in view of the fact that the fiscal deficit should have been 3 per cent (of GDP) at the most in order to maintain macroeconomic balance, as ordained by the Fiscal Responsibility and Budget Management Act (FRBM Act). These expenditures being mostly in the category of revenue expenditure inflated the revenue deficit as well. The revenue deficit was well above 3 per cent (of GDP) in these three years when the FRBM Act stipulates it to be zero.

The inflated fiscal deficit has a bearing on the price inflation. The price inflation was already high before the eruption of the global economic crisis in September 2008. The headline inflation based on the WPI measured 5.4 per cent in 2007–08. It increased to 7.7 per cent in the next year, that is, 2008–09. The origin of the price inflation in the domestic market at this time was rooted in the increase in international prices of essential commodities, in particular energy, food, metals, and energy-intensive products, witnessed towards the closing months of the year 2007. Mainly as a consequence, the prices of coal, iron ore, iron and steel products, and petroleum products, then not covered under the administered price mechanism, rose. However, it is true, the functioning and management of the Indian economy cannot be blamed for the inflation that crept into the domestic market at this time. It simply traversed from the international market.[4]

Beginning with the global economic crisis, the price inflation was high in the Indian economy for the next five years, 2009–10 to 2013–14, with the increase in the WPI averaging 7 per cent per year. The WPI, for reasons well known, is unable to reflect the price hike, which the consumers actually encounter in the market. It is not used to measure the erosion in income of the people as a result of price inflation. Instead, price inflation measured from the changes in CPI, which are available for rural and urban populations, are used. The increase in CPI for rural population, measured by the CPI-AL and that for urban population by the CPI-IW was 10 per cent per year during the period of 2009–10 to 2013–14. Such high price rise caused instability of macroeconomic parameters. The net result was slowdown of investment, from both domestic and international sources. Its ultimate victim was the growth rate of the economy. The economy entered into a cycle of low growth and low investment. A lower level of GDP reduced the per capita income and in its due turn decelerated consumption, savings, and investment.

A possible question at this stage is: To what extent could this increase in prices have been the off-shoot of the rise in the fiscal deficit, triggered by the contra-cyclical fiscal policy stance of the government? Or, from an opposite angle, to what extent did the inflated fiscal deficit have a bearing on the inflationary situation?

The extension of the scope of the fiscal stimulus measures and its prolonging was rooted in the perception that the Indian economy was interwoven with the international economy. However, there was considerable doubt about the actual impact of the global crisis by way of impinging on the growth potentials of the Indian economy. It has been shown in Chapter 6 that large areas of the real sector of the economy were not directly affected by the global economic crisis, and no one was sure about its influence on India's financial sector. The idea that the Indian economy could be impacted by the global economic crisis was perhaps taken too far, ignoring the fact that its growth rate was much less dependent on the state of the international economy than many countries with similar per capita income as India.

The continental size of the Indian economy with its GDP of USD 1.3 trillion and population of 1.1 billion people in 2008 had huge potential to keep domestic demand afloat. In actuality, the rural sector was largely insulated from the global economic crisis and that helped to keep the economy moving. A large segment of the economy being in the domain of unorganized sector provided considerable manoeuvrability to withstand the financial shocks originating from the industrial countries. The National Commission for Enterprises in the Unorganized Sector (NCEUS), a government appointed advisory body and a watchdog for the informal sector, estimated in 2007 that 93 per cent of the Indian workforce belong to the unorganized sector. A major chunk of the Indian economy does, therefore, have low level of external linkage and is unlikely to be affected by the global economic crisis to any great extent. The depth and intensity of the crisis was not the same for every area of the economy; the different segments of the economy were not uniformly affected by the crisis and neither were the different segments of the population. Such issues were either not considered at all or ignored while prolonging the stimulus measures.

The slowdown of the growth rate of the Indian economy from 2011–12 onwards was largely caused by factors emanating from the domestic economy rather than being triggered by the international economy. How this happened can be elucidated.

The aggregate GDP growth rate in India has traditionally been influenced by the growth rate of agriculture. There is a statistical basis for such an explanation. For the period 1951–2011, the correlation

coefficient between the yearly growth rate of agriculture and the aggregate growth rate of the economy works out to 0.82. The dependence
of the overall rate of economic growth on agriculture has waned since
the beginning of the economic reforms when years of low growth
were not necessarily the years of low agricultural growth. It is mani-
fested in the correlation coefficient between the yearly agricultural
growth rate and the overall rate of economic growth estimated as 0.95
for the four-decade pre-reform period, 1951–90, as compared to the
correlation coefficient as 0.59 for the two-decade period of economic
reform, 1991–2011. The lowering of the correlation coefficient in the
period of economic reform is a reflection of the lowering of the share
of agriculture in GDP. The share of agriculture in GDP reduced from
an average of 44 per cent in 1951–90 to 24 per cent in 1991–2001.
This is quite a significant change, enough to alter the pattern of inter-
sectoral relation in the economy.

Two pieces of evidence emerge from the pattern of sectoral growth
around the time when the global economic crisis struck. First, the
low growth rate in 2008–09 (4.3 per cent) was on account of both
agriculture and industry; the agricultural growth in this year declined
(–0.2 per cent), and the industrial growth rate lowered sharply to
5 per cent from the average of 11.2 per cent per year during the
previous three years, 2005–06 to 2007–08. In the next year, 2009–10,
agricultural growth rate declined (–0.9 per cent), but the overall
growth rate was modest (6.9 per cent) due to the high growth rate
of industry and services sectors, which was around 9 per cent. The
growth rate in agriculture, as has been shown earlier, could not
be affected by the global economic crisis, but the industrial growth
rate could. On this presumption, the impact of the global crisis
seemed to have faded in 2009–10.

Second, the elevation of the growth rate of the Indian economy to a
higher trajectory (8 per cent) in 2010–11 is viewed as withering away
or at least weakening of the global crisis. With this, the low growth rate
of the economy for three consecutive years from 2011–12 to 2013–14
becomes an issue that has to be reckoned with. Of these three years,
only one witnessed low agricultural growth—1.5 per cent in 2012–13.
In any case, the growth rate in agriculture was not associated with
the global economic crisis. The unusual dip in industrial growth rate
averaging 3.9 per cent per year in the other two years, 2012–13 and

2013–14, from the average of 8.2 per cent per year in 2009–10 and 2010–11, is considered to be the main reason behind the lower growth rate of the economy. It is plausible that the surge in the international price of crude oil throughout the three years, 2011 to 2013, retarded the industrial growth rate. The average price of crude oil in these three years rose to USD 111 per barrel from an average of about USD 67 per barrel in the previous seven years, 2004 to 2010. Apart from oil prices, the question that arises is: to what extent was the global economic crisis, and especially its impact on the industrially developed countries, responsible for such low growth in Indian industry?

In the past, and especially since the beginning of the economic reforms in 1991, high rate of growth of the Indian economy had been attained through industrial growth, and specifically through manufacturing, as industrial growth hinges on manufacturing. The years of high industrial growth have necessarily been the years with high rate of economic growth. The reverse is also true as the years with low industrial growth were also the years with low rate of economic growth. Industrial growth rate exceeded 10 per cent in 2005–06 and 2006–07; the rate of economic growth exceeded 8 per cent in these two years. Industrial growth lowered in 2008–09, and the rate of economic growth also lowered. In the next two years (2009–10 and 2010–11), industrial growth recovered, averaging 8.2 per cent per year, and the rate of economic growth became as high as 7.5 per cent per year. During the years 2012–13 and 2013–14, industrial growth lowered to 3.9 per cent per year and the rate of economic growth reduced to a low level of 5.8 per cent per year. It is evident that there is a strong positive association between industrial growth and the rate of economic growth. This association, measured from the correlation coefficient between the growth rate of industry and aggregate GVA for the period 2005–06 to 2019–20, is quantified as 0.79.

The dominant issue is the slower industrial growth rate, as it has been the prime reason behind the slowdown of the growth rate of the Indian economy. The decline in the rate of economic growth in 2012–13 and 2013–14 was exclusively due to the decline in industrial growth. The factors responsible for the decline in industrial growth rate can shed considerable light on the reasons behind the slide of the economic growth rate from 2011–12.

The private sector, which shoulders the major responsibility of investment and growth, faced insurmountable problems in matters related to land and labour, the two main factors of production. There are persistent problems with land acquisition, which is an essential prerequisite for setting up an industrial unit. Land acquisition rules often proved to be restrictive. The process of land acquisition is lengthy and time-consuming with the rules related to the conservation of forests posing intractable problems. The land legislation that was attempted by the government went through a complex process and never saw the light of the day due to environmental and other concerns. The labour-related regulations are also restrictive. There is no flexibility in the labour laws and it continues to remain rigid. It prevented private industrialists from starting new units or even from expanding the existing ones. These seem to have hurt growth prospects of the Indian economy in a major way.

The situation became worse with several proactive administrative measures of the government, which weakened the investor confidence. The problem was compounded by the inertia of the central government to take decisive action on key economic issues which were considered essential to raise the level of investment and, by implication, the growth rate of the economy. This particular crack in the government administration, surfacing from its inability or unwillingness to act decisively to find a solution to the emerging issues at that time, has been widely labelled as policy paralysis. It eroded the credibility of the government, and adversely affected the flow of investment, both domestic and foreign. Some of these may be mentioned here to comprehend the lamentable situation that the economy was going through then.

The government amended tax laws and implemented them in a retrospective manner. This placed the investors in a quandary and is considered to be a major causative factor in diluting the confidence of foreign investors. This had a domino effect on domestic investors. A specific order of the central government required Vodafone, a British mobile operator, to pay the withholding tax related to its acquisition of what later became Vodafone India from the Hutchison group. The matter went to litigation and Vodafone won the case in the Supreme Court of India in 2012. The government retrospectively amended a tax law allowing it (the government) to still tax the transaction. This reopened a tax dispute worth USD 2 billion. Several other corporate entities, such as Royal Dutch Shell and Nokia, automatically came under the purview of this amendment. The view of the transnational corporations of the developed capitalist world as well as the entire domestic corporate sector was that such a measure contributed to building an image of India as a country that pursues archaic tax policies or, to put it in a somewhat assertive manner, 'tax terrorism'. The tax dispute dented India's image as an international investment destination, at least for the time being, thus vitiating the investment climate, particularly in the industry and infrastructure sectors.

The moot point is how far the amendment to reopen an old case is ethical. In other words, is it ethical on the part of the government to resort to retrospective changes in tax law to get its way? The finance ministry was taking the call ignoring the advice of the Planning Commission that the retrospective part of legislation may be taken out to make it prospective. An identical suggestion came from Aravind Panagariya, who later became the vice chairman of the NITI Aayog. However, the finance ministry did not listen.

Another decision of the central government that undermined business confidence relates to the introduction of the General Anti-Avoidance Rules (GAAR) in 2012. It aims at companies routing money through tax havens (such as Mauritius). The investors, both domestic and overseas, viewed the GAAR as a tool to unusually empower the tax authorities. They were frightened as the instruments of this Act granted unbridled powers to tax authorities and these could be used effortlessly against the corporate sector. Owing to the hue and cry made by the corporate sector, the GAAR was deferred by two years.

Allegations of corruption surfaced from various and often unsuspected angles. It may be rather easy to cope with the form of corruption familiar to the society. However, new economies and rules of governance gave rise to novel forms of corruption, which the government found difficult to deal with. The investment atmosphere was vitiated by charges and counter-charges of corruption. Corruption-related issues have been a part and parcel of India's development story in a manner that is usually observed in developing countries. India is neither an exception nor a rule in this nexus between development and corruption. Even so, never before had such charges of corruption been levelled simultaneously against so many high-profile officials, including ministers in the Union Cabinet. It began with the allocation of coal blocks in the early 1990s, whose ripple effect was felt when the economy went downhill in 2011. Similar allegations of corruption surfaced in other sectors of the economy, important among them being the allocation of a spectrum band. These were magnified by irresponsible and unscientific estimates of potential losses to the state exchequer as a result of corrupt practices. A unique case relates to the grant of second generation (2G) licences for mobile networks. In November 2010, the Comptroller and Auditor General (CAG) of India reported that these licences were given at throwaway prices instead of conducting free and fair auctions, causing a notional loss of INR 1.76 lakh crore to the national exchequer. It was common knowledge that neither the office of the CAG nor the finance ministry possessed the requisite technical expertise to estimate the amount of loss, if any. The only organization which could have possibly done some justice to this issue, despite entering into its twilight years, was the Planning Commission. However, the Planning Commission was never consulted. It became a daily news item in the Indian print and electronic media. The hype in the media was so intense that the American weekly newsmagazine *Time* termed it the biggest abuse of power in the world after the Watergate scandal of the 1970s, which led to the resignation of US President Richard Nixon. The media hype on corruption was enough to damage the reputation of the government. The reputation of the government could be salvaged after six years of trial, in December 2017, when the judiciary pronounced the verdict that there was no proof of corruption in the 2G case and acquitted all the accused. Nevertheless, the damage done to the economy in the meantime was permanent, and there was no scope for repair. It is an embodiment of the policy paralysis that the government could not effectively confront these allegations. It was enough to undermine investors' confidence.

The policy paralysis plaguing the Indian economy can best be explained by the manner in which critical decisions in economic areas were taken around 2011. The government constituted a number of Group of Ministers (GoMs) and Empowered Group of Ministers (EGoMs) to decide on issues such as determination of gas price, disinvestment in public sector undertakings, investment in mega power projects, and projects pertaining to economic ministries. Between

2009 and 2014, the government constituted 68 GoMs and 14 EGoMs. When these were abolished by a new government in 2014, 20 GoMs and 9 EGoMs were still functional.

The EGoMs and GoMs are inter-ministerial panels, headed by cabinet ministers. They serve similar purposes. The difference lies in their power and authority to decide projects. The projects considered by the EGoMs are large key projects, and usually spread over more than one ministry of the central government. For the sake of economic growth, it is important that the EGoMs clear the projects as quickly as possible. It may sound strange that there seemed a dearth of able ministers, but how else how can one explain the then finance minister alone being the chairman of more than two dozen GoMs and EGoMs? Obviously, decisions were delayed. Its first and foremost casualty was economic growth. Observing such delays in the decision-making process, it became a saying in those days that projects were sent to GoMs and EGoMs when the government was not too willing to take a decision!

The most shining example of policy paralysis in the government can be found in the way it dealt with the social activists who wanted their imprimatur on a range of subjects from food security to reservation of jobs for backward classes, to land acquisition for development of industry and infrastructure, and even on technical issues such as capital account convertibility. Their domain knowledge, in most cases, is ephemeral, and certainly cannot be used as the only input in the decision-making process of the government. Social activists churned out sinking stories concerning mega projects, which are mostly in the industry and infrastructure sector. This impaired the investment climate. Private investment was the key to growth in the years of economic reform, and neither the private sector, which actually was investing money in the projects, nor the government, which had a say in its development in order to keep the momentum of economic growth, was anywhere in this picture. These social activists wielded enormous power to influence the policies and programmes of the central government and, in many cases, its decisions. However, they had no responsibility for the consequence of their statements or assertions, which were not fully based on facts. They did not even have a clear idea about what they would have liked to have, let alone prescribing a road map. This led to stalling, and eventually withdrawal, of several private sector entities from key industry and infrastructure projects. It was enough to hurt the growth prospects of the Indian economy during the critical period of 2011 to 2013.

The way poverty in India is defined, basically makes it a case of food poverty. The people who lack food are mostly spread over the backward and drought-prone areas, deserts, and tribal and hill areas. Besides low income and purchasing power, their access to food is restricted due to disadvantageous geographical location and lack of communication. Picking up isolated instances of food shortage, social activists created a hue and cry about the poverty situation in the country, ridiculing the basis of estimation of poverty, especially the poverty line. A section of them demanded that 75 per cent of the population be provided free food, completely ignoring the fact that many of them are capable of procuring food themselves. These social activists could have played a facilitating role in meeting the immediate needs of the poor by acting as a bridge between the poor and the administrative machinery that implements state-sponsored income transfer programmes. That the redistributive schemes are financed by growth and to widen the ambit of these schemes there should be growth maximization was beyond their comprehension. Strangely, the government could not engage with the social activists properly and virtually gave in. In the end, the people lost confidence in the government. The entrepreneurs and industrialists followed suit. The government was in the midst of an existential crisis.

Economic Growth in the 2010s: 2015–19

The Parliamentary election in May 2014 brought about a change of government at the centre. In India, psephological studies do not point out economic issues shaping election results; usually, non-economic issues take precedence in deciding election outcomes. In 2014, perhaps the noise around the state of the economy became a factor to reckon with: first, for the high price inflation during the previous five years, and second, the media hype on the so-called policy paralysis in the economy, some of which have been touched upon in the previous section.

In 2014, the government may have changed as a result of the price inflation and policy paralysis plaguing the economy. Ironically, these two factors impacted the economic situation, and eventually the growth rate in the second half of the 2010s, though in a somewhat different manner. The spate of price inflation is a major causative factor behind the rate of economic growth in the first half of the 2010s (2010–14) falling below the peak level of 8 per cent per year, whereas the growth rate in the second half of the 2010s (2015–19) began to decline despite the price inflation being at an exceptionally low level. Then, the second half of the 2010s was marked by a kind of policy activism, replacing the policy paralysis witnessed in the first half. The policy paralysis in the first half of the 2010s prevented the growth rate to scale new heights, whereas the policy activism in the second half pushed the growth rate below the medium-term trend.

Before analysing the features of the growth rate in the 2010s, a comparison of the growth rate in the two halves of the decade may be useful.

The economic growth rates in the two halves of the 2010s, namely (a) 2010–11 to 2014–15 (6.4 per cent per year); and (b) 2015–16 to 2019–20 (6.5 per cent per year), are pretty close. In the 2010s, the annual growth rate in four years exceeded 7 per cent, which is considered to be high in the present circumstances, and these four years were evenly spread over its two halves.

The savings and investment rates, which are available until 2017–18, show that both peaked in 2010–11 and declined thereafter. The decline has been sharp since 2013–14. The behaviour of savings, investment, and growth rate in the eight-year period of 2010–11 to 2017–18 can be divided into two segments of four years each: (a) 2010–11 to 2013–14; and (b) 2014–15 to 2017–18. Between these two periods, the decline in average investment rate (5.6 percentage points) was nearly twice of that in savings rate (3.1 percentage points). It brings home the message that much of the savings generated in the initial four-year period (2010–11 to 2013–14) did not translate into investment in the later four years (2014–15 to 2017–18). This may point to a structural bottleneck for converting savings into investment. Such a feature is usually associated with inept handling of the factors that the investors consider indispensable to make investment decisions. This is a reminiscence of the so-called policy paralysis that engulfed the economy around 2011 and continued until 2014.

In the first four years of the 2010s (2010–11 to 2013–14), the average investment rate was 37.8 per cent and the growth rate was 6.2 per cent per year, whereas in the latter four years (2014–15 to 2017–18), the average investment rate lowered to 32.2 per cent and the growth rate rose to 7.5 per cent per year. The higher growth rate in 2014–17, despite decline in the investment rate, may seem to be a puzzle. There can be two theoretical explanations: (*a*) the economy became efficient in 2014–17 and, as a result, less amount of investment yielded a higher growth rate; or (*b*) the years 2014–17 were able to benefit from the investment made in the previous four years, 2010–13. There is no evidence to demonstrate that the economy became more efficient in capital use in 2014–17. The natural conclusion is that the higher growth rate in 2014–17 was the outcome of the investments made in 2010–13; that is, the growth rate in 2014–17 was simply aided by the gestation lag of investments made in 2010–13.

In an analogous manner, the lowering of the investment rate in the four years from 2014–15 to 2017–18 can impact the growth rate as soon as the benefits from the higher level of investment of the earlier years taper off. The low investment rate in 2014–17 in all probability has impacted the growth rate of the later years, and that is already in evidence from the growth rate of 2017–18 and afterwards. The slowing down of the growth rate from 2017–18 onwards, which was due to the decline in investment rate, led to a corresponding decline in income, which eventually impacted savings, and in due turn, investments. This cycle of low income, low savings, low investment, and low growth is prominent in the second half of the 2010s. The search for the measures to lift the growth rate to the medium-term trend should begin against the backdrop of these events.

Decline in Growth Rate: 2016–17 to 2019–20

In the second half of the 2010s (2015–16 to 2019–20), the rate of economic growth began to decline after 2016–17. The growth rate, which averaged 7.7 per cent per year in the three years from 2014–15 to 2016–17, lowered to 5.5 per cent per year in the next three years, 2017–18 to 2019–20.[5] The worry initially was about why the growth rate was not picking up to 8 per cent, since this is the new benchmark for India to raise the level of the GDP to USD 5 trillion within five years from 2019–20.

The decline in the average growth rate from 2014–16 to the next three-year period, 2017–19, was 2.2 percentage points. Between these two periods, the industrial growth rate declined by 3.6 percentage points and the growth rate in services sector by 2.5 percentage points. Within industry, the growth rate of the manufacturing sector in 2017–19 (4.1 per cent per year) became less than half of that in 2014–16 (9.6 per cent per year).

Interestingly, the situation that unfolded in the second half of the 2010s (2015–19) was exactly opposite of what happened in the first half (2010–14), or even in the second half of the 2000s (2005–2009). Price inflation was high in the first half of the 2010s, with the increase in the WPI being close to 7 per cent per year and the increase in the CPI in rural and urban areas, measured by CPI-AL and CPI-IW, being 10 per cent per year. Its impact on the growth rate could be contained to a great extent through policy measures, monetary and fiscal. The growth rate in the first half of the 2010s at the back of such high inflation rates averaged 6.4 per cent per year.

On the issue of price inflation, the second half of the 2010s present a contrasting scenario. The inflation rate has been low from 2014–15 onwards, and it remained so until 2018–19. In this period, 2014–15 to 2018–19, the inflation rate measured by the WPI was as low as 1.2 per cent per year and the increase in the CPI in rural and urban areas measured by CPI-AL and CPI-IW were 3.9 per cent per year and 4.9 per cent per year respectively. The economic growth rate in the second half of the 2010s (6.5 per cent per year) is almost identical to that in the first half (6.4 per cent per year). The opposing nature of the impact of price inflation on the rate of economic growth in the two halves of the 2010s is worth noting.

In the second half of the 2010s, the policymakers in the government may have been obsessed with the idea that a low price level is the main recipe for growth maximization. Perhaps they were taking half-hearted lessons from the experience of the high inflation rate witnessed from 2009–10 to 2013–14, when prices rose in almost all areas and sectors of the economy. The hue and cry about the price inflation in this five-year period (WPI increasing by 7 per cent per year and CPI-AL and CPI-IW rising by 10 per cent per year) missed the growth

scenario. The growth rate in this period at the back of such high inflation averaged more than 6 per cent per year. The government failed
to notice the enormous amount of expenditure that it incurred in this
period of high inflation to generate wage employment and on income
redistributive programmes, including food subsidy, which could raise
the real income of those sections of the population whom inflation
hurt most.

The government lost sight of the reality that lower level of price
inflation depresses profit rate and impedes the inducement to invest.
The investment rate in the period of high inflation, 2009–10 to
2013–14, was 38 per cent; it lowered to 32.2 per cent in the period of
low inflation, 2014–15 to 2017–18; the data on investment rates are
available until 2017–18.

The low prices from 2014–15 onwards were mistakenly perceived
as beneficial for the economy (by way of pushing up the growth rate)
and the people (from erosion in the value of money, a la, income).
This, unfortunately, is born out of an immature assessment of the
economic situation. A large part of the agricultural distress throughout the second half of the 2010s owes to depressed farm product
prices. The agrarian distress in this period was not the outcome of
loss of output because agricultural growth rate in the three years
from 2017–18 to 2019–20 rose to 4.1 per cent per year, from 2.5 per cent
per year in the previous three years, 2014–15 to 2016–17. This happened when the overall rate of economic growth in 2017–19 lowered
to 5.5 per cent per year, from 7.7 per cent per year in 2014–16. Despite
the higher agricultural growth, the farmers have been hit on two
counts. First, farm prices are low, as a result of which farm income
has been low, affecting the net sellers of farm produce. Second, the
government's experiment with the minimum support price (MSP) for
major agricultural produce has not been successful. The increase in
MSP-based support has not been commensurate with the price rise.
As a result, the farmers have been the most affected group in agriculture in the regime of low prices.

The ills of agriculture, and specifically the hardship of the farming community, lie in an entirely different area, which has been
rarely visited by planners and policymakers in the era of economic
reform. Agriculture, right since the beginning of the planning era,
has been dependent on, and in the course of time benefited from,

public investment. Throughout the 1950s and the 1960s, that is, in the first four to five Five Year Plans, agriculture benefited from public investment in multipurpose projects. The private sector was not inclined to invest in these areas. Public investment in agriculture began to decline from the 1980s onwards, and the decline sharpened from the 1990s. The revival of public investment in agriculture is essential to remove the major bottlenecks faced by the agriculture sector. It is also in the interest of the agriculturists, especially the small and marginal farmers who do not have the capacity to invest. After all, increased public investment in agriculture has the potential to raise rural output and thus rural demand.

The low rate of inflation can create a series of problems for the economy, in addition to a depressing investment rate. It squeezes the nominal value of GDP, which, in turn, lowers the revenue collection. It may compel the government to cut down expenditure. This, in its due turn, has the potential of hurting the growth prospect of the economy.

That high inflation adversely affects economic growth and that the relation between the two is negative are not disputed. However, there is considerable divergence of opinion among economists about the level of price inflation in a country that can be defined as high. This level is found to differ between developed and the developing countries. The safe rate of inflation to ensure growth is usually higher in developing countries as compared to developed countries. The RBI, being guided by the decision of the monetary policy committee taken in 2016, uses the CPI as the benchmark for price inflation with the threshold inflation rate as 4 per cent on a band of plus or minus 2 percentage points. The band takes care of the volatility of food and energy prices. On this consideration, it may be prudent to treat the threshold inflation as 5 per cent.

It appears that in the second half of the 2010s, the policymakers confused a stable inflation rate with zero inflation, and gladly accepted the latter as the target. State action at every stage reflected the earnestness to maintain a low price level. It was a one-sided measure. In the process, the growth rate took a beating.

In order to maintain the growth rate at a higher level, monitoring of the macroeconomic parameters at almost every stage is necessary. It also necessitates state intervention at the right spot (of economic activities) and at the right moment. Unfortunately, this was not done. The government, instead of taking proactive measures to maintain the growth rate at the higher level, seemed to be satisfied with a 1 per cent annual inflation rate.

That India's growth performance in the second half of the 2010s is worrying can be deciphered from the state of the macroeconomic parameters and especially the investment rate. It does not compare well in relation to the member countries of the World Bank. That as per the estimates of the IMF's World Economic Outlook the Indian economy in 2019 was the fifth largest in the world or that only 44 out of 193 member countries of the IMF could have a growth rate of 5 per cent or more in 2019 does not bring any solace until the growth rate of the Indian economy reverts to the medium-term trend.

Spanners in Growth

Two decisions of the central government have been identified which hurt the growth prospects of the Indian economy in the second half of the 2010s (2015–16 to 2019–20). These are: (*a*) demonetization, to eliminate the unaccounted economy, or what is known in common parlance as black money, so as to make economic activities transparent; and (*b*) the implementation of the goods and services tax (GST), aimed at creating in India a unified common market. The economic activities entered the doldrums with demonetization in November 2016. It was accentuated by a half-hearted and hurriedly implemented GST in July 2017. These two events were akin to self-inflicted injury on the economic growth and serve as examples of policy activism.

Several research institutions, prominent among them being New Delhi's National Institute of Public Finance and Policy, which is under the Ministry of Finance, have conducted studies on black money. Earlier, the Planning Commission used to examine this issue. On black money, there is general consensus on two aspects. First, the existence of the black economy is real and it embraces a wide range of economic activities. Second, its precise estimate is not known and the size of the black economy has remained a conjecture.

Several governments in the past had avoided demonetization in view of the general consensus among economists that it harms the economy more than the gains it is likely to accrue. The reason is simple: people do not hoard black money in cash. They find other instruments for this purpose. The planners and policymakers never prescribed demonetization as the antidote.

In spite of the advice of the economists and civil servants, the government had taken recourse to demonetization in the past, and needless to say, without much success. In 1978, currency notes valued at INR 1,000 and more were demonetized, despite the advice of the then governor of the RBI against this measure. This measure did not succeed in mopping up black money. In any case, the people in general were left untouched as only high value currency was demonetized. The yearly per capita income in 1978–79 was INR 1,642 and most people may not have even seen the currency notes of such high denomination; in those days INR 1 and 2 notes were used as currency.

It was a different situation in November 2016 when the government withdrew the currency notes with denominations of INR 500 and INR 1,000 from circulation, which then amounted to 86 per cent of the value of currency under circulation in the country. Its stated objective was not only to weed out unaccounted income. It had other objectives too, namely 'to eliminate fake Indian currency notes, to strike at the root of financing of terrorism and left-wing extremism, to convert non-formal economy to a formal economy, and to give a big boost to digitalization of payments to make India a less cash economy'.[6]

The demonetization in 2016 seemed to be a reckless decision as even the most ordinary person would possess the currency notes of INR 500 and INR 1,000 because yearly per capita income in that year was INR 1.05 lakh. It is usual for a decision on such a critical issue, which has bearing on the economy and the lives of the people, to factor in suggestions of expert policymakers and civil servants. The final call is taken by the concerned ministry, which in this particular case is the finance ministry. It is not known whether there was any discussion within the government (union council of ministers) before resorting to demonetization. It is also not known exactly what the civil servants or economists advised the government. The main advisory body in such areas, the Planning Commission, no longer existed. Its replacement, the NITI Aayog, does not seem to have a concerted opinion on the issue of demonetization either.

The demonetization, along with its antecedent objectives, as is well known, turned out to be an utter failure. Of the total value of currency declared void through demonetization in November 2016, more than 99 per cent was exchanged by its rightful owners, showing proof or evidence that they held the cash legally. Therefore, less than 1 per cent of the total value of the currency that was demonetized did not come back to the government. Even this small amount of money is by no means unaccounted. It is very much accounted for, but did not return to the government due to 'owner's inertia, forgetfulness, even damage'. It proved the previously held conviction that unaccounted wealth is not stored as currency. The government argued that demonetization-related measures would lead to digital transactions and there would be less use of cash in the economy. No one took this assertion seriously, and this did not happen either. In actuality, the use of cash in the economy increased at a faster pace, by 25 per cent in the next three years following demonetization, that is, between 2016 and 2019. As things turned out, the related objectives such as combating terrorism was found to be totally unrelated to demonetization, and there was no sign of the non-formal economy going the formal way.

The government, in the same statement delivered by the Union Finance Minister in the Lok Sabha as late as 2019 conceded that 'it is difficult to pin-point the impact of demonetization on the economy'. The idea that the adverse impact of demonetization has fizzled out with the currency being back into circulation is a myth. Demonetization has left a permanent legacy. Due to its impact, millions of small-scale and informal sector units have gone into oblivion as these are managed and run entirely through cash. It will take years for these units to develop and grow. In the formal and organized sector, automobiles and real estate stand as glaring examples of the casualties of demonetization.

In a similar way, though the GST had been on the cards for quite some time, its roll-out in July 2017 may have been hurried. There were numerous changes in the early months of its rollout, creating considerable confusion across stakeholders. The small businesses were affected the most. A large segment of the economy, including mostly the informal sector, found it difficult to keep pace with the speed with which GST was enforced. No one doubted the advantages of the GST for its ability to create a unified Indian market and eliminate inefficient tax cascading. If some experts are to be believed, proper implementation of GST could have boosted the GDP growth rate by up to 2 percentage points. However, the situation in India has not been so. Even after three years of its enactment, the GST is not in full bloom. The informal sector is yet to adjust itself with the process. The government should have taken lessons from the discussions and parleys with the stakeholders, especially the state governments that implemented the process of introduction of the value added tax (VAT) in the country a few years earlier.

The decision-making process of the government in India is well-defined and, at the same time, transparent. The manner in which the GST rollout was decided is well within the knowledge of the business community and the people. The same, however, cannot be said for demonetization. The idea of demonetization had earlier (in 1978) come from the political class. In 2016, it is believed by some to have come from certain religious institutions too, in a manner in which the Church used to issue diktats to the government in sixteenth- and seventeenth-century Europe. Demonetization may have been good politics, but certainly not good economics. Because of its total failure, and the resulting unimaginable distress to the industry and loss of life and livelihood of the common man, it is important that the government discloses the manner and method of arriving at the decision of demonetization. It may also serve posterity.

In the 2010s, if derailment of economic growth rate in the first half was due to the policy paralysis that tanked the economy, then the slow-down of the growth rate in the second half was the direct consequence of the policy shocks transmitted through demonetization and GST.

Missed Opportunities

Two factors which have been instrumental in increasing the resources at the disposal of the government in the second half of the 2010s (2015–16 to 2019–20) have been identified. These could have been utilized to raise the level of investment, and in its due turn, the rate of growth. This did not happen due to the absence of proper planning, and hence can be termed as missed opportunities. These two factors are: (*a*) the tax–GDP ratio; and (*b*) the international price of crude oil.

The average tax–GDP ratio in the second half of the 2010s (2015–16 to 2019–20) has been 1 percentage point higher than that in the first half (2010–11 to 2014–15). The rise in the tax–GDP ratio means extra resources at the disposal of the government during the second half, over and above the availability in the normal course. The additional amount of resources should have been used to increase the level of investment. That this has not been the case is amply clear from the decline in the average investment rate by 3.5 percentage points between 2012–14 and 2015–17. The question thus arises: where has the additional money from the increase in the tax–GDP ratio gone? The expenditure on social welfare programmes as proportion of GDP has not increased. The money has also not been used to contain the budgetary deficit in any manner or form. Its destination remains unknown.

The additional money arising from the increase in the tax–GDP ratio in the absence of productive use can be harmful for the economy and the people, especially as three-fourths of the increase in the tax–GDP ratio has taken place on account of indirect taxes. It is likely to hurt the poor and the lower deciles of the population more, as the incidence of indirect taxes falls disproportionately more on them.

The other issue relates to the international price of crude oil. The international price of crude oil averaged USD 102 per barrel in the first half of the 2010s. It lowered to USD 57 per barrel in the second half. Thus, the average international price of crude oil that India faced in the second half of the 2010s is 56 per cent of that in the first half. The lower price of crude oil in the second half of the 2010s proved to be a bonanza for the government in two important ways. First, the government expenditure on crude oil and petroleum products reduced. Second, taking advantage of the lower international prices of crude oil, the government raised the domestic taxes on petroleum products; the revenue realization of the government increased as a result. These two factors, namely, lower import bill on crude oil and increased revenue (income), together yielded a kind of windfall gain for the government, which created elbow room for additional investment. However, the money was not utilized to increase investment. The investment rate declined in the second half, provoking a similar question as in the case of rise in the tax–GDP ratio. The utilization of this implicitly accrued money to the government as a result of the lower oil prices remains unknown. This was a great opportunity to raise the investment rate and, by implication, growth rate of the economy. The government policies withered this away.

The growth rate in the first half of the 2010s was 6.4 per cent per year when the oil price was high, and it is 6.5 per cent per year in the second half when the oil price is low. With regard to the nexus between oil price and the rate of growth, two issues surface. First, the growth rate in the first half of the 2010s could be achieved despite the high international price of crude oil. Second, the economy could not utilize the advantage of lower international price of crude oil throughout the second half of the 2010s to jack up the growth rate. In the natural course, there can be a question mark on the efficiency in management of the economy in the second half of the 2010s.

Misplaced Emphasis

Two initiatives of the government in the second half of the 2010s that were focused on raising the rate of economic growth seem to have got lost mid-way. These are (a) the 'Make in India' campaign to promote the manufacturing industry; and (b) the aim to convert India into a USD 5 trillion economy.

The 'Make in India' campaign was launched in 2014 with the aim to turn the country into a global manufacturing hub. It did not make even the slightest impact in the next five years. Its aim is to increase the share of manufacturing in GDP from 16 per cent in 2014 to 25 per cent in 2022, and generate 100 million additional jobs. The share of manufacturing in GDP has remained at the same 16 per cent throughout the five-year period, 2014 to 2019, and there is no tangible employment generation. These targets for the manufacturing sector are adopted from the National Manufacturing Policy (NMP), which was announced by the government in November 2011. In fact, the NMP 2011 has been repackaged as Make in India. In its 2011 edition, there was at least a blueprint for the strategy. In 2014, even that was missing and there was no specific plan to attain the targets of Make in India.

Increasing the size of the GDP to USD 5 trillion by 2024–25 is another such target that the government has set for itself. This was announced by the prime minister in 2019. There is another statement in the finance ministry's *Economic Survey 2018–19* that the GDP would be increased further to USD 10 trillion by 2032.

There are three essential factors which must be in place to increase the GDP to USD 5 trillion in 2024–25. First, the rate of growth of GDP should be at least 8 per cent per year during the five-year period of 2019–20 to 2024–25. Second, the annual inflation rate should be no more than 4 per cent. Third, the real effective exchange rate of the rupee should not appreciate. It is well-recognized by planners and policymakers that these three issues in any economy are related in a very complex manner.

The GDP growth in the recent past has to a great extent been driven by consumption. However, growth in GDP as high as 8 per cent per year cannot be sustained by consumption alone. It would be necessary to rely on export.

Investment is the major instrument of GDP growth. The present level of investment, which is around 32 per cent of GDP, is unlikely to yield the GDP growth rate of 8 per cent per year. The exchange rate of INR vis-à-vis USD may be a disruptive factor. The target would be missed if the exchange rate depreciates more in the next five years as compared to the actual depreciation that has taken place in the past five years. Rise in oil price above USD 80 per barrel may also spoil the party.

There is no official announcement about the manner and method or the strategy that is to be adopted to make India a USD 5 trillion economy by 2024–25. In order to attain the GDP growth of 8 per cent per year for the next five years, which is the driving force behind the target, the *Economic Survey 2018–19* postulates the centrality of investment as the key driver of growth. This is not very different from what had been attempted in the Five Year Plans during the first four decades of planning when the economic scenario was not as unpredictable as it is today in the environs of a globalized world. The only ingenuity the *Survey* shows is in the area of investment, which is treated as the key driver of growth; and it is the private sector which is responsible for a larger share of investment. In any case, this has been the strategy since the initiation of economic reforms in 1991.

The *Economic Survey 2019–20* theorizes that India's aspiration to become a USD 5 trillion economy depends critically on strengthening the invisible hand of the markets and supporting it with the hand of trust. It is obvious that it is the state which has to extend its hand of trust. Reminding the people of India that for more than three-fourths of the known economic history it had been the dominant economic power globally, the *Survey* underlines the importance of creation of wealth and respect for those who create it to increase income and thereby the GDP.[7] There can be no problem insofar as dependence on market is concerned, as this has been the leitmotif of the era of economic reform. However, such a theorization on wealth creation can be a matter of concern for its impact on the economy and the people. If creation of wealth alone could meet the multidimensional objectives related to growth and development, then the indispensability of the state in matters of economic management would come under doubt. There would also be no occasion for the state to intervene in the market. The exclusive emphasis on creation of wealth may lead to a situation which the European countries experienced in the course of the Industrial Revolution, when wealth was created in sufficient measure but it accrued only to a small number of people, chiefly to those who created the wealth, leaving the vast majority of the population in poverty. The people became isolated from the development process. There is a known philosophical statement, though it may not be as old as the known economic history, that those who believe that only the past was a golden era are bound to be disappointed with the present. There could have been very few Indians who had as much knowledge and respect for India's glorious past as Jawaharlal Nehru and his ideological mentor, Mahatma Gandhi. However, neither of them ever felt that India should be taken to the ancient days.

The state governments have been announcing their contribution in meeting this target of GDP from time to time and with great fanfare. It is a kind of self-declaration that seems to be prompted by emotion rather than being based on statistical evidences. How the states have arrived at these estimates remains unknown. It is necessary for the states to draw up plans in areas and sectors of the economy to meet the targets that they have set for themselves. This is a job specifically for planners and trained experts. The planning boards in many states do not function. In a number of states, they do not even exist on paper. It is beyond the capacity of the bureaucrats in the ministries to prepare such plans.

The aggregate GDP being the sum total of sectoral GDP, it becomes necessary to identify the areas and sectors of the economy which have the potential to grow. In this context, the contribution of specific sectors in GDP growth at the national level becomes more relevant. Then, these national estimates may be decomposed into state-wise estimates. Bypassing this, the state governments are found determining their own targets. It is not going to help even if these targets are indicative.

In the normal course, such an issue of national importance as raising the level of GDP to USD 5 trillion within five years is finalized after discussing with the state governments as the plans and programmes to meet the target depends to a great extent on them. It is doubtful whether the states were taken into confidence before announcing this move. Whether it was discussed in the Union Cabinet also remains unknown. It appears that the target is not based on quantitative reasoning and nothing extraordinary is going to be achieved by meeting or missing this target. Does the government expect a place at the high table with the developed countries? Perhaps not. The GDP of USD 5 trillion in 2024 would not lead India to the group of middle-income countries as per the categorization of the World Bank. All things considered, the zeal to become a USD 5 trillion economy is born out of misplaced emphasis, and may leave the economy stranded.

Strategy to Lift the Growth Rate

There are reasons to worry when the economic growth rate falters and goes down, especially to a level below the medium-term trend, as has been the situation in the second half of the 2010s. In this half, the growth rate declined by 1.4 percentage points on average every year from 2016–17 to 2019–20. The decline in the growth rate is usually the culmination of a series of mismatches in the economic system. It is necessary to isolate the reasons behind the decline in order to take necessary measures to bring the growth rate back to the trend level. The initiative has to come from the government even as the private sector is responsible for a larger share of investment in the economy and carries a greater responsibility for growth than the public sector.

India's approach to restore the growth rate to the trend level has always been pragmatic. It has resorted to both monetary and fiscal policies, balancing these two in a prudent manner, relying on supply-side and demand-side measures in the management of growth rate. The supply-side and the demand-side measures are operated in tandem. The balancing of these two is done keeping in view the assessed economic situation covering the real and financial sectors. In a democratic polity such as India, economic measures are usually decided first on the basis of their likely impact on the lives of the people in the short run; then, the long-term consequences of these measures are taken into account. The purpose has been to ensure that the measures to lift the growth rate to a higher level, which may often be painful, do not adversely affect the people deeply and for a long enough time.

The bottom line is that the policies to restore the rate of economic growth to the previously held high level should comprise supply-side as well as demand-side measures. The contours of the supply-side measures are determined by the monetary policy, the main purpose of which is to contain inflation and maintain a stable price level. The demand-side measures are the focus of the fiscal policy.

The role of monetary policy in enhancing investment and growth rate becomes limited when the price level is low and demand is subdued. This has exactly been the situation in the second half of the 2010s. In contrast with the first half of the 2010s, the price inflation measured from both WPI and CPI has been low throughout the second half. It has been mentioned earlier that the WPI during the five-year period of 2014–15 to 2018–19 lowered to 1.2 per cent per year from 7 per cent per year in the previous five-year period of 2009–10 to 2013–14. The CPI-AL and the CPI-IW increased by 10 per cent per year in 2009–13; these lowered to 3.9 per cent per year and 4.9 per cent per year respectively in 2014–18. It is only towards the end of 2018 that the RBI took note of the low inflation rate, and as a part of the monetary policy, began to reduce the interest rate from December 2018 onwards. In a bid to increase liquidity, the RBI reduced the repo rate (the rate at which the central bank lends to commercial banks and, therefore, signals the overall interest rate reduction) five times within nine months of the year 2019, that is, in February, April, June, August, and October. The quantum of reduction in 2019 is 110 basis points, which may be considered enough to increase liquidity in the system, which is necessary to boost investment and hence the growth rate. The attempt to strike a balance between the rate of economic growth and inflation using interest rate as the instrument of policy is visible in 2019, though it should have come earlier. The question, of course, remains whether the lower interest rates masterminded by the RBI will be enough for the industry to revive investment. Investment depends on many factors, and interest rate is just one among them. Over and above, monetary policy can be effective in promoting investment and growth in the short term or medium term, but not in the long run.

There is a limit to the use of monetary policy to boost investment and, by implication, economic growth. The interest rate on its own cannot propel investment to a higher level. The decision to invest is taken on the basis of long-term prospects of the economy, and most of all, business profitability. As monetary policies begin to run out of steam, it is crucial for economies to rely on fiscal policy.

The lowering of GDP growth rate results in the lowering of disposable income, which, in turn, affects consumption expenditure of the people. The measures to increase the income of the people, especially those belonging to the lower deciles, is an essential element for countering the decline in consumption arising from loss of income eventuated by the lowering of the growth rate. In such a situation, there is a specific role of the contra-cyclical fiscal policy stance in generating investment and growth. It makes the factors on the demand side equally important as the supply-side, in which the role of public spending to generate income, specifically for the poor and the lower deciles of the population, surfaces. The savings propensity of these people being close to zero, increase in their income is instantly translated into consumption. It is a sure-fire way to create demand for goods and boost consumption. Such increases in consumption demand may eventuate in inflating the price level, especially of food, as food usually makes the first draft on poor peoples' income or consumption. The increase in demand induces investors to invest, which in the process can propel the economy to a higher growth path. This was the approach in the similar situation (of low-growth cycle) during the period of economic reform. This has also been the approach in the period of 2009–10 to 2013–14 to maintain the growth momentum. The government succeeded in coming out of demand-related problems by transferring income and purchasing power to the lower deciles of the population through liberal and hassle-free income redistributive and wage employment programme.

The moral of the story is that the initiative to increase income and consumption of the people in years of low growth in the second half of the 2010s should have come from the state. The problem in this regard may rest with expenditure. The government may not have sufficient funds at its disposal to finance the expenditure on income redistributive programmes that are capable of increasing the income of the people who can actually make an impact on demand. There are a number of ways in which the expenditure can be financed at this juncture. A part of the transfer (INR 1.76 lakh crores) from the RBI may be used. However, the more substantive part of the strategy should be to raise the expenditure at the cost of fiscal deficit. There is nothing sacrosanct with the target of fiscal deficit set in the budget. It is widely known that the target set by the FRBM Act lacks scientific basis. It is also not known whether a seigniorage analysis has been conducted recently to find out the level of fiscal deficit that can be considered safe from the angle of price inflation. In the mid-1990s, such analysis used to be conducted by the Planning Commission to explore the feasibility of a higher level of fiscal deficit than that decided by the finance ministry, so as to enable the government to spend the extra money on income redistributive and social welfare programmes. Going by the tenets of the analysis conducted a quarter century ago, there could be no harm in breaching the fiscal deficit by a couple of decimal points (of GDP) now and channelizing the equivalent amount of money for income redistributive purposes or even in social welfare programmes. The fiscal deficit could be restored to its normal level when growth rate picks up. As already mentioned, a similar policy measure was pursued in the first half of the 2010s, when growth faltered, and it yielded the desired results. There is no reason why this should not have been effective in the second half of the decade to infuse confidence of the entrepreneurs to ward off the dipping investment sentiments.

Half-Hearted Measures

As the economy faced a downswing in the growth rate in the second half of the 2010s, the government initiated a series of measures in 2019, especially after the presentation of the Central Budget 2019–20, to boost investment and, in turn, the rate of economic growth. Most of these measures do not manifest a clear long-term view of the economy and seem to have been taken in a hurry. Again, the speed with which some of these budgetary proposals were either withdrawn or amended in less than a month show signs of nervousness of the government, besides pointing out that the ideas were not well thought out. These relate to core areas of the Budget such as taxation, corporate obligations, labour laws, and so on. For example, a tax was levied on very rich people in the Budget, only to be withdrawn within a month. Such actions of the government go against building confidence of the private entrepreneurs who are expected to lead the investment in the economy to charge up the growth rate.

The lowering of the rate of corporate tax by 10 percentage points in September 2019 will certainly fall in this category of measures. It is a significant reduction, no doubt guided by the singular expectation to stimulate investment, and in due time, the growth rate. However, it would be naive to expect this to be effective in the short run, let alone immediately. It would be equally naive to expect that additional profits as a result of lower taxes would be diverted towards investment. This is not the reality of business in the private sector. A host of factors come in the way of fund availability and its diversion to investment, important among them being profitability.

Moreover, the idea of lowering the corporate tax rate to kick-start investment is not founded on sound empirics. Earlier, on a number of occasions, the corporate tax rate was used as an instrument to channelize investment into less-developed areas of the country. The tax rate was lowered and, in many cases, exemptions were given for a long period of time in specific areas so as to promote investment. This has not been successful, and the regional disparity in investment remains unchanged.

As a result of the lowering of the corporate tax, the government may end up losing revenue (to the tune of INR 1.5 lakh crores in a year) without a commensurate gain in the form of investment or growth. As 40 per cent of the revenue loss from the reduction in corporate tax will have to be borne by the state governments, their finances will be in jeopardy.

The decision to lower the corporate tax may have been cheered by the stock market, but this is without any basis. Such a large cut in one stroke is unwarranted when there is excess capacity in the system and the interest rate is low. It will increase the income of large industrialists, and carries with it the potential of increasing the level of income inequality by raising their profit margin.

Unemployment and Poverty in the 2010s

That the rate of economic growth declined in the second half of the 2010s has been mentioned earlier. It has also been mentioned that the decline in growth rate accelerated after 2016–17. The lowering of the growth rate is likely to impact the unemployment rate and poverty ratio in the second half of the 2010s. As the growth rate plummets to a new low after 2016–17, unemployment and poverty will rise further. The living standard, especially of the poor and of the people located in the bottom deciles, will deteriorate.

In May 2019, the NSO, through its Periodic Labour Force Survey (PLFS), came out with an unusually high estimate of the unemployment rate for the year 2017–18. This is much higher than the unemployment rate estimated from the Employment–Unemployment Surveys of the NSS in 2011–12, or for that matter for any year since 1972–73. The Centre for Monitoring Indian Economy (CMIE), a premier research institution, also came out with an estimate of unemployment rate in 2017–18 that is as high as that in the PLFS.

The unemployment rate is known to be negatively associated with the rate of economic growth. However, the high unemployment rate in 2017–18 may not be explained entirely by the decline in the growth rate. It needs some elucidation. The usual status unemployment rate, a measure of long-term unemployment, as estimated by the NSO have been given in Table 8.3.

The methodology of estimation of unemployment in the PLFS (2017–18) is different from that employed to estimate the unemployment rate during the period of 1972–73 to 2011–12. The latter were estimated using the methodology of the 'Expert Committee on Unemployment Estimates', known as the Dantwala Committee, named after its chairman, M. L. Dantwala. The unemployment rates estimated from this method for nine points of time during the period

Table 8.3   Usual Status Unemployment Rate in India (Per Cent)

Year	Rural		Urban	
	Male	Female	Male	Female
1972–73 (NSS 27th Round)	1.2	0.5	4.8	6.0
1977–78 (NSS 32nd Round)	1.3	2.0	5.4	12.4
1983 (NSS 38th Round)	1.4	0.7	5.1	4.9
1987–88 (NSS 43rd Round)	1.8	2.4	5.2	6.2
1993–94 (NSS 50th Round)	1.4	0.9	4.1	6.1
1999–2000 (NSS 55th Round)	1.7	1.0	4.5	5.7
2004–05 (NSS 61st Round)	1.6	1.8	3.8	6.9
2009–10 (NSS 66th Round)	1.6	1.6	2.8	5.7
2011–12 (NSS 68th Round)	1.7	1.7	3.0	5.2
2017–18 (PLFS)	5.8	3.8	7.1	10.8

Source: National Statistical Office.

of 1972–73 to 2011–12 shows that in rural areas, it ranges from 1.2 per cent to 1.8 per cent among males and 0.5 per cent to 2.4 per cent among females; the unemployment rate in urban areas ranges from 2.8 per cent to 5.4 per cent among males and 4.9 per cent to 12.4 per cent among females. These are much lower than the estimated unemployment rate in 2017–18 yielding from the PLFS. Hence, there is the contention that the unemployment rate increased in 2017–18 and that the country did not witness such a high rate of unemployment in the previous four decades.

The wide gap between the unemployment rate in 2017–18 yielding from the PLFS and the unemployment rates in earlier years derived from the Dantwala methodology should not be entirely attributed to the declining growth rate of the economy as methodological issues may stand in between. The higher unemployment rate in 2017–18 revealed in the PLFS, in comparison with the relatively lower and more or less stable unemployment rates over a long period of four decades, 1972–73 to 2011–12, derived on the basis of Dantwala methodology, throws up intricate issues related to comparability of these two sets of estimates. In view of this, it would not be prudent to conclude that the decline in growth rate is the cause of the high unemployment rate in 2017–18. It should be remembered that there are instances, for example, the Sixth and the Seventh Plans, when the GDP growth rate targeted in the Plan could be met but not the employment target.

It is a similar story in respect of consumption expenditure, an important determinant of poverty. The sole source of estimate of consumption is the quinquennial survey of consumer expenditure conducted by the NSO, the latest of which is available for the year 2011–12 (NSS 68th Round). The next consumer expenditure survey was conducted in 2017–18 (NSS 75th Round). The data was gathered, but in November 2019, the NSO decided to scrap these data on account of methodological issues. The NSO is not going to undertake another consumer expenditure survey before 2020–21. Therefore, assessment of the level of consumption, and by implication, poverty will be possible only after 2020–21.

As an alternative, for occupation groups in the population, the statistics on earnings gathered in the PLFS 2017–18 can be compared with the per capita consumption gathered in the NSS 68th Round consumer expenditure survey (2011–12) so as to get an idea about the change in their levels of living during this period. The estimates of consumption in 2011–12 and earnings in 2017–18 are available at current prices, that is, at the prices prevailing in the respective years. These are converted into comparable prices by eliminating price inflation, using CPI of rural labour in rural areas and CPI of industrial workers in urban areas. At comparable prices, the earnings of regular wage and salaried employees in 2017–18 turn out to be less than their consumption in 2011–12 in both rural and urban areas. It is a similar story for the self-employed in rural areas, but not in urban. The earnings and consumption of the casual labourers in these two years are more or less similar. Though earnings are compared with consumption, these on the whole present a situation in which the living conditions may have deteriorated between 2011–12 and 2017–18. The declining living standard in this period is quite in contrast with the phenomenal increase in per capita consumption between 2004–05 and 2011–12, the details of which have been discussed in Chapter 7.

Ravi Srivastava and Balakrushna Padhi are of the view that both the Employment–Unemployment Surveys based on the Dantwala methodology and the PLFS provide robust estimates of wages. Comparing the changes in weekly real earnings from wages/salaries between two time periods, namely 2004–05 to 2011–12 and 2011–12 to 2017–18, they arrive at the conclusion that wage growth collapsed in the latter period and even turned negative for several employment segments.[8]

Using a range of socio-economic surveys conducted by the NSO, Himanshu found convincing evidence of decline in real per capita consumption expenditure in both rural and urban areas during the period 2015–16 to 2017–18.[9] The stagnation and decline of real wages, as brought out by Srivastava and Padhi, and the decline in real per capita consumption expenditure as illustrated by Himanshu's study, are symptoms of a deeper economic malaise. It will not require much introspection to find out that these are the end results of a bunch of ill thought out policies pursued by the state, especially since 2016.

The Role of the State

It is the responsibility of the state to formulate authentic policies to promote investment and growth. The state cannot perform this job efficiently and successfully without an organization that can take a holistic view of the economic growth and development of the country. The absence of such an organization is felt more when the growth rate dips, and it becomes imperative for the state to locate the reasons behind the slip in the growth rate and take requisite steps to lift it to the trend level. The task becomes complicated when the state has to intervene in the market. It is not possible for the central ministries or the state governments, or even the Prime Minister's Office to perform this job. They do not possess the requisite expertise and talent pool to cope with the problems when growth falters.

The formulation of policies to lift the sinking growth rate to the trend level requires constant monitoring of the situation at the detailed areas and sectors of the economy. Usually, two kinds of problems are encountered in this effort. First, the prescriptions may not always be foolproof. Second, the efficiency in implementing the prescribed measures may not always be at the desired level. These two factors, despite the best of intentions and efforts, may not be successful in bringing back the growth rate to the trend level. It is a kind of experimental economics that the government has to resort to in its bid to apply the different instruments to restore the growth rate to a healthy mark. In the planning era, the Planning Commission used to perform this job.

The measures to set the nuts and bolts of the economy to kick start the growth rate are now being initiated by the RBI and the finance ministry. The RBI has a limited view, and is capable of supervising the monetary policy. The monetary policy has limited ability to stimulate growth, and that too in the short term, because the decision to invest in a market economy is taken on the basis of long-term interest rate and not a short-term one. The RBI can keep track of the measures to ensure price stability. However, the responsibility of growth should not be reposed entirely with it. The finance ministry alone cannot perform this job; it can, at best, formulate a well-designed fiscal policy which can boost consumption and promote economic growth. The central ministries are responsible for the implementation of the plans and programmes falling exclusively within their domain, and their expertise does not go beyond financial accounting.

An institution such as the erstwhile Planning Commission can ideally take a holistic view on the economic situation related to both demand and supply sides of the economy, embracing monetary, fiscal, and price policies. In the era of economic reform, the flow of investment into different areas and sectors of economic activity is decided by market forces and the growth responsibilities are largely borne by the private sector. Even then, the Planning Commission had acted as the bridge between the short-term measures to lift the growth rate and the long-term objectives of the economy, and also as a link between the central government and the state governments. These have important connotations for growth.

In the absence of an institution such as the Planning Commission, each sector formulates its own policies in isolation, and implements them in silos. It has the potential to hurt the growth prospects of the economy not only in the long run but also in the medium term. Two issues surface in this context. First, has replacing the Planning Commission with the NITI Aayog helped the Indian economy to devise policies to maximize the growth rate or lift the growth rate to the trend level when it faltered? Second, in the event of the NITI Aayog failing to rise to the occasion, will it be necessary to bring back the Planning Commission? These two issues are pertinent to the growth and development of the Indian economy, especially in times of crisis situations and in the context of taking care of the long-term goals.

It may be worthwhile to mention in this connection that several experts who were earlier associated with the planning and policymaking on behalf of the government have raised a debate around the role of the Planning Commission and the relevance of the NITI Aayog. Y. K. Alagh, who was a member of the Planning Commission in the 1980s and the Minister of Planning in the 1990s, has been candid in stating that absence of the Planning Commission is sure to hurt the long-term growth prospects of the Indian economy. Alagh wants the NITI Aayog to be a more focused body concentrating on issues such as energy, land, water, and demographics, which have a long-term perspective.

Echoing a similar view, C. Rangarajan, a former governor of the RBI, wants the NITI Aayog to be transformed into an institution that looks at long-term problems of the country and to come up with strategies and solutions.[10] Vijay Kelkar, chairman of the Thirteenth Finance Commission, feels that replacing the Planning Commission with the NITI Aayog has reduced the government's policy reach and it is essential that the NITI Aayog is allowed more space in the decision-making process, and especially in the allocation of capital and revenue grants to the states. Kelkar asserts that reposing these responsibilities with the NITI Aayog are in the interest of long-term growth and development of the Indian economy.[11]

There is a near unanimity in the assertion that the standards set by the Planning Commission in the 1950s and the 1960s, or in other words, during the Nehru era, were allowed to deteriorate; certainly after the 1980s, the Planning Commission was unable to maintain its earlier standards. The role of the Planning Commission evolved over the years with the change in the structure of the economy as well as the altered socio-economic landscape as a result of economic growth. Its function changed after the country embarked on the economic reform programmes in 1991 when the economic decisions became market-based. The emergence of a market economy and withdrawal of the state from large areas of economic activity that occurred in this period called for rewriting the role of the Planning Commission. This did not happen. As a result, the Planning Commission began to suffer from a kind of identity crisis. With projects and programmes related to economic growth being shifted to the private sector, the role of the Planning Commission was eclipsed dramatically. It became more of a facilitator, discharging the function of releasing central funds to the state governments. These engagements became ceremonial in nature, as the dependence of state governments on central funds reduced greatly with the policies of economic reform taking shape. The Planning Commission needed to reorient its role to suit the demand of an open and market economy. It was unable to do so. It failed to establish a foothold in the administrative set-up of the government and willy-nilly became rudderless. It was disbanded in this maelstrom, like the proverbial case of throwing the baby out with the bathwater.

The Finale

The growth rate in the second half of the 2010s (2015–16 to 2019–20) was on a downward sloping curve whereas that in the first half (2010–11 to 2014–15) was U-shaped. This happened even when the average growth rate in the two halves (first and second) in the 2010s were quite similar. On this count, the decline in growth rate in the second half, however steady it may appear from the year 2017–18, cannot be attributed to structural factors. It is a slowdown of the growth rate occurring as a part of the cyclical pattern embedded in the long-term growth rate that is witnessed at regular intervals, especially since the beginning of economic reform in 1991. The slowdown in the growth rate, to begin with, was triggered by ill-conceived policies, some of which have been mentioned earlier in this chapter. The lowering of the growth rate to less than 4 per cent in the last year of the 2010s, that is, in 2019–20, has been caused by domestic factors as well as the crisis in the international economy. The World Bank has quantified the extent of the slowdown of the growth rate of the Indian economy caused by the events in the international economy. Hans Timmer, the World Bank's chief economist for South Asia, stated that international sources could be responsible for as much as 80 per cent of the slowdown in India's economy that occurred in the year 2019–20.[12]

The facts that in 2019 the fiscal deficit was not alarmingly high, inflation rate was under control, and the balance of payments was not in serious disequilibrium point out that the slowdown in the growth rate is more cyclical than structural. The lowering of the growth rate at the level of major sectors of the Indian economy is proportional or across the board. In the event of a structural breakdown, the sectoral growth rates are likely to be topsy-turvy. There is evidence of increased unemployment rate and depressed consumption expenditure, which in isolation can be treated as the outcome of low growth but is not enough to suggest structural flaws.

The slowdown of the growth rate in the 2010s, and especially in the second half, may not be alarming because this low growth is preceded by the high growth rate of several years. The growth rate exceeded 7 per cent per year during the six-year period of 2005–06 to 2010–11, which could create a large base for the economy. This is going to sustain for quite some time. The lowering of the growth rate to less than 4 per cent in 2019–20 still means per capita income growing by about 3 per cent per year, which is not a meagre number. That such a level of growth would be unable to satisfy the aspirations of the youth who are born and brought up in an environment of a globalized world, which is far removed from the early days of planning, is a separate issue. The irony is that deceleration in growth rate from 2016–17 onwards is the result of ill-conceived policies of the government.

It may take time for the growth rate to revert to the trend level and the recovery may not be as quick as in the past. There are reasons for this. The decline in the growth rate has been caused largely by the withering away of the informal sector of the economy in the wake of demonetization. This damage to the economy by way of income and employment generation is permanent. It will take years for the informal economy to develop and regrow.

There is some uncertainty within the system, as a result of which the industrialists and business class are in no mood to invest in the domestic economy when it is needed most to lift the sinking growth rate. At the same time, they are moving out of the country to invest. This is a demonstration of their lack of confidence and faith in the system which borders on the idea that the environment many not be congenial.

Investment decisions are not as simple as to be shaped by the improvement of 'ease of doing business'. Evidently, the industrialists and entrepreneurs are not impressed by the phrase 'minimum government, maximum governance' coined by the government because it hardly made any impact on the administrative apparatus of either the central government or the state governments, and remained symbolic in nature. This is clear as investment is not picking up. The different departments of the government which are responsible for creating enabling conditions for growth are willy-nilly creating an environment which deters private investors from taking positive steps. This is happening when corporate governance is becoming increasingly complex. The circumstances may not be conducive as the investors are yet to familiarize themselves with the new rules of engagement. This is a situation that is compelling them to wait and watch.

India's growth rate moves along with the international economy, though there may be a debate on the extent to which it is intertwined with global economic growth. In order to get back to the higher growth trajectory of 8 per cent in 2020, India need not have to wait for the revival of the global economic growth. The East Asian financial crisis in 1997–98 affected the industrial growth rate of the Indian economy for two years at the most. It was more or less a similar situation in 2008–09, when the global economic and financial crisis struck.

In order to attain the growth rate of 8 per cent per year and make it sustainable, India should rely more on the financial sector as there are plenty of constraints on the growth of the real sector. There are limits to capacity utilization in the real sector in the absence of a booming export market. Besides, India lacks competitiveness in export. As such, evidences point out India's declining competitiveness.[13] In contrast, the scope in the financial sector is unbounded, and efforts should be made to develop the financial sector with all seriousness. That, for the moment, is the route to realize the growth rate of 8 per cent in a year, and make it sustainable.

The potential reasons behind the economic slowdown and the remedial measures to lift the growth rate to a higher trajectory need to be discussed and debated threadbare. Besides the government agencies such as the NITI Aayog, the RBI, the central ministries, the state governments, and the think-tanks in the country should be involved in this discussion. Only then can solutions emerge, and the road-map to recovery be decided. Before the year 2014, the Planning Commission was the main forum of such discussions. In its absence, it has become important for the government to strengthen the institutions which can engage in issues related to economic growth and development. Since 2014, several institutions located in New Delhi's central vista have been abolished (for example, the Planning Commission) while some others have been weakened (for example, the Independent Evaluation Office) to such an extent that these can be treated as virtually non-existent. This has restricted the ability of the government to devise suitable measures to take the growth rate back to the previously held higher trajectory. It can hurt the growth prospect of the private sector, as the private sector entities look towards these institutions and their deliberations before making any commitment for investment. In the absence of these institutions, the investment decisions of the private sector would have to depend entirely on the dynamics of the market economy, which means that it would not be able to factor in long-term considerations. This is not going to help either the private investors or the economy.

Though the growth rates in the two halves of the 2010s are more or less similar, these are the outcomes of widely differing policies and approach to growth and development. The growth rate in the first half was realized against the backdrop of high inflation rate which threatened the macroeconomic balance, whereas the growth in the second half came in the environs of very low inflation. The first half may have been subjected to policy paralysis in respect of economic management whereas the second half witnessed policy activism expressed through demonetization and a hurriedly implemented GST, which adversely affected the growth rate.

In the first half of the 2010s, the monetary policy was used in tandem with the fiscal policy so as to maintain the growth rate at the trend level. In the second half, the growth rate began to decline after 2016–17, but the monetary policy was not set in motion before December 2018, even though the price level was low. The fiscal policy measures were also not contemplated until the beginning of 2019. In this phase of declining growth, it is essential that the income level of the poor and the lower deciles of the population are protected so as to boost the consumption demand. The government seems to have shied away from these demand-related measures, fearing a possible distortion of the macroeconomic balance which they thought could occur through increased public expenditure.

Some attempts have been made to increase the income of the people in rural areas in the second half of the 2010s, but these are distinctly different from those of the first half. In the second half, the expenditure is not oriented towards the poorest of the poor in rural areas, as was the case in the first half. In the first half, government expenditure was diverted to wage employment, which catered mostly to the landless agricultural labourers who are the poorest of the poor; in the second half, the thrust of the expenditure has been on small and marginal farmers who are poor but not the poorest of the poor in rural areas.[14]

The nature of the income- and consumption-enhancing measures in the second half of the 2010s are very different from those in the first half. In consequence, their effectiveness to keep the momentum of economic growth varied between the two halves.

India is a large country and over time its economy has developed and diversified such that it cannot be controlled and regulated from the centre. Large swathes of power are concentrated with the state governments, and without their cooperation, if not participation, it is not possible to transform the country's economic structure even when the market predominates. State laws in a large number of areas continue to be the catalysts of growth. The growth- and development-related policies conceived by the central government have to be implemented through the state governments. The cooperation of the states and their efficiency in implementing these policies are important to foster economic growth. In the planning era, or specifically until 2014, the central government used to discuss the growth- and development-related issues with the state governments, mostly through the NDC and the Inter-State Council (ISC). With the abolition of the Planning Commission in 2014, the NDC withered. The core economic issues are not discussed in the ISC under the usual circumstances. Earlier, the NDC would discuss for days together not only the Five Year Plans but also specific sectoral issues, or even issues that the states would consider relevant. The NITI Aayog hardly discusses these issues with the state governments. Even if it does, the state governments do not engage with the NITI Aayog seriously for two reasons. First, the NITI Aayog is not armed with sufficient power and authority to influence government decisions. Hence, the states feel that interacting with it is a mere wastage of time and energy. It may not be beyond conjecture that such a state of affairs induced a scholarly person such as Aravind Panagariya to quit the NITI Aayog somewhat prematurely. Second, the NITI Aayog itself does not have a plan for the problems the states usually face in implementing government decisions. In form and content, the NITI Aayog pales before the erstwhile Planning Commission. The disbanding of the Planning Commission and the absence of a capable organization to address serious growth- and development-related issues is proving to be costly for the country, and its impact is likely to be felt in the medium term. With the growth rate of the economy dipping to a pernicious low and the dire need for a concrete road map from the government to lift the growth rate to the medium-term trend, perhaps the time has come to take the states into confidence for the overall growth and development of the economy.

Annexure 8.1

On the Estimates of Macro-aggregates

The time-series of macro-aggregates from 1951–52 to 2011–12 used in Chapter 1 to Chapter 7 to assess the performance of the Indian economy have been worked out by the CSO with 2004–05 as the base year. This long data series has been constructed based on the underlying concept and methodology of compilation that has been standardized under the 2008 System of National Accounts (SNA 2008) of the United Nations.

In January 2015, the CSO shifted the base year of the estimates of macro-aggregates from 2004–05 to 2011–12. In addition, it made some changes to the database, using a larger dataset as available from the statistical system, which covers some of the new and emerging areas; this altered the methodology of measurement of the macro-aggregates marginally. Based on this new method and 2011–12 as the base year, the CSO estimated the macro-aggregates from 2004–05.[15] These have been used to assess the economic situation in the 2010s in Chapter 8.

The change in the methodology of measurement of macro-aggregates made by the CSO in January 2015 is important mainly on two counts. First, economic performance is now measured from GVA evaluated at basic prices (using the actual expenditure incurred by consumers) as against factor cost, which was the practice earlier. The shift from factor cost to basic prices is considered a step forward in the attempt to align the estimate of the GVA with the international practice.

Second, there are some changes in the database that have been used to work out the GVA in the new series, that is, with 2011–12 as the base year. In agriculture, there is not much of a change in the data source in the new series, from that in the earlier series (that is, 2004–05 as the base year). The estimate of GVA in the new series uses some recent and up-to-date data in mining and quarrying, mostly sourced from the Ministry of Corporate Affairs or from the financial statements of the companies in the stock market. Earlier, these were obtained from the Indian Bureau of Mines, which used to be dated and with a smaller coverage. In the new series the change is significant in the case of manufacturing sector, both organized and unorganized. The value added in manufacturing sector in the new series is worked out using an expanded dataset of the corporate sector provided by the Ministry of Corporate Affairs. It is based on the data of about five lakh companies registered with the Ministry of Corporate Affairs, which means that the estimates in the new series use enterprise-level data from annual financial reports for corporate manufacturing. It amounts to taking into account the selling and marketing expenses. The details are not recounted here as the CSO's methodology has been referred to earlier in this section.

The CSO changes the base year of calculation of macro-aggregates in order to incorporate the changing structure of the economy in a more precise manner. The ultimate aim is to bring the methodology in India closer to global practices and making it at par with international standards (SNA 2008), so as to facilitate inter-country comparison.

In the new series, the size of the GDP is increased, and along with this, a structural change is witnessed by way of significant rise in the share of industry in aggregate GDP that might change the perception of India's growth trajectory. However, the state of the economy does not change with this upward revision of GDP estimates.

It is the usual practice of the CSO to compile back series of the macro-aggregates whenever there is a change in the base year. In November 2018, the CSO released the macro-aggregates from 2004–05 with the changed methodology and 2011–12 as the base year.[16]

A debate on the estimate of GDP in the new series, and inter alia its growth rate, was ignited by Arvind Subramanian, a former chief economic adviser of the Government of India, through research work at Harvard University, published in June 2019.[17] The new series of macro-aggregates estimated by the CSO yields the GDP growth rate during the period of 2011–12 to 2016–17 as about 7 per cent per year. Subramanian's Harvard research paper pegged the same at around 4.5 per cent per year.[18] It renders the CSO's officially measured GDP growth rate overestimated by 2.5 percentage points. He concludes that the overestimation of GDP growth rate is on account of the change in the methodology introduced by the CSO while changing the base year of calculation from 2004–05 to 2011–12. An important ramification of Subramanian's estimate is that India cannot claim to be the fastest growing economy, a position which it had been holding for the past decade or so.

Subramanian's GDP estimates are based on an elegant mathematical model which uses a wide range of variables from India and other countries. The analysis is based upon 17 key economic indicators, which enjoy a higher interdependence with the GDP growth for the period of 2001–02 to 2017–18. The indicators include index of industrial production; production of steel, petroleum, and cement; electricity consumption; sales of two-wheelers, commercial vehicles, and tractors; airline passenger traffic; foreign tourist arrivals; railway freight traffic; credit to industry; and exports and imports. The model results show the following: (*a*) before 2011, the growth rate of a number of economic indicators were found to be positively correlated with the GDP growth rate, whereas after 2011 the growth rate of most of these indicators are negatively correlated with the GDP growth rate; and (*b*) in case of cross-country regressions India has a normal relationship between growth in standard indicators and GDP before 2011, but not so afterwards. Subramanian finds the value added of the manufacturing sector by the CSO as overestimated and attributes this overestimation to the change in the methodology. He substantiates this from the evidence that before 2011, manufacturing value added used to be closely correlated with the manufacturing component of index of industrial production (IIP) and manufacturing exports, whereas this link has broken down in the later period.

The mathematical model used by Subramanian, however elegant it might be, should take note of the fact that some of the indicators used in the model are correlated. The IIP is correlated with the production of steel, cement, electricity, and also vehicles. It is also important to note that in the new method and 2011–12 base, the CSO measures the GVA in the manufacturing sector and not production, as reflected in the IIP. This may dilute some of the solid stands that Subramanian has taken against the CSO methodology.

What Subramanian, in effect, has done is a check of the macroestimates by way of a 'smell test' on the conclusions about GDP growth arrived at by the CSO. He asserts that the GDP estimates of the CSO are not precise, and questions its methodology on the plea that its growth rate does not correlate well with certain indicators of economic growth. Correspondingly, Subramanian has not estimated the GDP, let alone the macro-variables, conceding that 'since the underlying data are not available publicly, nobody outside the CSO can estimate GDP'. He has tried to find out whether the GDP estimates as derived by the CSO are plausible, broadly satisfying some macro-consistency checks. Thus, his is not an attempt to estimate but to cross-check and to validate the CSO estimates. In this endeavour, he arrives at the conclusion that the GDP estimates are not precise and goes on to suggest that it is necessary to revisit the CSO's methodology by an independent task force comprising both national and international experts. Instead of dismissing Subramanian's analysis, there should be a theoretical answer to his recommendation. That answer is: The bottom line is that discarding of CSO's methodology is not warranted simply because the GDP growth rate does not correlate well with certain indicators of economic growth.

Notes

1. The CSO was subsumed in the newly constituted National Statistical Office (NSO) in May 2019.
2. In January 2015, when the new estimates (that is, new method and 2011–12 as the base year) were released, 2013–14 was the latest year for which the GDP estimates with 2004–05 as the base year were available. The impact of the new estimate on the size of the economy can be viewed from the fact that the GDP growth rate in 2013–14 from the new estimate is 2.6 percentage points more than in the previous estimate, that is, the estimate derived from 2004–05 as the base year. More strikingly, the growth rate of the manufacturing sector in 2013–14 becomes 5.3 per cent in the new estimate in place of –0.7 per cent in the previous estimate.
3. It is a World Bank assessment conducted in its International Comparison Program (ICP), and covers 199 countries. The PPP is the conversion rate for a given currency into reference currency (in this case, the USD). The PPP rate is an implicit foreign exchange rate at which a given amount of money has the same purchasing power in different countries. It can be used to work out the money that would be needed to purchase the same goods and services in two places.

4. A mix of demand-pull and cost-push factors caused the inflation. The sectors and items principally affected by the price rise were mineral oils, iron and steel, chemicals, and edible oils. These together contributed to around 40 per cent of the total inflation. Food articles contributed to less than 10 per cent of the overall inflation, and yet it attracted considerable attention in view of its predominant weight in the consumption basket, especially of the poor.

5. The growth rate of GVA declined consistently for the eight quarters spread over the two years 2018–19 and 2019–20; from 6.9 per cent in the first quarter of 2018–19, it became 3 per cent in the fourth quarter of 2019–20.

6. Statement by the Union Finance Minister in the Lok Sabha in reply to Unstarred Question No. 2261 on Demonetization, 2 December 2019.

7. Based on Angus Maddison, *Contours of the World Economy, I—2030 AD,* Oxford University Press, 2007. For details, see *Economic Survey 2019–20,* Chapter 1, Vol. I, Ministry of Finance, Government of India.

8. Ravi Srivastava and Balakrushna Padhi, *Collapse in Wage/Salary Income Growth in India, 2011–12 to 2017–18,* Institute for Human Development, Delhi, Working Paper No. 01/2020.

9. Himanshu, 'What Happened to Poverty during the First Term of Modi?', *Mint,* 15 August 2019, New Delhi.

10. C. Rangarajan while addressing an interactive session titled 'An Overview of the Indian Economy: A Policymaker's Perspective', at the MICA, Ahmedabad, on 15 March 2017; Press Release: MICA, dated 16 March 2017.

11. Vijay Kelkar, 'Towards India's New Fiscal Federalism', Professor Sukhamoy Chakravarty Memorial Lecture, presented at the 55th Annual Conference of the Indian Econometric Society, Mumbai School of Economics and Public Policy, and National Institute of Securities Market, Mumbai, on 8 January 2019; printed under the same title as NIPFP Working Paper No. 252, 25 January 2019, National Institute of Public Finance and Policy, New Delhi.

12. 'India Still Fast-Growing Economy with Lot of Potential: World Bank Economist', *The Times of India,* 13 October 2019.

13. India's rank in the Global Competitiveness Index slipped from 2010–11 to 2014–15. The rank improved marginally in 2015–16, but then deteriorated throughout the years 2016 to 2019.

14. In December 2018, the Pradhan Mantri Kisan Samman Nidhi (PM-KISAN) was introduced to provide direct cash transfers to the tune of INR 6,000 a year to the families of small and marginal farmers. This is a half-hearted attempt to boost consumption. With the average size of

rural household as five persons, the income transfer through PM-KISAN works out to INR 100 per capita per month, which is just 8 per cent of the poverty line expenditure.

15. The details of the methodology can be found in 'Changes in Methodology and Data Sources in the New Series of National Accounts, Base Year 2011–12', CSO, Ministry of Statistics and Programme Implementation, Government of India, New Delhi, June 2015.

16. Press Note on National Accounts Statistics, Back Series 2004–05 to 2011–12, Base 2011–12, CSO, Ministry of Statistics and Programme Implementation, Government of India, 28 November 2018.

17. Arvind Subramanian, 'India's GDP Mis-estimation: Likelihood, Magnitudes, Mechanisms, and Implications', CID Faculty Working Paper No. 354, Centre for International Development at Harvard University, June 2019.

18. Subramanian's model yields the GDP growth rate between 2011–12 and 2016–17 at around 4.5 per cent per year, with a 95 per cent confidence interval of 3.5–5.5 per cent.

Index

acquisitive economy, 17, 188
additional central assistance (ACA),
    39, 53n12
administered price mechanism, 32,
    215–6, 224, 304
adult education, 43
adult franchise, 192–5
adult suffrage, 194–5
Advisory Planning Board, 16;
    constitution of, 52n6
Africa, 194, 279
age–sex–activity distribution, of the
    population, 289, 292
agrarian, distress, 316
agricultural, commodities, 68,
    136–7; development, 190;
    economy, 167; employment, 249;
    GDP, 94; growth, 68, 84, 90, 92,
    94–5, 98, 101, 104–5, 124, 132, 149,
    151–2, 220, 222, 225, 306, 316;
    investment, 112, 137; land, 191;
    operations 48, 132, 215, 225;
    output, 68, 103–4, 127, 132, 150,
    152, 218; plan/planning, 69, 145;
    production 68, 94, 104, 123, 127–8,
    131, 137–8, 190–1, 220, 316;
    productivity, 68, 137, 190, 247;
    products, 59, 136; projects, 146;
    season, 105, 245; strategy, 137–8;
    sub-model, 68–9; wage rate, 247;
    year, 264
agricultural growth rate, 94–5, 151–2,
    222, 316; decline in, 101, 104, 149,
    306; in Second Plan, 124
agricultural labourers (wage earners),
    145, 147, 190–1, 245, 341
agricultural operation, in India, 48,
    132, 215, 225
agricultural output/production, 94,
    103–4, 123, 127, 131–2, 137–8,
    150, 152, 190–1, 218; under
    economic reforms, 220
Agricultural Trade Development and
    Assistance Act (1954), 136
Ahluwalia, Montek Singh, 28–9, 153
Air India, 178
Alagh, Y. K., 87n9, 336
All India Congress Committee
    (AICC), 16, 199, 204n15
Ambedkar, B. R., 200–1
animal husbandry, 36; products, 291
annual, budget, 27, 209, 212–3; plan
    19–20, 27, 42, 93, 202n3
anti-poverty, measures, 24;
    programmes, 11, 257, 260
asset generation programmes, 78,
    148, 242
Avadi Resolution, 182

About the Author

K. L. Datta completed his graduation and postgraduation in economics from University of Calcutta and received a subsequent masters degree in economics from The University of Machester, England. He joined the Indian Economic Service in 1975. He has held various positions in the Government of India, specifically in the Planning Commission, including as adviser and head of various committees; deputy secretary, Ministry of Finance; and chief economic adviser, Ministry of Rural Development. He also served as adviser for development planning, Ministry of National Economy, Sultanate of Oman, Muscat. He was the international consultant at a World Bank project for the Government of Bangladesh, Dhaka.

Datta has worked extensively on input–output and growth models, and poverty and income distribution. He has delivered a number of lectures on Plan models, poverty, and inequality in various institutions at home and abroad.

He has published several articles in technical journals and authored three books: *Facets of Indian Poverty* (2002); *Central Planning: A Case Study on China* (2004); and *Poverty and Development Planning in India* (2014).